D1294623

THE GOVERNORS

OF VIRGINIA

1860–1978

THE GOVERNOR'S MANSION

(Executive Mansion)

of Virginia

The GOVERNORS of

VIRGINIA

1860–1978

Editor
Edward Younger

Editor (1979–1982)
James Tice Moore

Associate Editors
James W. Ely, Jr.
Ronald L. Heinemann
Jack T. Kirby
Richard G. Lowe
John H. Moore

University Press of Virginia
Charlottesville

THE UNIVERSITY PRESS OF VIRGINIA
Copyright © 1982 by the Rector and Visitors
of the University of Virginia

First published 1982

Library of Congress Cataloging in Publication Data
Main entry under title:

The Governors of Virginia, 1860–1978.

Includes index.
1. Virginia—Governors—Biography—Addresses,
essays, lectures. 2. Virginia—Politics and
government—Addresses, essays, lectures.   I. Younger,
Edward, 1909–1979.   II. Moore, James Tice.
F225.G77   975.5'04'0922 [B]   81-16359
ISBN 0-8139-0920-1   AACR2

Printed in the United States of America

Contents

CONTENTS

Preface

The University of Virginia has been aptly described as the "lengthened shadow" of Thomas Jefferson. This study of the Old Dominion's governors from 1860 to 1978 could with equal justice be characterized as the "lengthened shadow" of another individual closely associated with the university, Professor Edward Younger of the Corcoran Department of History. In a fundamental sense, this book represents the culmination of a career of selfless devotion to his profession, to his students, and to the principles of humane, cooperative scholarship.

Dr. Younger's influence pervades much of the modern-day writing of Virginia history. When he began his thirty-three years of service in Charlottesville in 1946 the study of the state's post–Civil War past was for the most part a neglected field. A few path-breaking works had been published, but the interest of scholars had focused to a much greater extent on the colonial and Revolutionary periods. By the close of Dr. Younger's career, however, a very different situation prevailed. Inspired by his efforts in classroom, seminar, and study, a generation of graduate students had transformed Virginia's historiographical landscape. Those who worked under his direction had illumined the Commonwealth's history from the 1860s to the 1960s in scores of theses and dissertations, dozens of articles, and at least nine books (with others in various stages of preparation).

Dr. Younger's influence affected more than the course of state historical scholarship; it also touched the lives of individuals—as the contributors to this volume will readily attest. Of the thirty-two authors whose efforts are published herein, twenty-nine did graduate work with him at the University of Virginia. As students, they came to share his love of intellectual inquiry, his insistence on depth of research and clarity of expression, his distrust of cant and dogma. As individuals, they grew to appreciate his inexhaustible patience, unfailing courtesy, and sincere concern for their welfare. Even during his hectic, relentlessly active years as department chairman (1962–66) and Dean of the Graduate School of Arts and Sciences (1966–69), he always found the time—or made the time—to help his students in any way he could. Dr. Younger demanded the best work of which they were capable; he gave no less in return. Dignified but never pompous, he was, in the best sense of the term, a gentleman. Loyalties to him endured far beyond the completion of dissertations and the acquisition of degrees. More than a teacher, he was a friend.

These personal and professional legacies permeate this book, but Dr. Younger's "lengthened shadow" also manifests itself in these pages in a more immediate and comprehensive way. He was, throughout, the driving force in the decade of planning and effort that led to the completion of this volume. With characteristic enthusiasm and resolve, he created the guidelines for the project, spearheaded essential fund-raising activities, enlisted the services of the authors, and devoted countless hours to the editorial tasks for which he was so well suited by experience, talent, and temperament. Better than any other individual, he knew and understood the history of Virginia in the period under consideration. Just as important, if not more so, he was personally acquainted with those who were writing the essays. As a friend, he knew each one's strengths and weaknesses. By turns criticizing and complimenting, cajoling and encouraging, he labored to transform rough drafts into polished, comprehensive chapters. Deadlines came and went, but he never listened to those who doubted the feasibility of a project dependent on thirty-two individuals with disparate schedules, interests, and obligations. He did not despair; amid phone calls, letters, and memoranda, the work went on.

Unlike Thomas Jefferson, who saw his dreams of a university accomplished in brick and mortar, Edward Younger did not live to witness the fruition of his labors on this volume. Stricken with cancer during the first months of 1979, he died in June of that year. Even during this period of declining health, "the book" was never far from his thoughts. Manuscript revisions were at his bedside—to be read whenever pain and medication would allow. Anxious to conclude publication arrangements, he visited the offices of the University Press of Virginia a few days before his death. Ever the optimist, he hoped that he would be granted the time to complete the work. Ever the realist, he asked his associate editors to finish the task if he could not. To the best of their ability, they have attempted to maintain his standards of excellence. To the extent that this book is deserving of praise, the lion's share of the credit belongs to him. Its completion is, in itself, a testimony to his character, influence, and example. Like the founder of the university he loved, Dr. Younger left his mark on the future as well as the past. He cast a long shadow.

The completion of this project placed demands of one sort or another on hundreds of individuals, only a small fraction of whom can be noted here. To those not cited, the editors extend apologies and assurances that their help was appreciated.

Financial donations to further the work were provided by Mr. and Mrs. John S. Battle, Jr.; Mr. FitzGerald Bemiss; the Honorable Harry F. Byrd, Jr., U.S. Senator from Virginia; Mrs. Gulielma T. Hooper; Mrs. Gay Montague Moore; Mr. J. V. Rainbolt; Mr. T. N. Rainbolt; Mrs. Harry Carter Stuart; Mr. Langbourne M. Williams; Mr. J. H. Tyler Wilson; the Old Dominion Foundation; and the Westmoreland Davis Foundation, Inc., Leesburg, Virginia.

Fund-raising activities at the University of Virginia were facilitated by the active support and involvement of University President Frank L. Hereford, Jr.; Mr. John J. Owen, Vice-President for Development; Mr. Alexander G. Gilliam, Jr., Special Assistant to the President; and Miss Lindsay Jones, Foundation Relations Officer. Ms. Margaret M. Jones and Ms. Patricia A. Hawk, Research Administrators, handled financial disbursements.

The Corcoran Department of History of the University of Virginia extended its help to Professor Edward Younger in the form of released time for editorial work, and the College of Humanities and Sciences and the Department of History and Geography at Virginia Commonwealth University provided similar support and encouragement for James Tice Moore after he assumed chief editorial responsibilities in 1979.

All illustrations were provided by the Virginia State Library and are reproduced herein with that agency's consent.

Research librarians and staff at numerous institutions provided indispensable aid and courteous assistance. Particular recognition is due the following depositories for granting permission to quote from manuscript collections in their holdings: Archives Branch, Archives and Records Division, Virginia State Library; Earl Gregg Swem Library, College of William and Mary; North Carolina State Archives; University of Virginia Library; Virginia Historical Society; and William R. Perkins Library, Duke University.

Permission to incorporate previously published materials in articles appearing in this volume was provided by *Civil War Times Illustrated* with reference to F. N. Boney's article on Governor John Letcher and by the Department of History of East Carolina University and *The Virginia Magazine of History and Biography* with reference to Alvin. A. Fahrner's article on Governor William Smith.

A host of typists contributed their services to this project, but a particular debt is owed to Mrs. Wanda P. Clary, Secretary, Department of History and Geography, Virginia Commonwealth University. Through several lengthy and sometimes vexatious drafts of the manuscript, she remained cheerful, efficient, and cooperative.

Lastly, those who edited and those who wrote extend a special word of thanks to their friends, colleagues, and families—who encouraged and endured.

THE GOVERNORS

OF VIRGINIA

1860–1978

VIRGINIA AND ITS

GOVERNORS

1860–1978

James Tice Moore

Virginia's ties with custom and tradition were readily apparent when John Letcher took the oath of office in January 1860. Although Richmond, Norfolk, and a handful of other towns showed signs of commercial growth and industrial development, the Old Dominion remained overwhelmingly rural in appearance and character, a patchwork of fields and forests, plantations and farms. Most of the state's people, white and black, still looked to harvests of tobacco, wheat, and corn for their livelihoods—as they had for generations. Exhausted soils had threatened the vitality of the countryside in the first decades of the nineteenth century, but improved methods of tillage had sparked improved crop yields and rising land values by the 1850s. Nevertheless, ominous shadows loomed as the antebellum era drew to a close. Endangered from without and from within, the outmoded "peculiar institution" of slavery clung to existence in the Piedmont and Tidewater, where fears of Negro revolt and abolitionist agitation were deeply ingrained. Long-developing antagonisms between the eastern and western sections of the state continued to simmer, only partially allayed by democratic features of the Constitution of 1851. Conservative biases circumscribed the intellectual horizons of gentry and yeomanry alike and were intensified by the annual exodus of thousands of the Old Dominion's ablest and most ambitious citizens in search of new lands and new opportunities. Hampered by this loss of human capital and individual initiative, since 1810 Virginia had forfeited more than half of its congressional seats, and its influence was on the wane, even within the circle of slave states. Reformers launched repeated efforts to halt this decline, but results were disappointing. The state government invested heavily in banks, canals, and railroads in the pre–Civil War years, only to be met by outcries against high taxes and deficit spending. Demands for enhanced educational opportunities for the lower classes foundered on the rocks of elite hostility and mass inertia, while poorly constructed and inadequately maintained county roads perpetuated rural isolation and provincialism. Tightfisted local oligarchies kept welfare outlays to a parsimonious minimum. Reconciling themselves to frustrated hopes and diminished expectations, Virginians increasingly looked to achievements of bygone days, to the renowned "dynasty" of George Washington and Thomas Jefferson, James Madison and James Monroe, for solace in a period of decline. The Old Dominion's "golden age," it appeared, lay in the past, not in the future.

Already weakened by internal discontent, John Letcher's Virginia suffered massive damage in the Civil War. Invading armies ravaged the state, leaving a trail of devastated towns and looted farms. Unionist West Virginia officially severed its ties with the Commonwealth in 1863, depriving the mother state of a third of its territory and a fourth of its people. Slavery, too, was driven from the scene, although true equality remained an elusive goal for Virginia's blacks. The postwar decades brought additional turmoil, and the advent of the twentieth century hastened the pace of change still more.

John Letcher's Commonwealth was gone, and a very different Virginia had emerged by the conclusion of Mills E. Godwin, Jr.'s second gubernatorial term in 1978. By that time less than 10 percent of the state's work force was employed in an agricultural system which devoted an ever-increasing share of its land to timber lots and to pasturage for beef cattle. Emerging from its meager antebellum origins, industry now bestrode the Old Dominion. Coal mines in the Southwest bore witness to the rise of the new order, as did the presence of textile mills in Danville, furniture plants in the Southside, shipyards in Hampton Roads, cigarette factories in Richmond, chemical works in Hopewell, and a host of other enterprises dispersed across the Commonwealth. Heightened business activity and the development of an extensive highway system had prompted spectacular urban growth, especially in the decades after World War II. From the apartment complexes of Fairfax County and Alexandria to the high-rise condominiums of Virginia Beach, a growing portion of the state's people resided in the so-called urban corridor, the southern extension of the Boston–New York–Washington megalopolis. Further dramatizing the extent of change, out-migration had given way to a massive influx of new citizens. By the mid-1970s one Virginian in four had been born outside the South. Boosted by these economic and demographic trends, per capita income in the Commonwealth approximated the national average—a significant accomplishment after generations of relative backwardness and poverty. This progress had not been achieved without cost. Industrial wastes poisoned streams and rivers; coal miners contracted black lung disease; much of the urban landscape exhibited a dreary sameness and an unbridled commercialism; ignorance and underemployment continued to plague the urban ghettos and rural hinterlands. Still, change and modernization were omnipresent. For better or worse, a new Virginia had arisen from the ashes of the old.

Governmental activities in Mills Godwin's Commonwealth mirrored this revolution in economic and social patterns. Outlays for educational and welfare services skyrocketed in the 1960s and early 1970s, while state regulatory and promotional agencies played an ever-expanding role. Tax receipts from personal incomes, corporate revenues, consumer purchases, and gasoline sales enabled the General Assembly to approve budgets ranging into the billions of dollars, dwarfing by several thousandfold the miniscule appropriations of the antebellum period. The simple and circumscribed administrative machinery of John Letcher's day had been submerged as well—replaced by a bureaucratic hierarchy employing tens of thousands in schools, offices, and agencies from the southwestern mountains to the Eastern Shore. A less dramatic (but nonetheless significant) index of change was apparent in another branch of government. In the 1970s annual legislative sessions replaced the old biennial ones, enabling Virginia's lawmakers to deal more effectively with the challenges of a new era.

The Old Dominion's government had undergone a remarkable transformation, but what of the governorship, the state's highest office? How had the position evolved in the century and more since John Letcher took the gubernatorial oath? At the outset of Letcher's term the powers and duties of the job were already far from negligible, however limited they might appear by twentieth-century standards. According to the Constitution of 1851 (in effect at the end of the antebellum era), Virginia's governor was to enforce the laws, command the state's military forces, represent the Commonwealth in negotiations with other states and with foreign countries, and—at his discretion—grant pardons and reprieves to those convicted of criminal offenses. The General Assembly exercised absolute control over the making of laws and the appropriation of funds, but the executive could influence the legislators' conduct by calling them into special session and by submitting messages to them on matters of public concern. Although the Assembly had the final say concerning appointments to state offices, the governor could fill vacancies in those posts on an ad interim basis when the lawmakers were not in session. With its incumbent chosen by statewide election for a four-year term, the governorship was, in 1860, a position of some influence and considerable prestige.

Building upon these antebellum prerogatives, Virginia's governors soon acquired new ones. The so-called Underwood Constitution, under which the "reconstructed" Commonwealth returned to the Union in 1870, brought the governor into the lawmaking process by authorizing him to veto legislation. The votes of two-thirds of those present in the Senate and House of Delegates would be necessary to override his veto. The 1870 constitution also expanded the scope of executive clemency; the governor was now permitted to "remove political disabilities" from citizens who had forfeited their right to vote and hold office through convictions for criminal misconduct.

The radical Republican authors of the Underwood Constitution soon disappeared from Virginia's political arena, but the trend toward increased gubernatorial influence continued. The Constitution of 1902 furthered the process by allowing the governor to veto individual items in appropriations bills and to return defective legislation to the General Assembly with suggested amendments. Thus augmented, the executive's veto power approximated its modern-day form. The fundamental law of 1902 also authorized the governor to remove negligent or malfeasant state officials and appoint their successors during periods when the legislature was not in session. After the lawmakers resumed their work they could either sustain or reject the executive's decisions in these matters; in either case, ultimate power of removal remained with the General Assembly.

Yet the Commonwealth's administrative machinery was poorly equipped to deal with twentieth-century demands. Scores of state agencies and offices came into existence after 1900, but they lacked centralized coordination and supervision. Distressed by the resulting waste and inefficiency, the legislature in 1918 placed the governor in charge of the budget-making process for Virginia's administrative bureaucracy. The General Assembly retained the last word with reference to appropriations, of course, but establishment of the budget system was clearly a victory for gubernatorial prerogative.

The emphasis on improved managerial practices bore even more significant fruit in a series of constitutional amendments initiated by Governor Harry F. Byrd in 1926 and ratified by the electorate in 1928. Consolidating power (and patronage) in the hands of the executive, these changes empowered him to appoint the secretary of the Commonwealth, the state treasurer, the superintendent of public instruction, the commissioner of agriculture and immigration, and the members of the State Corporation Commission—all of whom had previously been selected by the voters. Although General Assembly confirmation was required for the occupants of these posts, the governor now clearly enjoyed the initiative in filling them. A similar approach was also apparent when the legislature approved a Byrd-sponsored reorganization program in 1927 which eliminated many state agencies and consolidated the remainder into twelve major departments—each with an administrative head responsible to the governor. These reforms worked to general satisfaction, and gubernatorial powers have remained essentially unchanged since that time. Indeed, the most significant alteration in these arrangements (embodied in the Constitution of 1971) could well be considered a belated capstone to Byrd's efforts. The most recent version of the Commonwealth's fundamental law mandates that the chiefs of state administrative departments "shall serve at the pleasure of the Governor," a provision allowing the executive to remove them at will. With power to veto legislation, oversee the preparation of the budget, and appoint and remove public officials, Virginia's governor has emerged—in the twentieth century—as one of the strongest in the nation.

The governorship underwent great changes from 1860 to 1978, but the personal characteristics of the thirty individuals who occupied the post during those years exhibit a striking degree of continuity and homogeneity. All were white males; all but seven were between forty and sixty years of age when they took the gubernatorial oath; all—in so far as they evinced a religious preference—were Protestants. Drawn from throughout the state's major geographical regions, the great majority were native-born Virginians of middle-class or upper-class origins. Reflecting their relative affluence, twenty-five had received at least some schooling at the college or university level. Eleven had attended the University of Virginia; eight, Washington and Lee. Twenty-one of the thirty worked as lawyers at one time or another in their careers, while four agriculturalists and three editors comprised the next largest vocational groups. Prior political experience also typified the governors, whose ranks included eight men who served in the U.S. House of Representatives and fifteen who held seats in the General Assembly before moving to the Executive Mansion. Four erstwhile lieutenant governors and four attorneys general won the state's highest office during the period as well. The import of these statistics is clear: with rare exceptions, the governorship was the province of the well-to-do and the well-connected.

Although broadly similar in occupations and origins, Virginia's governors differed to a much greater extent in their political ideologies and objectives. This was especially true in the period from 1860 to 1900—years when the state was torn by disputes between wartime secessionists and Unionists, Reconstruction radicals and Conservatives, debt-paying Funders and repudiationist Readjusters, deflationist goldbugs and inflationist silverites. Reflecting the pervasive character of these antagonisms, each of these groups had at least one spokesman in the Executive Mansion during this turbulent era. The Commonwealth's Democrats ensured their preeminence by disfranchising the mass of black Republicans in the Constitution of 1902, but internal clashes between "organization" and "independent" elements of the dominant party enlivened the scene for the next half century. Led at first by U.S. Senator Thomas S. Martin and then by Harry F. Byrd, organization forces generally enjoyed the upper hand, but the independents nevertheless managed to capture the governorship on several occasions. The Democratic hegemony was also marked by bitter disputes on a variety of issues, disputes which intensified old rancors and engendered new ones. Prohibitionist "drys" battled anti-Prohibition "wets" over liquor controls; supporters of bond sales for highway construction crossed swords with advocates of the ascendant "pay-as-you-go" creed; champions of improved educational and welfare services clashed with low-tax adherents of fiscal restraint. Inevitably, governors from the major Democratic factions had to choose sides in these controversies, just as those who served after 1932 had to deal with disputes over New Deal–Fair Deal economic programs and, later, with the consequences of federally sponsored drives for racial equality. The revival of Republican strength in the Commonwealth after World War II further complicated the situation. Exploiting Democratic schisms, the GOP survived repeated defeats and emerged victorious in hard-fought gubernatorial races in 1969 and 1973. One-party rule had given way to two-party competition, and the long-range outlook for state politics was more unpredictable than it had been since the 1890s. Partisan alignments were fragile; individual affiliations, ephemeral. Mills Godwin's career provided the most graphic illustration of the uncertainties of the new era. Winning the governship as a Democrat in 1965, he regained the post eight years later as a Republican.

Caught up in these struggles over issues and organizations, men and measures, Virginia's governors could scarcely avoid involvement with the great forces that were transforming the Commonwealth. Indeed, as their powers and prerogatives increased, the men who occupied the state's highest office had to shoulder growing responsibility for the problems generated by economic and social change. For better or worse, Mills Godwin's Virginia was very different from John Letcher's, and the governors through the years had helped to make it so. From the military and political struggles of the 1860s to the energy and environmental crises of the 1970s, executive after executive had thrown his influence into the balance—sometimes to the Old Dominion's benefit, sometimes to its detriment. The governors' successes and failures, strengths and weaknesses, affected the lives of millions of their fellow citizens. To that extent this book is more than the story of thirty individuals. It is also the story of a state and its people, of Virginia and Virginians, in one of the most eventful periods in their history.

SOURCES

Jean Gottmann's *Virginia in Our Century* (Charlottesville, 1969) provides the best analysis of the economic, social, and demographic changes that characterized the period. Virginius Dabney surveys historical developments in *Virginia: The New Dominion* (Garden City, N.Y., 1971).

State constitutions from 1776 to 1971 offer indispensable insights into the evolution of gubernatorial powers. The Commonwealth's fundamental laws prior to 1902 are conveniently grouped in Armistead R. Long's *The Constitution of Virginia: An Annotated Edition . . . Together with a Reprint of the Previous Constitutions of Virginia* (Lynchburg, 1901). Official publications containing subsequent constitutions are available at the Virginia State Library (Richmond). For a superb discussion of the development of governmental institutions and practices, see A. E. Dick Howard, *Commentaries on the Constitution of Virginia* (2 vols., Charlottesville, 1974).

The impact of individual governors on the evolution of the office provides a central focus for the articles in this volume. In addition to the sources listed at the end of each article, those interested in specific governors should consult Richmond and hometown newspapers, gubernatorial messages in the Senate and House *Journals,* pertinent legislation in the *Acts* of the General Assembly, and the *Annual Reports* of state institutions.

During preliminary work on this book Professor Edward Younger compiled statistics concerning the governors' family and geographical origins, their educational and occupational backgrounds, and their military and political experience. Arranged in tabular form, this information is very helpful in understanding the men who served in Virginia's highest office. Dr. Younger's findings (together with other documents pertinent to the book's completion) are on deposit at the University of Virginia Library.

JOHN LETCHER

Governor of Virginia

1860–1864

JOHN LETCHER

Pragmatic Confederate Patriot

F. N. Boney

John Letcher was born into a comfortable, middle-class household in Lexington, Virginia, in 1813. To the dismay of his stern Methodist parents, as a youth he took up smoking, drinking, and lively parties. This adolescent phase of John's resistance to parental authority also included lackadaisical academic efforts. Squandering his opportunities, young Letcher dropped out of local Washington College during his freshman year. His disgusted father then put him to work as a carpenter's apprentice—an abrupt tactic which had the desired effect.

In due course he followed his father into the ranks of the Jacksonian Democrats where he became the protégé of James McDowell (a future governor) and also commenced the study of law in the office of another local Democratic leader, William Taylor. Tall and loose-jointed, florid-faced and a little awkward, Letcher certainly was not handsome, but his open manner and gregarious disposition made him a popular young man around Lexington. He enjoyed the social whirl and after an erratic courtship married Susan Holt in 1843. An ideal antebellum wife, she became the dutiful, loving mother of a fast-growing family and the quiet, strong helpmate of a rising lawyer-politician.

An ambitious young man, Letcher charged forth with characteristic optimism, indomitable energy, and the not inconsequential support of McDowell, who in 1839 had put him in charge of the Lexington *Valley Star,* a new Democratic newspaper. Editor Letcher lashed out at the Whigs relentlessly, but he usually refrained from the more extreme partisan excesses of this passionate period. Concentrating on issues instead of personalities, he championed hard money, states' rights, and strict constitutional construction and opposed monopolies, protective tariffs, abolitionism, and federally financed internal improvements. On the state level he took liberal stances in favor of public schools, state-sponsored internal improvements, and sweeping, democratic reform of Virginia's government. The Whigs denounced Letcher as a Loco Foco, a radical Democrat, and he willingly accepted the partisan characterization. Regardless of labels and slogans, within the generally conservative context of Virginia politics John Letcher was clearly a liberal, a champion of change.

In the western half of Virginia democratic reform was a popular cause; most westerners, Whigs and Democrats alike, resented the east's traditional domination of the state. A majority of white Virginians lived west of the Blue Ridge Mountains, but the eastern minority still controlled the government. Hammering away at this inequity, Letcher got so angry during a debate on this matter in 1847 that he even threatened division of the state and gradual emancipation in the west if the east did not grant basic reforms. Finally, in 1850 a state constitutional convention was called, and after recanting his brief flirtation with emancipation, Letcher was elected a delegate. Tempering idealism with practicality, fighting hard but sometimes accepting half a loaf, he played a major role in the creation of a new constitution which granted universal white manhood suffrage, gradually equalized sectional representation in the legislature, multiplied the number of elected officials, and ushered cautious old Virginia into the new age of mass democracy.

The Jacksonian crusade had finally triumphed in the Old Dominion, and Letcher quickly exploited his new popularity by running for Congress. Again recanting his single, superficial stand for emancipation, he won easily, gaining the support of the usual Democratic majority in his congressional district as well as the votes of many Whigs willing to reward him for his convention performance. His electoral base in the Valley was secure as long as he wanted to remain in Congress. The first phase of Letcher's political career had ended; the liberal crusader had won his fight at home.

Now the moderate liberal became a moderate conservative, contented with the new, democratic status quo. But as a congressman, Letcher soon realized that this status quo might be short-lived: he was a member of a shrinking minority, a spokesman for a southern way of life threatened by a hostile world. A Virginian, he represented a state that had once dominated the whole Union but could no longer even lead the Southland. In the North the abolitionists grew stronger, and the secession reaction in the South was gaining strength too. The traditional middle ground of moderates like Letcher was fast disappearing. Reacting within the context of his Jefferson-Jackson heritage, Letcher rejected the doctrines of Calhoun and the secessionists but also defended the rights and traditions of Virginia and the South. At best this was an awkward holding action, a forlorn attempt to halt the drift toward disaster.

The Lexington congressman fought hard for honesty and economy in the federal government, becoming a financial expert and winning the nickname "Honest John Letcher, Watchdog of the Treasury." His speeches contained too many facts and statistics to be eloquent, and he sponsored no significant legislation. Nevertheless, his tireless work on the powerful Ways and Means Committee earned him a reputation as a capable and conscientious lawmaker. Rising sectional tensions nudged him a little to the right, but throughout his eight years in Congress he remained a moderate conservative who usually came down on the side of compromise and reconciliation. Although hampered by nagging attacks of fever and rheumatism, he remained as gregarious as ever. Letcher loved to chat informally for hours, sipping brandy and smoking a pipe, and he associated with persons of every political persuasion—even with such abolitionist radicals as Joshua Giddings. His closest friends in Washington were successful businessmen, but he mixed widely in a society increasingly fragmented by political pressures.

In 1858 he launched a cautious campaign for the governorship. The Democrats controlled the state, but Governor Henry A. Wise was an old enemy, and the other state party leader, Robert M. T. Hunter, was not a close ally. But the time was right, and Letcher won his divided party's gubernatorial nomination at a tumultuous convention in Petersburg in 1859. His Whig opponent, William L. Goggin, was a better speaker with a more attractive stage presence, and all through the campaign Letcher was passionately attacked for his flirtation with emancipation a decade earlier. Letcher won, thanks to heavy support in his native west, but his victory margin was uncomfortably narrow. Many Virginians, especially states' rights extremists, continued to harbor serious doubts about their new chief executive.

Governor Letcher's four-year term began on January 1, 1860. Anxious to discourage the drift toward secession, Letcher appealed in his inaugural address for a convention of all the states to resolve problems that threatened the Union. Conscious of the fears aroused by John Brown's raid, however, he also recommended modernization and expansion of the Commonwealth's military forces as a necessary precaution. The new governor was trapped in a classic dilemma of the modern age. He knew that he had to prepare his people for any eventuality, but he also realized that such preparation—the physical and psychological conditioning of the masses for conflict—greatly increased the likelihood of war. Responding to his appeals, the General Assembly quickly voted large military appropriations, but it delayed a whole year before calling for a convention. The so-called Peace Convention would eventually gather in Washington in February 1861, but by then the time for compromise had passed. Perhaps, just perhaps, if it had met earlier, war might have been averted—or at least postponed.

Dismayed by the continued increase in sectional antagonisms, the governor aligned himself with moderate, pro-Union forces in Virginia and the nation at large during the fateful 1860 four-man presidential race. Although most Virginia Democrats eventually united behind the southern Democratic nominee, John C. Breckinridge, Letcher did not. On August 22, less than three months before the presidential election, the governor publicly announced his stand. Characteristically appealing for "prudence and moderation . . . conciliation and compromise," he proclaimed his support for Stephen A. Douglas, the northern Democrats' candidate and in Letcher's opinion the only legitimate Democratic nominee. In November a plurality of Virginia voters went for a third candidate, John Bell, the Whiggish nominee of the

Constitutional Union party. Bell defeated Breckinridge in the state by the razor-thin margin of 74,681 to 74,323. Over 16,000 Virginians followed Letcher's lead and voted for Douglas, more than enough to deprive the southern Democrats of the Commonwealth's electoral votes. By the narrowest of margins Virginia had refused to follow the secessionist "fire-eaters" of the cotton South, and the governor's decisive role in producing this outcome was not forgotten by secessionists in or out of the state.

Bell carried Virginia, but Republican Abraham Lincoln won the presidency, and the old Union began to disintegrate. In December 1860 South Carolina seceded, and by February 1861 the rest of the Deep South had followed that disaffected state into the nascent Confederacy. The upper South, including Virginia, wavered in an agony of indecision. The most populous and powerful of the southern states, weighted with the responsibility of past glory, the Old Dominion held the key to the situation. Without Virginia the new Confederacy was incomplete and terribly vulnerable; with Virginia the new nation would have a fighting chance of survival.

In spite of growing secessionist sentiment, Governor Letcher remained optimistic that his state could be kept in the Union and that war could be averted. Stalling for time, he initially opposed the calling of a state convention but in January 1861 agreed to summon one to meet the following month. Encouraged by the governor and other moderates, a majority of delegates at first refused to vote for secession. Meanwhile, Letcher sought reassurances concerning southern rights from the president-elect, but the strange, enigmatic man from Illinois refused to commit himself before his inauguration.

Although the Unionist ranks in Virginia were thinning rapidly, Letcher remained (in his own words) "calm and conservative." He moved very cautiously in directing Virginia's military preparations, doing what he could to soothe rising passions. Then the rush of events suddenly nullified all his efforts. Confederate batteries opened fire on Fort Sumter, and President Lincoln called for militiamen to suppress the rebellion. Recognizing that further delay was hopeless, Letcher rejected the federal request for Virginia troops and awaited the will of the convention. On April 17, 1861, the delegates voted to secede. Despite the efforts of moderates like Letcher, the Civil War had finally come.

Letcher was now the wartime chief of the most powerful southern state, a vital leader in the experiment in rebellion. In the prime of life, the forty-eight-year-old governor worked frantically to prepare his state for war. In this initial period of feverish activity Letcher occasionally became bogged down in administrative trivia, but generally he functioned effectively in the face of a host of new and urgent problems. Indeed, no rebel governor surpassed his energetic mobilization efforts during the first months of the conflict—and none was to experience the full fury of the Union onslaught more quickly. Soon even the most rabid prewar secessionists were willing to admit that the former Unionist was now a vigorous rebel leader. Basically Letcher was what he had always been, a Virginian first and last, a states' righter with a practical bourgeois aptitude for flexibility in an emergency.

The governor made a few mistakes in his appointments of officers for the state forces, but he usually placed capable men in command. He made Robert E. Lee the overall chief of Virginia's troops and did not interfere with purely military operations, a policy which President Jefferson Davis and many other Confederate political leaders would have done well to emulate. Despite opposition, Letcher also offered a colonelcy to an eccentric Virginia Military Institute professor named Thomas Jonathan Jackson and later defended the redoubtable Stonewall in a bitter dispute with Confederate Secretary of War Judah P. Benjamin. Although he himself had no military experience, Governor Letcher thus played a significant role in the emergence of two of the greatest rebel generals.

More so than other southern leaders he realized that unity was the key to Confederate success and stressed that this unity could be achieved only if the rebel states cooperated fully with the Confederate government. This meant yielding many traditional rights and privileges to the demands of the hour. Letcher's great admiration for Jefferson Davis made this cooperation much easier. He considered the aloof, austere Mississippian indispensable, the best man available to lead the South, but this confidence did not extend to some of the president's closest advisers. Even so, for the sake of harmony Letcher usually refrained from attacking Confederate authorities publicly, a sensible policy not followed by many rebel politicians and journalists. However, in private letters to friends he bitterly condemned what he considered ineptitude in high places.

By early 1862 the rebel armies were in danger of withering away as troops who had enlisted for one year prepared to return home. Determined to retain these veterans and mobilize new manpower, the Confederate government in April 1862 instituted the first national draft in American history—a decision which provoked a storm of criticism against this infringement on state and individual rights. Letcher joined the general condemnation of the draft in private correspondence with other rebel governors. Assailing the measure as unnecessary and unconstitutional, he decried it as "the most alarming stride toward consolidation that has ever occurred." As a practical matter, on the other hand, Letcher counseled going along with this unconstitutional act until victory was achieved and then challenging it in the courts. This willingness to subordinate his individual judgment to central government decisions was characteristic of Governor Letcher. While some of the South's leaders were beginning to resist the ever-increasing demands of the Confederate bureaucracy, Letcher continued to cooperate, realizing that the temporary abandonment of ancient rights was preferable to military defeat, which would mean the permanent loss of much more.

Letcher's pragmatism, reinforced by the constant menace of Union military power, triumphed over his states' rights heritage again and again as the war continued. Not only did he support the draft, but he also activated the Commonwealth's dwindling militia units whenever Confederate generals requested these temporary (and often timid) reinforcements. The governor even tolerated the hated practice of impressment, the seizure of civilian property by government agents. Quietly shelving traditionalist views, the governor subordinated himself and his state to Confederate authority.

But support of the Confederate war effort became politically risky as war-born disaffection grew with every passing month. An experienced politician, the governor quickly spotted the rising hostility to his cooperation with Confederate officials and his wide-ranging use of his executive powers. Many state legislators, especially prewar secessionists, had old scores to settle with Letcher, while others criticized his expanded authority. In particular, the General Assembly resented his constant proddings and pleas for forceful action, and the lawmakers began to investigate Letcher's prompt agreement with virtually every Confederate request for the mobilization of state militia units. No formal rebuke followed, but the Assembly's warning was clear: the governor should not be so quick to support the Confederacy at the expense of Virginia's rights and privileges. Recognizing political realities, Letcher began to bend with the popular tide occasionally, but fundamentally he did not alter his course. Instead he continued to serve as a buffer between the hypersensitive Virginia legislature and the hard-pressed Confederate government.

Overall, Letcher was an effective leader, possibly the most proficient of all the rebel governors, but his leadership was not without flaws. He was not an inspirational public speaker, his formal addresses too long and saturated with facts and statistics. Legalistic by training and conscientious by nature, Letcher (like President Davis) sometimes studied a problem to death, planning and procrastinating in order to postpone a hard decision. Both Letcher and Davis occasionally acted more like chief clerks than chief executives.

Letcher's greatest administrative failure involved the severe shortage of salt that plagued Virginia and the entire Confederacy. The Virginia legislature, finding no simple solution to the problem, passed the matter on to the governor in the fall of 1862. Letcher suddenly became the salt czar of the Commonwealth with power to do practically anything to secure and distribute the vital commodity at a reasonable price. A lifelong democrat, the governor made a poor czar. Moving too hesitantly and cautiously, he buried himself in the bureaucratic details of organization. He appointed a host of agents and administrators, but the new system, so impressive on paper, did not function well. Disappointed with the outcome, the General Assembly intervened early in 1863 and transferred most of the salt czar's powers to the Board of Public Works, which also performed ineffectively. The Commonwealth's inability to deal with the salt shortage mirrored the Confederacy's larger failure to mobilize its limited resources on the home front; the agrarian South proved unequal to the demands of total war.

Baffled by salt, the governor also faced other problems. Although he had become a financial expert while in Congress, he could exercise only limited control over the legislature's financial policies, and Virginia's public debt soared as the state poured more and more funds into the war effort. Letcher proposed that this ballooning debt be sharply reduced by selling all state interests in banks, canals, and railroads, but the General Assembly failed to act, leaving the debt problem to vex postwar politics for a generation or more. The governor exerted even less influence on soaring commodity prices and inadequate supplies of consumer goods—problems which struck at every home and every table. He repeatedly denounced "speculators" and "extortioners" (once equating them with drunkards, adulterers, fornicators, and other undesirables), but no one could stop the rampant inflation that was ravaging the home front. In April 1863 he helped to prevent a full-scale riot by dispersing a hungry mob which had started to loot food stores in Richmond. The fundamental problem remained, of course, but Letcher's bold action helped to hold back the forces of unrest a little longer.

Sometimes the governor supported the war effort too vigorously. He championed the harsh concept of guerrilla warfare and even directed the organization of a few innovative but largely ineffective "ranger" units. Angered by the rising tide of disaffection that eventually created West Virginia, Letcher initially favored trying some captured Union soldiers from the breakaway counties for treason. Confederate authorities declined to hand over any Unionist prisoners of war to Virginia "justice," however, and, as usual, the governor quietly accepted the central government's decision. He also wanted to try some captured Union army officers in state courts for inciting slave insurrections, another capital crime in Virginia.

These retaliatory proposals reflected an increasing preoccupation with military affairs. Before the sectional crisis of 1860–61 the lawyer-politician from Lexington had shown little interest in such matters, but once he became a wartime governor, combat considerations influenced practically every decision he made. His conversations with such confidants as Lexington lawyer James D. Davidson, Virginia Military Institute Superintendent Francis H. Smith, Secretary of the Commonwealth George W. Munford, Attorney General John Randolph Tucker, and aide-de-camp S. Bassett French centered increasingly on the lethal test of strength between Lee's Army of Northern Virginia and the powerful, persistent Army of the Potomac. In a nation of armchair generals even Letcher finally evolved into something of a military "expert."

By May 1862 the governor was so worried about gaps in Confederate defenses that, with the legislature's permission, he began to organize an auxiliary combat unit known as the Virginia State Line. Made up of men ineligible for the draft, the Line at its peak never numbered over 3,600 troops. Campaigning in western Virginia, the Line got in the way of Confederate army operations, won no significant victories, and eventually was disbanded by the General Assembly in 1863, much to the disappointment of the governor.

During 1863, the last year of his administration, Letcher was relieved of some duties by an ever-expanding Confederate bureaucracy and by a jealous state legislature. Although such moves may have hurt his pride a little, the reduced workload enabled him to spend more time with his wife and children in an informal, unpretentious, and friendly family setting which impressed visitors to the Governor's Mansion, including even a few Union army officers who briefly experienced the Letchers' hospitality before being transferred to regular prisoner-of-war facilities. Wartime inflation steadily reduced the purchasing power of the governor's $5,000 annual salary, but the Letchers continued to entertain visitors. Friends like Richmond Mayor Joseph Mayo, lawyer William H. Terrill, and banker C. W. Purcell and their families came more and more often. These bourgeois gentlemen were much like Letcher's previous acquaintances in Lexington and Washington, and he welcomed them with his usual informality and good humor. Shrouded in tobacco smoke and lubricated with bourbon and brandy, these lively gatherings now extended later into the evenings, giving the weary governor badly needed relaxation.

These occasional respites did not dilute Letcher's ambition and optimism. Early in 1863 he carefully analyzed his political prospects. Forbidden by the state constitution to seek reelection as governor, he decided to resume his career in the House of Representatives—this time the Confederate one in Richmond. On April 22, 1863, he announced his candidacy in his old congressional district in the Valley, and the election was held on May 28. Letcher enjoyed a narrow lead in the soldier vote, but overall he was decisively defeated. The victor, incumbent John B. Baldwin, was an able man, but before the war Letcher would have brushed aside such Whig opposition. Voters who had sent him to Washington four consecutive times by large majorities in the 1850s now rejected him emphatically. The reason was clear. The people of the Valley—and of all Virginia—disapproved of Letcher's wartime administration. In their opinion he had subordinated the state too much to Confederate authorities in Richmond, surrendering too many of their traditional rights and privileges. He had asked too much of a provincial, conservative people who were psychologically and philosophically unprepared for modern war. By the standards of the mid-nineteenth-century South he had been too demanding, too forceful, in a sense too successful a chief executive.

Already stunned by the recent death of his friend Stonewall Jackson, the governor was shocked by this defeat, the only major political setback of his career. Nevertheless, he continued to stress the need for unity and harmony, and his belief in eventual Confederate victory never wavered. Although he remained loyal to President Davis, Letcher increasingly placed his faith in the military genius of Robert E. Lee and the fighting spirit of his troops. Never a religious man, the governor had always prided himself on being hardheaded and realistic, yet he continued to believe that somehow the gaunt, tattered ranks of the rebel army would rise up and sweep the hated foe from southern soil.

One of Letcher's last offical acts was to host a farewell banquet at the Governor's Mansion on December 29. Old friends and colleagues gathered to pay tribute to the retiring chief executive, a decent and able man who had done his best in difficult circumstances. The festivities continued long into the night and included lengthy addresses by Letcher, his friend James D. Davidson, and Governor-elect William ("Extra Billy") Smith. Like Letcher a lifelong Democrat, Smith had been governor from 1846 through 1848 and had served in Congress with Letcher in the 1850s.

Early in January 1864 Letcher returned to Lexington where, as a private citizen, he continued to support the rebel cause. Wartime inflation in Richmond had ruined him financially, and the strain of gubernatorial duties had weakened his health. In the spring his personal cares increased even more when his eldest son, sixteen-year-old Samuel Houston Letcher, marched off to war with the Virginia Military Institute cadets. A month later the former governor had to flee from a Yankee army which invaded Lexington, burned VMI and some other buildings (including his home), and then marched to the outskirts of Lynchburg before being repulsed. The destruction of Letcher's residence—in a sense northern recognition of his contribution to the rebel war effort—left him more destitute than ever but still confident that Lee could somehow salvage final victory.

But the aging general and his exhausted troops had run out of miracles, and the Confederacy's last hopes in Virginia expired at Appomattox on April 9, 1865. Stunned, Letcher accepted defeat stoically, but the war was not quite over for him yet. Before dawn on May 20 a detachment of Union cavalrymen rode quietly into Lexington and surrounded the Letchers' rented home. The former governor was abruptly awakened, given only enough time to pack a few items and to say a few goodbyes, and then carried off to Washington in an army wagon. There he was imprisoned for seven weeks, first in a cell by himself, and later in a larger cell with several other former Confederates, including deposed rebel Governors Zebulon B. Vance of North Carolina and Joseph E. Brown of Georgia. Letcher was not treated harshly, and old friends (northerners as well as southerners) saw that he was well supplied with food, tobacco, and brandy. On July 4, 1865, Letcher watched from his barred window with mixed emotions as the victors celebrated Independence Day—an event he too had celebrated for so many years before the war. Six days later he finally received his parole. After a "pleasant and satis-factory" interview with the new president, Andrew Johnson, a fellow Demo-crat in Congress in the 1850s, he went home to Lexington to begin a new life at the age of fifty-two.

Although financially ruined, Letcher refused to join many of his fellow southerners in the refuge of bitterness and hatred. Instead, he resumed the full-time practice of law, handling everything from routine debt collections to murder cases. In January 1867 he received a full pardon from President Johnson. During these lean postwar years the former governor was too busy recouping his finances to get deeply involved in politics. An advocate of national reconciliation, he championed President Johnson's lenient Recon-struction plan as the best arrangement the defeated South could hope for, but he played only a minor role in the Conservative movement that guided Vir-ginia through its short, superficial Reconstruction experience at the end of the 1860s.

Indeed, for a time Letcher allowed himself to be diverted from his grow-ing law practice by only one significant public activity—the rebuilding and revitalization of the Virginia Military Institute. From his initial appointment to the college's board of visitors in 1866 until his health failed in 1881, the former governor labored tirelessly as VMI slowly rose from its ashes—a mon-ument to the Confederate past and a commitment to the American future.

Reasonably prosperous once more, Letcher finally returned to the politi-cal arena. In 1875, at the age of sixty-two, he was elected to the House of Delegates from Rockbridge County. Returning to his true calling, the veteran politico from the Valley was not just a legislative ornament from the past; he put in long hours and carried his share of the work load, championing honesty and economy in government and strongly supporting Governor James L. Kemper's penny-pinching Conservative administration. But in March 1876, just as he was getting back into the swing of things in Richmond, he suffered a cerebral stroke and the following year was swept from office by the surging Readjuster movement that demanded partial repudiation of the state debt. This demand was anathema to a fiscal conservative like "Honest John" Letcher, and for the second time he paid the price for ignoring a groundswell of popular opinion.

Letcher continued to practice law and to preach the same moderation that had marked his prewar career. Always a battler, he now fought hard against the encroachments of old age and infirmity, but by 1880 he was bedridden most of the time—still mentally alert and still skeptical of religion. Finally, on January 22, 1884, the long struggle ended. Surrounded by friends and relatives, John Letcher died peacefully at the age of seventy—once again a Virginian, a southerner, *and* an American.

The people of the Old Dominion paused only briefly to mark his passing. They had never fully appreciated Letcher's merits or achievements, and now they were too busy building a "New South" to do more than salute another old rebel going to join his fallen comrades. John Letcher deserved better. A moderate, conscientious politician forced into a war he never wanted, he became an outstanding war governor. He faltered occasionally, but overall he effectively marshaled the Commonwealth's resources. Selflessly cooperating with the Confederate government, he set an example which obstreperous governors like Vance of North Carolina and Brown of Georgia would have done well to follow. Flexible and realistic, Letcher coaxed his fellow Virginians much farther along the path of sacrifice than they wanted to go, and for his pains he reaped only rejection and defeat. A plain, unpretentious man of the middle class, he was one of the unsung heroes of the Confederacy—a pragmatic patriot who ably led the Old Dominion during its greatest ordeal.

SOURCES

The Letcher Executive Papers are at the Virginia State Library. Some private papers and records are owned by his grandson, Brigadier General John Seymour Letcher of Lexington. Other Letcher correspondence is located at the Virginia Military Institute, Duke University, and the State Historical Society of Wisconsin. Washington and Lee University has some issues of editor Letcher's Lexington *Valley Star*.

F. N. Boney's *John Letcher of Virginia: The Story of Virginia's Civil War Governor* (University, Ala., 1966) is a comprehensive account of Letcher's life and career. Briefer accounts by the same author are: "Governor Letcher's Candid Correspondence," *Civil War History* 10 (June 1964): 167–80; "Virginian, Southerner, American," *Virginia Cavalcade* 17 (Summer 1967): 11–19; and "Governor John Letcher, Virginian," *Civil War Times Illustrated* 11 (Dec. 1972): 10–19.

WILLIAM SMITH

Governor of Virginia

1864–1865

WILLIAM ("EXTRA BILLY") SMITH

Governor in Two Wars

Alvin A. Fahrner

William Smith served one full term and part of another as war governor of Virginia—a full term of three years during the Mexican War and a frantic fifteen months of a four-year term during the Civil War as the Confederacy was collapsing. Smith was an energetic, even dramatic, political leader who demonstrated administrative skill and imagination, but the drift of history has covered his role and image. A popular vote-getter, Smith was an inveterate politician who possessed genuine qualities of leadership.

He was born at Marengo, the ancestral home of his father Caleb, in King George County, Virginia, on September 6, 1797. Caleb Smith, considered a man of wealth and influence in his community, frequently occupied places of honor and served several terms in the state legislature. William Smith's mother was Mary Anne Waugh Smith, cousin of his father and daughter of William and Elizabeth Donaphan Smith of Mount Eccentric of Fauquier County, sometimes called the "cradle" of the Smiths in Virginia. William Smith took particular pride in his maternal ancestry, especially the Donaphan branch—lineal descendants of Alexander Donaphan, a Spaniard by birth, who had immigrated to Virginia by way of England. The Donaphans were identified as gentry in the official records of King George County as early as the reign of William and Mary.

Although Smith's family traced its roots to the colonial squirearchy, little remained of aristocratic tradition in his childhood home of three brothers and four sisters; instead the Smiths of the early 1800s exemplified middle-class tastes and values. At the age of seven William Smith entered an old-field school six miles from home; at ten he journeyed to Fredericksburg, Virginia, for private tutoring; and at fourteen he enrolled at Plainfield Academy in Plainfield, Connecticut. Remaining in Connecticut only a short time, Smith returned to Virginia and entered Thomas Nelson's English and Classical School in Hanover County. Smith soon demonstrated the ambition and intellectual qualities considered necessary for the study of law, and his father sent him to study in the office of Green and Williams at Fredericksburg. From there he went to work with Thomas L. Moore, a Warrenton attorney, and finally completed his legal training in the office of William H. Winder of Baltimore, Maryland.

The twenty-one-year-old Smith commenced law practice in 1818 in the small town of Culpeper, Virginia, and three years later married Elizabeth Bell, the eldest daughter of a Culpeper family noted for its wealth and influence. Eleven children, three of whom died in infancy, were born to the couple. Elizabeth Smith proved to be a loving mother and an inspiration to her husband—applauding his successes and comforting him when he failed.

Smith's ambition and exuberance naturally propelled him into business ventures. As the drive for internal improvements gathered momentum in the 1820s, he seized the opportunity to make his fortune. In 1827 he organized a mail-coach service from Fairfax Courthouse to Culpeper and rapidly expanded the system overland from Washington, D.C., to Georgia. Eventually Smith added steamboat connections from Washington to Baltimore, Norfolk, Pensacola, and Galveston. He won postal delivery contracts from the federal government for each leg of this system and kept the Post Office Department so busy making "extra" payments for his services that he came to be known as "Extra Billy" Smith, a nickname he bore for the rest of his life.

Dabbling in local governmental affairs as a Democratic-Republican, the Culpeper entrepreneur moved up rapidly in politics as well. In 1828 he took the stump for Andrew Jackson and zealously supported Old Hickory's conduct of the presidency with one significant exception: he would not endorse Jackson's threat to states' rights in the South Carolina nullification crisis. In 1836 Smith was elected to the Virginia Senate as a Democrat and was subsequently reelected to a second term, gaining valuable experience and taking an active part in deliberations. He was especially interested in financial issues, and he emerged as one of the chief architects of banking legislation.

The question of state banking policy was a major source of political and sectional strife. The western counties clamored for the incorporation of numerous independent state banks, while eastern communities called for an increase in the capital stock of existing financial institutions (most of which were headquartered in the Tidewater and Piedmont) and the establishment of additional branches only. Reflecting the views of his Piedmont constituency, Smith pressed for strict regulation of banks, large-scale investment of state funds in banking projects, reliance on a "hard money" currency, and continuance of existing emphasis on a few large banks with additional branches rather than establishment of a large number of independent banks. Although hostile—like many other Jacksonians—to banks in general, Smith considered them necessary evils, instruments through which the Commonwealth could finance its ambitious and vital program of internal improvements.

Overcoming strong Whig opposition, in 1841 Smith won a seat in the U.S. House of Representatives. This post allowed the freshman congressman a new forum for the exposition of his Jacksonian principles, and he took full advantage of the opportunity. He advocated economy and retrenchment in federal expenditures, and one of his speeches in opposition to the protective tariff was considered a masterpiece by his Democratic colleagues. Such accomplishments did not, however, ensure political success. Virginia's Whigs, who controlled the state legislature, gerrymandered Smith's district, and he failed in his bid for reelection.

Defeated and out of office, Smith moved from Culpeper to Warrenton in 1843 in order to take advantage of superior educational advantages for his growing family. He resumed the practice of law, but political affairs continued to attract his attention. He campaigned actively in 1844 for James K. Polk, the Democratic presidential nominee. Colorful, emotional, and sometimes acrimonious in his rhetoric, Smith faced Whig leaders in prolonged debate throughout Virginia, winning widespread popularity among the voters and his party's managers alike. When Polk carried the state, the Old Dominion's Democrats (who now controlled the legislature) rewarded Smith's campaign endeavors by electing him governor in 1845. Extra Billy was forty-eight years old at the time.

In those days—before the constitutional convention of 1851—the General Assembly elected the governor for a three-year term, and the legislators clearly played the dominant role in state affairs. Even so, Virginia's chief executive could exert considerable influence through his appointive powers. He chose the county sheriffs from nominations submitted by the county courts, for example, and filled vacancies in the county courts themselves. He also appointed directors of state banks, a power which enabled him to award control of those politically and financially potent agencies to his supporters, and he controlled the selection of administrators for the state's charitable institutions as well. In the last analysis, nevertheless, Smith's ability to persuade the General Assembly to adopt his policies would determine the success or failure of his administration.

Beginning his term on January 1, 1846, Smith had barely settled into office when President Polk took the country into war with Mexico, and the new governor was at once overwhelmed with the problems of recruiting and outfitting Virginia's share of the volunteer army. Despite opposition from Whigs and Calhoun Democrats, Smith vigorously supported the war effort. He showed imagination and administrative competence, cutting through legal barriers and parrying with skill the clamor for commissions and offices. When legislative sanction was lacking for the efficient handling of details, he acted on his own authority and subsequently persuaded a reluctant Assembly to approve what he had done. In all he recruited and transferred to federal service one regiment of 1,303 officers and men. Smith's energetic activities in this conflict constituted a rehearsal for the more pressing responsibilities he would assume during the last months of the Civil War.

Successful in his mobilization efforts, Smith watched with growing concern the heated congressional debates of the late 1840s over the extension of slavery into the territories. He chafed at the Wilmot Proviso, which would have barred slavery forever from the lands acquired from Mexico, and began to move toward the extreme southern rights wing of the Democratic party. Convinced that free blacks were a threat to the "peculiar institution" in Virginia, he attempted with almost religious fervor to ram legislation through the General Assembly to require their expulsion from the state. A sizable bloc of moderate lawmakers opposed the measure, however, and thwarted Smith's repeated efforts to attain this goal.

The governor enjoyed greater success in his more constructive endeavors for internal improvements, constitutional reform, and public education. He urged the legislature to use the state's resources to construct two main railroads instead of a variety of lesser projects. Both lines would extend from the coast across the mountains to the Shenandoah Valley; from there one line would proceed to the Tennessee border, eventually connecting with the Deep South and the Southwest; the other would make its way northward through the Kanawha Valley to the Ohio River. These great trunk lines, Smith argued, would make the Old Dominion independent of the North, "wean away" western Virginians from their economic affinities for the free states, flood Virginia markets with produce, and transform the Tidewater into a vast shipyard.

To further cement western Virginia to the east, Smith pushed for a constitutional convention and democratic reform of the county courts. Ever the Jacksonian, he wanted to see disgruntled westerners share more equally in the powers and privileges of government—a goal which would in large measure be attained after his term of office in the constitutional convention of 1851. Smith also manifested his democratic proclivities by supporting legislation that increased educational opportunities for the masses. During his term the General Assembly acted to improve the primitive primary school arrangements then in effect and authorized local officials to create district school systems. By 1850 primary schools were operating in 126 counties and towns, and about 40,000 children were enrolled at one type of educational institution or another. A full-fledged tax-supported school system would not be created until the Reconstruction years, but Smith's administration had witnessed significant steps toward this goal.

In all of these areas Smith foreshadowed the more dynamic, program-oriented governors who would emerge in the twentieth century. He left office on January 1, 1849, enormously popular but financially weakened by the suspension of his law practice and, more importantly, by losses from his postal business. The country was seething with excitement over the discovery of gold in California, and one of Smith's sons had already joined the rush to the "Golden West." Anxious to recoup his fortunes, the irrepressible former governor soon made his way to California as well. He practiced law in San

Francisco for three years, successfully speculated in real estate, participated in civic affairs, and was drawn irresistibly into Democratic politics once again. In 1852 he served as the presiding officer of the California Democratic state convention. Also, although not a member of the state legislature, he received scattered support in that body for one of the new state's seats in the federal Senate. Smith's essential loyalties remained with the Old Dominion, however, and financial success enabled him to return there in December 1852.

In spite of his three-year absence, Extra Billy retained his popularity with the Virginia masses, and he resumed a prominent political role with surprising ease. In 1853 he was elected to the U.S. House of Representatives from the Warrenton district and kept the office for the next eight years, often against bitter Whig opposition. In Congress Smith was colorful and flamboyant, at one time engaging in a fistfight in the halls of the House. Predictably, he functioned as a hard-line Democratic regular, although in 1855, 1857, and 1859 he had to accept Know-Nothing support in order to be reelected. An advocate of the Gadsden Purchase and the Kansas-Nebraska Act, Smith vigorously opposed the admission of free states, homestead measures, and federal land grants to railroads. In the presidential election of 1860 he backed the states' rights Breckinridge wing of the Democratic party but reacted to Republican Abraham Lincoln's victory with surprising moderation; Smith approved the secession of the Deep South but urged Virginia and the border states to remain in the Union to mediate between the North and the cotton states. When Lincoln called for volunteers in April 1861, however, the Old Dominion joined the Confederacy, and Extra Billy proffered his services to the southern war effort.

Although sixty-four years old, Smith was in excellent health and eager for a leadership role in the army. Governor John Letcher rejected Smith's request for a brigadier general's commission because of his lack of military experience but did appoint the former chief executive to the colonelcy of the Forty-ninth Virginia Regiment. From 1861 to 1863 Smith served under Generals Pierre G. T. Beauregard, Joseph E. Johnston, D. H. Hill, William Mahone, Jubal A. Early, and Richard S. Ewell—the last of whom repeatedly praised him for courage and boldness. He participated in the bloody engagements at First Manassas, Seven Pines, Seven Days, and Antietam, where he was seriously wounded in the shoulder. While recuperating at home during the next eight months he was promoted to brigadier general and given command of Early's famous Fourth Brigade. Returning to the field, he provided that unit with "devoted if unskilled leadership," according to military historian Douglas Southall Freeman. After an undistinguished performance at Gettysburg, Smith was relegated to service behind the lines. Promoted to the rank of major general in July 1863, he was assigned to recruiting duties— tasks which enabled him to put his Mexican War experience to good use.

Smith's primary mission was to urge deserters and stragglers to return to their units, a role for which he was better qualified than active command of troops in the field.

As a military leader, Extra Billy was bold and colorful, but he had demonstrated little talent for strategy or tactics. He had won a reputation for reckless bravery, nevertheless, and was popular with soldiers throughout the army. This popularity soon found expression at the polls, and even as the war raged the indefatigable Smith responded to the magnetic tug of politics. He served two stints in the Confederate House of Representatives, where he played an unobtrusive role and generally supported President Jefferson Davis's programs.

In 1863, as his military career was entering its final phase, Smith launched his second drive for the governorship. In 1845 he had been elected to the office by the legislature; this time (as required by the Constitution of 1851) he needed the support of the voters. His opponents in the race were George Wythe Munford, a Democrat, and Thomas S. Flournoy, a Whig and an erstwhile Know-Nothing gubernatorial aspirant in 1855. This campaign was unique in a number of respects. Conducted under wartime conditions with the enemy literally "at the gates" in some localities, the race was also notable because General Smith did not leave his command to solicit votes. Instead, the electioneering in his behalf was performed by partisans who were for the most part his supporters from the antebellum years. Smith's adherents stressed their candidate's military heroism and his previous experience as war governor during the Mexican conflict. Winning a decisive majority of the soldier vote, Extra Billy emerged victorious in the May 28, 1863, election.

The sixty-seven-year-old Smith was inaugurated as governor of Virginia on New Year's Day, January 1, 1864. Following an inaugural address in which he reviewed the history of the sectional conflict and made a variety of proposals to the General Assembly, Smith was honored at a reception which President and Mrs. Davis held for him at the Confederate White House. This affair attracted a large number of prominent civilian and military officials, including outgoing Governor Letcher and incoming Lieutenant Governor Samuel Price.

By the start of 1864 conditions in Virginia were approaching a crisis stage, primarily because of the South's deteriorating economic and military strength. Smith recognized the gravity of the situation and hastened to come to grips with the problems that he considered most pressing. The first of these, naturally enough, was the need to strengthen local defenses against the impending Union onslaught. He believed that the state's so-called second-class militia (composed of youths between sixteen and seventeen years of age and men from forty-five to fifty-five) was entirely inadequate, and on January 22, 1864, he urged the General Assembly to make all white men not subject to Confederate conscription liable for local defense service. The governor was less tactful than usual in this case, reprimanding the legislators severely for neglecting this grave matter so long. The Assembly considered Smith's criticism an insult and contemptuously tabled his request. Undaunted, the ingenious Extra Billy—reverting to the practices of his Mexican War days—proceeded on his own authority to organize a substantial force of aliens, draft-exempts, and individuals previously discharged from Confederate service because of age and disability. Reflecting the success of his endeavors, this force totaled 13,073 officers and men by September 1864.

Smith's zealous efforts on behalf of local defense caused some conflict with the Davis administration. James A. Seddon, Davis's secretary of war, believed that all military forces should be under the control of the central government, and the Conscription Act of February 17, 1864, added white men between seventeen and eighteen and between forty-five and fifty years of age to the list of those subject to the draft. Extra Billy, along with other Confederate governors, protested against this act because it threatened to destroy their local defense units. When Seddon insisted, however, Smith reluctantly complied with the law and was pleasantly surprised to discover that he was still able to maintain a viable force in spite of the loss of some men to the Confederacy. Historians have contended that the maintenance of these home-guard organizations materially contributed to the southern defeat by draining off vital manpower, but this was not the case in Virginia. Although he did so reluctantly, Governor Smith deferred to the manpower requirements of the central government, and his second-class militia was still sufficiently strong to contribute to the defense of Richmond and its environs.

The problem of supplies for the civilian population had also reached an extremely critical stage by 1864. Facing the issue squarely, Smith concluded that the Commonwealth should adopt a policy which he had proposed in his inaugural address—state participation in blockade-running through its own agent. He further insisted that Virginia should send a representative to purchase supplies in other states where destruction was less severe. To his dismay, the Senate refused to fund his proposals. Once again, this time in desperation, Extra Billy implemented his own plan. Withdrawing $40,000 from the Civil and Military Contingency Fund and borrowing $30,000 from a Richmond bank, he employed an agent to run the blockade and furnished him with cotton to exchange abroad for commodities desperately needed in Virginia. Smith also arranged with Confederate authorities for the exclusive use of a railroad train under the control of another of his agents, who proceeded through several southern states to purchase corn, rice, and other much needed supplies. Smith reported to the Assembly in December 1864 that although this scheme failed to live up to his expectations, it had met with reasonable success. Following in the footsteps of Governor Zebulon Vance of North Carolina, Smith also moved to involve the Commonwealth of Virginia directly in blockade-running by state-owned ships. The governor's venture in blockade-running paid off handsomely for a time and served to alleviate the supply problem. After the fall of Wilmington and Charleston early in 1865, however, provisions procured in this manner rapidly dwindled.

The maintenance of food stocks plagued Extra Billy throughout his Civil War governorship, and clothing supplies demanded his attention as well. Most of Virginia's cotton and woolen resources had been turned over to Confederate control during Letcher's administration, but Smith decided that the state would have to assume more responsibility for clothing its civilian population. Appealing to the General Assembly in March 1864, he convinced the legislators to create the post of commercial agent and to appropriate funds to enable that officer to carry out his mission. The commercial agent was charged with the responsibility of purchasing raw cotton and cotton and woolen cards to sell to the civilian population at cost. On the governor's orders, textile mills in Virginia were required to process the people's cloth and to charge them no more than they charged the Confederate government. With an appropriation of $400,000 from the Assembly, Smith's agent, S. Bassett French, purchased a considerable amount of goods in other states but far from enough to meet the needs of the people of the Commonwealth. Lack of sufficient transportation further aggravated the situation.

Already exorbitant when Smith took office, prices of foodstuffs and other essentials climbed even higher as the war dragged on. Reluctantly the beleaguered governor appealed to the legislature in December 1864 to adopt price controls. The lawmakers rejected this approach; nevertheless, the increasingly desperate situation ultimately compelled the Assembly to pass regulatory laws. In order to guarantee wool production, for example, the lawmakers prohibited the slaughter of sheep, and they also authorized the governor to impress certain types of private property when he deemed it necessary.

The General Assembly and Smith also clashed repeatedly over exemptions from military service. Confederate conscription enactments authorized draft exemptions for officials engaged in administering the government and laws of each state. Since all state officials were eligible for such exemptions if so certified by the governor, minor state offices were much sought after, and officials who had fled from enemy-occupied territory continued to insist upon exemption even though they had no duties to perform. The governor declared that he would follow a policy of "limited" exemption based solely upon genuine administrative needs. In spite of legislative opposition, Smith for the most part certified only those whom he considered "necessary." In comparison with such states' rights obstructionists as Zebulon Vance of North Carolina and Joseph E. Brown of Georgia, therefore, Extra Billy's record on exemptions was good. He defied his exemption-oriented legislature, subordinated particularistic needs to the overriding demands of the Confederate war effort, and certified "necessary" exemptions with painstaking moderation.

The Confederate government's policy of impressing slaves to work on

fortifications also embroiled Smith in controversy, placing him squarely between the planter-dominated General Assembly on the one hand and the
increasingly desperate Davis administration on the other. Appreciating the
property rights that were at stake, the governor sympathized with the planters' opposition to the policy, but his military experience and Virginia's precarious situation compelled him to recognize the necessity for the forced
recruitment of slave labor. Unlike his predecessor, John Letcher, who had
occasionally opposed such impressment, Smith exerted himself once again in
a vexatious and controversial attempt to meet the demands of the
Confederacy.

As the war entered its final phase, moreover, Extra Billy stood in the
vanguard of the movement to reinforce the dwindling Confederate armies
through the use of Negro troops. Sherman's capture of Atlanta and Grant's
protracted siege of Petersburg convinced the governor that drastic measures
were required. As early as October 1864 Smith met with the governors of
North Carolina, South Carolina, Georgia, and Mississippi in a common advocacy of the use of black troops. In December 1864 he informed the General
Assembly that the time had come to use slaves as soldiers "even if it resulted
in the freedom of those organized." He exhorted the lawmakers to act immediately, but it was not until March 4, 1865, that they authorized him to
furnish black troops to the Confederate army. After the Confederate Congress
passed the necessary enabling legislation twelve days later, both Governor
Smith and President Davis moved with alacrity to get black soldiers to the
field, and the process of requisitioning slaves for this purpose was well under
way when the Confederacy collapsed.

Bedeviled with supply and manpower problems, the governor also had
to contend with a rapidly escalating state debt. Although his predecessor,
Letcher, had characterized Virginia's financial condition as "highly prosperous" at the end of his term, Smith inherited a debt of $35 million. Most of
this sum stemmed from the Commonwealth's antebellum investments in railroads and other internal improvements, while the remainder consisted of
wartime bond issues scheduled to be refunded by the Confederate government at the end of the struggle. As the state assumed more responsibility for
the defense and welfare of its people, the Commonwealth's tax revenues
lagged still further behind its disbursements. As a result, frequent borrowing
was necessary—no easy task in a time of spiraling inflation and fiscal collapse.
With guidance from the veteran state auditor, Jonathan M. Bennett, however,
Extra Billy managed to meet the financial needs of Virginia's government
until the end of the war. Even so, he left a bitter legacy: the state's bonded
obligations totaled $40,040,718.16 as of July 1, 1865, setting the stage for
the prolonged and divisive debt controversy of the postwar years.

Smith also had to devote much of his time to routine matters, some
unrelated to the war but generally aggravated by it. He spent onerous hours

on appointments to minor offices, and he seriously considered each pardon, reprieve, and commutation that came before him. At times he was swamped with letters describing the personal hardships of individuals on the home front and in the front lines. The governor took time to read much of this correspondence and to discuss it with his assistants. When unable to help, he directed the able secretary of the Commonwealth, George Wythe Munford, to prepare tactful letters of regret. There can be no doubt that the burdens of the people bore heavily on the conscientious Extra Billy.

Although civilian and military morale declined precipitously in 1864 and 1865, Governor Smith, always the epitome of hospitality, continued to maintain a degree of social life in the Executive Mansion. He and his wife held weekly receptions on Friday evenings from eight to ten. One visitor, Colonel Tom August, was asked how he had enjoyed himself at one of these affairs. "First rate," he replied. "All we did was promenade and lemonade."

Finally time ran out for the Confederacy, and the governor was in attendance at St. Paul's Church in Richmond on the morning of April 2, 1865, when President Davis received General Lee's notification that he should prepare to abandon the city. When Davis ordered the Confederate capital evacuated, Smith took the necessary action to move the state government as well. It was not until one o'clock on the morning of April 3, however, that the governor departed Richmond with his son and aide, Lieutenant Colonel P. Bell Smith, on a trek which took them along the James River to Lynchburg and later across country to Danville. Mrs. Smith and the rest of the Smith household left Richmond about six hours later. En route to Lynchburg, the governor's horse stumbled and fell into the water, and both horse and rider narrowly escaped drowning. Informed of Lee's surrender at Appomattox, the redoubtable Extra Billy—unwilling to accept defeat—resolved to continue the struggle. He wrote to President Davis asking for control of all Confederate forces in Virginia, but Davis refused. Undaunted and undeterred, Smith decided to resort to guerrilla warfare if he could win support from the people. Traveling through the state, however, he found to his disappointment that the mass of Virginians yearned for peace. A mass meeting of Augusta County citizens, among them the prominent and respected Alexander H. H. Stuart, adopted resolutions calling for cooperation with federal authorities in the reorganization of the state government. Smith realized that further resistance on his part was futile. On the next day, May 9, 1865, President Andrew Johnson declared all acts of the Confederate state government of Virginia null and void and recognized Unionist Francis H. Pierpont as the chief executive of the Commonwealth.

Assailed from all sides, Extra Billy accepted the inevitable. On June 8, 1865, he returned to Richmond and turned himself in to the occupation forces. A reward of $25,000 had been offered for his capture, but the conquerors proved lenient. After transferring the property of the state to Pierpont on June 13, Smith was allowed to return to his home in Warrenton. He subsequently petitioned the president for a pardon and in July took the prescribed oath of loyalty to the United States. Finally, eighteen months after the collapse of the Confederacy, Johnson pardoned Smith—along with many other erstwhile leaders of the southern cause.

Extra Billy's military struggle against the federal government was over, but he continued to do battle against one of the major consequences of the northern victory, the enfranchisement of the Negro. He joined the white supremacist Conservative party in the postwar years and participated in the brief but bitter struggle to overthrow the carpetbag Republican regime in the state. In 1875, at the age of seventy-eight, he was elected for a term in the House of Delegates, where he served with his old war-governor colleague, John Letcher. In the General Assembly Smith supported proposals designed to curtail the political activities of blacks, and he also opposed incipient Readjuster efforts to scale down the state debt. Retiring from politics, he showed great interest in scientific agriculture during his last years at his Monterosa estate and carried on an extensive correspondence with old friends.

William Smith died on May 18, 1887, almost ninety years of age. His devoted wife, Elizabeth, had died nine years earlier. Only three of his eleven children still lived. Extra Billy was buried in Hollywood Cemetery in Richmond, and his statue stands in Capitol Square today, a fitting tribute to the man who as governor during the Mexican War had supervised the landscaping of those grounds.

Of average height, Smith was freckled as a youth, ruddy in his prime, and courtly and chivalrous in his later years. Confident and exuberant, he rigorously disciplined himself: he abstained from the use of both tobacco and alcohol; he walked "straight as an arrow" even in old age. Although never a formal communicant of a church, he firmly upheld Christianity and its moral teachings.

Smith always considered himself a Jeffersonian-Jacksonian Democrat, and he was popular with the masses throughout his political career. As governor during the Mexican War he displayed political skill and administrative daring. As governor during the hectic final months of the Civil War he gave evidence of similar traits, courageously supporting the Davis administration, while at the same time seeking pragmatic solutions to Virginia's problems. Caught in an almost untenable position between a demanding Confederate government and a recalcitrant Virginia legislature, he conducted the affairs of state in a forceful and constructive manner. He was, as historian Nathaniel W. Stephenson concluded in 1919, one of the "strong men" of the Confederacy who had not had his "due" from scholarly interpreters of the conflict. William ("Extra Billy") Smith merits respect as a devoted servant of Virginia—and of the South.

SOURCES

No useful collection of Smith's personal papers exists. A contemporary and friend, John W. Bell, collected and published a number of letters, reminiscences, and speeches in *Memoirs of Governor William Smith of Virginia* (1891). The most valuable manuscript sources are Smith's Executive Papers (Virginia State Library); the William C. Rives Papers and Martin Van Buren Papers (Library of Congress); the Charles Ellis and George Wythe Munford Papers, Jefferson Davis Papers, and John Francis Hamtramck Papers (Duke University); and the E. M. Law Papers and Charles W. Dabney Papers (University of North Carolina).

The most extensive treatment of Smith's life is Alvin A. Fahrner, "The Public Career of William 'Extra Billy' Smith" (Ph.D. diss., University of North Carolina, 1953). See also Fahrner's "William 'Extra Billy' Smith, Democratic Governor of Virginia, 1846–1849," *East Carolina University Publications in History* 2 (1965): 36–53, and "William 'Extra Billy' Smith, Governor of Virginia 1864–1865: A Pillar of the Confederacy," *Virginia Magazine of History and Biography* 74 (1966): 68–87.

FRANCIS HARRISON PIERPONT

Wartime Unionist,

Reconstruction Moderate

Richard G. Lowe

As a young lawyer and businessman in antebellum western Virginia, Francis Harrison Pierpont had an idealized vision of his state—a land of middle-class farmers, merchants, and industrialists, working together to make Virginia prosperous and enjoying equal political rights and privileges in a progressive community. This Whiggish conception did not include aristocratic slaveholders or propertyless slaves. In his seven-year political career Pierpont was successful as long as he worked with and governed the groups included in his ideal Virginia—essentially the white, nonslaveholding middle class. But as soon as he was forced by postwar circumstances to deal with aristocratic planters and penniless former slaves, Pierpont faltered.

Francis H. Pierpont was born on the family farm near Morgantown (now in West Virginia) on January 25, 1814. His family soon moved a few miles to the southwest where his father farmed and operated a tannery in the small village of Fairmont. As young boys, the future governor and his four brothers worked on the farm, but they also helped at their father's tannery located in a region dotted with iron furnaces, brick factories, tanneries, and flour mills. Young Francis had little time for formal schooling. He probably attended a log schoolhouse near Fairmont for a few months, but most of his education was obtained at home under the tutelage of his parents. Armed with a basic knowledge of the three Rs and some familiarity with the classics, at the age of twenty-one he enrolled in Allegheny College in Meadville, Pennsylvania, a small Methodist college where he was graduated with honors in September 1839.

Pierpont tried his hand at teaching for two years but also read law in preparation for a career as an attorney. Admitted to the bar in 1842, he quickly established a successful law practice in Fairmont. The rising young lawyer aligned himself with the Whig party, perhaps because of his intense dislike of the Democratic-controlled legislature across the mountains in Richmond. In the minds of Pierpont and thousands of other antebellum westerners, their region was treated in a high-handed manner by the eastern-dominated General Assembly. Eastern slaveholders, they said, had written

FRANCIS H. PIERPONT

Governor of Virginia

1865–1868

the state constitution to favor slaveowners at the expense of nonslaveholders. While $1,000 of slave property was taxed at $1.20, every $1,000 of other property was taxed $4.00. By 1860, Pierpont later observed, three-fourths of the state government's income was being spent to protect slave property, to provide higher education in slaveholding eastern Virginia, and to construct internal improvements east of the Appalachians. This official discrimination was made possible, westerners complained, by unfair overrepresentation of eastern counties (and consequent underrepresentation of western areas) in the legislative halls. These and other sectional protests were an important part of Pierpont's early life, and they served to intensify his allegiance to the Whig party.

In 1848 he became attorney for the Baltimore and Ohio Railroad, a new line connecting the Atlantic coast to the growing Ohio River valley. Five years later he opened a coal mine in Fairmont and was soon selling coal, bricks, and leather goods. The income from these various enterprises (together with law fees) made Pierpont a well-to-do, eligible bachelor, and one month before his fortieth birthday he married Julia Augusta Robertson, a governess in the home of a neighbor and the daughter of abolitionist New York parents. Although his wife never converted him into an abolitionist radical, her background combined with his western sectionalism tended to alienate him even further from the slaveholding elite of eastern Virginia.

In the presidential campaign of 1860 Pierpont remained true to his old Whig attitudes and supported John Bell of the Constitutional Union party. Although happy that Bell carried the Old Dominion in 1860, Pierpont realized that southern secession was a definite possibility. When the Old Dominion joined the movement in April 1861, trans-Appalachian Virginians with no slaves to protect feared their region would become a bloody battleground between secessionists and Unionists. After several large protest meetings they agreed to hold a convention in Wheeling on May 13 "to consult and determine upon such action as the people of Northwestern Virginia should take in the present fearful emergency." Each northwestern county was instructed to elect five delegates.

The May 13 gathering was more a mass Union meeting than a constituent assembly. Only twenty-seven northwest counties were represented; twenty-four others which would later become part of West Virginia sent no delegates at all. Of the 436 convention members (one of whom was Pierpont), 162 (or 37 percent) were from four counties in the northern panhandle squeezed between Ohio and Pennsylvania. After a confusing debate, the delegates decided to campaign against the secession ordinance, scheduled for a popular vote on May 23; if the hated proposition should pass, they would elect delegates to a second Wheeling convention which would "take such action as the safety and welfare of Virginia may demand." In addition, the first convention established a central committee to act as a link between the two meetings. One of the nine members was the prosperous Fairmont lawyer and businessman Francis H. Pierpont.

Thus, at the age of forty-seven Pierpont became a pivotal figure in the histories of Virginia and West Virginia. It was he who devised the plan that the central committee and later the western counties would ultimately adopt to combat secession. The Pierpont plan, solidly rooted in constitutional law, was based on the old and well-established idea that an abused people could remove their abusers from power and on a relevant decision by the U.S. Supreme Court (*Luther* v. *Borden,* 1848). It provided for the quick reestablishment of law and order through the creation of a loyal state government and opened a legal path toward the formation of a new state. It was the most reasonable, commonsense approach to the situation and the path finally followed by the people of the northwest.

Exactly as Pierpont feared, Virginia voters approved the secession ordinance on May 23 by a margin of 128,884 to 32,134, but in the fifty counties of what would soon become the new state of West Virginia, the vote was almost two to one against it. The next stage of the northwest's resistance to secession was initiated on June 11 when representatives from thirty-five western and northern counties assembled for the second Wheeling convention. This convention, like the one in May, included many self-appointed delegates, but, ignoring legal and constitutional problems, the members began to set Pierpont's plan into motion. They declared vacant all state offices occupied by Confederates, and on June 20 they appointed Pierpont governor of the entire state of Virginia to replace rebel Governor John Letcher. Daniel Polsley of Mason County was named lieutenant governor, and a five-man Governor's Council, which included four former Whigs and a Republican, was appointed to assist Pierpont.

The national government's official recognition of these proceedings arrived in Wheeling on June 25 when Secretary of War Simon Cameron assured "Governor" Pierpont of federal aid. President Lincoln himself mentioned the Pierpont "Restored" government in his July 4 message to Congress, noting that "those loyal citizens, this government is bound to recognize, and protect, as being Virginia." Nine days later the U.S. Senate added its official recognition, and Pierpont's upstart Restored government became the de jure authority for the entire state of Virginia.

Governor Pierpont's method of restoring loyal government in Virginia was regarded throughout the North as a model to be used in other southern states. Although the Civil War proved to be longer and harder than most had foreseen, thus preventing quick duplication of the Pierpont formula in other Confederate states, many aspects of the Virginia experience were visible in President Lincoln's 1863 "Ten Percent Plan" of Reconstruction. Both Pierpont and Lincoln assumed that the seceding state governments were invalid, that loyal citizens in Confederate states should erect Unionist governments, and that these governments would serve as nuclei around which a fully operational administration could be constructed after the war. Thus, Pierpont's formula for Virginia had significance far beyond the borders of the Old Dominion.

The new Unionist governor took his position seriously. Leaving his coal mine and tannery in the hands of relatives and removing his wife and young children to the safer environs of Pennsylvania, Pierpont devoted his full attention to the Unionist state government in Wheeling, working twelve to fourteen hours a day. Fortunately, he had a strong constitution and held up well under the grueling strain. Although of average size, the governor appeared to be a powerful man. His large, square face was ringed by a full head of curly brown hair and a thick set of chin whiskers. Serious, intense eyes and thick, dark eyebrows gave him the appearance of one accustomed to hard work and difficult decisions.

Pierpont soon acquired office space for the Restored government in the recently completed federal customs house in Wheeling. On his authority the government borrowed money from prosperous northwestern Unionists and from the federal government. By borrowing, collecting old debts, seizing bank funds of the Richmond government, and tightening the purse strings, the Unionist government became a going concern. By 1862 it was collecting taxes in twenty-nine counties, all that could be protected from Confederate troops and southern sympathizers. Governor Pierpont also expanded authority to a handful of eastern Virginia counties, those occupied by the Union army around Washington, Norfolk, and the Eastern Shore. Throughout the war, however, the Pierpont regime extended only as far as the blue line of the U.S. Army.

In order to solidify and extend that line, Pierpont devoted much time and energy to cooperation with military authorities. With the permission of the Lincoln administration, Governor Pierpont commissioned officers and enlisted troops for the Union forces. By 1862 he had organized sixteen infantry regiments and five artillery batteries. Raising troops, appointing regimental officers, forming local militia units, issuing passes for travel on the Baltimore and Ohio Railroad, providing supplies for the army, fending off Confederate raiders, protecting public records from southern supporters—the tasks to be accomplished and the problems to be overcome seemed endless. A more volatile chief executive might have broken under these pressures. A less committed Unionist might have concluded the situation was hopeless. But Pierpont, the calm, tireless, systematic workhorse, was a man who could deal with such conditions. The Unionists of the northwest were fortunate to have him as their leader during those desperate days.

While the governor struggled to keep Unionism and his Restored government alive, others were working to create an entirely new state in western Virginia. The second Wheeling convention reassembled in August 1861 and set this plan in motion. In the winter of 1861–62 a constitutional convention drew up a proposed state charter, and northwestern voters approved it by a margin of 18,862 to 514 in April 1862. Under Pierpont's leadership, the Restored legislature, acting for the state of Virginia, gave its consent to the formation of the new state of West Virginia in May, and the governor lobbied in Congress for federal approval of the statehood bill. Pierpont's actions eventually earned him the sobriquet "Father of West Virginia," a strange title for a governor of Virginia who did not become a citizen of West Virginia until several years after its formation.

On December 31, 1862, President Lincoln signed the statehood bill. In the following months several western political leaders offered the governorship of the new state to Pierpont, but he declined, saying that his term and his work as governor of Virginia were not finished. This was doubtless the only instance in American history when the governor of one state was offered the governorship of a neighboring state. Finally, on June 20, 1863, Unionists of the northwest celebrated the official birth of West Virginia.

But what of Pierpont's Restored government? Did it still exist now that the northwestern counties had become a different state? Legally, Pierpont's government still claimed authority over the remainder of Virginia. But now that the Unionist counties of the northwest were part of the new state of West Virginia, the Restored government consisted only of a handful of counties around Washington, the Eastern Shore, and the area held by Union forces near Norfolk. For the last two years of the Civil War the Restored government, relocated in Alexandria, clung to legal existence by claiming to represent all of Virginia and by governing regions under Union control.

The Alexandria years of Pierpont's administration were marked by many difficulties. Virtually all of these problems stemmed from the Lilliputian size of Restored Virginia now that the western counties had separated and from wartime conditions. One of the most perplexing difficulties was relations with the military. Restored territory was under both civil and military government. Theoretically, all districts within Union lines were under the authority of the Restored government, recognized by the president and Congress. Yet war conditions forced the United States to occupy eastern and northern Virginia with federal troops. Who was to have ultimate authority in occupied regions? No general agreement was ever reached between Pierpont and army officers, and President Lincoln never established an official policy on the matter.

An even more embarassing problem involved Virginia's representation in Congress. In July 1861 Congress had accepted representatives and senators from Restored Virginia. But in 1863 and again in 1865 Congress refused to seat both representatives and senators. These men were told that conditions were too unstable in Restored Virginia and too few voters had participated in the elections. Even the Republican party's national nominating convention of 1864 refused to allow Unionist Virginians to vote in convention proceedings.

Restored Virginia, limited to a small area, appeared more than ever to be an anachronism, a useful device once, perhaps, but now somewhat of an embarassment to the federal government. In its original form the Pierpont government served as a nucleus around which Unionists of the northwest could rally, as a possible model for Reconstruction in other states, and as a friendly government which would approve the formation of a new state. But now that northwestern Unionists were safe, Lincoln's Ten Percent Plan of Reconstruction had been spurned by Congress, and West Virginia was an accomplished fact, the Restored government was for the most part simply ignored by Congress and the North. The Restored government's only hope for real power and authority lay in Union victory. Then Governor Pierpont and the Restored legislature—as the officially recognized government of the state—would be installed in Richmond to administer whatever Reconstruction plan the federal government devised for the South. Only then would the governor and his General Assembly have real power and respect. And by late May 1865, the Pierpont regime was indeed in Richmond in a political environment totally unlike that of Wheeling and Alexandria. The governor now faced a broad spectrum of Virginians, ranging from radical Republicans to moderate former Whigs, former slaveholders, and Confederates. His task was to put together, through flattery and cajolery and compromise, a coalition of radicals and moderates capable of carrying the state through Reconstruction. Although Governor Pierpont enjoyed considerable success as a Unionist administrator during the war, he was to be far less successful as a peacetime Republican politician.

If the governor and his fellow Unionists had traveled overland from Alexandria to Richmond, perhaps they would have understood better the difficulties they were about to encounter. Instead of riding through the human and physical debris of war, however, the governor and his party traveled by steamboat down the Potomac River and Chesapeake Bay and then up the James River to Richmond. Even there, among the charred skeletons of downtown buildings, Pierpont's attention was distracted from the bitterness and suffering of the war by a welcoming parade of Union troops and a twenty-one-gun salute.

After establishing himself in the Governor's Mansion recently vacated by William ("Extra Billy") Smith, Pierpont made his first and greatest political mistake. He naively assumed that the war had settled all the important questions dividing the nation and the state. His only task as governor, he concluded, would be to reestablish local and state government and meet the minimum requirements of Reconstruction laid down by President Johnson. Pierpont sincerely believed that former Confederates had learned their lesson at Appomattox, that they would heed the counsels of the North, that they would repudiate their old leaders and deal fairly with the freedmen—and that they would do all these things of their own free will. In his mind, the war had destroyed slavery and secession, and all that remained was to establish the Restored government in Richmond and start the work of rebuilding.

With these attitudes firmly fixed, Governor Pierpont urged the Restored legislature (which had followed him from Alexandria) to grant voting and officeholding privileges to any Virginian who would take President Johnson's loyalty oath. There were not enough wartime Unionists in the state to reorganize local government and resume normal affairs, Pierpont stressed, and therefore reenfranchisement of former Confederates was necessary. Under his leadership the Restored General Assembly in June 1865 granted voting and officeholding privileges to the overwhelming majority of former rebels and set a referendum for October which could also restore officeholding powers to those who had held positions under the Confederacy. Moreover, the governor automatically signed all applications for presidential pardon and forwarded them to the White House. Richmond newspapers were effusive in their praise of Pierpont and his General Assembly. Ex-Confederates could hardly have hoped for easier terms or a more lenient governor.

Unfortunately for Pierpont, his conciliatory and forgiving policy toward former Confederates virtually destroyed his political base among Unionists and Republicans. They held numerous local meetings to denounce the governor's course and appealed to congressional Republicans for protection. One Republican gathering in Alexandria even asked for a military government to replace Pierpont's administration. In addition, these anti-Pierpont Republicans for the first time began calling for black suffrage to offset the new political power of ex-Confederates, and several local conventions of freedmen sent petitions to Congress calling for the vote. Despite these protests, Governor Pierpont persisted in his policy of conciliation.

When state elections in October 1865 installed ex-Confederates in virtually every state and local office and removed the ban on officeholding from former Confederate officials, Republicans foresaw only doom unless Congress intervened. Fortunately for Virginia Unionists, Congress refused to seat the southerners elected to national office in 1865, and Virginia entered into four years of Reconstruction politics that would bring changes unimagined a few years earlier.

Governor Pierpont soon realized that he had misjudged the political climate. When the General Assembly convened in December 1865, it stunned the governor by ignoring his advice and adopting numerous reactionary measures. The Assembly removed from office every Unionist it could legally touch, mainly those who had served with Pierpont in Alexandria during the war. The legislature also repealed the act that had given Virginia's permission for the formation of West Virginia, asked President Johnson to free Jefferson Davis from prison, requested the repeal of the federal test oath, and passed a repressive vagrancy law aimed at the freedmen, a law that Union General Alfred H. Terry voided as "slavery in all but its name." The Assembly then guaranteed payment of the total prewar state debt, including wartime interest, but ignored Governor Pierpont's request to appropriate funds for public schools. Reeling from so many political blows by men he had thought to be reformed by military defeat, the governor finally realized in early 1866 that his faith in the former Confederates had been misplaced, and he attempted to realign himself with moderate wartime Unionists and Republicans. But most Republicans, especially radicals, generally spurned him for the remainder of his days in office. The governor's political naiveté had isolated him from the freedmen and strong Unionists, and his wartime Unionism had alienated former Confederates.

Pierpont nevertheless pressed on, hoping to reestablish himself as a respected leader by concentrating on economic recovery, a cause he hoped would attract widespread support and avoid political partisanship. In addition to lobbying in Congress for a protective tariff on coal and working to attract immigrants to the Old Dominion, he plunged into a project to consolidate various Virginia railroads into a strong network of lines connecting Norfolk with railroads penetrating into the Mississippi Valley.

Even in these economic matters, however, Pierpont discovered that politics were involved and that he had to choose sides, thus alienating still other Virginians. Essentially, the railroad controversy boiled down to a contest between two powerful groups. Former Confederate General William Mahone, a dapper and crafty promoter who would become a powerful political figure in the 1870s, had concocted a scheme to consolidate three south Virginia lines into one grand railroad connecting Norfolk in the southeast corner of the state to Bristol in the southwest corner of Virginia. At Bristol, Mahone's line would connect with other railroads stretching into the upper and lower South and the Mississippi Valley, thus funneling a potentially rich traffic flow to Norfolk. Opposing Mahone were the powerful Baltimore and Ohio Railroad, which owned a subsidiary line extending from the Washington area into southern Virginia (and was thus a rival for the trade of southwest Virginia), and Richmond businessmen who feared that Mahone's consolidated line would bypass the capital. Governor Pierpont, despite his prewar connections with the Baltimore and Ohio company, sided with General Mahone, believing that state interests would be best served by a Virginia business concern. The price of taking sides, however, was that Pierpont alienated powerful businessmen and politicians in Richmond and northern Virginia.

The governor attempted once again to lead Virginia along a moderate postwar path when the General Assembly convened in Richmond in December 1866. He urged the legislature to ratify the recently adopted Fourteenth Amendment which granted citizenship and civil rights to the freedmen and disqualified some ex-Confederates from public officeholding. Ratification, he warned, was the only means of convincing Congress that Virginia was ready for restoration of its full rights as a state in the Union. Once again the General

Assembly ignored Governor Pierpont and refused to ratify the proposed amendment.

Virginia's action in this instance, together with its behavior throughout 1865 and 1866 and similar developments in other southern states, finally forced moderate Republicans in Congress to abandon moderation and ally with radical Republicans in drawing up a more stringent Reconstruction program. In March 1867 Congress placed the South under martial law, required the southern states to draw up new constitutions that would give freedmen the vote, and ordered each former Confederate state to ratify the Fourteenth Amendment. Civil governments that had operated under President Johnson's plan of Reconstruction, including Pierpont's government in Virginia, would be allowed to remain in office and handle routine matters, but they were now under the control of the military. Thus, as Pierpont himself realized, congressional Reconstruction made him a mere figurehead. Real power was now in the hands of the Union army.

The new program, by extending the vote to adult black males, had the effect of ballooning the size of Virginia's hitherto small Republican party. What had been a small minority of moderate Whigs and Unionists and a few carpetbaggers from the North suddenly became a major force in state politics. In order to incorporate the new black element into the party and to prepare for the election of delegates to a state constitutional convention, the Republicans held a state convention in Richmond on April 17, 1867. The radicals immediately seized control and discussed several resolutions that sent shudders through the moderate wing of the party. Led by the Reverend James W. Hunnicutt, a white South Carolinian whose Unionism had forced him to flee from Virginia to the North during the war, the radical majority cheered a proposal to confiscate rebel land and redistribute it to poor loyal men. A few moderates, mostly whites, managed to have the motion tabled, but the damage had been done. The state's Republican party was branded in the minds of white moderates and conservatives with the stamp of extreme radicalism.

Although Governor Pierpont had been repeatedly rejected and insulted by former Confederates, he had never joined forces with the Republican radicals. The April meeting convinced him that the party was in danger of losing all moderate white support and becoming a minority organization of freedmen and a few radical carpetbaggers and scalawags. In order to retain white Unionist support, the governor called in reinforcements from the North. At Pierpont's urging, Republican Senator Henry Wilson of Massachusetts, New York *Times* editor Horace Greeley, New York abolitionist Gerrit Smith, and other prominent northern Republicans visited Virginia in an attempt to forge an alliance between moderates and radicals. They discouraged all talk about land confiscation, assured the freedmen that such proposals had no chance of passage in Congress, and urged cooperation with Governor Pierpont in the upcoming elections for the constitutional convention.

This "cooperator" movement resulted in a June 10 meeting at the Governor's Mansion between representatives of the radical and moderate wings of the party. Acting as mediators, several New York and Philadelphia Republicans managed to obtain the approval of the radicals for a second state Republican convention. This gathering, both sides agreed, would allow moderate whites, including many interested antebellum Whigs and even some former Confederates, to walk into the embrace of a quieter, less strident Republican party. The prestige and financial resources of these white moderates would combine with the power of black votes to make the Virginia Republican party an influential, perhaps dominant, force in state politics.

Unfortunately for Governor Pierpont and his fellow white moderates, the second convention, held on August 1, 1867, in Richmond, was a disaster. The radicals, led by the Reverend Mr. Hunnicutt and a few prominent black delegates, flooded the meeting hall an hour early, repeated the actions taken in April, and adjourned before any moderates could speak. When Governor Pierpont attempted to address the gathering after adjournment, his speech was cut short by a fistfight in the crowd. It hardly mattered, however, for most of his fellow white moderates had already abandoned the party in disgust.

Despite the humiliation he suffered at the hands of the radicals, Governor Pierpont did not give up. He had his name placed on the ballot for a seat in the upcoming constitutional convention, hoping to serve as a stabilizing influence in that body. But on October 22, 1867, long lines of voters, including for the first time Virginia's blacks, sent a radical majority to the convention. Pierpont suffered one more humiliation when he was defeated by James Morrissey, a radical carpetbagger and close ally of Hunnicutt. Most of the other Virginia white moderates who had dared to run were also overwhelmed.

One result of the crushing radical victory was that conservative former Confederates, hitherto unhappy but also unorganized, were shocked into action. On December 11 and 12, 1867, some eight hundred native whites from all sections of Virginia met in Richmond and formed the Virginia Conservative party. Forgetting their antebellum conflicts, former Whigs and Democrats united in opposition to the now-dominant Republicans and promised to deliver the Old Dominion from the grasp of "Negro supremacy." This new development held no promise for Pierpont, however. Conservatives had rejected the western Unionist from the very beginning, and now that they were organized in opposition to the Republicans, their resistance to the governor would be even more powerful.

Reduced to an administrative figurehead by the radical plan of Reconstruction, humiliated by radical Republicans and spurned by Conservatives, Pierpont was truly a leader without a party by early 1868. The Union general in charge of Virginia Reconstruction, John M. Schofield, realized that Pierpont's usefulness as governor was now destroyed and replaced him on April

4, 1868, with Henry H. Wells, a former Union general, carpetbagger from Michigan, and personal friend of Schofield. Thus, Pierpont's basic conservatism and his inability to deal with war-induced passions led to his downfall during the tempestuous years of Reconstruction. His naive cooperation with and pardoning of former Confederates in 1865 had isolated him from most of his fellow Unionists, and Virginia conservatives responded to his soft, forgiving policy with insults and rejection. When he attempted to form a moderate white and black Republican party in 1867, he was greeted with radical vituperation and defeat at the polls. Events had passed him by. New, more radical leaders had caught the fancy of freedmen and carpetbaggers, and Governor Pierpont seemed to them a relic of the past.

Pierpont, after serving seven years as Virginia's Unionist chief executive, quietly left Richmond in the spring of 1868 and returned to his old home in Fairmont, now in West Virginia. Soon involved in state politics as a Republican, he supported Grant for the presidency in 1868 and served one term in the lower house of the West Virginia legislature. But once again Pierpont found himself an isolated figure, and his service as a state legislator was generally unproductive and undistinguished. The former governor gradually dropped out of public life, and from 1869 onward he busied himself with other matters, especially his brick factory and tannery and his law practice. As old age closed in on him, in 1897 he moved to Pittsburgh, Pennsylvania, to live with his daughter. Finally, on March 24, 1899, thirty-eight years after the whirlwind excitement of his election to the governorship, Francis H. Pierpont died at the age of eighty-five. He was given a military funeral in Fairmont, and his coffin was covered with a Union flag sewn by his wife during the thrilling summer days of 1861.

Pierpont's career as governor was one of the most unusual in Virginia's history, for he was both elected to and removed from office in an extralegal fashion. At Wheeling and at Alexandria Pierpont was at his best. What Virginia Unionists needed in those frightful years was a calm, strong, persistent leader to shepherd them through the fire and storm of war. This, Pierpont was willing and able to do, and his record as a staunch Unionist war leader and efficient administrator was his greatest accomplishment.

His failings as a political leader became clear only after the war when it was necessary to guide Virginia through Reconstruction and at the same time build a coalition of Unionists and Republicans to maintain loyalists in power. Pierpont had no experience in dealing with warring, hostile factions. The people he had led in Wheeling and Alexandria were of his own type—Union-loving, middle-class whites. When he moved to Richmond to govern all of Virginia, however, he was plunged into a boiling cauldron of war-inspired fears and hatreds. His record as the Unionist governor of Virginia and "Father of West Virginia" had already embittered former Confederates, and he had neither the political experience nor the political instincts to pull suspicious and hostile groups together during the maelstrom of Reconstruction. Francis H. Pierpont was an admirable and successful wartime Unionist but a naive and inept Reconstruction political leader.

SOURCES

The most revealing primary materials are the Pierpont Letters and Papers (West Virginia University) and the Pierpont Executive Papers (Virginia State Library). The Archibald Campbell Papers and the Waitman T. Willey Papers (West Virginia University) and the John C. Underwood Papers and Scrapbook (Library of Congress) throw additional light on Pierpont's career as governor.

The most complete biography is Charles H. Ambler's *Francis H. Pierpont: Union War Governor of Virginia and Father of West Virginia* (Chapel Hill, N.C., 1937), but a useful short sketch is provided in Thomas Perkins Abernethy's entry on Pierpont in Dumas Malone et al., eds., *Dictionary of American Biography*.

Insight into northwestern Virginia Unionism and the statehood movement is available in Richard Orr Curry, *A House Divided: A Study of Statehood Politics and the Copperhead Movement in West Virginia* (Pittsburgh, 1964). Reconstruction in Virginia is examined in Richard Grady Lowe, "Republicans, Rebellion, and Reconstruction: The Republican Party in Virginia, 1856–1870" (Ph.D. diss., University of Virginia, 1968), and in Jack P. Maddex, Jr., *The Virginia Conservatives, 1867–1879: A Study in Reconstruction Politics* (Chapel Hill, N.C., 1970).

HENRY H. WELLS

Governor of Virginia

1868–1869

HENRY HORATIO WELLS

The Rise and Fall of a Carpetbagger

Patricia Hickin

Of all the governors of Virginia, probably none was less popular with the state's white establishment than Henry Horatio Wells. In his year-and-a-half administration (April 1868–September 1869), the Old Dominion was, technically, no longer the Commonwealth of Virginia. Its official title was Military District Number One, and Wells was governor, not because anybody elected him, but simply because a military commander appointed him chief executive. Hostile newsmen soon dubbed him "the Michigan adventurer" and the "prince of carpetbaggers"; Virginians said his middle initial stood for "Harpy," "Hellhound," and "Hotspur." After Wells left office an erstwhile supporter charged that he had so alienated Virginia voters, black and white, that he could not win a hundred votes if he ran for dogcatcher.

Surprisingly, when General John M. Schofield first announced Wells's appointment on April 4, 1868, the new governor was not an especially unpopular choice. Schofield and many others considered him, in fact, the one Republican in the state around whom all other Republicans could unite. Even many native Virginians were disposed to look upon him with favor, but this approbation was short-lived. On April 7, immediately after he was sworn into office, Wells delivered a brief address to the radical-controlled state constitutional convention then in session at the State Capitol. To moderate and conservative Virginians his few remarks were a bombshell. Though his primary concern, said Wells, was to restore Virginia to the Union, he called for radical and fundamental changes in the laws of the state. All men in Virginia, he declared, "are today . . . free and equal, not simply in theory and in principle, but as a living fact. . . . The law must rise entirely beyond any and all discrimination on account of color." Taxation must fall principally on property and not on heads; every child regardless of color must be educated for the duties of citizenship. Only the Republican party, he insisted, could be entrusted with the reconstruction of Virginia. Less than an hour after he was sworn into office Wells had made the first surprise move of his administration. It was not to be his last.

Though Wells had come into office with a reputation for moderation, there was much in his background to suggest that he was a firm advocate of egalitarian principles. Born in Rochester, New York, in September 1823 of parents who had recently migrated from Connecticut, young Henry grew up in the years when fiery evangelists began to stress the equality of all men before God and began to convert western New York into a hotbed of democratic religious fervor. Moving to Detroit, Michigan, he completed his education and began practicing law. He saw fugitive slaves attempting to flee to Canada and defended several white men who had assisted some of them to escape.

Wells supported the fledgling Republican party's hostility to the expansion of slavery and in 1854 was elected to the Michigan House of Representatives where he spoke out for free schools, temperance, emancipation, and the extension of certain civil and political rights to free blacks. In the mid-1840s he married Millicent Leib, daughter of a Michigan judge, and by 1860 had several children, including one son named for himself. The outbreak of the Civil War offered the ambitious attorney still more opportunities. In 1862 he helped to recruit a regiment, the Twenty-sixth Michigan Infantry, and in October of that year was mustered into service as its lieutenant colonel.

The unit was ordered to Virginia, but Wells did not accompany it into combat, for he was detached as provost marshal of Alexandria and then as provost marshal general of the defenses south of the Potomac River. Over the next two years the Michigan colonel coped admirably with a variety of intractable problems—with the notorious Virginia mud, filthy streets, federal prisons, deserters, bounty jumpers, camp followers, inebriates, and refugee slaves. His only real failure was his inability to capture Confederate Ranger John Singleton Mosby, who taunted and harassed the invading forces with style and spirit.

The Michigan colonel had better luck with another notorious southerner. In April 1865, after Lincoln's assassination, Wells played a significant role in the successful manhunt for John Wilkes Booth and was brevetted a brigadier general as a reward for his services. More prosaic duties then occupied his attention for a time: robbers, horse thieves, prostitutes, and drunken sentinels. Finally, at the end of the summer, civil authorities once again assumed responsibility for the enforcement of police regulations.

But Wells did not return to Detroit. Attracted by the economic opportunities in postwar Virginia, he had already brought his family to Alexandria and had become quite friendly with the radical federal district judge, John C. Underwood. Returning to the practice of law, Wells soon built up a substantial business in admiralty and confiscation cases, and he also became deeply involved in transportation matters. At the end of the war he and two other men leased the Alexandria Canal and soon put it back into operation.

Though Wells showed little of the reformer's zeal in the first postwar years, he did write one letter in which he indicated his adherence to policies that were eventually to become the mainstay of the radical Reconstruction program. Published in the Alexandria *Gazette* in June 1865, it urged the continuation of military rule in the South, protection of freedmen's rights, and disfranchisement of Confederate sympathizers.

After this one letter, Wells ceased to comment on such controversial matters, at least in public. Instead he came to be considered "a very agreeable" man. Quiet and unostentatious, endowed with a "pleasant address," he was said to be scrupulously correct and moral in his habits. Industrious and well-versed in constitutional law, he soon won a host of friends, particularly among fellow attorneys. During the months that followed, the ranks of those holding conservative, moderate, and radical views began to take shape. Some men took their stand on principle, some on economics, others on sheer opportunism. Wells, primarily involved in business and professional affairs, appeared to the public as an individual with moderate, economic-oriented proclivities. To close friends, however, at least to those holding similar opinions, he expressed his egalitarian ideals—views which aligned him with the radicals. Consequently he came to the favorable attention of both moderate and doctrinaire Republicans, and his political prospects soared as a result.

Meanwhile Virginia was being restored to the Union under the terms of the 1867 Reconstruction Acts. In December 1867 a state constitutional convention, controlled by radical Republicans and presided over by Wells's friend Judge John C. Underwood, began its deliberations. The adoption of a new state constitution, the end of military rule, and the election of public officials—including a governor—seemed possible by the beginning of the next summer. After the constitutional convention assembled, a group of leading Republicans submitted a petition to General John M. Schofield, commander of Military District Number One, asking him to name Wells as governor. Schofield, a moderate, proved responsive to their appeal, although he did not act until the spring of 1868. By the end of March, fearing that radical James W. Hunnicutt might capture the Republican gubernatorial nomination, he removed Governor Pierpont from office and appointed Wells to the post, asserting that Wells was one of the few men who could unite all "the friends of reconstruction."

To reassure radical supporters (and to blunt Hunnicutt's appeal to the blacks) Wells decided to shed his moderate image. His open support of the radicals would eventually play a major role in his downfall, but at the time it appeared politically sound. His first public address as governor had aligned him with majority sentiment in the Virginia Republican party, at least in so far as that sentiment found expression in the proposed state constitution which had just been completed under the eye of Judge Underwood. Meeting on May 6, 1868, the Republican convention endorsed Wells for the governorship by an overwhelming majority.

Yet there were obvious political risks in Wells's radical stance. Native whites, for the most part either indifferent or hostile to black aspirations, composed the bulk of Virginia's population, and many were thoroughly imbued with elitist principles. Even so, Wells and his radical associates had good reason to believe that they could carry the state and win ratification of the Underwood Constitution. Unionist whites in the Shenandoah Valley and the mountain counties found many measures of the Underwood Constitution highly desirable, and the business community would support almost any policy that promised normal commercial and political relations with the federal government. More significant still, many apathetic and demoralized whites had not registered to vote, and Wells endeavored to prevent them from participating in the upcoming elections.

Further enhancing radical chances for victory was the Conservative obstructionist policy which offered few prospects for success and the fielding of a weak candidate, an ex-Confederate colonel, Robert E. Withers of Lynchburg. Yet the radical drive never gained momentum, for opposition emerged from an unexpected but powerful source. General Schofield, disillusioned by the proscriptive disfranchisement and "test-oath" (officeholding) provisions of the Underwood Constitution and by Wells's endorsement of them, decided not to submit the document to the voters in June 1868. Using as his excuse a lack of funds in the state treasury, he argued that Congress would have to appropriate special funds before the referendum could be held and new state officials elected. In the meantime, he hoped that sentiment against the new constitution—or at least against its two "obnoxious clauses"—would lead to revision of the document. Having stemmed the radical tide, Schofield departed for Washington to become secretary of war in Andrew Johnson's cabinet, and his place was filled by another moderate, General George Stoneman.

Recognizing the threat that these developments posed to his campaign, Wells went to Washington but found Congress little disposed to order an election in Virginia. A tight presidential race was in the offing, and congressional Republicans had no desire to bring a state into the Union that might well wind up in the Democratic column in November. In addition, many northern Republicans and almost all northern Democrats were—like Schofield—fearful of a constitution that disfranchised so many men of education and experience and enfranchised so many who were illiterate.

Wells continued to serve as governor, but his powers were few. General Stoneman exercised ultimate control over officials in the counties and municipalities and continued Schofield's efforts to rid localities of "disloyal" officials. But like Schofield he found it difficult and sometimes impossible to find competent Union men. By mid–1869 only about one-fourth of the twenty thousand local offices in Virginia had been filled with Unionist appointees.

While Stoneman struggled with patronage, Wells gave speeches to the hundred of blacks who gathered repeatedly in Capitol Square, and he also traveled about the state extolling the equality of all men regardless of race. Despite his limited authority, Wells did carry out minor official duties. He was responsible for the appointment of notaries public, oversaw the upkeep of the penitentiary, and had the power to pardon criminals. In this latter capacity, in fact, he did more than many Virginians believed necessary. Wells, they charged, was issuing pardons to win black votes. The governor responded that it was impossible for blacks to get equitable treatment in county courts still controlled by native Virginians and that he had to issue pardons to offset unjust sentences.

Wells also showed considerable interest in state finances. The Commonwealth had gone deeply into debt before the war to finance internal improvements, and by the time Wells assumed the governorship in 1868 the state had accumulated obligations of almost $40 million in outstanding bonds and unpaid interest—even after repudiating its Confederate debt. In July 1868, with its treasury virtually empty, the state failed to make its semiannual interest payment to creditors, and the condition of Virginia's public finances continued to deteriorate. Wells responded by working with the military authorities in a vain effort to induce West Virginia to assume a portion of the prewar debt; the Old Dominion's civil and military authorities also made arrangements with railroads that were indebted to the Commonwealth so that some revenues found their way into the state treasury.

Partly as another move to reduce expenses, partly because its commanders were said to be biased against the blacks, Wells persuaded Stoneman to abolish the old Virginia State Guard (popularly known as the Public Guard), which had been founded in 1801 after the Gabriel slave revolt to protect the capital from slave insurrections and to ensure the security of the state penitentiary. Throughout these months the gubernatorial campaign continued in a desultory fashion, but the failure of Congress to arrange for an election gave an air of unreality to the affair. Matters had reached an impasse—with no readily perceivable end in sight.

The question of white oligarchy versus interracial democracy was not the only burning issue in postwar Virginia. In the decades immediately preceding the war Virginians had discovered a new love: railroads. Significantly, in railroad matters Wells enjoyed real power. As chief executive he was a member of the three-man Board of Public Works, and the two other members, the state treasurer and the state auditor, were gubernatorial appointees. The most significant railroad embroglio of his brief administration involved the battle for control of the Virginia and Tennessee Railroad, a strategically located but financially troubled line from Lynchburg to Bristol. William Mahone, an ambitious entrepreneur from Petersburg and a former major general of the Confederate army, was attempting to consolidate the Virginia and Tennessee with two other lines under his control so as to create a unified system extending from Norfolk to Bristol. His efforts were opposed, for obvious reasons, by the powerful Baltimore and Ohio Railroad. When Wells came into office, he was thought to be a Mahone supporter, but by the fall of 1868 it became clear that Wells was aligning himself with out-of-state interests in order to secure their support in his struggle against the Conservatives.

A number of influential Virginians heavily involved in railroads soon decided to throw their weight into the political balance against Wells and the radicals. Avoiding open talk of railroad matters and declaring their support for "home rule," Mahone and his associates rallied powerful support for a "New Movement" against northern political and economic domination. The Richmond *Whig,* which Mahone had secretly purchased in August 1868, led the outcry against Wells. Soon Conservative leader James B. Baldwin and Alexander H. H. Stuart (his widely respected Augusta County brother-in-law) joined hands with Mahone.

Denouncing Wells was easy enough, but driving him from office promised to be a more difficult task. Nevertheless, the advocates of the New Movement worked diligently. Baldwin and Stuart—with Mahone's behind-the-scenes support—organized a conclave of prominent business and political leaders to develop strategy. Meeting in Richmond, they agreed to accept wholesale black enfranchisement as provided in the Underwood Constitution if some of the more "obnoxious clauses" of the constitution were submitted to the voters separately. In particular they hoped to see the test-oath clause, which prohibited most leading ex-Confederates from holding political office, and the disfranchisement clause, which prohibited many former Confederate sympathizers from voting, submitted separately—and defeated.

Having contrived this daring strategy, the organizers of the New Movement endeavored to secure the approval of Congress and President-elect Ulysses S. Grant. They appointed a committee of nine men to journey to Washington to convince federal authorities that white Virginians were loyal to the Union and were willing to abide by the tenets of congressional Reconstruction, including the recently ratified Fourteenth Amendment with its declaration of black citizenship and equality before the law. Alarmed, Wells and several of his supporters hastened to Washington to present their views. Additional delays occurred, but in April 1869, soon after taking office, President Grant gave his support to the New Movement. The Congress authorized a separate vote on the test-oath and disfranchising clauses of the constitution, and the referendum on that document and the accompanying election of state officials was scheduled for July 6, 1869.

As these developments were taking place, moderate Republicans, a number of whom were from Norfolk, worked to undermine the radical Republican organization. In quick order they adroitly reaffirmed the nomination of Wells but saddled him with a black running mate, Dr. J. D. Harris, for lieutenant governor and then deserted the party. In March 1869 this breakaway moderate bloc held a convention in Petersburg. Calling themselves "True Republicans," they chose as their gubernatorial candidate one of Mahone's cohorts,

Gilbert C. Walker, a native of Binghamton, New York, who had settled in Norfolk during the Civil War. Although he was by definition a "carpetbagger," Walker had been a Union Democrat before the war and had not converted to Republicanism until 1867. He had become prominent in Tidewater banking and manufacturing circles, and his close association with Mahone rendered him an apt spokesman for the New Movement.

At first Wells believed that the True Republicans would enhance his chances by draining off moderate voters from the Conservative Withers. But in the spring of 1869 the Conservative leadership convinced Withers to withdraw from the race, endorsed Walker for the governorship, and wheeled their massive white support into a unified campaign against Wells. The radical cause had suffered yet another devastating setback. Wells suddenly realized that the opposition might overwhelm him.

Now there were two Republican candidates in the field, both of them supporting the new constitution, the enfranchisement of the blacks, and the establishment of public schools. For a time the chief discernible difference between the parties lay in the radicals' support of the test-oath and disfranchisement provisions of the Underwood Constitution and the True Republicans' strong opposition to those "obnoxious clauses." As the campaign went on even that distinction became blurred. As Wells saw his chances for victory threatened, he suddenly changed tactics. In a public letter to a native Albemarle County Republican, Thomas Garland, the embattled governor announced his support for the New Movement plan for a separate vote on the test-oath and disfranchisement clauses, indicating he no longer insisted on the acceptance of the two proscriptive measures. Blacks and diehard Republicans felt betrayed. Though most radicals continued to support Wells (since they lacked any real alternative), their enthusiasm for his candidacy cooled considerably.

In the meantime the governor's campaign suffered more damaging blows. Charges circulated, never proved or disproved, that he had stolen a political letter from the U.S. mails and that he was pardoning black convicts for political purposes. Then in April 1869—in a move that surprised even the ever-observant Mahone—General Stoneman suddenly removed Wells from office. The governor's friends registered strong protests, and he soon was restored to his former position; meanwhile, President Grant replaced Stoneman with a far more radical officer, General Edward R. S. Canby. Even so, Wells's prestige had been irreparably damaged, leaving him open to absurd attacks by his opponents, who charged that he had stolen at least $300,000 from the state in the course of his carpetbagging activities.

When election day came, the Underwood Constitution, endorsed by both candidates, won overwhelming approval. More than 200,000 votes were cast in its favor, fewer than 10,000 against it. Both of the "obnoxious clauses" were defeated by margins of about 40,000 votes. In the gubernatorial race the vote, as expected, seems to have been cast largely—but not entirely—along racial lines. More than 125,000 whites and 97,000 blacks voted, and Walker was elected, 119,535 to 101,204. Walker's 18,000-vote majority was better than the Conservatives had dared hope for.

Though soundly defeated at the ballot box, Wells attempted to cling to the governorship. His supporters charged that the Walker forces had employed fraudulent and corrupt methods to carry the day, but investigations turned up numerous instances of fraud on both sides and General Canby found insufficient evidence to justify overturning the results. The Wells men then approached the triumphant True Republicans with an offer to withdraw their opposition to Walker's installation as governor if the victors would support Wells for a seat in the U.S. Senate. Disgusted by such intrigues, Canby ordered Wells to submit his resignation and appointed Walker provisional governor until he could be installed under the new state constitution. Canby's order took effect on September 21, 1869, and the troubled career of Henry H. Wells as governor of Virginia came to an end.

To compensate Wells in some measure, in 1870 the Grant administration appointed him U.S. attorney for the Eastern District of Virginia. The next year he suffered a near-fatal injury while serving as counsel for his old friend George Chahoon, a radical who was trying to keep his position as mayor of Richmond. During the course of the trial the crowded Court of Appeals room of the Capitol fell in. Sixty-two people were killed in the disaster, and Wells was among more than two hundred who were injured. For a day or two his life hung in balance, but he recovered. In 1872 he resigned, turning the office of district attorney over to his son, who had become his assistant, and moved to Washington to enter private practice and to look after his interests in the newly formed Alexandria Canal, Bridge, and Railroad Company.

As usual, Wells was highly successful in his business and professional endeavors. He built a handsome town house on the northern outskirts of Washington, which still stands on the northwest corner of Ninth and M streets, and his name appeared on the city's "Elite List." In 1875 Wells became a U.S. attorney once again, this time for the District of Columbia, and continued in the office for five years. In 1880—at the age of fifty-seven— he gave up his federal post but continued to practice law in the city. Weakened by advancing years and a prolonged illness, he died on February 12, 1900, at the home of his daughter in Palmyra, New York.

As governor, Wells was—like Pierpont before him—a classic example of an able and intelligent administrator who lacked the flair for effective political leadership. As the wartime provost marshal general of northern Virginia and as an attorney and businessman, he exhibited a large measure of savoir faire and won the respect of those who knew him. But as a political leader he lacked the instinct for compromise and the force of personality needed to bind discordant elements into a winning combination. Despite his intelligence, he often failed to make the right move at the right time. Remaining steadfast in his principles too long, he attempted to compromise only after his opponents had already gained the upper hand. It is doubtful whether any man sincerely committed to egalitarian principles could have been a successful governor of Virginia in the late 1860s, but Wells clearly was not the man for the job.

SOURCES

Since there are few Wells papers, one has to rely upon conservative (and critical) Richmond newspapers and the radical Washington *Chronicle* for an assessment of his political career. The small collection of his Executive Papers (Virginia State Library) consists largely of requests for appointments to minor offices but does include drafts of some significant letters. More extensive and far more important are the William Mahone Papers (Duke University) and the Mahone-McGill Collection (University of Virginia). The Alexander H. H. Stuart Papers (Virginia Historical Society) are helpful in understanding the New Movement. The best and most unbiased reporting of the progress of Reconstruction in Virginia, however, is to be found in Record Group 393: Records of United States Army Continental Commands, 1821–1920, Department of Virginia and North Carolina, Letters Sent, 1867–70, vol. 1–8, First Military District (National Archives, Washington, D.C.). In addition, the John McAllister Schofield Papers, Letters Sent, 1867–68 (Library of Congress) contain material concerning Schofield's decision to replace Pierpont with Wells. Although recent secondary accounts, including several Ph.D. dissertations, have dealt with political Reconstruction in Virginia, the authors have relied excessively on such outdated works as Hamilton J. Eckenrode's *Political History of Virginia during the Reconstruction* (Baltimore, 1904); Alexander H. H. Stuart's *Narrative of the First Popular Movement in Virginia in 1865 to the "Committee of Nine" in 1869* (Richmond, 1888); and Nelson M. Blake's *William Mahone of Virginia: Soldier and Political Insurgent* (Richmond, 1939). These studies are still of value, but a comprehensive history of postwar Virginia politics that includes a detailed examination of the relationship between railroads and political interests is sorely needed.

GILBERT C. WALKER

Governor of Virginia

1869–1874

GILBERT CARLTON WALKER

Carpetbag Conservative

Crandall A. Shifflett

The governor's chair in Virginia in 1869 was not a post which many politicians of today would relish. Memories of the Civil War lingered like old wounds—often festering and bringing an edge to most political issues of the period. How a Republican carpetbagger brought opposing factions together, "redeemed" the Old Dominion, and dealt with the debt issue is one of the most fascinating stories in southern political history and the major legacy of the governorship of Gilbert Carlton Walker.

Walker was born near Binghamton, New York, on August 1, 1832. His parents were able to give him a good education, first at Williams College in Massachusetts, which he left after a dispute over commencement exercises, and then at Hamilton College in Clinton, New York, where he graduated in 1854. After a year of law studies in the office of Judge Horace J. Griswold in Binghamton, he was admitted to the New York state bar. On April 15, 1857, Walker married Olive Evans, the daughter of a wealthy sheet metal manufacturer in Binghamton and the sister-in-law of Judge Griswold. Two years later Walker and his wife moved to Chicago, where he quickly became a prominent lawyer and businessman and began to display an interest in politics.

A Douglas Democrat in 1860, Walker loyally supported the Union cause during the Civil War. Business commitments and tuberculosis kept him out of uniform, but an improvement in his health after an 1864 business trip to Tidewater Virginia convinced Walker to settle in Norfolk early in 1865 where he quickly emerged as one of the port city's leading businessmen. He organized the Exchange National Bank, functioned as its first president, and played an active role in other commercial ventures, too. Soon he was closely associated with one of the state's most prominent businessmen, General William Mahone, president of the Norfolk and Petersburg Railroad. Mahone hoped to merge his company with several other Virginia lines in opposition to the Baltimore and Ohio Railroad, a northern corporation which also sought to control area trade. Walker's bank financed a million-dollar stock subscription for the general's railroad in 1867, after which Walker became one of the line's directors. Mahone and Walker also collaborated in an effort to encourage European immigration and settlement in Virginia. Frustrated in earlier attempts to win political office in New York and Illinois, Walker now found the perfect milieu for his talents.

His appearance and personality also enhanced these prospects. His angular face and high cheekbones were accentuated by bushy eyebrows, an imposing mustache, and neatly groomed, dark, wavy hair. Over six feet tall, his erect carriage and handsome features added to his appeal. Observers thought him "gracious" and "dignified." There is evidence however, that his public image was a facade for coldness and a certain unapproachability; as a result, he acquired uncomplimentary nicknames such as "His Highness" and "The Serene Gilbert." He could also be indiscreet, once appearing drunk in public while returning from a political rally.

Although he failed to win a seat in the constitutional convention in 1867, his effort struck one important note. Campaigning as a Conservative, he had argued that the Republicans, in seeking to secure the vote for blacks, had no right to deny that privilege to former Confederates. This was a significant stand, one which suggested a formula for compromise because it did not foreclose the possibility of full political rights for either blacks or whites.

Two months after the election of convention delegates Walker displayed for the first time the political expediency that was to typify his political career in Virginia. In a letter published in the Norfolk *Journal* (December 6, 1867), he renounced his membership in the Conservative party and sounded the theme of compromise once more. The Conservatives had announced that they would oppose any constitution drafted by the Republican-dominated convention, but Walker declared that he would support such a document if it conformed to his views. He also made ardent pleas for early restoration of the state to the Union and called as well for prompt acceptance of federal terms as the most effective means of achieving that goal. "Business is prostrated," he argued, "commercial enterprise palsied, uncertainty and distrust exist everywhere." These were themes which more and more Virginians were beginning to air, and Walker sensed a changing political climate—a chance for new and more promising approaches to the problems of the day.

As it turned out, the new, radical-sponsored Underwood Constitution was easier to draft than to ratify. General John M. Schofield, commander of the Military District of Virginia, convinced that the document's suffrage and officeholding restrictions against ex-Confederates were unwise and unworkable, recommended that Washington authorities should not allow a vote on the constitution until the test-oath was modified and a separate referendum on the disfranchisement clause was permitted.

These delays sapped radical momentum and permitted hard-pressed Conservatives to launch a determined counterattack against their opponents. Officially they continued to take a hard line toward the entire Underwood Constitution. Unofficially, they began to focus their opposition on the test-oath and disfranchisement clauses. If these objectionable provisions could be deleted, a growing number of influential Conservatives privately indicated their willingness to accept the rest of the document, including black suffrage. In December 1868 Alexander H. H. Stuart called for "universal suffrage and universal amnesty" and elicited a positive response throughout the state. In a dramatic way, a bridge toward possible reconciliation had been built, and Conservative leaders selected a "Committee of Nine" to go to Washington to lobby for acceptance of these moderate terms. Walker quickly joined this campaign, spending ten days in the federal capital rallying support among Republican senators and congressmen. Winning the respect and gratitude of Virginia's Conservatives, Walker once again sensed the future direction of political change. Ultimately, Stuart's Committee of Nine convinced President Ulysses S. Grant and the Congress to postpone the referendum on the Underwood Constitution and to allow a separate vote on its test-oath and disfranchisement provisions. The forces of moderation had won a significant victory, and Walker had gotten in on the ground floor of an emerging political consensus.

The support of Walker and other Republicans for universal amnesty and suffrage revealed a growing split within Virginia's Republican party—a split which deepened in the early months of 1869. One faction, led by provisional Governor Henry H. Wells, became increasingly identified with radical Republicanism and with the unpopular provisions of the Underwood Constitution. The party's other element, who called themselves "True Republicans," rallied the support of a small but growing body of GOP conservatives and moderates. This group included individuals like Gilbert Walker, men who supported the Committee of Nine's formula in order to restore Virginia to the Union as soon as possible. When the Radicals overwhelmed the moderates in March 1869 and nominated Wells for a full term as the state's chief executive, eight insurgent party leaders nominated a state ticket of their own. This True Republican cabal chose Gilbert C. Walker as its gubernatorial candidate, Valley Unionist John F. Lewis for lieutenant governor, and James C. Taylor of Montgomery County for attorney general. Walker was a natural choice to head the ticket. His northern background would ease congressional apprehensions about the split in Virginia's Republican ranks and might also attract the support of a sizable number of blacks. By the same token, the dissidents also recognized the appeal which Walker's well-known hostility to Confederate disfranchisement might hold for the state's white voters. Yet another important, if not decisive, factor was the support of William Mahone, who had been working behind the scenes to secure a nominee sympathetic to his railroad manipulations.

Soon after the True Republicans nominated their ticket, a movement began to build to ease Conservative nominee Robert E. Withers out of the race in order to prevent a split in the anti-Wells vote. Withers, a weak candidate, finally withdrew from the race in April 1869, and two months later the

Conservatives officially endorsed Walker. Instantly, the True Republican movement was transformed into a powerful challenge to radical Republicanism. Without the Conservatives, the insurgent Republicans constituted a small group of disgruntled politicians with little or no hope of victory. Once the Conservatives joined them, however, they had solid prospects of winning. Less obvious, perhaps, the True Republicans were so weak that traditionalist white Conservatives, who would supply the bulk of Walker's vote, would also dominate his administration.

More than 200,000 Virginians trooped to the polls on July 6, 1869, and the outcome constituted a decisive victory for Walker. He won 54 percent of the ballots, and his 18,000-vote advantage topped all previous gubernatorial margins in Old Dominion history. Completing the moderate triumph, the test-oath and disfranchisement clauses of the Underwood Constitution went down to a crashing defeat, while the remainder of the document was approved by an overwhelming margin. Even more significant for the state's political future, Conservative candidates gained well over a two-thirds majority in both houses of the legislature and won five of eight congressional seats. The election had been a thumping defeat for the radical Republicans, a political masterpiece for the forces of compromise.

Marking the end of radical Reconstruction in Virginia, the 1869 election was one of the most momentous political battles in the state's history, and the mass of the Commonwealth's citizens recognized the significance of the outcome. Spontaneous celebrations erupted across the state on election night, but the festivities in Norfolk were particularly noteworthy. Bonfires, musical salutes, and general merrymaking lasted late into the evening as the port city's Conservatives celebrated the election of the thirty-third governor of the Old Dominion. Traveling to Richmond the following day, July 7, Walker received the accolades of thousands. Caught up in a mood of rejoicing after years of war and military occupation, Richmond well-wishers lifted Walker to their shoulders and carried him to a waiting carriage which took him on a mile-long procession through the streets of the former capital of the Confederacy. Richmonders, the *Whig* observed, had not provided such an enthusiastic audience even for Henry Clay, their prewar idol.

Taking office amid general rejoicing, Virginia's youthful chief executive moved to complete the task of restoring Virginia to the Union. Walker called the General Assembly into special session on October 5, 1869, and the legislators acted with dispatch to conform to congressional demands. They promptly ratified the Fourteenth and Fifteenth Amendments, elected Conservative Robert E. Withers and True Republican John F. Lewis to the U.S. Senate, and submitted the newly adopted Underwood Constitution (minus the test-oath and disfranchisement clauses) to Washington for approval. On January 26, 1870, Congress officially recognized that the Old Dominion had fulfilled the requirements of the Reconstruction Acts. Virginia, once again, was a state among states, the master of its own destiny.

It was ironic that the Old Dominion had been redeemed by a carpetbag governor elected on a Republican ticket, but the irony did not stop there; this same Republican governor was to preside over the progressive deterioration of Republican strength in the Commonwealth between 1869 and 1873. Although he had pledged to support "impartial suffrage," he did nothing to prevent his Conservative allies in the General Assembly from gerrymandering electoral districts and enacting discriminatory voter registration laws—measures that reduced black membership in the legislature from 27 in 1869 to 17 in 1871. Walker's willingness to countenance such manuevers appeared to contradict not only his previous moderation in racial affairs but also his tactics in the pivotal 1869 campaign, when he and his cohorts had actively courted the Negro vote. To anyone familiar with the governor's checkered career, however, this conduct should have come as no surprise.

From the outset, opportunism had played a central role in Walker's rise to prominence, complementing such previously noted assets as a good marriage, a dignified demeanor, advantageous friendships, political acumen, and good luck. Consequently his movement away from Republicanism—after the Conservatives manifested their power in 1869—was predictable. During his first months in office Walker sided with Conservatives against Republicans in several local power struggles, notably for control of the Richmond municipal government, and Virginia's Republicans countered by officially expelling him from their party. The governor then proclaimed himself a Conservative once again, although he remained at heart a political maverick, seeking the aid of any party which would support his ambitions. In 1870 he considered running for a seat in the U.S. Senate, an option which he abandoned in hopes of winning the Liberal Republican nod for vice-president in 1872. Spurned again by the GOP, he returned to the fold of the Virginia Conservatives in a vain attempt to convince them to run an independent national ticket. Thus, Walker's zeal for office rendered him a party man in name only—a political chameleon in an era of political flux.

These partisan and personal intrigues continued throughout Walker's gubernatorial term, but his administration also focused on matters of much greater concern. One major question, Virginia's public debt, consumed an ever-increasing share of his attention. All other issues—railroads, schools, taxes, welfare expenditures, and governmental efficiency—became inextricably intertwined with the debilitated condition of the Old Dominion's credit. Of necessity, therefore, the governor had to grapple with this central problem of state finance, and his approach to the debt question generated bitter controversy for decades to come.

When Walker took office in 1869 the Commonwealth owed more than

$45 million to its creditors as the result of bond issues dating back to pre–Civil War years. Essentially the government of Virginia had functioned as a giant joint-stock investment bank in the decades before 1861, borrowing private capital to finance state investments in railroads, canals, and other public improvements. The Old Dominion had sold roughly three-fourths of its securities to out-of-state investors, primarily northern and British capitalists, while Virginians had purchased the remainder. In the absence of alternative sources, state financing had constituted a sensible, even essential, approach to economic development. The Civil War transformed a debt already becoming burdensome into a serious financial drain. The war destroyed many of the state's transportation lines, interest payments to the bondholders ceased during the conflict, and the market value of the Commonwealth's securities plummeted to a third of their former value by 1865. Falling land values and the loss of the slaves as tangible assets further accentuated these difficulties, as did the excision of a third of the Old Dominion's prewar territory by breakaway West Virginia.

The Walker administration inherited not only the debt problem but a proposed solution as well: the 1866 legislature declared that the Old Dominion would repay the entire prewar debt and issued yet another series of bonds to fund the interest accrued during the war. Other southern states had appealed to their bondholders for relief or had simply repudiated their debts after Appomattox, but Virginia's leaders rejected such a course. Proclaiming their commitment to fiscal integrity, they made preservation of public credit a matter of personal and collective honor. A depleted treasury (along with the advent of congressional reconstruction in 1867) temporarily nullified the General Assembly's bold pledge, but a significant commitment to the state's creditors had nevertheless been made, one which Walker—as Virginia's chief executive—would attempt to fulfill.

A banker by occupation, Walker continued to stress the importance of fiscal integrity after he assumed the governorship. On March 7, 1870, he outlined a state debt proposal of his own, calling on the legislature to permit the funding of all previous liabilities up to January 1, 1871, in new bonds that would mature in from ten to thirty years. Walker encouraged the General Assembly to authorize a uniform annual interest rate of 6 percent on these securities (which included West Virginia's share of the debt), and he also insisted that interest coupons from the new bonds should be receivable for all taxes or other financial demands due the Commonwealth. Reflecting the "Funder" philosophy of the Old Dominion's elite, this plan was exceedingly generous to bondholders. In December 1870 the General Assembly's Joint Committee on Finance reported a bill similar to Walker's proposal. It called for funding of two-thirds of the debt in new bonds bearing 6 percent annual interest and carrying interest coupons acceptable for all state taxes. The legislators expected West Virginia to pay the remaining third of the debt. The bill proposed to retire the debt through creation of a sinking fund financed with proceeds from the sale of the Commonwealth's investments in railroads and other properties.

Although the funding bill was less generous than Walker's initial proposal, Virginia's business community in general and the bondholding interests in particular, along with railroad entrepreneurs who stood to gain from the sale of state investments in their lines, rallied to its support. Yet many Virginians, including a sizable bloc of state legislators, believed that the committee's proposal would either increase the state debt or require massive tax increases to implement its provisions. Expressing the views of hard-pressed farmers, especially in the western counties, these dissidents insisted that either the debt principal or its interest (or both) be scaled or "readjusted" downward in accordance with wartime property losses and the state's reduced ability to pay. The break between these "Readjusters" on the one hand and the bondholders' Funder advocates on the other was a serious one, reflecting a deepseated disagreement on an essential matter of public policy, and the division was exacerbated still more by the closely balanced popular strength of the opposing forces.

The funding bill sailed through the Senate with ease but encountered powerful opposition in the House of Delegates. Working to force their debt plan through the House, the state credit men launched a highly orchestrated pressure campaign to win a majority of the delegates to their side. Lobbyists filled the halls of the legislature, while a syndicate of northern bondholders employed a Conservative, General Bradley T. Johnson, and a Republican, John W. Jenkins, to sway wavering lawmakers. The Pennsylvania Central Railroad even bought an influential newspaper, the Richmond *Enquirer,* and transformed its previous opposition into enthusiastic support. Gilbert C. Walker also played a pivotal role in the effort by inviting undecided legislators to the Governor's Mansion where he brought his well-known powers of persuasion to bear—with significant results. Most of the Readjusters resisted these blandishments, but enough shifted sides to tip the balance. The controversial debt proposal passed the House of Delegates on the last evening of the session. The Funding Act of 1871 had become law.

The public credit had been preserved—but at tremendous cost in public confidence. Rumors of graft and conflict-of-interest charges were widespread, and many Virginians shared the Readjuster belief that the Funding Act was excessively generous to the creditors. And in 1871 they registered their dissatisfaction in no uncertain terms by reelecting only 26 of 113 incumbent legislators.

In spite of this setback, Walker doggedly continued to support his debt program—even in the face of mounting opposition from the General Assembly. In December 1871 the newly elected senators and delegates voted to suspend the funding process, but Walker vetoed the suspension, and the

Senate sustained his action. Legislative dissidents then proceeded to repeal the tax-receivable coupons, a move which threatened to deprive bondholders of one of their most valuable privileges. The governor vetoed this measure, too, but this time the increasingly impatient lawmakers overrode his veto. Events soon vindicated Walker's course. In December 1872 the state Supreme Court declared the General Assembly's attack on the coupons unconstitutional. Roughly a third of the debt remained to be funded at the time of the decision, however, and a loophole in the court's ruling allowed the Commonwealth to issue bonds without tax-receivable coupons for this share of the outstanding securities. Even so, the overall tenor of the judges' stand served to reinforce the governor's position, supplying additional legal authority for his defense of the state credit.

Exactly what lay behind Walker's persistent support of the Funding Act is not entirely clear. It seems remarkable, for instance, that a man usually so sensitive to changing political trends refused to trim his sails or retreat on the debt issue. The governor's critics had a ready explanation: he had invested heavily in state bonds and would gain a financial windfall from the continued operation of the funding program. A more plausible reason for Walker's firm stance can be found in constraints imposed by state and federal judges who consistently backed the bondholders' demands for the fulfillment of legally binding contractual obligations. Furthermore, there is every reason to believe that the governor sincerely regarded the Funding Act as the best way to deal with Virginia's financial difficulties. The national economy was booming at the start of the 1870s, and Walker maintained that the Old Dominion would attract a flood of outside capital if the state government could get its fiscal house in order. New tax revenues, in turn, would enable Virginia to repay public creditors with ease, thus securing the state's honor and its future prosperity at the same time. Unfavorable economic trends (notably the financial panic of 1873)—together with mass antagonism toward the Funding Act—eventually nullified these grandiose plans, but there can be no doubt that such considerations influenced Walker.

On March 8, 1870, as part of his drive to straighten out Virginia's finances, Walker urged the General Assembly to approve the sale of the state's railroad assets to corporate interests. Justifying his position in terms of the laissez-faire dogma of the Gilded Age (and ignoring the importance of state aid in the construction of the rail network), Walker maintained that the government should stay out of private business. State interference, he argued, was responsible for the current problems of the lines. In fact, although the Commonwealth had financed the internal improvements, it had exercised little control over their day-to-day operations, and the governor neglected to mention the devastating impact of the Civil War. Taking an even more controversial stand, Walker followed in the footsteps of the previous governor,

Henry H. Wells, by urging sale of the state's stock at current market value—even though Virginia's antebellum investment had been much greater.

Once more the lobbyists descended upon Richmond, and the lawmakers agreed to sell the state's stockholdings. The results of this laissez-faire, "free railroad" policy soon became apparent: well-financed northern corporations gobbled up the most desirable blocs of shares at bargain-basement prices. The Orange and Alexandria passed into the hands of the Baltimore and Ohio Railroad, while the Pennsylvania Central gained control of the Richmond and Danville and the Richmond and Petersburg. Although Walker had predicted a financial windfall for the Commonwealth, the railroads—and not Virginia's treasury—emerged as the prime beneficiaries of his program. By 1874 the revenues from the free railroad policy had enabled the Old Dominion to discharge only a little more than $3.7 million of the public debt—about one-tenth of its outstanding obligations. All in all, the state received approximately $11 million less from the sale of its railroad stock than it had initially invested in the lines themselves.

Walker's railroad policy, like his funding scheme, brought him into conflict with the man most responsible for his election to the governorship, William Mahone. Bitterly opposed to this northern takeover of Virginia's transportation network, Mahone fought the free railroad program with all his energies—to no avail. And in spite of his vital services to the antiradical cause in 1869, the Petersburg entrepreneur encountered serious difficulties in pushing his long-delayed Atlantic, Mississippi, and Ohio consolidation bill through the legislature. Lobbyists for the Baltimore and Ohio fought him at every turn, and he counterattacked with lobbyists of his own, luring undecided lawmakers with liquor and money. Responding to these inducements, the General Assembly passed the consolidation measure in the spring of 1870. Mahone then shifted his attention to the governor, caught in the middle in this struggle between his erstwhile political ally and the financially potent northern capitalists. Fearful of a veto, Mahone rallied public opinion to his side, and Walker—on this occasion—conformed to the drift of local sentiment. He signed the controversial bill into law, declaring petulantly that the legislature was responsible for its provisions.

The governor's conduct in this struggle blackened his reputation still further. Critics accused him of speculating in railroad stock and of taking bribes from railroad officials, but no solid proof exists to support these claims. He did own shares in the Virginia and Tennessee Railroad, one of the companies which became part of the Atlantic, Mississippi, and Ohio, but he sold them in the midst of the consolidation controversy—apparently in order to fend off attacks on his personal integrity. More to the point, perhaps, the governor's subsequent financial status offers no evidence of graft or speculative profiteering. At the time of his death, some eleven years after he vacated the Governor's Mansion, Walker left his wife a modest estate of $1,000, and when she died the family's personal property and real estate holdings were valued at only $2,600. If the governor actually did attempt to exploit his position for personal gain (and even this is subject to debate), he was singularly unsuccessful.

Yet Walker must bear some responsibility for the perversion of the political process during his administration. Virginia's officials could not make decisions concerning railroad charters and the state debt with decorum and detachment under the pressures exerted by corporation lobbyists and bondholder syndicates. Business interests were well represented in the deliberations on these issues, but farmers, laborers, educators, and the general taxpayer had little voice. The governor failed to take vigorous steps to allay suspicions of malfeasance that surrounded his funding and railroad programs, and this inaction was widely viewed as proof of guilt. Regardless of Walker's personal integrity, his administration plumbed new depths in terms of public morality and popular esteem.

Although the governor focused his energies on bond issues and stock sales, he did not entirely neglect progressive concerns or humanitarian needs. Proclaiming himself an advocate of "free education for all," he championed the public school system mandated by the Underwood Constitution, and his able and efficient superintendent of public instruction, William Henry Ruffner, did yeoman service in putting the new educational machine into operation. Under Walker's leadership the legislature created Virginia Agricultural and Mechanical College (Virginia Polytechnic Institute and State University), and he spoke out in behalf of improved conditions at the state's mental hospitals and prison facilities. Even so, debt payments consumed such a large share of the Commonwealth's revenues that charitable, educational, and penal institutions remained on an insecure financial footing throughout the 1870s. As a result, the brutal convict-lease system flourished, scores of the insane had to be confined in local jails, and many public schools closed their doors. Walker's verbal support for the poor and the unfortunate notwithstanding, the lower classes received comparatively little from his administration. The major beneficiaries of his programs were bondholders, railroad promoters, financial speculators, and business developers.

After leaving office in 1874, Walker parlayed his ties to the Commonwealth's business and political elite into continued success at the polls. He was elected to the U.S. House of Representatives from the Richmond district in 1874 and reelected to the post in 1876. Now a loyal adherent of the Conservative-Democratic cause, he supported Samuel J. Tilden for the presidency in 1876 and was outraged when the election fell to Rutherford B. Hayes, the Republican contender.

In 1878 Walker's wife convinced him to move back to Binghamton, New York, where he resumed the practice of law until 1881, when he moved to New York City to serve as counsel (and subsequently as president) of the Underground Railway Company. Weakened by tuberculosis, Gilbert C. Walker died on May 11, 1885. Fifty-three years old at the time of his death, he was buried in Spring Forest Cemetery near Binghamton.

Walker's sojourn in the Old Dominion had been brief, extending only from 1864 to 1878, but his impact on the Commonwealth—for good or ill—was a lasting one. His debt policy sparked rancorous debate into the 1890s, crippling social services and hampering educational progress, while his free railroad program deprived the state of potentially valuable assets without securing adequate compensation in return. And through it all an aura of corruption pervaded his administration. Yet it would be wrong to place a wholly negative evaluation on his stewardship. The Old Dominion benefited from Walker's pragmatic flexibility in the highly charged political climate of 1869. The state needed a man of compromise who could resolve the prolonged deadlock over Reconstruction, and Walker proved to be such a man. He sought (and in large measure achieved) universal amnesty for the ex-Confederates of his adopted state, and he also convinced Virginia's whites to acknowledge—on paper, at least—the political equality of their black fellow citizens. He took the Commonwealth back into the Union sooner than would have been the case under more dogmatic leadership. In this respect the New York–born carpetbagger aided both Virginia and the nation at large.

SOURCES

With the exception of a small box of Executive Correspondence (Virginia State Library), Walker left no papers. Insights into his career may be derived from his correspondence with important figures of the time, especially as reflected in the William Mahone Papers (Duke University).

A number of University of Virginia theses and dissertations are also helpful: Audrey Marie Cahill, "Gilbert Carleton [sic] Walker: Virginia's Redeemer Governor" (M.A. thesis, 1956); Richard Grady Lowe, "Republicans, Rebellion, and Reconstruction: The Republican Party in Virginia, 1856–1870" (Ph.D. diss., 1968); James Douglas Smith, "Virginia during Reconstruction, 1856–1870: A Political, Economic and Social Study" (Ph.D diss., 1955); and Robert Maurice Ours, "Virginia's First Redeemer Legislature, 1869–1871" (M.A. thesis, 1966).

Published studies of the Walker period include Jack P. Maddex, Jr., *The Virginia Conservatives, 1867–1879: A Study in Reconstruction Politics* (Chapel Hill, N.C., 1970); Charles E. Wynes, *Race Relations in Virginia, 1870–1902* (Charlottesville, 1961): James Tice Moore, *Two Paths to the New South: The Virginia Debt Controversy, 1870–1883* (Lexington, Ky., 1974); Alrutheus A. Taylor, *The Negro in the Reconstruction of Virginia* (Washington, D.C., 1926); and Hamilton J. Eckenrode, *The Political History of Virginia during the Reconstruction* (Baltimore, 1904).

JAMES L. KEMPER

Governor of Virginia

1874–1878

JAMES LAWSON KEMPER

Native-Son Redeemer

Robert R. Jones

Among the Commonwealth's major political figures of the turbulent era from mid-century to the late 1870s, none was more representative than James Lawson Kemper, a leader in both the antebellum and the postwar years. He was born on June 11, 1823, in Madison County, on the eastern fringe of Virginia's Blue Ridge Mountains, the fourth son and the sixth child in a family of eight children. His boyhood at Mountain Prospect mirrored the comfortable, well-ordered life of antebellum rural Virginia. Kemper's mother was an expressive and deeply religious woman. His father, many years her senior, was less demonstrative, but he taught Kemper the value of industry and self-discipline and instilled in him a strong sense of duty and responsibility. His earliest formal education was at a field school maintained by his father and a neighboring planter. At age sixteen Kemper entered Washington College in Lexington where he pursued a traditional, classical course of study, indulged a fascination for military affairs by joining the Cincinnati Cadets, and participated in the debating, public speaking, and fraternal activities of the Washington Literary Society. Although described by a classmate as "fond of company . . . [and] of humor," Kemper approached college with an uncommon seriousness and sense of purpose, noting that his future would depend principally upon his "own exertions." He graduated in June 1842, within a few days of his nineteenth birthday.

During the next few years Kemper attended to his enfeebled father's far-flung estate and conducted a primary school near Mountain Prospect. Subsequently he crossed the mountains to study law under Judge George W. Summers of Charleston and was admitted to the bar in October 1846. Then, shortly after being commissioned a captain of volunteers in February 1847, he embarked from Old Point Comfort for Mexico on a voyage that proved to be a long and traumatic "series of sufferings," a "vomite . . . more dreadful" (as he described it) than anyone could have imagined. When the First Virginia Regiment reached Mexico some two weeks after the battle of Buena Vista, Kemper lamented that he and his comrades were "too late for Laurels." He remained in Mexico over fifteen months, earning a reputation for industry and commitment to duty.

In August 1848 when he returned to Madison County, Kemper stood on the threshold of his professional career. Predominant political influences in his formative years had been Democratic and Jacksonian. Madison County was staunchly Democratic, and Kemper's early predilections were reinforced at Washington College where in public oratory he employed Jacksonian rhetoric to rail against "aristocratical monopolies," to champion "popular supremacy," and to eulogize the "hardy yeomanry" of the soil. Influenced by Washington College's liberal president Henry Ruffner, he urged the establishment of public education in Virginia and called slavery the "blackest curse" of the age. Young Kemper was unabashedly patriotic, but his nationalism was conditioned by reverence for Virginia. He reflected perfectly the extraordinary attachment and loyalty to his native state that was characteristic of antebellum Virginians. Virginia was the "noble old mother state," and the essence of patriotism was disinterested devotion and service to its cause.

Although not of imposing stature, Kemper was striking in appearance. Broad-shouldered and thick-chested, he cut an impressive figure in his officer's uniform in the mid-1840s. A photograph of a dozen years later shows a clean-shaven, handsome man, of serious countenance, with a high forehead, prominent nose, resolute mouth, and dark, deep-set, intense eyes.

In personality and character Kemper was complex and contradictory. Intelligent and able, he was highly self-disciplined and exceptionally industrious, a person of impeccable honesty and integrity. On the other hand, there was a darker side to his character. Kemper's early letters and his Mexican War diary reveal a pretentiousness and conceit which did not diminish with age. His ambition, hypochondria, and excessive preoccupation with his own reputation reflected an underlying and pronounced egotism. Many of his contemporaries thought him pompous, bombastic, and imperious. Even with close friends and family, he was frequently inconsiderate and insensitive. Like most egotists, Kemper was self-righteous, argumentative, and thin-skinned, defects which embroiled him in fisticuffs, aborted duels, and numerous verbal or written altercations.

In mid-1848 Kemper opened a law office in Madison Courthouse and began his courtship of the beautiful, vivacious Belle Cave, daughter of Belfield Cave, longtime Madison clerk of court and scion of a prominent Piedmont family. On July 4, 1853, when Belle was sixteen, she and Kemper were married. That same year he won a seat in the House of Delegates, a position he would hold for almost a decade.

State and national political campaigns of the mid-fifties were of major importance in Kemper's incipient political career. He was an early supporter of Henry A. Wise for governor and played an active role in the campaign of 1855 that swept the Democrats to victory over the Know-Nothings. In 1856 he was among a coterie of Wise followers who rallied Virginia to the support of James Buchanan and who subsequently claimed credit for the election of an administration sympathetic to southern needs.

But despite the South's triumph in the election of 1856, during these years he pressured the General Assembly to reform the state militia, and in March 1858 the legislature finally passed his comprehensive militia reorganization proposal. John Brown's raid of the following year greatly alarmed Virginians, galvanizing support for military preparedness, and Kemper's fight was no longer a lonely one. The legislature of 1859–60 appropriated nearly $838,000 for public defense, and the special session of early 1861 voted an additional $1 million. Other Virginians also contributed to the state's military revival, but Kemper was the architect and prime mover of the preparedness program, and his leadership on this critical issue made him one of the most powerful legislative figures in the state.

A champion of southern rights and unity, he sincerely wanted to preserve the Union but insisted that the South had a natural right to defend itself, and he warned in 1860 that increasing northern encroachments on southern rights must cease. If not, he threatened, "we will tear down the pillars of the temple though we perish in its ruins."

In complete disregard of Governor John Letcher's pleas for moderation, he sponsored legislation early in 1861 calling for a state convention to consider Virginia's status in the Union, and with secession Kemper dedicated himself wholly to the cause of southern independence. After participating in the carnage at First Manassas, he devoted most of the following winter to his new duties as speaker of Virginia's House of Delegates. Then, as a regimental and brigade commander, he led his troops in nearly all of the early battles of the Army of Northern Virginia, including Williamsburg, Seven Pines, Gaines's Mill, Frayser's Farm, Malvern Hill, Second Manassas, South Mountain, Sharpsburg, and Fredericksburg. Consistently lauded by his superiors, he was also a favorite with his men, admired for his dash, impetuosity, and impassioned oratory.

Kemper's battlefield career ended at Gettysburg, where his brigade was one of the two lead units of Pickett's fabled charge. At a point less than fifty yards from the famous stone wall on Cemetery Ridge, Kemper was knocked from his horse, desperately wounded. The retreating army left the paralyzed Kemper in the hands of the enemy, and neither Confederate authorities nor his family learned until late July that he had survived. He had been struck in the left thigh by a minié ball that had glanced upward and lodged near the base of his spine, to remain there for the rest of his life. Because of the seriousness of his condition, he was exchanged for a Union general in late September 1863.

In the spring of 1864 he was appointed to command all reserve forces of Virginia and in September was promoted to major general. Despite his physical condition, he plunged into his new work with enthusiasm and diligence, reorganizing the reserve forces and invigorating the conscription service to provide replacements for Lee's army. But these efforts could not turn the tide, and some three weeks after Lee's surrender Kemper was paroled at Danville.

Both his life and body shattered, Kemper struggled to get his bearings.

From 1865 to the early 1870s he tried a variety of business projects, including a brokerage agency to secure pardons for former Confederates. Convinced that Virginia was the Eldorado of the South, he worked enthusiastically to attract northern capital, labor, and railroads. But these ventures met with only limited success, and he eventually fell back upon his antebellum profession, the law. By dint of hard work he was able to build up his practice, settle most of his debts, and make sound investments in land and property. By the early 1870s he had regained a solid financial position.

In the meantime Kemper devoted considerable attention to politics. Along with other conservative whites, Kemper was especially alarmed by the radical state constitutional convention and in December 1867 played an active part in founding of the Conservative party, an organization designed to combat the radical threat to native white control of the state's political affairs. By the spring of 1869 the path had been cleared for Virginia's restoration to the Union, contingent upon ratification of the Underwood Constitution. State officials and representatives to Congress would be chosen the same day. Although Kemper opposed the withdrawal of Conservative Robert E. Withers from the gubernatorial race, emphatically favored a native Virginian for the governorship, and had longtime political and personal ties with railroad opponents of William Mahone, by early June he came out strongly for "True Republican" Gilbert C. Walker and for the Mahone-backed candidate for the local seat in the House of Delegates. It is unclear whether Kemper's dramatic shift of position resulted from his realization that the first priority was the defeat of the radicals or from a perceptive reading of his personal political prospects. In any case, his enthusiastic support of Mahone candidates opened the possibility of reciprocal support from the railroad executive in the future.

A little over a year after the True Republican–Conservative forces swept to victory, personal tragedy struck. Kemper's wife died in the early fall of 1870 of complications from her seventh childbirth. Only thirty-three years old, Belle had been her husband's most valued supporter and confidante. He was devastated, lamenting that he was a man "broken in health, in energy and in spirits." Only the passage of time could change his perspective and restore his sense of purpose. By the summer and fall of 1872 Kemper had become politically active once again, seeking unsuccessfully the Conservative nomination for Congress from the Seventh District, winning plaudits for his resolution at the Conservative convention in support of the Liberal Republican presidential slate, and conducting a vigorous statewide campaign, as elector-at-large, for the Greeley-Brown ticket. Greeley failed to carry Virginia, but Kemper had made a "profound impression" as an enthusiastic and forceful campaigner, and his heightened visibility brought him increasing attention as a strong gubernatorial prospect for 1873.

Kemper possessed several distinct assets. No figure in postwar Virginia politics combined as distinguished an antebellum political career with as gallant a Confederate record. Kemper's cane and his pronounced limp were constant reminders of his loyalty to that Virginia of bygone days, and no one stood to gain more than he from the rising wave of disillusionment with the Walker government and from the mood of nostalgia that disaffection spawned. From the beginning Kemper backers identified their favorite as a "true son" of Old Virginia; he was, they emphasized, " 'One of the few Old Romans' left."

Among Conservative gubernatorial prospects, Kemper and Robert E. Withers soon emerged as the dominant candidates. Withers and his supporters thought the Conservative party owed him the nomination since he had "stepped aside" in 1869. Associated with the Pennsylvania Central Railroad, Withers could rely on the wealth and power of that huge corporation. Kemper, on the other hand, had an organizational problem. He very much wanted to be governor, but (in conformity to Virginia tradition) he wanted "the office to seek him."

In the meantime William Mahone was looking for a suitable candidate. A bitter opponent of the Pennsylvania Central, Mahone adamantly opposed Withers. Mahone lieutenants were wary of Kemper; but, unable to find alternative candidates, in June 1873 they began the critical, behind-the-scenes work of securing city and county delegations pledged to Kemper. Mahone did not create the Kemper candidacy, but his contribution to it was substantial. At the state convention in August, Kemper displayed solid strength on the first ballot, and subsequently the nomination was his by acclamation.

The Conservatives approached the contest as an aroused, confident, and united party. They wanted not only to win but, in words of a Richmond merchant, "to roll up such a majority . . . that the Radicals . . . [would] never dare make another nomination in V[irgini]a." The task would not be easy. The Virginia Republican party was still a formidable force, with great strength in the black belt counties of the Southside and the Tidewater and some potential for attracting the support of poor and disaffected white farmers and laborers. Robert W. Hughes of Abingdon, a member of a distinguished southwest Virginia family and a prominent newspaperman, loomed as a strong Republican gubernatorial nominee. A former Democrat, the moderate Hughes had assumed the leadership of the Republican party after 1869 and had won the 1873 nomination with the support of Mahone's GOP associates.

In keeping with increasing Republican moderation and Conservative acceptance of the "new order," the two parties adopted similar platforms; both endorsed the public schools, advocated the development of state resources, and pledged equal justice to all citizens. Nevertheless, significant differences continued to divide them. The Republicans, representing a new political alignment in Virginia, saw themselves as American loyalists, legitimate heirs to the national revolution that had destroyed the antebellum order. They believed that they constituted the only party suited to govern the "new system of society" that had evolved. The Conservatives, on the other hand, consistently viewed themselves as the "true people of Virginia." Their fundamental purpose had not deviated from that espoused in 1867, to preserve the civilization and liberty of the Old Dominion by preventing the misrule of blacks and carpetbaggers.

Kemper, a dynamic and effective speaker, conducted a vigorous, forceful campaign. Still a handsome, striking-looking man with erect, military bearing and a formidable black beard, he possessed a great deal of personal magnetism. His almost messianic view of his role in the reestablishment of "True Virginia" leadership and his ingrained paranoia imparted a keen sense of urgency to his campaign effort. In a whirlwind canvass, he traveled over 4,000 miles, making some sixty speeches. He grew optimistic in the late stages of the campaign, confidently admonishing a Farmville crowd in late October that they were "looking on the face of the next Governor of Virginia."

Beautiful weather and vigorous campaigning brought large numbers of voters to the polls on November 4. Kemper won only four counties in the Southside, where the Republicans got out a heavy black vote, but he captured fifteen of thirty closely contested Tidewater counties. He swept the rest of the state with the exception of two counties. Kemper had a substantial margin of 25,745 votes, an increase of 7,000 over Gilbert Walker's majority in 1869. Kemper's smashing victory dealt a death blow to radical Republicanism in Virginia, and the Conservatives were ecstatic. The destiny of the Old Dominion was again in the hands of a "true and devoted patriot," they boasted, and under his leadership the state would become again the "grandest Commonwealth" in the South. They awaited eagerly a redemptive administration that would cleanse the state government of what was Yankee and un-Virginian and reaffirm traditional Virginia principles of integrity and commitment to duty.

The new governor still saw himself as a disinterested, devoted Virginia patriot who had neither material interests nor political ambitions that conflicted with a faithful performance of duty. Preoccupied with his own reputation, he believed that recognition of devoted service to Virginia was the highest honor one could receive. Thus, in a curious way, his egotism reinforced his extraordinarily strong commitment to duty and obligation. Kemper wanted his administration to be characterized by dignity, simplicity, and prudence; hence, after his election he "authoritatively forbad" all public celebrations of victory, refused handsome gifts, and assembled only a small personal staff. His inauguration on January 1, 1874, was so simple and brief that the Richmond *Dispatch* noted that the governor "was sworn in almost before he knew it."

Grave problems quickly arose, the most dramatic being a Conservative attempt to gain control of Petersburg's Republican-dominated board of commissioners. Kemper realized that he was dealing with an emotion-packed issue, but—after days of deliberation—he vetoed an undemocratic legislative revision of the city charter as a violation of the political rights of Petersburg's citizens. Angry mobs in Petersburg and Richmond burned the governor in effigy, and he was subjected to a torrent of verbal abuse. On the whole, however, reaction to the veto was strongly favorable, both within and outside the state.

By his veto Kemper sought to demonstrate to the North and to the federal government that Virginia recognized the equality of the races before the law and would defend the rights of black Virginians. He also wanted to impress upon white Virginians, especially the arrant negrophobes among them, that his administration would not tolerate any infringement of black rights or disruption of racial harmony. Under Kemper's leadership white Virginians largely accepted the "new constitutional order," including black education, suffrage, officeholding, and even limited participation in Conservative politics. Kemper was particularly proud of his record in race relations; his administration proved, he felt, that it had both the will and the capacity to protect the personal rights of blacks and to "enforce justice, order and law." It was the governor's belief, reinforced by experience, that most blacks acquiesced to white domination, conducted themselves peacefully, and showed deference and respect to Conservative leaders. Kemper, in turn, sought to protect "the weaker . . . race," to promote black education and personal development, and to treat black citizens with kindness, fairness, and magnanimity. Although their racial policy did not encompass real racial equality, Kemper and Conservatives of his ilk considered themselves the true friends of the freedmen.

While the Old Dominion was still in an uproar over the Petersburg charter affair, Kemper was struggling with another grave issue, the state's financial crisis. The Funding Act of 1871 required interest payments that constituted an enormous drain on the state's reduced revenues, and Virginia's inability to repay its creditors was severely depressing the public credit, a situation which Kemper feared would seriously retard economic recovery. Against the advice of Nathaniel B. Meade, his closest adviser during the first six months of his administration, the determined and combative governor took the "dangerous" question of the public debt to the Assembly in March and to an official conference with Virginia's creditors in November. He told the bondholders frankly that the state could not afford to pay the required 6 percent interest, warned them that there was "profound dissatisfaction" with existing funding arrangements, and urged them to work with the state to achieve a mutually agreeable resettlement of the debt carrying 4 percent interest initially. In turn, Kemper warned the legislators in December that if they did not solve the debt problem quickly, they risked engendering "such internal difficulties and agitations as may be strong enough to tear the vitals of the state." But the General Assembly failed to act. Creditor intransigence, legislative inertia, and public apathy were too strong.

Failing in his initial efforts to negotiate a cut in the interest rate, Kemper radically altered his approach. Hand in hand with continuing efforts to achieve a debt settlement, he led what historian C. C. Pearson called a "truly heroic attempt" to meet the state's existing obligations by reducing expenditures and increasing revenues. In the executive branch Kemper practiced careful frugality and insisted on the strictest accountability, and he hounded the legislature to inaugurate a rigorous system of retrenchment in the public service. But the General Assembly consistently lagged behind the governor in its commitment to reform. Some modest reductions in governmental expenses were achieved, but significant economies resulting from several of Kemper's retrenchment initiatives—such as his successful campaign to reduce the size of the House of Delegates by constitutional amendment—were not felt until the early 1880s.

At the same time, Kemper was making a concerted effort to increase state revenues, primarily through a more equitable distribution of taxes. His basic approach was to oppose increases in the general property levy, the burden of which fell heavily on farmers and the poor; instead he urged the legislature to widen the tax base to include such untaxed or undertaxed subjects as personalty, liquor, the oyster industry, and church property. With the passage of the "Moffett Punch Act" in 1877, the Assembly finally heeded the governor's repeated requests for heavier taxes on alcoholic beverages, but otherwise the lawmakers did little to increase revenues or to equalize the burdens of taxation.

In December 1875 Kemper reached the midpoint of his term. He had coped with the challenges of his office in admirable fashion, and, although he suffered increasing paralysis and ever-decreasing "powers of locomotion" as a result of his war wound, he enjoyed a modest social life. He had occasional overnight guests in the Governor's Mansion, held open house each New Year's Day, hosted a number of informal breakfasts, dinners, and other social events, and entertained such guests as Stonewall Jackson's widow and President Hayes at formal receptions. The governor also got away for quiet weekends in Madison, and in 1876 he took an entire month to travel and to rest. At other times his family visited him in Richmond. "You ought just to see me," he wrote to a friend during the Christmas holidays of 1875. "Although in pain, my children have made me younger and my bosom is full of roses."

Kemper consistently urged the legislature to support the insane asylums, the state penitentiary, the school for the deaf and dumb, and the institutions of higher learning, but the Commonwealth's financial crisis made it impossible to provide adequate social services. As a country lawyer who had lived and worked for thirty years among the common people, he was sensitive to the needs of Virginia's masses. He advocated prison reform, believed it wrong that Virginians had to send mentally ill relatives out of state because the asylums were filled, and lamented that youthful offenders had to be sent to the penitentiary because of the absence of a reformatory for juveniles. Even so, the state's poverty and its ongoing debt problem meant that there was little he could do to alleviate such conditions.

As a youthful and idealistic Jacksonian, Kemper had been an advocate of free mass education, and he had no difficulty in accepting wholeheartedly the tax-supported public schools mandated by the Underwood Constitution. Indeed, he thought that the schools constituted one of the state's "great interests," and he was committed to giving them "unceasing and fostering care." Nevertheless, financial shortages ensured that schools would suffer uncertain and limited funding. These financial difficulties did not result from a lack of commitment on the part of Kemper's administration, which gave strong support to public education despite the problems of the day. The $443,000 appropriated in 1875–76 was Virginia's largest disbursement for schools up to that time, and more children attended the schools in 1876–77 than ever before. Reflecting his concern for the future of public education, the governor recommended in his farewell message that a constitutional amendment be adopted to put the schools on a more dependable financial basis. When he left office, Kemper could honestly say that he had supported the school system "fairly, efficiently, and in the spirit of its founders."

Kemper's positions on two other major issues, constitutional reform and sectional reconciliation, provide striking evidence of the ambivalence of the era. The new Underwood Constitution, he thought, aside from making some necessary changes in the fundamental law, had unnecessarily laid violent hands on Virginia's ancient traditions and patterns of life. Kemper favored a thoroughgoing revision that would conform to the "habitudes, ideas and necessities" of Virginians, but in the absence of strong public support he had to content himself with piecemeal, partial alterations through the amendment process.

On the other hand, Kemper and the Conservatives changed profoundly Virginia's relations with other sections and with the federal government. Despite his antebellum record as an ardent southern nationalist and his conviction that the South was still being persecuted as a conquered section, Kemper vigorously championed the cause of reconciliation. He entreated his people to leave the past "severely alone," to ignore patiently the "passions of the hour," and to assume a "magnanimous bearing under wrong." Kemper's firm commitment to the Union and to reconciliation was demonstrated early in his term when he spurned the objections of unreconstructed Virginians and held a lengthy meeting at the White House with President Grant on the political affairs of Virginia and the South. Fittingly, the last major activity of Kemper's governorship was hosting President Hayes's short but pleasant visit to Virginia in October 1877.

Kemper provided Virginians with four years of forceful, spirited, and independent-minded leadership. He came to office with the help of William Mahone and at first welcomed Mahone's counsel on patronage and railroad matters. Mahone, however, had little substantive influence on the course of Kemper's administration, and by late 1876 the governor had made it clear that he would no longer rely on Mahone's advice, even in patronage cases. Kemper was not the tool of any class or faction, and he rejected out of hand the special interest politics in which his predecessor had been so deeply involved. Kemper dodged no issues, no matter how controversial, no matter how powerful his opponents. He tackled the debt issue and was bitterly denounced by bondholders; he appointed tobacco inspectors to protect the interests of tobacco planters and earned the wrath of warehouse owners and tobacco dealers; he interfered with efforts to deprive blacks of a voice in the government of Petersburg and was hung in effigy; he urged the abolition of a number of state offices and was ridiculed by former friends and allies.

Perhaps no governor of Virginia ever came to office with a more definite and coherent view of what he wanted to achieve, but Kemper was only partially successful in carrying out his plans. The major difficulty was the nature of the problems Virginia faced in the mid-1870s. The problems—race relations, state finances, economic recovery, public schools, and social services—were simply overwhelming in their magnitude. Nevertheless, Kemper's administration was an able and notable one. He restored honesty and integrity to Virginia government and revived the idea of governmental impartiality and concern for the welfare of all Virginians. In his support of public education and sectional reconciliation he focused the state's attention on the future and on progressive development, and his administration may have provided the best race relations in the South in the mid-1870s. His governorship faltered on the rocks of economic hard times and financial insolvency, but the fault was not his. Indeed, Kemper made the boldest and most persistent attempts of the decade to free the state from the financial burdens that prevented fulfillment of his dreams of a New Virginia of "contentment, peace, [and] prosperity."

When he left Richmond on January 1, 1878, Kemper intended to retire forever from public office and from active politics. He had for a quarter of a century given Virginia his best effort; "I have," he asserted, "earned an honorable discharge." Only once, when he was enticed to take the stump against the newly organized Readjusters in the heated legislative campaign of 1879, did Kemper abandon his voluntary retirement. Instead, the ex-governor devoted himself, in his own words, to "the task of consolidating my domestic affairs—so long neglected—and achieving peace and repose for my declining years." In the early 1880s he moved his family to a 350-acre farm in the Blue Ridge foothills near Orange Courthouse, where he built a handsome country estate called Walnut Hills. Here, despite declining health, the deaths of two of his children, and the disappearance of another, Kemper enjoyed the comfortable life of a Virginia country gentleman. During the final half dozen years of his life, however, he was beset by severe financial problems and was tortured by deteriorating health aggravated by his old wound.

On Sunday, April 7, 1895, at ten o'clock in the evening, the seventy-one-year-old Kemper breathed his last. Newspapers throughout the state showered praise upon the "intrepid soldier" and the "great statesman" and bemoaned the loss of another link with Virginia's illustrious past. But the Richmond *Dispatch* penned the words that Kemper himself would have appreciated most of all: "Virginia never had a more loving son, nor one that served her from more unselfish purposes."

SOURCES

There are excellent collections of Kemper Papers at the University of Virginia, the Virginia Historical Society, and the Virginia State Library. The William Mahone Papers at Duke University and the University of Virginia are indispensable for an understanding of the politics of the late 1860s and the 1870s. Important Kemper material is also found in the manuscript collections of such contemporaries as John C. Rutherfoord, F. W. M. Holliday, and Nannie Tunstall at Duke University, and S. Bassett French at the College of William and Mary.

Several studies provide background on Kemper. See Robert R. Jones, "Forgotten Virginian: The Early Life and Career of James Lawson Kemper, 1823–1865" (M.A. thesis, University of Virginia, 1961) and "Conservative Virginian: The Post-War Career of Governor James Lawson Kemper" (Ph.D. diss., University of Virginia, 1964); and Jack P. Maddex, Jr., *The Virginia Conservatives, 1867–1879: A Study in Reconstruction Politics* (Chapel Hill, N.C., 1970), based on his senior thesis and doctoral dissertation. Jones deals with particular aspects of Kemper's life in "The Mexican War Diary of James Lawson Kemper," *Virginia Magazine of History and Biography* 74 (1966): 386–428, and "James L. Kemper and the Virginia Redeemers Face the Race Question: A Reconsideration," *Journal of Southern History* 38 (1972): 393–414.

Other works dealing with Kemper and the politics of Reconstruction and redemption include C. C. Pearson, *The Readjuster Movement in Virginia* (New Haven, 1917); James Tice Moore, *Two Paths to the New South: The Virginia Debt Controversy, 1870–1883* (Lexington, Ky., 1974); Charles E. Wynes, *Race Relations in Virginia, 1870–1902* (Charlottesville, 1961); and Nelson M. Blake, *William Mahone of Virginia: Soldier and Political Insurgent* (Richmond, 1935).

FREDERICK W. M. HOLLIDAY

Governor of Virginia

1878–1882

FREDERICK WILLIAM

MACKEY HOLLIDAY

Paradoxical Patrician

James Tice Moore

Frederick William Mackey Holliday emerges from the context of Virginia history as one of the most paradoxical figures ever to serve as governor. Few individuals have been better suited for the office (at least by conventionally accepted standards), but few—if any—have enjoyed less success. Superbly trained as a lawyer, talented as an orator and writer, imposing in appearance and affable in personal bearing, he had demonstrated courage and leadership during the Civil War, and his reputation for personal integrity was a byword in a Gilded Age redolent with accusations of fraud and malfeasance. Recognizing these virtues, Virginia voters accorded him an unopposed election to the state's highest office in 1877—a rare distinction in a period marked by virulent political partisanship. Despite great promise, however, his gubernatorial tenure proved to be an almost unmitigated disaster.

Born in Winchester, Virginia, on February 22, 1828, young Fred Holliday grew up in a home conducive to intellectual development and cultural refinement. His Scotch-Irish father, Robert J. McKim Holliday, was the son of a successful merchant. A physician by trade, he commanded the respect of his neighbors through hard work and conscientious care for his patients, and his practice enabled him to purchase several slaves, a commodious home, and a variety of real estate holdings. Fred's mother, Mary Catherine Taylor Holliday, herself the daughter of a local physician, conformed closely to the prevailing Victorian ideal of womanhood. Together Robert and Mary Holliday provided a secure and comfortable home for Fred, his sisters Mary and Margaret, and his brother Taylor. All in all, the little world of antebellum Winchester was a happy one for young Holliday, and he fully appreciated its virtues. By his late teens he was already an ardent champion of Virginia and, by extension, of all things southern—from the beauty of the region's women to the desirability of Negro servitude.

Holliday's conservatism also was nurtured by an education which conformed to the highest standards of the antebellum Virginia elite. He attended Winchester Academy, the oldest and most prestigious of the town's schools, and then in the autumn of 1845 enrolled as a junior at Yale College, long known as a training ground for the sons of the southern aristocracy. Working with diligence in his courses, Fred honed his oratorical skills as a member of Calliope, a debating society composed of students from the South. Pleased with his solid—if less than brilliant—academic record (and with college life in general), Holliday graduated from Yale in 1847.

Returning to Winchester, the future governor decided to become a lawyer. He first read law at the local firm of Barton and Williams and then enrolled at the University of Virginia School of Law in the fall of 1848. After less than a year at the university, Holliday gave abundant proof of personal enterprise and intellectual capacity. He received diplomas in law, philosophy, and political economy and was chosen by the school's Jefferson Society to deliver the valedictory address. In his speech, "The Influence of Intelligence upon Our Republican Institutions," he praised the conservative wisdom of the Founding Fathers as expressed in the federal Constitution and stressed the need for educated men to exert a restraining and elevating influence on the masses, whose potential for mischief was great in an age of democratic suffrage and demagogic excess.

After graduation Holliday returned to Winchester, where he began law practice in the autumn of 1849. His trial notes indicate careful preparation for courtroom appearances, and he exercised his oratorical skills to the fullest. Recognition came quickly; in 1851 Holliday was elected Commonwealth's attorney for Winchester and nearby Frederick County. Maintaining his reputation for diligence, he represented the public in actions ranging from a crackdown on unsavory "bowling saloons" to prosecutions for rape and murder, and the voters reelected him without opposition in 1856 and again in 1860. His prospects appeared limitless, as he acknowledged by absentmindedly but repeatedly scribbling his own name beside that of George Washington on the back of a sheet of trial notes.

At the onset of the sectional crisis, Holliday, innately conservative and fearful of disorder, deprecated all radical elements, whether abolitionist or secessionist; but—with the continuance of North-South strife—he shifted resolutely into the camp of the hard-line states' rights advocates and began to look upon the North as a land populated by "ambitious demagogues" and "foolish fanatics" bent on converting "this fair garden of ours into a gloomy wilderness." He vigorously supported John C. Breckinridge in 1860 and regarded Republican Abraham Lincoln's triumph as the death knell for southern rights within the Union. Organizing rallies and drafting resolutions, Holliday emerged as the leader of secessionist sentiment in Frederick County and Winchester during the winter of 1860–61. These extremist maneuvers placed him well in advance of public opinion in his locality. In February 1861 more moderate neighbors rejected his bid for a seat in the state convention by a resounding two-to-one margin. The youthful "fire-eater" had suffered the first defeat of his political career, but Virginia's decision to join the Confederacy offered a belated vindication for his stand.

Several dozen Frederick County volunteers who called themselves the "Mountain Rangers" then asked him to serve as their captain. He accepted without delay, and his unit became Company D of the Thirty-third Virginia Regiment. Assigned to General Thomas J. Jackson's famed Stonewall Brigade, Holliday and his men took part in the brilliant Shenandoah Valley campaign and the hard-fought Seven Days battles on the outskirts of Richmond. Absorbing some of Jackson's legendary zeal for combat, Holliday displayed an aggressive spirit bordering on recklessness. This disregard for personal safety won him rapid promotion (he became a colonel in less than two years), but it also set the stage for the end of his military career. Rallying his troops in the battle of Cedar Run on August 9, 1862, Holliday was severely wounded during an assault on the Union line. Amputation of his right arm above the elbow ensued, and he began an agonizing struggle to rebuild his strength. Service on the battlefield, graphically symbolized thereafter by his empty sleeve, had come to an end.

Gradually recovering his health, he campaigned successfully for the Winchester district's seat in the Confederate House of Representatives, beginning his term in the spring of 1864 in a political climate which bordered on despair. But the defiant Holliday spurned this defeatist mood. Steadfast in opposition to the northern invaders, he stood by the embattled Davis regime on issue after issue. Even as the conflict drew to its close, Holliday struggled to keep up the fight. On March 18, 1865, as the Confederate Congress prepared to adjourn for the last time, he introduced a resolution calling on House members to devote their energies "to the maintenance of our great cause and to the prosecution of the war to a successful issue."

With the conclusion of hostilities Holliday returned to Winchester. His hometown, which had changed hands more than seventy times during the course of the war, lay in shambles, and the surrounding countryside had been despoiled by roving bands from both armies. Thirty-seven years old, Holliday demonstrated his usual resolve and set to work rebuilding—so far as possible—the congenial and orderly existence that he had enjoyed before 1861. Although he no longer held the prestigious post of Commonwealth's attorney, the popular ex-Confederate had little difficulty in reestablishing his law practice and, within a decade, thanks to shrewd investment, his financial situation was secure.

Holliday also made important contributions to Winchester's economic revival and sought to mend the community's war-torn social and cultural fabric as well. His first moves centered on his own household. But twice married and twice a widower within four years (1868–72), the future governor never tried a third marriage. Instead he began to look beyond the grief-stricken confines of his family circle to the broader and more promising realm of community involvement and service. He spearheaded a successful drive to establish an Episcopal academy for girls in the 1870s and held office on the administrative boards of at least three other private schools in the town during the same decade. He also participated in the Frederick County Bible Society, worked with the Winchester YMCA, and engineered fund-raising efforts for a Valley-wide farmers' organization. Such public-spirited activities made him more popular than ever before, and he became for his neighbors the embodiment of patrician rectitude and noblesse oblige.

Successful in his business and cultural endeavors, Holliday assumed an increasingly prominent role in the political arena, too. Unswervingly enunciating his conservative principles, Holliday campaigned for white supremacy and local self-government in the Reconstruction era; yet he soon reconciled himself to life in the reconstituted Union. Indeed, in 1871 he accepted an appointment from Governor Gilbert C. Walker as the Commonwealth's representative on the U.S. Centennial Commission, a post which consumed an ever-increasing share of his time as the Philadelphia Exposition of 1876 drew near. Regarding this world's fair as an excellent opportunity to advertise Virginia's resources, Holliday set to work rallying public support and collecting materials for the state's exhibit. His efforts were hindered by inadequate appropriations from a penny-wise legislature, but his diligent—and unpaid—efforts won favorable notice from one end of the Old Dominion to the other. During the Centennial year he also made a highly regarded address on social and political trends to the University of Virginia's Society of Alumni in June, and in the same month the Conservative state convention selected him to campaign as an at-large elector for the Democratic presidential ticket. Endorsing party nominee Samuel J. Tilden in speeches throughout Virginia, Holliday relentlessly excoriated the misdeeds of President Ulysses S. Grant and his Republican henchmen—all the while enhancing his own stature as an oratorical champion of morality in government.

Holliday's sudden political prominence (after eleven years in which he had held no elective office) stemmed, in part at least, from voter desire for new and more effective leadership—not just in Washington but in Richmond as well. No longer so concerned about the fading specter of Negro rule, Virginia's white majority was becoming increasingly critical of the state's dominant Conservative organization. The party had successfully smashed the radical threat in the late 1860s, but it had demonstrated little aptitude for dealing with the hard times of the subsequent decade. In particular, the state debt issue had emerged as the inescapable nemesis of Virginia's governing elite. Exasperating public sentiment throughout Virginia, this financial crisis had split the Conservative machine. One faction, the "Readjusters," demanded that the legislature should arbitrarily "adjust" the debt burden downward. This repudiationist element found its most devoted following among democratic-minded farmers in counties west of the Blue Ridge. The other wing of the Conservative organization, known as "Funders" because of their efforts to uphold the state's credit, insisted that cuts in the debt principal or interest could only be made with the consent of the bondholders—a stand supported by the business elite and the traditionalist gentry of the Piedmont and Tidewater.

Laying bare the shortcomings of Virginia's governmental policies, the debt crisis provided Holliday with his supreme political opportunity. He feared that repudiation would undermine the very structure of law and morality, and he instinctively adopted Funder views. Still, as a private citizen he had avoided involvement in the controversy and seemed to offer the electorate a chance for a new beginning, a fresh start toward resolution of the problem. His popularity in the Shenandoah Valley, a hotbed of Readjuster sentiment, further enhanced his prospects as a spokesman for compromise, and his reputation for personal integrity augmented his appeal still more. Lastly, Holliday's distinguished appearance and dignified bearing also served to elevate him in the public's esteem. His empty sleeve evoked memories of wartime heroism; his graying hair suggested maturity of judgment; a solemn voice added conviction to his words. Approximately six feet tall and inclined toward portliness, he personified the Victorian ideal of solidity and decorum. To a people weary of turmoil and unrest, therefore, he represented the promise of certainty and serenity, restoration and repose. Rallying support from friends and neighbors and from well-wishers throughout the Commonwealth, he entered the 1877 gubernatorial campaign.

Holliday enjoyed real advantages, but he nevertheless encountered significant obstacles on his road to the Governor's Mansion. He was less well known than some of the other aspirants, and his supporters were less organized, too. As a result, county caucuses gave him only third place in a field of six candidates when convention delegates were chosen in June and July 1877. Petersburg railroad magnate William Mahone shared the initial lead with Lynchburg's John W. Daniel (reputedly the best orator in Virginia), while Holliday headed a list of lesser hopefuls which included William B. Taliaferro of Gloucester, Fitzhugh Lee of Fairfax, and William Terry of Amherst. Yet the preconvention vote suggested the likelihood of a deadlock—with the "one-armed hero of the Valley" a distinct possibility for dark-horse honors. Daniel and Mahone had engaged in bitter clashes over railroad matters, and there was every reason to suspect that either of them would support a third candidate before he would permit the nomination to go to his hated rival. Furthermore, the emergence of state finances as a campaign issue worked in Holliday's favor. Mahone, stung by attacks on his railroad dealings and desperate for popular support, endorsed Readjustment in a letter issued to the press only a month before the convention. This move forced the other five candidates to announce their views, and all (including Holliday) expressed support for Funder principles. The Winchester native's statement, however, made him even more acceptable as a compromise nominee. He declared that although he opposed repudiation, he regarded the debt as an issue "belonging properly to the Legislature, not to the executive"—an ambiguous phrase implying that as governor, he would follow the General Assembly's lead in the matter.

Meeting in Richmond on August 8, 1877, the Conservative convention followed a predictable course. Funder sentiment predominated, but neither Mahone nor Daniel could muster a majority. Meanwhile Taliaferro, Lee, and Terry withdrew, and most of their adherents moved into Holliday's camp. Mahone's floor leaders (determined to block Daniel) then shifted their support to Holliday, giving him victory on the seventh ballot. The delegates rounded out the ticket by nominating Funders James A. Walker and Raleigh T. Daniel for the posts of lieutenant governor and attorney general. Completing their work, the assembled Conservatives adopted a platform opposing repudiation and calling for retrenchment in governmental expenditures. Holliday—and debt payment—had triumphed.

What followed was one of the strangest election campaigns in Virginia history. Demoralized by previous defeats, the Republicans fielded no gubernatorial candidate, focusing instead on legislative races, where Mahone and his adherents (still determined to slash the debt) made a vigorous bid for control of the General Assembly. Stunned by the death of attorney general nominee Raleigh T. Daniel a few days after the convention, the party's executive committee awarded the post to James G. Field, a moderate Readjuster from Culpeper. Field subsequently enunciated his debt-scaling views in several speeches, while lieutenant governor candidate James A. Walker assailed Readjustment as "larceny" and its advocates as "highway thieves." Caught in this crossfire, Holliday maintained a discreet silence. The November elections reflected the confused state of affairs. Holliday swept to unopposed victory, garnering more than 100,000 votes, but Readjuster and Independent gains rendered control of the legislature problematical.

Taking office on January 1, 1878, the new governor abandoned his previous reticence and reminded an inauguration day crowd of 12,000 of his belief in debt payment. He also called for an end to political agitation over the issue, but the Readjuster lawmakers had different plans and soon produced two significant proposals. The first of these, the Barbour bill (named after House Finance Committee Chairman James Barbour), specified that 50 percent of the Old Dominion's tax receipts should be earmarked for general government expenses, 20 percent for public schools, and no more than 30 percent for interest payments on the debt. Individuals would be allowed to pay only the last 30 percent of their taxes in bond interest coupons, while the rest would have to be remitted in currency. A second bill, devised by Albemarle Senator John E. Massey, required that all levies for the support of schools—including the poll tax—be paid in cash. Stressing the importance of preserving the educational system, the lawmakers approved both measures early in 1878 and sent them to Holliday for his signature.

This placed Holliday in a difficult situation. During his bid for the governorship he had acknowledged the General Assembly's control over state finances, but to the surprise of the Readjusters, he vetoed both proposals. Soul-searchingly moralistic in his approach to the debt issue (as he was to life in general), Holliday could find no ethical justification for either of the bills. The Commonwealth had pledged to accept the coupons for any and all of its taxes when it had issued the bonds, and he believed that it could not in good faith unilaterally retract or limit this privilege. Appalled by Readjuster assertions that schools enjoyed a higher claim on the Commonwealth's resources than bondholders, he defiantly responded with the most controversial statement of his career. "Our fathers did not need free schools," he informed the legislature, "to make them what they were." "Public free schools are not a necessity," he added. "They are a luxury . . . to be paid for, like any other luxury, by the people who wish their benefits." The Funders rejoiced at this defense of the public credit, but the Readjusters countered with a torrent of abuse. Denounced from the mountains to the Chesapeake for thwarting the popular will and undermining the schools, Holliday nevertheless held fast to his conservative beliefs. His last—and most frustrating—battle had begun.

The governor's resolute stand did nothing to increase his popularity, but it did enable him to win his first clash with the Readjusters. Unable to override his vetoes and anxious to avoid a prolonged deadlock, the Senate asked Holliday for his own recommendations for dealing with the financial crisis. He replied with two suggestions: the General Assembly could either raise the property tax ("I think the people would not feel it," he blandly noted, "were it a little more or a little less"), or it could seek a compromise settlement with the bondholders. Confronted with these alternatives, a coalition of Funders and moderate Readjusters pushed a new debt proposal through the legislature. Coauthored by Thomas S. Bocock of Appomattox and Isaac C. Fowler of Bristol, this Bocock-Fowler bill invited Virginia's creditors to exchange their old bonds (most of which paid annual interest of 6 percent) for new securities bearing only 3 percent per annum for eighteen years and 4 percent for the following thirty-two years. Holliday endorsed the measure with alacrity. The General Assembly also sought to take concrete action on behalf of the schools. Legislative investigations revealed that almost $400,000 had been diverted from education to debt payments from 1870 to 1874, and the two houses authorized the Commonwealth's auditor of public accounts (if he found it "practicable") to make special payments of $15,000 every three months until the schools had been compensated for these losses. Governor Holliday approved this measure as well, and the legislators adjourned in the spring of 1878—hopeful that they had taken decisive steps toward resolving the Old Dominion's financial problems. Unfortunately, both of these major achievements proved stillborn. The bondholders refused to accept new securities, and the state auditor, faced with a depleted treasury, found it "impracticable" to make any reimbursements to the schools. A significant effort at compromise had failed.

Beset—like its predecessors—by insufficient revenues and obstinate bondholders, the Holliday administration plunged ever deeper into debt throughout 1878. Tax receipts remained grossly inadequate, while the flood of interest coupons crested at a record annual rate of $1.2 million. State outlays for primary education dropped to $241,000 in 1878, slightly more than half as much as had been expended a few years earlier. Enrollments slipped by 100,000 pupils in a matter of months, and the future of tax-supported education in Virginia appeared in doubt. Holliday, meanwhile, continued to espouse his Funder creed. A 60 or 80 percent increase in the property tax was all that was needed, he declared, to enable the Commonwealth to meet its obligations. It would be better, he piously exhorted his depression-racked people, "for us . . . to invite the debt into our houses to partake of our daily bread, than to ignore or renounce it." Prospects of an orderly and enduring settlement of the Old Dominion's financial problems seemed more remote than ever.

When the legislature reconvened in December 1878, Holliday included one hopeful note in his generally somber message to that body: alarmed by the rise of Readjuster sentiment, a number of influential capitalists had informed him of their desire to work out a compromise. The governor urged the General Assembly to take advantage of this opportunity, and a special legislative joint committee began to meet with representatives of two prestigious creditor syndicates. Hugh McCulloch, erstwhile secretary of the treasury under Andrew Johnson, headed the bondholder delegation, and the resulting proposal came to be known as the McCulloch bill. This measure provided for funding of Virginia's outstanding securities (valued at approximately $33 million) in new bonds bearing 3 percent annual interest for ten years, 4 percent for the next twenty years, and 5 percent for the final ten years before maturity. This represented a substantial reduction from the current 6 percent rate, and the Funder press estimated that the compromise could save the Commonwealth $26 million. The two syndicates would handle the funding process, and—to encourage creditors to make the necessary exchanges—the new bonds would be exempt from all Virginia revenue levies and would continue to feature the much maligned tax-receivable coupons. These provisions attracted inevitable criticism from the Readjusters, who argued that even with the reduced payments, the state would still be unable to maintain its schools and other social services. Advocates of the settlement then agreed to support a major reform in appropriations procedures suggested by David W. Henkel, a Readjuster from the Valley. The Henkel bill sought to ensure a reliable income for education by requiring that three-fourths of the school taxes should be retained in the counties—thereby preventing Richmond bureaucrats from diverting the revenues to interest payments. Having thus compromised their differences, Funders and moderate Readjusters cooperated to pass the McCulloch and Henkel bills in March 1879. Holliday had placed the full power and prestige of his office behind this drive, even authorizing an extension of the legislative session to complete the work, and he promptly signed both measures. Within six months the syndicates funded more than $8 million of the debt in the new reduced-interest securities.

The McCulloch Act promised an end to Virginia's financial difficulties, but it was never given a chance to prove its effectiveness. Instead the voters, in one of the most dramatic uprisings in the state's political history, blasted the debt scheme into oblivion in the 1879 legislative elections. This stunning development was engineered by extremist insurgents led by William Mahone. Breaking completely with the old Conservative organization (which had endorsed the McCulloch settlement), these uncompromising, "Simon-pure" Readjusters established their own party and went on the attack. The new law, they argued, was far too generous to the bondholders, and its tax-receivable coupons would mortgage away control of the Commonwealth's finances for a generation to come. What was more, the McCulloch Act had turned the funding process over to outside "brokers" and "Shylocks" who stood to profit at public expense. Appealing to black voters as well as whites, to disorganized Republicans as well as disaffected Conservatives, the insurgents hammered incessantly at these issues throughout the state. The overconfident Conservatives mounted only a lackluster counterattack, and aggressive Mahoneites won majorities—albeit small ones—in both houses of the General Assembly.

The impact of the election became apparent when the legislature convened in December 1879. Holliday's annual message urged the lawmakers not to overturn the McCulloch settlement, but the victorious Readjusters focused their energies instead on consolidating their hold on Virginia politics. They quickly put their own men in local and state offices and elevated Mahone to the U.S. Senate. The implications of this trend were not lost on the state's creditors. Recognizing the realities of the situation, the bondholder syndicates abandoned efforts to fund the debt. The McCulloch Act—with its promise of order and stability—was dead.

Having scuttled Holliday's financial program, the Readjusters then devised a settlement of their own. Put into final form in February and March 1880 by Harrison H. Riddleberger, a state senator from Shenandoah County, the Riddleberger bill repudiated roughly two-fifths of the debt. Under its terms all of Virginia's outstanding obligations were to be exchanged for $19.6 million in new bonds maturing in fifty years and bearing only 3 percent annual interest. The new securities would carry no tax-receivable coupons, and the bill placed drastic restrictions on the use of coupons from the old bonds as well—thus implying that only creditors who acquiesced in the settlement would receive any interest revenues at all. This repudiationist document came before Governor Holliday for his signature in March 1880. Predictably, he vetoed the measure. The Readjusters lacked the votes to override the veto, but there was no rush to compromise. The government was deadlocked, and it would remain so for the rest of Holliday's term.

The governor and his traditionalist compatriots advanced a simple explanation for the demise of the McCulloch settlement and the ascendancy of their Readjuster opponents: venal demagogues had misled the ignorant and the gullible, especially blacks, into overthrowing the rule of Virginia's "best people." Although widely accepted at the time, this partisan assessment left much to be desired. The insurgents had used misleading and inflammatory rhetoric, to be sure, but other factors contributed to their success. For one thing, the bondholders must bear a large part of the blame; exasperating popular sentiment, they had delayed for too many years before evincing willingness to compromise. The Conservatives' lackadaisical campaign of 1879 also contributed to the Mahoneite triumph, and Holliday must shoulder some responsibility for the collapse of his financial program. Resolute (as always) in the defense of his principles, he had nevertheless demonstrated a damning insensitivity to the needs and aspirations of ordinary citizens. Isolated from the masses by wealth, training, and temperament, he had angered thousands with his reference to the public school system as a "luxury," and his repeated demands for tax increases in the midst of a harsh depression had alienated still more. By awarding control of the General Assembly to the insurgents, therefore, Virginians had voted to repudiate not only the debt but Holliday's leadership as well. The Winchester native would remain in the Governor's Mansion almost two years after his Riddleberger bill veto, but he would no longer—in any meaningful sense—govern the Commonwealth.

Thwarted in his efforts to end the debt crisis, the hard-pressed chief executive experienced additional frustrations in carrying out routine duties. He successfully vetoed a legislative attempt to give the Readjusters complete control of the state penitentiary in February 1880, but he could not prevent them from filling the Commonwealth's other administrative and judicial posts with their spoilsmen. Holliday looked on the new functionaries with ill-disguised contempt. Still—short of resigning his post—he had no choice but to work with them, an enforced collaboration which inevitably generated friction and ill will.

Vexed by intractable problems and insubordinate bureaucrats, by a rebellious electorate and a hostile legislature, Holliday instinctively sought relief from political strife by minimizing social contacts with friends and enemies alike during his gubernatorial term, thus preserving the introspective solitude he had come to enjoy as a bachelor and widower. He gave evidence of this reclusive stance by closing off most of the Governor's Mansion, living in the few remaining rooms with a single servant. Not satisfied with this degree of isolation, Holliday made frequent visits to his beloved Winchester and absented himself from Richmond on numerous other occasions, too. He took a week-long trip up the James River and Kanawha Canal in 1879, traveled to a governors' conference in Philadelphia that same year, attended centennial observances in Tennessee and the Carolinas in 1880, and participated in similar activities in New York City in 1881.

Overshadowing these pastimes, however, was Holliday's involvement in the 1881 Yorktown Centennial. He viewed the celebration as an opportunity to reassert traditional virtues and threw himself unreservedly into preparations for the event. He rallied national support for the project during his northern trips and spearheaded planning and fund-raising efforts in the Old Dominion. Rewarding his efforts, the centennial proved to be a rousing success. Approximately 25,000 visitors, including President Chester A. Arthur and many other notables, flocked to Yorktown for three days of festivities in October 1881, and thousands more participated in a subsequent parade and reception in Richmond. Welcoming this multitude to Virginia, Holliday enunciated his vision of an America which, forgetting old sectional and partisan battles, could anticipate unparalleled progress through renewed commitment to individual liberty and constitutional law.

Yet less than a month after the Yorktown gathering Virginians went to the polls and awarded complete control of the state government to his opponents. The Readjusters retained their grasp on both houses of the General Assembly, and insurgent gubernatorial candidate William E. Cameron defeated Funder John W. Daniel by a resounding 12,000 vote margin. After January 1, 1882, the Mahoneites were free to enact their repudiationist sentiments into law.

Holliday was now only fifty-three years old—with more than eighteen years of life ahead of him—but he never reentered the political arena. He was so alienated by the Readjuster triumph, in fact, that he refused even to comment on state affairs. Instead he withdrew inward, pursuing the personal satisfactions that had eluded him in his previous career. He returned to Winchester, where income from his investments allowed him to live in the congenial style of a well-to-do Virginia gentleman. His parents had died during his stay in Richmond, but Holliday avoided total seclusion by sharing his home with his brother Taylor, a bachelor physician. Reading widely, expanding his library to more than eight thousand titles, and refurbishing his house according to high Victorian taste, the ex-governor enjoyed a welcome escape from partisan upheavals. He indulged another of his interests by purchasing a 436-acre farm in Frederick County. Although he employed tenants to maintain this estate, he became increasingly expert in directing the production of grains, grasses, and livestock. Lastly, his new leisure gave him time to travel. Beginning in 1882 and continuing for more than a decade thereafter, he embarked on tours of the art museums of Europe and the Hindu shrines of

India, the peaks of the Alps and the inner reaches of the Amazon, the isolated outposts of Australia and the teeming cities of China.

These wide-ranging excursions came to an end in 1893 when Holliday's health began to deteriorate, and his morale suffered a devastating blow in August of that year when Taylor, his brother and closest confidant, died. These misfortunes compelled the ex-governor to curtail his travels, but he did not abandon himself to lassitude or despair. Instead he became active once more in Winchester affairs, coordinating fund-raising efforts for a new water-works and other municipal improvements. He also began publishing seven volumes of letters written during his world tours. In March 1896 a stroke paralyzed his right side. Suffering another stroke three years later, he died on May 29, 1899, at the age of seventy-one. A contingent of Confederate veter-ans escorted Holliday's body to Winchester's Mount Hebron Cemetery, where a simple stone was erected to mark his grave.

What evaluation should be placed on Frederick William Mackey Holli-day as a man and as a governor? At the time of his death Virginia newspapers agreed that his administration had not been a success, but the obituary writers still maintained that he had been one of the most able, intelligent, and consci-entious individuals ever to have served as the Commonwealth's chief execu-tive. Such a judgment clearly has much to recommend it, but it does not resolve the essential paradox of Holliday's life. Why had such a competent man proved to be a failure in the state's highest office? Ironically, it appears that the same virtues which had brought Holliday to public favor also ren-dered him incapable of sustained political achievement in Gilded Age Vir-ginia. Superbly trained in the governmental theories and ethical principles of the antebellum order, he refused to modify those concepts in the transformed postwar environment. Consequently, his resolution degenerated into obstruc-tionism and his moral strength into self-righteousness—exacerbating the par-tisan excesses he abhorred. Viewed within this context, a sentence from a speech prepared for delivery shortly before his death provides insight into the fundamental tragedy of his governorship and his life. "Oh!" he wrote, "for one hour of the Statesmen and Statesmanship of the Olden Time!" During his four years in Richmond, Holliday had attempted to provide Virginians with just such statesmanship—with disastrous results. He had been, in essence, a paradoxical patrician, a man against his time.

SOURCES

The Frederick William Mackey Holliday Papers (Duke University) con-tain material pertinent to almost all phases of Holliday's career. Newspa-per files at the Handley Library (Winchester) and local tax records offer proof of his ascending economic and social status (1865–99). Holliday left a detailed account of his world tours in the seven volumes of his *Letters of Travel* (Baltimore, 1897).

Previous analyses of Holliday's life include Julian P. Porter, Jr., "Frederick William Mackey Holliday, Governor of Virginia, 1878–1881" (M.A. thesis, University of Virginia, 1969), and James V. Hutton, Jr., "The One-armed Hero of the Shenandoah," *Virginia Cavalcade* 19 (Summer 1969): 5–11.

Additional insight into men and issues of Holliday's administration is available in Nelson M. Blake's *William Mahone of Virginia: Soldier and Political Insurgent* (Richmond, 1935); Richard B. Doss's "John W. Daniel: A Study in the Virginia Democracy" (Ph.D. diss., University of Virginia, 1955); Elizabeth H. Hancock's edition of the *Autobiography of John E. Massey* (New York, 1909); Jack P. Maddex, Jr.'s *The Virginia Conservatives, 1867–1879: A Study in Reconstruction Politics* (Chapel Hill, N.C., 1970); and James Tice Moore's *Two Paths to the New South: The Virginia Debt Controversy, 1870–1883* (Lexington, Ky., 1974).

WILLIAM E. CAMERON

Governor of Virginia

1882–1886

WILLIAM EVELYN CAMERON

Restless Readjuster

Walter T. Calhoun and James Tice Moore

Elected by the Readjusters in 1881, William E. Cameron seemed to per-
sonify a spirit of youthful vigor and reform as he presided over enactment
of one of the most progressive legislative programs in the state's history. From
the outset, however, Cameron was plagued by factional intrigues, racial animosities, and bureaucratic blunders that sapped the vitality of his administration, and events soon demonstrated that he lacked both the will and the ability
to stem such disruptive forces. As a result, power ultimately passed into the
hands of his opponents. Leaving the Governor's Mansion, Cameron began a
prolonged political odyssey which took him from party to party in the 1880s
and 1890s—from Readjuster to Republican to gold Democrat to Democrat.
Brilliant but star-crossed, with more than a touch of the quixotic in his personality, he traversed Virginia's political landscape in a restless and controversial career extending from Reconstruction to the First World War.

Although Cameron rose to prominence as a political maverick, he was
by birth a patrician. Through his mother, Elizabeth Walker Cameron, he
could trace his ancestry to the Harrisons and Byrds; through his cotton
broker father, Walker Anderson Cameron, to the Reverend John Cameron,
an eighteenth-century classical scholar and Episcopal rector whose heirs prospered in business and the professions. In a genealogically minded society
which valued "good blood," his lineage ranked with the best.

Born in Petersburg on November 29, 1842, young Cameron attended
various local schools, read history and poetry, and cultivated an interest in
music, particularly the piano. But this life of ease ended suddenly with the
death of his parents. After a sojourn with two maiden aunts in Petersburg, in
1857 he moved to Hillsboro, North Carolina (where he had other relatives),
and enrolled at the North Carolina Military Institute. Two years later Cameron went to live with an uncle in St. Louis, where he obtained a position as
an assistant purser on a St. Louis and Memphis Packet Company steamboat.
Forming an acquaintance with fellow worker Mark Twain, he found adventure, but his long-term ambitions (like Twain's) lay elsewhere. Cameron had
acquired a taste for the soldier's life and dreamed of a career as an army officer.
In preparation for an appointment to West Point, he enrolled at Washington
College in St. Louis late in 1860.

The Civil War interrupted his studies; and, influenced by heritage and the extreme states rights' views of his uncle, Cameron became drillmaster for a company of secessionist "Minute Men" stationed on the outskirts of St. Louis. He and his unit (together with hundreds of other southern sympathizers) were soon captured by federal troops, but his imprisonment lasted less than a day. Escaping under cover of darkness, Cameron made his way to Memphis on the last steamer permitted to go south of Cairo, Illinois. From Memphis he headed for home, traveling much of the distance on foot. Shortly after returning to Virginia, he reported for duty at Norfolk and was assigned to the Petersburg City Guard, a unit which eventually became Company A of the Twelfth Virginia Infantry. In June 1861 he was a second lieutenant; in May 1862, regimental adjutant. Severely wounded at Second Manassas in August 1862, he was unable to return to action until just before the battle of Fredericksburg. Transferred to General William Mahone's brigade as brigade inspector, Cameron served in that position until June 1, 1863. This began a close association with Mahone (a fellow Petersburg resident) that was to last for more than two decades—with significant consequences for both men and, ultimately, for the entire Commonwealth of Virginia.

Promoted to captain in 1863 and reassigned to a Mississippi brigade in Heth's division, Army of Northern Virginia, Cameron saw action during the summer of 1864 in all the engagements from the Wilderness to the battle of the Weldon Railroad. Commissioned an assistant adjutant general in October 1864, he then returned to Mahone's old brigade, now under the command of General David A. Weisiger, remaining with that unit until Appomattox.

During the course of the war Cameron provided solid proof of his gallantry, but his conduct also revealed a flaw which would haunt him in years to come: a lack of attention to administrative detail. One of Cameron's few extant wartime letters (1863) confesses to an inability to keep up with paperwork, and the future governor also figured unfavorably in an 1864 report by the inspector of the Third Corps. After surveying the siege lines near Petersburg, Major R. J. Wingate suggested that Cameron's performance bordered on dereliction of duty. "The Twenty-sixth Mississippi," he observed, "was in the most discreditable condition. . . . I called the attention of the officers to the number of guns of sick men that had not been turned in to ordnance officers, as required by the orders. There was much in the appearance of the command to reflect upon the Brigade Inspector, Captain Cameron, whom I regretted to find absent, as I wished to call his attention to the irregularities which he allowed to go unreported. If he could not correct them it was his duty to have reported them, which he did not do."

After Appomattox, the twenty-two-year-old veteran returned to Petersburg where he read law under the direction of Judge William T. Joyner and was admitted to the bar in 1866. While engaged in these studies he also served as city editor of the Petersburg *Daily News,* commencing a journalistic career which would continue (with numerous interruptions) for more than half a century. The *Daily News* soon was suppressed by federal authorities for printing derogatory remarks about President Johnson. During the next six months he helped edit the Petersburg *Daily Index* and the Norfolk *Virginian,* returning to Petersburg in November 1866 when his old wartime commander, William Mahone, helped him purchase an interest in the *Daily Index.* Soon the future governor began to emerge as a figure of consequence as the influence of his pen—and his ideas—spread throughout the state.

Aligning himself with Virginia's new Conservative party, Cameron expressed his views with such fervor that—on one occasion—his editorials provoked a duel. In June 1869 he denounced the "venal pen" and the "specious" reasoning of Republican Robert W. Hughes of the Richmond *State Journal,* prompting a challenge to formal combat which took place just across the North Carolina line. Cameron was slightly wounded; Hughes was unharmed. Years later, recognizing his responsibility for provoking the affair, Cameron regretted that "in the heat of youth and political ardor" he had been "betrayed into language unjustifiable." "Fortune," he observed concerning the outcome, "not as blind as usual, awarded her decree with poetic justice."

Although Cameron's personal flamboyance and rhetorical excesses continued, he (along with most other ex-Confederates) began to accommodate himself to the new order of things. Close ties with William Mahone nurtured this pragmatic orientation. Mahone, seeking control of the railroads from Norfolk to the Tennessee border, was willing to deal with radicals as well as Conservatives to achieve this goal. Dependent in large measure on Mahone's patronage, Cameron also was aware of large majorities of blacks and laboring-class whites in Petersburg and neighboring counties. Local Conservatives stood little chance of "redeeming" the Southside unless they could win the support of such groups.

Responding to these realities, Cameron played a significant role in re-shaping Conservative priorities and programs. Under his editorial guidance the *Daily Index* began to champion free public schools, tax reform, and regulation of railroad rates. He endorsed the progressive features of the state's new constitution but argued that native Virginians could implement its provisions better than a Republican machine dominated by "foreigners." Most significant of all, he actively supported Mahone's "New Movement" crusade to elect Gilbert C. Walker, a moderate Republican, to the governorship and urged other Conservatives to do likewise. When Walker won in 1869, Cameron's prestige soared. The Petersburg editor's middle-of-the-road, accommodationist brand of Conservatism had triumphed; the radical threat was on the wane.

The Reconstruction years also witnessed successes of a more personal nature. Cameron was attracted by the charms of Louisa Clarinda Egerton, a Petersburg belle four years his junior. When Louisa went north in October 1868 to visit a sister who had married a Union soldier, Cameron, fearing she also might be "captured" by a handsome Yankee, followed, pled his cause, and married her in St. Paul, Minnesota. The couple returned to Petersburg, where they set up housekeeping. Three children—two sons and a daughter— were eventually born to them.

In September 1869 Cameron gave up editorial management of the *Daily Index* (while retaining a financial interest in the paper) to become aide and private secretary to Governor Walker. Resigning after only three months, he joined the Richmond *Whig* but encountered still more frustrations. The *Whig* was General Mahone's journalistic mouthpiece in the capital, and the railroad magnate and his youthful protégé soon were at odds. Cameron disliked the general's heavy-handed censorship; Mahone, in turn, became irked when Cameron did not publish articles prepared by his lieutenants. Cameron quit for a brief time in the spring of 1870, but family financial pressures and promises of greater editorial freedom ended this stalemate. Nevertheless, the seeds of distrust—and of future conflict—had been sown.

Cameron maintained a sporadic, on-again, off-again relationship with the *Whig* for the remainder of the 1870s. Struggling to pay creditors, he wrote Civil War articles and poetry and also accepted a post with the Richmond *Enquirer,* now entering the final phase of its long and distinguished career. Increasingly, however, his attention turned to Petersburg, where he supplemented his income by working briefly as a state inspector in two tobacco warehouses. In 1873 he severed most of his Richmond ties and rejoined the editorial staff of the *Daily Index.*

Cameron's return to the "Cockade City" was prompted by political as well as financial considerations. Determined to redeem his birthplace from Republican rule, he played a major role in Petersburg's Conservative organization, even during the years when he was closely associated with the Richmond press. In 1874 the Conservatives finally captured the municipal government, electing two-thirds of the city council. Throughout the Reconstruction years Cameron performed yeoman service with his pen and on the stump, activities which were finally rewarded in 1876. That year Petersburg Conservatives nominated the still-youthful journalist as their mayoral candidate against Dr. William G. Pearse, the radical aspirant. Buoyed by personal popularity, a distinguished war record, and ties with Mahone (the town's most influential citizen), Cameron swept to victory by more than 900 votes. Conservative nominees won every seat on the city council. The Cockade City had, at last, been fully redeemed.

Cameron's oft-demonstrated failings as an administrator did not prevent him from compiling a superb record in his new job. A cooperative city council shouldered the burdens of policymaking, while subordinate officials handled most of the day-to-day routine. Meanwhile, Petersburg's new mayor excelled in the tasks that remained to him: submitting annual messages to the council, appearing at ceremonial functions, and serving as judge of the Mayor's Court.

Cameron proved particularly adept in this latter capacity, dispensing a rough-and-ready justice to assorted gamblers, thieves, prostitutes, vagrants, and delinquents. He also exercised general supervision over law enforcement, an authority which led him to call for codification of municipal ordinances, strict compliance with the ban on Sunday liquor sales, and establishment of a civil service system for policemen. In official pronouncements he repeatedly voiced support for free schools, improved municipal services, and government regulation of private business for the public good.

Cameron's evolving liberalism enabled him to establish a new rapport with the blacks of Petersburg and surrounding counties. His Mayor's Court rulings with reference to youthful offenders and the indigent, many of whom were Negroes, displayed considerable leniency. He manifested similar concerns in an unsuccessful effort to move the state mental hospital for blacks from temporary quarters in Richmond to a permanent site in Petersburg (a shift later accomplished when Cameron was governor). And while campaigning for Conservative candidates in the Southside, he vigorously appealed for black votes. Such moves did nothing to harm Cameron's own political prospects. Retaining his hold on Petersburg's whites and attracting increased support from freedmen, he was reelected without opposition in 1878 and in 1880 achieved a crushing two-to-one victory over his old Republican rival, Dr. Pearse.

The emergence of the state debt issue provided the springboard for Cameron's sudden rise to the Commonwealth's highest office, although he experienced greater difficulty choosing sides than he had in the secession and Reconstruction crises. Emotional and family ties at first made him reluctant to "dishonor" Virginia by endorsing repudiation; as a result, he enunciated extreme debt payer views in the immediate post–Civil War years. By the mid-1870s, however, vexed by his own creditors, he became increasingly receptive to the tenets of the debt-scaling creed. By the same token, Cameron's essentially moderate approach to political affairs alienated him still more from the Funders' dogmatic emphasis on the rights of the bondholders. Cameron's decision also was shaped by his continuing, though somewhat frayed, ties with William Mahone—ties particularly evident during the general's campaign for the Conservative gubernatorial nomination in 1877. Seeking to rally popular support, Mahone emphatically endorsed Readjustment, and Cameron echoed this stand as his floor leader at the party convention. After a bitter contest, Frederick W. M. Holliday, a debt payer from the Valley, won the nomination and went on to an unopposed triumph in the general election. Even so, Mahone's candidacy had demonstrated the mass appeal of the Readjuster cause—a lesson not lost on the ambitious Cameron.

The years immediately following the 1877 campaign constituted a pivotal phase in the debt struggle. Spurred by unrelieved economic depression, chronic budgetary deficits, and an unprecedented wave of school closings in

1878–79, popular resentment soared to new heights. The Readjusters, sensing victory, declared their independence from the Funder-ridden Conservative machine early in 1879. With Mahone as chairman of their new party organization, that fall they won control of both houses of the General Assembly. Holliday's vetoes rebuffed the insurgents' debt proposals, but the beleaguered chief executive could not prevent them from filling administrative offices and county judgeships with Readjusters. Crowning this triumph, they elected Mahone to the U.S. Senate. After a decade of hard times and frustrated hopes, Readjustment had shaken the old political order to its foundations.

But the Democratic national committee's endorsement of Funder presidential electors in 1880 compelled insurgent leaders to reevaluate their situation. Buoyed by this endorsement, the Funders swept to victory in the Old Dominion, polling 96,449 votes to 84,020 for the Republicans and only 31,527 for the Readjusters. The national Democrats' stance showed that the insurgents could expect no help from that quarter. In addition, the 1880 election returns indicated that Readjuster success in 1881 could be assured only with the help of Virginia's Republicans.

Mahone spearheaded this coalition drive. Taking his seat in the U.S. Senate in March 1881, he sided with the Republicans and cast the decisive vote that gave them control of the previously deadlocked chamber. The new Garfield-Arthur administration rewarded him with a major voice in the distribution of federal patronage in Virginia. Not surprisingly, the Old Dominion's Republican hierarchy quickly discovered a new but fervent devotion to Readjuster principles. While these developments were transpiring, Cameron endeavored to secure the support of black Republicans by proclaiming his commitment to their civil rights, striving to secure them an equitable share of the government jobs, and working as backstage organizer of a Negro state convention which met in Petersburg in March 1881. Convention delegates enthusiastically endorsed the debt revolt, and within a few months opposition to Readjuster-Republican unity collapsed. Prospects for the impending campaign were bright indeed.

Cameron's prospects for the Readjuster gubernatorial nomination were bright as well. Popular with both wings of the new coalition, he emerged as a leading contender because of close ties with Mahone, oratorical and journalistic talents, and a distinguished ancestry (which belied Funder attacks on the insurgents as the disreputable "rag-tag and bob-tail" of Virginia society). Cameron mustered fervent support, particularly in his native Southside, but his road to the nomination was by no means free of obstacles. The most serious challenge loomed in the person of Baptist minister John E. Massey, reputedly the ablest stump speaker in Virginia and arguably the best-loved man in the Readjuster movement. Associated with the debt revolt for more than a decade—much longer than Cameron or Mahone—he had compiled an excellent record as state auditor of public accounts after being elected to that post in 1879. Yet Massey was out of step with recent trends in the Readjuster organization. He resented Mahone, was unenthusiastic about coalition with Republicans, and doubted the sincerity of many new converts.

As the delegates (a third of them Negroes) made their way to Richmond in June 1881, a final threat to Cameron emerged from an unexpected source. For reasons not entirely clear, Mahone launched a behind-the-scenes drive in behalf of Harrison H. Riddleberger, a state senator from Shenandoah County and author of a debt adjustment bill vetoed by Governor Holliday in 1880. Whatever the general's motives, this last-minute trial balloon failed to excite any enthusiasm. Forced to choose between Cameron and Massey, Mahone's agents threw their influence to Cameron, who won on the fourth ballot. After a brief recess, a crestfallen Massey asked that the nomination be made unanimous.

With a united party (including Mahone) behind him, Cameron began his general election campaign against Funder John W. Daniel. Daniel excelled as an orator—although Cameron was his equal in debate—and the race between them was hard-fought and sometimes acrimonious. The Readjusters, as always, stressed their debt views and support for schools. The Funders responded by accusing Cameron of inconsistency on the debt issue and, more importantly, of attempting to "Africanize" Virginia through coalition with the GOP. Bondholder syndicates contributed heavily to the Funder campaign, while Republican officials throughout the country funneled cash to the insurgents in an effort to break the Democratic "solid South." The two factions were closely matched, but on election day Cameron won by more than 12,000 votes, and the insurgents retained control of both houses of the General Assembly. Holding their own among the white farmers of the Valley and Southwest, the Readjusters carried almost all of the black counties in the Southside and Tidewater. Coalition—and Cameron—had swept the field.

What sort of man had Virginians elected as their governor? Reporters on the campaign trail described him as "ingenious" and "quick as lightning" in debate and possessed of an "easy and graceful" demeanor. Contemporary observers on both sides of the political fence called Cameron "brilliant," "gifted," and "incisive." Blessed with an ingratiating personality and a ready wit, he moved effortlessly from the drawing rooms of polite society to the smoke-filled back rooms of Gilded Age politics and seemed ideally suited as spokesman of a democratic movement in a traditionally aristocratic state.

The new governor's strengths were readily apparent, but he had his share of weaknesses, too. An impatience with administrative detail boded ill for the future, as did his financial insecurity and extravagant tastes. His health, never robust, had deteriorated in the 1870s, rendering him increasingly susceptible to respiratory infections, rheumatism, headaches, and other real or imagined ailments. Convivial drinking sometimes betrayed him into indiscreet statements, even in public. Another hint of trouble could be found in frequent business trips or vacation excursions—all suggesting a revival of the old wanderlust and a less than wholehearted commitment to political life.

During the first months of his term, Cameron's performance (and that of his party) seemed to justify the people's faith. Sworn into office with a minimum of ceremony, he presided over the enactment of one of the most wide-ranging reform programs in the state's history. His first official message—brief and to the point—urged the Readjuster-dominated General Assembly to implement the party's campaign proposals, and the legislators responded with alacrity. The Riddleberger debt bill, no longer blocked by a gubernatorial veto, received Cameron's signature in February 1882. Repudiating approximately a third of the debt, it authorized bondholders to exchange their securities for slightly more than $21 million in so-called Riddleberger bonds, reducing the annual interest rate from 6 to 3 percent. To encourage exchange, the General Assembly passed a pair of "coupon-killer" enactments to impede the use of coupons from previous issues for payment of taxes.

With the Commonwealth's interest burden alleviated, the insurgents channeled new revenues into other areas, notably public education. The 1882 General Assembly required that 90 percent of all taxes collected for schools be retained at the local level and mandated special annual payments of $100,000 to the schools until full restitution of revenues Funders had diverted to debt interest had been made. Taking advantage of a $500,000 settlement against the Norfolk and Western Railroad, insurgent lawmakers allocated $400,000 of it to the schools, with the remaining $100,000 earmarked for establishment of the Negro Normal and Collegiate Institute (Virginia State University) in Petersburg. These expenditures yielded spectacular results. The number of public schools for whites mushroomed from 1,816 in 1879 to 4,259 in 1883, while those for blacks increased from 675 to 1,715 in the same period. Enrollments for both races more than doubled. The Readjusters also increased appropriations for colleges and mental hospitals. In March 1882 the General Assembly finally approved the erection of permanent facilities for treatment of insane blacks. Like the new normal school, this asylum was to be located in Petersburg, the governor's hometown.

The same legislative session wooed farmers with a 20 percent cut in the property tax. Readjuster administrators compensated for this reduction by tripling revenue assessments on railroads, slashing routine expenses of government, and improving the efficiency of the state's tax-gathering machinery. These moves—together with reduced interest payments under the Riddleberger Act—revitalized the Commonwealth's finances. Chronic deficits gave way to a treasury surplus which swelled to more than $1.5 million by 1883. Retrenchment and reform, traditional watchwords of Gilded Age liberalism, took on new dimensions during the insurgents' dynamic regime.

The Readjuster crusade also attempted to alter the aristocratic tone of

Virginia government and society. Although the Funder press ridiculed the new pretensions of "niggers and poor white men," substantive changes in long-established modes of thought and behavior did occur. At the insistence of black members, the 1882 General Assembly abolished the hated whipping post, and the lawmakers also endorsed a state constitutional amendment eliminating the poll tax as a prerequisite for voting, which soon won voter approval. Combating a rash of duels inspired by the debt controversy, the legislature voted unanimously to impose harsh penalties on public officials who resorted to the "field of honor." One after another, the symbols and practices of the old order were being "readjusted" out of existence.

Cameron hastened the reform process by signing these enactments into law, and he also contributed to his party's record in another way—one more suited to his flamboyant personality. When authorities in coastal counties proved unable to deal with turmoil in the fisheries and oyster industries, Cameron made establishment of law and order among the watermen a major objective of his administration. In February 1882 he even led an expedition against the so-called oyster pirates. Chartering two steamboats, he ordered several Norfolk militia units (with artillery) up the Chesapeake Bay to the Rappahannock River. There, after an engagement in which Cameron himself fired several warning shots, the state forces captured seven vessels and seventy-two "pirates" (fifty-nine of whom were later sentenced to the penitentiary for illegal dredging). The governor's vigorous conduct won widespread acclaim in the press, even in such Funder organs as the Richmond *Dispatch* and the Richmond *State*. The raid did not end law enforcement problems on the Chesapeake, of course, nor did another well-publicized gubernatorial foray against the dredgers in February and March 1883. Nevertheless, these "oyster war" excursions provided a unique outlet for Cameron's energy, boldness, and resolve.

From debt legislation to attacks on oyster pirates, the Readjusters brought new life to moribund administrative apparatus. In one of the supreme ironies of Virginia history, however, this success led directly to their demise. As platform planks became law, as common objectives were achieved, the Readjuster coalition fell apart. Personal antagonisms and frustrated ambitions fueled the flames of discord. Massey, angered by failure to win the party's gubernatorial nod in 1881, moved into open rebellion the following year when the Readjuster legislative caucus rejected him (at Mahone's insistence) in favor of Riddleberger for a U.S. Senate seat. Four Readjuster dissidents in the state Senate backed Massey, threatening the party's control of the upper house. Mahone fought back, but the results were disastrous. Massey's allies in the 1882 General Assembly blocked a series of Readjuster caucus efforts to gerrymander Virginia's congressional districts, unseat Funder circuit court judges before their terms expired, and create a host of new offices for the party faithful. Emboldened by these legislative setbacks, the Funder press assailed

Mahone as a would-be dictator, an unscrupulous spoilsman interested solely in the preservation of power. In spite of the relative efficiency of their administration, Readjuster loyalists were stigmatized as well, lambasted from one end of the state to the other as "Mahoneite" tools of the "petty Boss."

Cameron's political fortunes paralleled those of Mahone and the party. Although increasingly offended by the "Boss's" administrative meddling and imperious ways, the governor stood by his embattled chieftain through the turmoil of 1882 and 1883, with calamitous consequences for his own popularity and prestige. Cameron called the legislature into special session in March 1882 in a vain effort to win approval of the controversial caucus bills. When this manuever failed, the governor and his associates (Attorney General Frank S. Blair, in particular) combed statute books and public records in a drive to purge opposition officeholders. Discovering that Funder school boards in Richmond and Petersburg had failed to take a prescribed oath, Cameron replaced them with his own appointees, several of whom were Negroes. A similar effort to unseat the board of visitors at the Medical College of Virginia was thwarted by an adverse ruling from the state Supreme Court. Such intrigues provoked howls of protest from the Funder press, which criticized the governor's morals and motives and even went so far as to demand his social ostracism. Cameron responded with an emotional outburst that only aggravated his plight. In a Petersburg speech in September 1882, he declared that he "would not give the parings of General Mahone's toe-nails for all the boasted chivalry, honesty, and aristocracy of all the Bourbon Funders in Virginia." For months Funder editorial pages teemed with contemptuous references to the "toe-nail governor," thus reinforcing their claims of "Mahoneite" degradation and subservience.

Weakened by wholesale defections, especially among white voters in eastern counties, the Readjusters approached the 1883 legislative elections in a spirit of near despair. Their opponents, on the other hand, recognizing that continued insistence on the rights of bondholders was futile, sacrificed their unpopular debt views on the altar of political expediency. At their state convention in Lynchburg, representatives of Virginia's traditional ruling class accepted the Riddleberger Act as the final settlement of the debt issue. "Mahoneism," not Readjustment, was the enemy, the flexible patricians announced, and they invited all opponents of "Boss rule" and Negro equality to join their crusade. Indicative of this new spirit, John E. Massey played a major role in the Lynchburg proceedings and helped to draft the platform of his onetime enemies. In another significant move the delegates jettisoned their "Conservative" label in favor of the more popular "Democratic" designation, underscoring their hostility to Mahone's alliance with Republicans at the national and state levels. To head their revitalized organization, the Democrats chose John S. Barbour, a railroad executive who rivaled Mahone as a political manipulator. These innovations paid handsome dividends at the polls. Aided by a tragic outbreak of racial violence in Danville on November 3, 1883 (denounced across the state as one of the "fruits of Mahoneism"), they garnered more than 53 percent of the votes. This edge translated into two-thirds majorities in both houses of the legislature, enough to override Cameron's vetoes on any issue. The brief heyday of the Readjuster-Republican coalition was over, and the long era of Democratic rule, extending into the last half of the twentieth century, had begun.

The election results did not signal an immediate return to financial conservatism. Instead, a strikingly liberal spirit prevailed when the General Assembly convened in December 1883. True to their campaign promises, the victorious Democrats endorsed a joint resolution in support of the Riddleberger debt settlement and reaffirmed this stance by eliminating—at Cameron's request—several loopholes in the "coupon-killer" laws. Educational and charitable institutions continued to benefit from increased expenditures, while new enactments mandated construction of a teachers' college in Farmville for white women and a mental hospital (also for whites) near Marion. Spurred by a special message from the governor, the legislature appropriated funds to create a permanent police force for the state's fisheries. By the end of 1884 a three-vessel "oyster navy" was patrolling the Chesapeake in search of lawbreakers. A Cameron proposal for the establishment of a regulatory commission for Virginia's railroads fell on barren ground, but the Democrat-controlled Assembly did require those corporations to maintain suitable depots, fence their lines, and discharge their tax bills in money instead of coupons. These developments reflected an obvious fact: although the Readjusters had suffered a crushing defeat at the polls, their influence lived on—to a surprising degree—in the legislative program of their opponents.

Yet the Democrats remained inveterately hostile to the personnel of the insurgent regime. Meeting in regular and then in special session through much of 1884, the General Assembly purged dozens of Readjuster officials at state colleges, mental hospitals, and penal facilities. The legislature also severely curtailed Cameron's patronage powers, vesting them instead in the Board of Public Works. The governor served as ex officio chairman but was generally outvoted by the other members—the state treasurer and the auditor of public accounts—both elected by the General Assembly. Tightening their grip still more, the Democrats gerrymandered the congressional districts to ensure control of at least seven of Virginia's ten seats in the U.S. House of Representatives. The culmination of this trend came with the Anderson-McCormick election law (named after Delegate William A. Anderson of Rockbridge and Senator J. Marshall McCormick of Warren) which transferred appointment of local election officials from county judges (most of whom were Readjusters) to county electoral boards chosen by the legislature. Democrats now would handle the registration books, count the votes, and certify the accuracy of the returns. Cameron was dismayed by such blatant partisanship and withheld his signature from bill after bill, only to see his vetoes summarily overridden. The foundations for more than eighty years of Democratic supremacy had been laid.

In the midst of these struggles, Cameron absorbed yet another blow, largely self-inflicted. After passage of the Readjuster debt settlement the state began to accumulate surplus revenues, and the governor had deposited these funds to the Commonwealth's account in various banks in Richmond, Petersburg, Norfolk, and Lynchburg. On May 19, 1884, the Petersburg bank suspended operations, with a loss to the taxpayers of $135,000. This default was bad enough in itself, but newspaper accounts disclosed that the bank had extended more than $31,000 in personal loans to the governor before closing its doors, while Mahone and other prominent Readjusters had also benefited from the institution's largesse. A legislative inquiry found no evidence of criminal wrongdoing on Cameron's part but castigated him for giving the appearance of conflict of interest and for failing to obtain adequate security for state deposits. The governor's popularity slumped to a new low.

Plagued by bad luck and bad judgment, Cameron and his associates looked to the national Republicans for help. After the Readjusters officially adopted the "Republican Party of Virginia" label at their state convention in April 1884, the governor made repeated trips to the North to seek campaign funds for the impending presidential and congressional races. In spite of these efforts, Cameron's place in the new Republican organization was far from secure. Senator Mahone had come to regard him as a political liability, and relations between them rapidly cooled. The Richmond *Whig,* Mahone's organ, began to criticize Cameron, who soon gave vent to more than a decade of pent-up antagonism and resentment. Moving into open revolt in the spring and summer of 1884, he denounced Mahone's imposition of the unit rule on Republican national convention delegates, and he also endeavored to prevent the senator from dictating selection of the party's congressional nominee in the Petersburg district. Cameron went so far as to endorse a black independent, even though the Republican national committee supported Mahone's choice, carpetbagger James D. Brady, who won easily in November. The governor maintained a nominal allegiance to the GOP after this rebuff, but his stand had made him a pariah to party regulars. Long distrusted and maligned by the Democrats, he had now forfeited the backing of the Mahoneites, too.

Meanwhile, Readjuster-Republican strength continued to deteriorate—a trend Cameron could neither halt nor reverse. In March 1885 Democrat Grover Cleveland became president; no longer would the GOP control the federal patronage in Virginia. In April the U.S. Supreme Court struck down the Riddleberger debt settlement, initiating another prolonged round of disputes with the bondholders. At the Republican state convention in July, an effort by Cameron and other anti-Mahone leaders to create a less authoritarian party structure was smashed by the Boss's adherents, who refused to allow reform proposals to come to a vote. Victimized by factional antagonisms and ballot-box fraud, GOP gubernatorial candidate John S. Wise lost to Democrat Fitzhugh Lee by 16,000 votes in November. When Cameron turned over the reins of the governorship to Lee in January 1886, the last vestiges of insurgent authority had been eradicated.

Now forty-three years old, Cameron still had a long and active career ahead of him. He practiced law in Petersburg for the balance of the 1880s, but the old urge for new places and new experiences took him to Chicago in 1892. As official historian of the Columbian Exposition, he composed an 800-page chronicle, *The World's Fair,* published in 1893. The next year he returned to Petersburg, where he became increasingly prominent in "Lost Cause" activities. His neighbors soon forgave his Mahoneite ties and elected him as city delegate to the state constitutional convention of 1901–2. He played a subdued but influential role, chairing the committee on the executive department and serving on the committees on the judiciary and on final revision. A few years later he became commissioner general for the 1907 Jamestown Exposition. Meanwhile, the ex-governor returned to journalism, his first love. He became associated with the Norfolk *Virginian* in 1906 and took charge of the newspaper's editorial page shortly thereafter. Cameron stayed at the helm of the *Virginian* (after 1915, the *Virginian-Pilot*) until his retirement in September 1919. He was then seventy-six years old.

During the years from 1886 to 1919 Cameron made a remarkable pilgrimage across the Old Dominion's political and ideological spectrum. Abandoning the liberalism of Readjuster days, he severed his ties with the Republican party in 1890, his sojourn in strike-torn Chicago only hastening a drift to the right. Back in Virginia, Cameron supported the gold Democrat ticket in 1896, denouncing the evils of Bryanism, populism, anarchism, and communism in speeches from one end of the Commonwealth to the other. The man who had risen to power on a platform of debt repudiation now was one of the state's foremost advocates of sound money and economic orthodoxy. This transformation was completed at the constitutional convention of 1901–2 where Cameron stood shoulder to shoulder with the Democrats in their successful crusade to disenfranchise Virginia's black voters. The liberal reformer of the 1880s was now a white supremacist conservative.

Cameron had returned to the Democratic fold, but he soon discovered that the Virginia branch of that party was as boss-ridden and hostile to dissidents as Mahone's GOP had been. His 1904 bid for the Democratic congressional nomination in the Fourth District was a disaster, and he reluctantly withdrew from the race. As editor of the *Virginian-Pilot,* Cameron repaid his detractors, lashing out against ring rule and the fee system for the payment of local officials. Yet, although Cameron employed the antimachine rhetoric of the early twentieth century, he was no progressive. Hostile to Prohibition and suspicious of woman suffrage, he looked askance at most manifestations of the new reform impulse. He was simply a crochety individualist—a man who had outlived his time.

Retirement from the *Virginian-Pilot* effectively removed Cameron from the arena of conflict. His wife had died in 1908, and the ex-governor spent his final years with two of his children, Mrs. Susie Cameron Whitfield of Tallahassee, Florida, and George V. Cameron of Louisa, Virginia. After a protracted illness, Cameron died on January 25, 1927, at his son's home. Newspaper obituaries recalled him as a figure from another day and time, a "picturesque" individual from the Commonwealth's "glorious past." Little was said of the accomplishments of his gubernatorial term—improvements in educational facilities and mental hospitals, abolition of the poll tax, and the temporarily enhanced status of black and poor white Virginians. Instead the Democratic press hailed the deceased as a brave soldier, a talented journalist, and a brilliant and cultivated gentleman of the old school.

Obituary writers laid special stress on Cameron's independence, particularly as manifested in his break with Mahone in the 1880s. By emphasizing the ex-governor's "independence," however, the press unwittingly revealed his major shortcoming as a man and politician. Cameron was undoubtedly one of the ablest Virginians of his day, but refusal to be bound by place or party or belief prevented him from attaining success commensurate with his abilities. Lacking fixed points on his ideological compass, he shifted erratically from one partisan stance to another, from one ephemeral crusade to the next— sometimes in step with public opinion, sometimes not. Dead at the age of eighty-four, he was buried in Petersburg's Blandford Cemetery adjacent to the church where his great-grandfather had served as rector, amid the graves of friends and foes (Mahone among them). A simple stone, bearing no reference to his gubernatorial service, was erected to mark the spot. After more than eight decades of controversy, Virginia's Readjuster governor was, at last, at rest.

SOURCES

The Virginia State Library has two small collections of Cameron manuscripts; another cache of material is in the papers of his daughter, Susie Cameron Whitfield (Florida State University). Many Cameron letters are available, however, in the William Mahone Papers (Duke University) and the Harrison H. Riddleberger Papers (College of William and Mary). The David Addison Weisiger Papers and the Chamberlayne Family Papers (both at the Virginia Historical Society) contain letters pertinent to Cameron's pregubernatorial career.

For Cameron's Civil War experiences, see *Official Records—War of the Rebellion,* ser. 1, vols. 42 and 46; and George S. Bernard, *War Talks of Confederate Veterans* (Petersburg, 1892). In addition to Cameron's official messages as governor, see *The World's Fair* (Philadelphia, 1893);

and "The Southern Cause," *Southern Historical Society Papers* 30 (1902): 360–68.

Secondary sources of particular value include Nelson M. Blake, *William Mahone of Virginia: Soldier and Political Insurgent* (Richmond, 1935); Allen W. Moger, *Virginia: Bourbonism to Byrd, 1870–1925* (Charlottesville, 1968); James Tice Moore, *Two Paths to the New South: The Virginia Debt Controversy, 1870–1883* (Lexington, Ky., 1974); Charles C. Pearson, *The Readjuster Movement in Virginia* (New Haven, 1917); William D. Henderson, *The Unredeemed City: Reconstruction in Petersburg, Virginia, 1865–1874* (Washington, D.C., 1977); and Lenoir Chambers and Joseph E. Shank, *Salt Water and Printer's Ink: Norfolk and Its Newspapers, 1865–1965* (Chapel Hill, N.C., 1967).

Mrs. Lou Whitfield Miller, Cameron's granddaughter, graciously provided genealogical data and family reminiscences during the preparation of this chapter.

FITZHUGH LEE

Governor of Virginia

1886–1890

FITZHUGH LEE

Confederate Cavalryman in the New South

Harry Warren Readnour

As head of the Commonwealth of Virginia from 1886 to 1890, Fitzhugh Lee presided over a land in which he had deep personal roots. Born on November 19, 1835, the son of Sidney Smith and Anna Maria Mason Lee, he was descended from two truly great Northern Neck families who had given birth to generations of gracious ladies and prominent planters, soldiers, and statesmen, creating in the process a distinguished tradition of genteel hospitality, achievement, and service. Fitzhugh Lee would uphold that tradition in an eventful career which took him from hand-to-hand combat with western Indians to cavalry battles against invading Union armies, from the Governor's Mansion to the consul-generalship in Havana, Cuba, on the eve of the Spanish-American War.

Fitzhugh's father was a naval officer, and his prolonged absences at sea compelled his wife and family (eventually six sons) to spend considerable time at the imposing Mason estate near Alexandria. Nearby lived Fitzhugh's widowed godmother and subsequent benefactress, Mrs. Anna Maria Fitzhugh, and Robert Edward Lee, his father's younger brother. Fitz—as he was called by his family, friends, and, in time, the public at large—attended a neighborhood private school where he distinguished himself in sports and boyish pranks rather than in classwork. Dispatched to a Baltimore boarding school at fourteen, he continued the same pattern of educational endeavor, augmented by a preoccupation with horses—a lifelong interest which would profoundly influence this young Virginian's career.

In 1852 Lee entered the U.S. Military Academy, thoroughly enjoying his first year but managing to avoid dismissal. However, his problems increased when Colonel Robert E. Lee assumed command of the academy in 1853. Superintendent Lee frequently invited his nephew to dinner but was determined to show no favoritism. Twice that year Fitz was caught leading a group of cadets to a forbidden nocturnal resort, and twice Superintendent Lee recommended dismissal. When fellow cadets pledged their good behavior as collateral for the young Virginian's retention, Secretary of War Jefferson Davis, more tolerant of the antics of spirited southern gentlemen, allowed him to remain.

Fitz's conduct subsequently improved, although when he graduated in

1856 demerits ranked him forty-fifth in a class of forty-nine; nevertheless, he attained first place in horsemanship, an achievement which won him a cavalry assignment. After graduation Lee was detailed for two years to Carlisle Barracks in Pennsylvania, the home of the Cavalry School for Practice; then, in January 1858 he joined Colonel Albert Sidney Johnston's Second Cavalry Regiment in western Texas. His first months were filled with garrison duty; during the spring and summer of 1859, however, he led one of three squadrons sent northward into the Oklahoma-Kansas region against the Comanches. During this campaign Lee not only performed ably but emerged a hero as the result of success in hand-to-hand combat.

When the battle-tested veteran returned to West Point in December 1860 as an instructor in cavalry tactics, his future seemed bright indeed. Unfortunately, the secession crisis soon overwhelmed Lee, his family, and his beloved state; and with tears in his eyes and cheers from the cadets for "Our Fitz" ringing in his ears, he left to join the Virginia forces commanded by his Uncle Robert.

By September 1861 he was a lieutenant colonel in Colonel J. E. B. Stuart's First Regiment of Virginia Cavalry, the nucleus of the cavalry arm of the future Army of Northern Virginia. In that most famous of Confederate armies, Fitzhugh Lee found his proper niche and remained there for the duration. By the spring of 1862 he had established a harmonious association with Stuart that would last until the latter's death in 1864. In July 1862 Lee was promoted to brigadier general (at the age of twenty-seven) in command of five Virginia regiments. "General Fitz" participated in most of the major Virginia campaigns and rendered especially commendable service during the Peninsula campaign and at Kelly's Ford and Chancellorsville. Wounded at Winchester in 1864, he managed to return to duty and served as cavalry commander for his uncle during the first months of 1865.

After the collapse of the Confederacy, Fitzhugh Lee and his family suffered less hardship than many Virginians because of the generosity of his well-to-do godmother who gave them the use of Richland, her Stafford County estate forty miles south of Washington. For the next two decades Lee engaged in agricultural pursuits, though not on the same grand scale as some of his ancestors. In 1871 he married Ellen Bernard Fowle, an eighteen-year-old Alexandria belle. As his family grew, Fitz changed from a slender, dashing cavalryman to a stout, jovial husband and father; and as an heir of his godmother, Lee became financially independent after her death in 1874. Meanwhile, he followed the example of General Robert E. Lee as he tried to effect a true reconciliation between North and South. His speech at the Bunker Hill centennial in Boston (June 1875) was especially well received throughout the nation.

Lee hoped national accord would bring northern investments and immigrants to Virginia and the South. As head of the Rappahannock and Potomac Immigration Society, he launched a campaign to attract northern farmers with capital to his own region, and, as president of the Convention for the Promotion of American Commerce (held in New Orleans in 1878), he was an ardent booster of all phases of economic endeavor to revive the South. Frustration of these schemes eventually led him into politics.

Lee was presented as a candidate for the gubernatorial nomination at the 1877 Conservative party convention by some of his impulsive wartime comrades, but the delegates finally selected Frederick W. M. Holliday, with Lee finishing a poor fourth. Not an extreme debt payer but rather a traditionalist concerned that the state's heritage might be disgraced by repudiation, General Fitz accepted the Conservative nomination for the House of Delegates from his home district in 1879. His campaign efforts were negligible, and his defeat by Readjuster Duff Green, a crippled Confederate veteran, was by approximately the same ratio as the Conservative loss throughout the state. Two years later the Readjusters won control of the state government and scaled down the debt, but then their machine began to fall apart. In 1883 Conservative party chairman John Strode Barbour thoroughly reorganized his forces, enticed Readjuster-Republican malcontents into the newly renamed Democratic party by belatedly accepting the Riddleberger debt settlement, and captured control of the General Assembly. Lee did not participate in these maneuvers, but he was soon performing yeoman service for the new party. After campaigning for Grover Cleveland in 1884, he received a tremendous ovation when he led a body of Virginia troops in the inaugural parade on March 4, 1885.

Returning to Virginia amid a clamor by rank-and-file Democrats for his nomination as governor, General Fitz was thrust into his only successful political campaign. Opportune circumstances favored Lee's candidacy in 1885. Both Barbour, the architect of the 1883 victory, and John W. Daniel, the defeated Funder-Conservative gubernatorial candidate of 1881, wanted the U.S. Senate seat that Mahone would vacate in 1887. Daniel planned to push Lee for governor and decrease Barbour's chances by stressing that two major officials should not be from the same section of the state. Since no one considered Lee a professional politician, he fitted into the category of "new faces" that Barbour said the party needed. Barbour temporarily lost control of the convention, and Lee, the political neophyte and symbol of the "Lost Cause," was nominated—as a result of intricate footwork by hardened politicians. When ex-Readjuster John E. Massey was selected as his running mate, the reconciliation of Funders and Readjusters was complete. Daniel's path to the Senate was clear in spite of his Funder past.

Disregarding this personal rebuff, Barbour quickly assumed control of the campaign and began to utilize Lee to best advantage against the Mahone coalition which now bore the Republican label. The Republicans had chosen ex-Confederate Captain John S. Wise, also the scion of a noble Virginia family and son of the state's last prewar governor, to oppose Lee. Since both party platforms were strikingly similar, the Democrats stressed the Negro's role in the Republican party when they appealed to white voters. Bitterness burst forth at times because of this tactic, amid fears that an honest ballot count under the 1884 Anderson-McCormick election law would be impossible since Democrats now controlled the voting process.

Barbour and the state executive committee mapped out a shrewd strategy. There would be no Lee-Wise debates; other stump speakers could dog Wise's footsteps while Lee, less able in debate, made solo appearances. Exploiting Lee as a symbol of the "Lost Cause," Barbour arranged campaign appearances preceded by mounted processions (the "Fitz Lee Cavalry") which aroused tremendous excitement. In often nonpolitical speeches, Lee pointed with pride to the past while espousing hope for progress in the future. His rhetoric was sincere as well as stirring, and he projected a better image than his opponent, the increasingly quick-tempered and unpredictable Wise. The Republicans ridiculed Lee's use of "Uncle Robert's" saddle in his campaign cavalcades, and Wise repeatedly asked if anyone would have seriously considered his opponent for the governorship if his name had been "Fitzhugh Smith" instead of Fitzhugh Lee. Such sallies were lost upon the mass of white Virginians, however, and the Democrats swept the state on November 3 with a majority of 16,000 votes, carrying the General Assembly by a margin of 101 to 39.

At noon, January 1, 1886, Fitzhugh Lee was quietly inaugurated. Ironically, since the martial hero did not wish to detract from the dignity of a civil ceremony, there were no marching troops, cavalry, and bands; however, the ball that followed was one of the most notable galas in the state's history. The occasion was more than a partisan celebration of a Democratic triumph, for ex-Governor Cameron and John S. Wise were among the special guests; rather it was a commemoration by Virginians of myriad backgrounds and conflicting opinions of all that was glorious and good in the life of the Old Dominion. The traditionalist Lee regarded the celebration as a manifestation of the true Virginia heritage and a good omen for the future. In reality, Lee's installation constituted a significant benchmark in Virginia's political history, for his administration ended two decades of turmoil and ushered in an era of uninterrupted Democratic rule.

The new governor, viewing himself as the visible symbol of all Virginians and an emblem of their unity, hoped to avoid the conflicts that had vexed his immediate predecessors. Such hope was realistic since Democrats now were in firm control, and Lee was essentially a nonpolitical figure who avoided controversy. The governor, he believed, should enhance the dignity of his office and not grasp for personal power or challenge the judgments of the General Assembly. This concept conformed to reality since Democrats had reduced the powers of Cameron, Lee's Readjuster predecessor, after their

1883 victory. The new system generally bestowed prestige rather than authority on the governor—with the General Assembly being the true locus of power, both legally and politically. It elected major officials in the executive department as well as the judges of county and municipal courts. Nominees for these judgeships, leading figures in the "courthouse cliques," usually were recommended by Democratic county chairmen. Further, the Anderson-McCormick election law authorized the legislature to choose local electoral boards. Hence local officeholders and party officials were tied not to the governor but to the state chairman and other members of the Democratic central committee who gave advice, instructions, and financial aid at election time. This system, which reduced even a Democratic governor to the status of an ancillary figure, was in its infancy during the Lee administration, but its outlines nonetheless were firmly established.

Governor Lee seldom provided dynamic leadership, viewing himself as the chief of staff, rather than the commander, of the governmental apparatus which would achieve his goal of promoting "the prosperity of the State." Although he refrained from slavishly catering to the legislative whim, he avoided major clashes which, in his opinion, were not only futile but possibly dangerous since the Republicans were by no means defunct. For example, during Lee's first year in office—with Barbour on vacation in Europe—the Democrats captured only four of the state's ten congressional seats.

Although the debt was no longer so volatile an issue, it continued to be the chief matter of public concern affecting all government functions. For four years Lee struggled with this complex topic and the related problem of insufficient revenues. Despite Readjuster claims, the Riddleberger Act reducing the total debt and issuing new bonds bearing lower interest rates had not brought relief. Some creditors, fearing wholesale repudiation, accepted the law, but most hoped that a more favorable agreement might be reached. Many holders of older bonds refused to exchange them for new ones since coupons from the former could be used in tax payments. Non-Virginians often discounted coupons to local taxpayers so as to receive more return from old bonds than they could expect from new "Riddlebergers"—a practice which significantly diminished state revenue.

Lee firmly believed in enforcing the Riddleberger settlement, and his first message to the General Assembly maintained that Virginia's obligation to support and operate the free schools, charitable institutions, and prison facilities was higher than that to its creditors. He proposed that the Assembly appoint a commission to work out a compromise with the bondholders, but the legislature ignored this advice. Meanwhile, coupons forced on the state treasury rose from $50,000 in 1885 to $250,000 by 1888, while total annual revenues remained static at less than $2.5 million. Lee's vision of the governor's office as a pleasant sinecure evaporated in March 1886 when the legislature left him to cope with the debt as best he could. Disliking paperwork and financial intricacies, he found himself embroiled in laborious and extensive correspondence with foreign bondholders.

In the spring of 1887 Lee called the Assembly into special session and suggested new laws to make the redemption of coupons an even more complicated process. Once again, he urged the establishment of a commission to deal directly with the bondholders. The legislature passed even tougher laws than Lee proposed, and the Joint Committee on the Debt was authorized to remain in existence during legislative recesses. These actions helped the Democrats win large majorities in the legislative elections that fall, but a final settlement of the debt continued to elude Virginia's leaders.

Lee's acute concern with finance was related to his interest in preserving and strengthening the public school system, a question with both political and racial overtones. He firmly believed that an adequate state-supported system for both races was a key factor in promoting progress and prosperity and worked to commit fellow ex-Conservatives to his belief. Local school revenues did rise, but Lee's efforts to secure ample increases in state expenditures were not rewarded to the degree he desired. Nonetheless, at the close of his term the governor could note with pride that the necessity of maintaining an adequate school system was no longer questioned.

Lee's major triumph, and the principal redeeming feature of his administration, was in the broad area of public relations. Since the governor felt his chief role was to be the symbol of the Commonwealth, he put great emphasis upon official and quasi-official public activities. Lee's adeptness was bolstered by his attractive family. Mrs. Lee, gifted with all of the social graces, demonstrated her hospitality at numerous receptions. All of the Lee children were well liked, but the fifth and youngest child became the darling of the state; the entire Commonwealth celebrated the birth of this baby (appropriately named Virginia) at the Executive Mansion in 1886. Perhaps Lee's greatest success was his increasing personification of the "Confederate cult," which flowered during his tenure amid monument dedications, memorial services, and reunions. Yet public appearances, deference to the legislature, and stumping for Democratic candidates did not win Lee much influence in the party's inner councils. At the close of his term, he remained a respected celebrity but one who exerted little impact on Virginia political affairs.

During his incumbency an estimated $100 million in new capital investment came into the state partially, Lee believed, because he had helped to create a favorable image for investors. After retiring in 1890 he continued to devote himself to advancing the prosperity of the Old Dominion through the so-called New South movement, that many-faceted effort to bring industry and its supposed blessings to the region. He accepted the presidency of the Rockbridge Company, which was able to establish the town of Glasgow, but its dreams of being "The Grandest Enterprise in the New South" failed to materialize as a result of the panic of 1893. That year also proved to be politically disastrous for Fitzhugh Lee when he decided to seek a seat in the U.S. Senate. He had campaigned actively for Cleveland once more in 1892, as well as for state congressional candidates, and, gratified with the Democratic success, believed his own political fortunes were at their apex. The depression, however, soon caused Cleveland's popularity to decline, and his progold monetary policy became a burden to Virginia Democrats in the state elections of 1893.

When U.S. Senator John Barbour died in 1892, the contest for his seat became a significant turning point in Virginia political life. Lee and the astute Thomas Staples Martin, an attorney from Albemarle County, emerged as the two leading candidates for the selection to be made by the Democratic caucus following the legislative elections of November 1893. Bound by his own conventions and those of his party as well, Lee did not openly seek the office and instead relied on appearances in behalf of Assembly candidates to reveal his "availability." The acclaim he received gave him an unrealistic opinion of his chances, and the homage he was accorded at state and national party functions (he had even been suggested as a vice-presidential nominee in 1888 and 1892) increased the delusion of widespread support. All too often Lee ignored the fact that politicians, not the people, were the electorate in the senatorial election.

Martin, in comparison with Lee, was virtually unknown, his circle of friends confined to politicians throughout the state. The middle-aged bachelor shunned publicity and had never held public office, but as a district counsel for the Chesapeake and Ohio Railroad he devoted considerable time to politics and dispensed essential railroad campaign contributions to Democratic candidates. Martin, an effective, behind-the-scenes worker, had experienced a remarkable rise since 1883. His services as a Barbour lieutenant won him an appointment to the state central committee as early as 1885, and he used that post to secure Lee's nomination as governor and the election of Daniel to the Senate. As a member of the prestigious executive group of the committee Martin continued to earn the respect of Democratic officeholders and candidates and by 1892 had acquired a considerable fund of political obligations.

Lee, because of an inflated self-confidence, could not fathom the possibility that a former VMI cadet, especially one who had missed the famed battle of New Market in 1864 (Martin had a cold and was left behind when the Cadet Corps marched off to war), might be the victor over an ex-Confederate general named Lee and the former governor of Virginia as well. Moreover, Lee had been successful thus far without becoming too deeply involved in intrigues and relished his reputation as an uncompromised public servant. The reception of the press was encouraging, his activities were well publicized, and newspaper accounts contained the usual laudatory comments about past achievements; yet most newspapers saw little need to actively promote his senatorial bid. He and most of his contemporaries failed to perceive the significance of recurring suggestions by the Richmond *Dispatch,* the leading Democratic organ, that Martin, too, was a viable candidate. Lee exhibited an almost cavalier unconcern for the Senate race as he continued to be absorbed in business matters and refuting criticisms levied against his uncle by General James Longstreet in the so-called Gettysburg controversy.

These liabilities were compounded by the ex-governor's failure to establish an effective campaign organization. Lee received endorsements from a few members of the state central committee, but none of them worked actively for him. His lack of dependable, skilled political allies was fatal. This meant that Lee had few ironclad commitments among the legislators after the 1893 election, even though he had been soliciting their support for almost a year and a half. Lee and the nonpolitical friends upon whom he increasingly relied were satisfied that a majority of the legislators seemed to be in sympathy with his cause.

In contrast, Martin, a shrewd and calculating politician, used all of his considerable talents to secure his goal. He received initial commitments from a majority of the 1891–92 legislature and resolved to repeat that feat in the 1893–94 session. He perfected a superb campaign apparatus headed by Henry D. ("Hal") Flood, a rising young delegate from Appomattox. Martin also attended numerous local party meetings and functions but, unlike Lee, avoided the money question and other controversial subjects. Instead, he and his lieutenants carefully cultivated pro-Martin men and tried to attract neutral legislative candidates by personal and small campaign contributions.

Lee's ultimate disadvantage involved campaign funds from the railroads, especially important in a depression year. Many candidates, sorely pressed for money in 1893 and thinking of the future as well, contemplated the wisdom of allying themselves with Martin. Lee had little to offer them. For example, his candidacy had President Cleveland's sympathy, but no effort was made to distribute federal patronage in his behalf since the administration regarded the choice of senator as a state matter.

The Democratic legislative caucus convened in Richmond on the evening of December 7, 1893. As Martin had predicted, he led on the first ballot, and the totals boded ill for Lee: Martin 55, Lee 46, others 20. Martin finally emerged as the winner on the sixth ballot in one of the great upsets of Virginia politics: Martin 66, Lee 55, others (Governor Philip W. McKinney) 1. Caucus participants adjourned with jubilant shouts of the Martin supporters ringing in their ears, a marked contrast to the stunned silence of the dazed Lee partisans. However, the outcome was not a great surprise to Virginia politicians and others who understood the internal workings of the Democratic party. And, although Martin's campaign methods were a matter of some concern, Lee's contributions to his own defeat should not be ignored—as they often have been by both his contemporaries and historians who have examined this very significant election.

Basically a congenial and forgiving man, Lee never completely forgot this defeat, but he remained a loyal Democrat and spoke to enthusiastic crowds in behalf of party candidates in the congressional elections of 1894. For a time, following his appointment as the collector of internal revenue for the Western District of Virginia in April 1895, he was viewed by some as the potential leader of "sound money" or Cleveland Democrats in Virginia. That possibility evaporated a year later when the president named him consul general in Havana, the highest American official in war-torn Cuba. During his two years in Cuba he worked to protect American lives and property threatened by the protracted insurrection. Lee came to believe that any policy other than American intervention bordered on being callous and inhumane. Recognizing his honesty, dependability, and familiarity with the situation, Republican William McKinley retained this stalwart Democrat in Havana, although there was official concern that Lee was too outspokenly in favor of intervention.

Early in April 1898 Lee left Cuba, and the war he had predicted erupted a short time later. His knowledge of Cuban conditions led the press and numerous citizens (both North and South) to urge his appointment as commander of the American invasion force being sent to Cuba. Lee, a longtime proponent of sectional reconciliation, soon found himself portrayed as a symbol of national reunion. On May 4, 1898, the ex-Confederate general, aged sixty-two, was formally confirmed as a major general in the Volunteer Army of the United States by the Senate. After nearly four decades the cycle of reunion was complete—a U.S. Army lieutenant (1861), resigned; a major general, Confederate States Army (1865), paroled; and a major general, U.S. Volunteers (1898), eager to serve his country in "Federal blue" once more. As if to augment the significance of his appointment, two first lieutenants were assigned to his staff—Fitzhugh Lee, Jr. (his son), and Algernon Sartoris (grandson of Ulysses S. Grant).

Lee helped to restore order near Havana after the brief war ended, retiring from active service in 1901. Until his death on April 28, 1905, he busied himself with plans for the Jamestown Exposition of 1907. The end came suddenly when he suffered a paralyzing stroke while en route by train from Boston to Washington. Within hours he was dead.

This good and basically able man was always a gentleman, but his delightful digressions saved him from becoming pompous and stodgy. Even in his old age he loved a joke—whether on himself or on a friend. His setbacks resulted from his own action, bad luck, or unfavorable circumstances he could not control. The first of an unbroken line of twenty-one Democratic governors (1886–1970), Lee unconsciously initiated the basic pattern of unobtrusive yet diligent service from which few of his successors deviated. This was especially true of the next three governors, McKinney, O'Ferrall, and Tyler. His 1893 senatorial defeat foreshadowed the fate of future outsiders or independents who challenged the inner party councils.

Fitz Lee remained a man who could be overwhelmed by adversity but never vanquished by it. In good times and bad he exhibited an animated faith in himself, in Virginia, and in his country. A symbol of Democratic unity as governor, he also was the embodiment of much that Virginians admired: a facile writer, a skillful public speaker, an excellent horseman, and a spirited individual who, firmly rooted by lineage to his state's historic past, always looked to the future with keen anticipation.

SOURCES

A biographical study of Lee would be impossible without the manuscript collection of his great-grandson Fitzhugh Lee Opie of Alexandria, Xerox copies of which are on deposit at the University of Virginia Library. Other manuscript collections pertaining to Lee and his contemporaries are available there and at the Virginia Historical Society, the Library of Congress, Duke University, and the Henry E. Huntington Library.

For a review of pre–Civil War cavalry, see George F. Price, *Across the Continent with the Fifth Cavalry* (New York, 1883) and Robert M. Utley, *Frontiersmen in Blue: The United States Army and the Indian, 1848–1865* (New York, 1967). Lee's role in the Civil War is analyzed in Douglas Southall Freeman's monumental works, *R. E. Lee, a Biography,* 4 vols. (New York, 1934–35), and *Lee's Lieutenants,* 3 vols. (New York, 1942–44).

Sources on the immediate postwar period include Jack P. Maddex, Jr., *The Virginia Conservatives, 1869–1879: A Study in Reconstruction Politics* (Chapel Hill, N.C., 1970); James Tice Moore, *Two Paths to the New South: The Virginia Debt Controversy, 1870–1883* (Lexington, Ky., 1974); Raymond H. Pulley, *Old Virginia Restored: An Interpretation of the Progressive Impulse, 1870–1930* (Charlottesville, 1968); and Allen W. Moger, *Virginia: Bourbonism to Byrd, 1870–1925* (Charlottesville, 1968).

The most extensive treatment of Lee's career is Harry W. Readnour's "General Fitzhugh Lee, 1835–1905: A Biographical Study" (Ph.D. diss., University of Virginia, 1971). For the 1893 Senate race, see James A. Bear, Jr., "Thomas Staples Martin: A Study in Virginia Politics, 1883–1896" (M.A. thesis, University of Virginia, 1952).

PHILIP WATKINS McKINNEY

Southside Party Workhorse

John Hammond Moore

On January 1, 1890, Philip Watkins McKinney, limping slightly as the result of a Civil War wound, entered the House of Delegates on the arm of a state senator and made his way to the front of the crowded chamber. A stalwart, impressive figure with a bountiful head of white hair and an equally luxuriant mustache, McKinney smiled as applause swelled up to greet him. After glancing at his wife, he took the gubernatorial oath of office and signed it. James Hoge Tyler then took his oath as lieutenant governor, and small Bibles were presented to the new state officials as gifts for their young daughters. Despite appeals from onlookers, both men refused to speak. A short time later McKinney walked across the snow-covered ground to the Executive Mansion to rejoin his family. Virginia thus entered the Gay Nineties without fuss or fanfare, and that was precisely the way the new governor wanted it.

Few men have become Virginia's chief executive so quietly, and few of them have had less prior experience in the art of governing. Yet only a handful have earned more scars in the front line of political combat; during the previous quarter century both victory and defeat greeted McKinney as he did battle with carpetbaggers, blacks, Republicans, and Readjusters. Now, at fifty-seven, he stood at the pinnacle of his career. Since he believed lawmakers should make laws and chief executives should execute them, it was obvious he seldom would display innovative or aggressive leadership. Above all else, McKinney would pursue policies designed to help his Democratic party gain complete mastery of the Old Dominion. In short, this solid-appearing man espoused the views of the conservative, probusiness wing of his party—views conforming closely to those nurtured by his rural, small-town background—and only rarely would he depart from this central path.

Virginia's thirty-eighth governor was born at New Store in Buckingham County on March 17, 1832, the son of Charles and Martha Guerrant Mc-Kinney. His father, a prosperous farmer, operated a crossroad store and owned about three dozen slaves. Philip got his basic education at a local old field school and graduated with honors from Hampden-Sydney College in June 1851, receiving a special medal for debating ability. After studying law with Judge John W. Brockenbrough at Washington College in Lexington, he returned to Buckingham County to begin practice.

PHILIP W. McKINNEY

Governor of Virginia

1890–1894

In 1854 he married Ann Fleming Christian of New Kent County. Two years later she gave birth to a son, Robert Christian. The following year (1857) McKinney, a Whig like his aging father, was elected to the General Assembly where he served until 1861. In 1859 his wife died. With the outbreak of war, McKinney became commander of a unit which he helped raise in his native county, Company K of the Fourth Cavalry, Army of Northern Virginia. After action with J. E. B. Stuart in the Richmond area and in Maryland, Captain McKinney was seriously wounded at Brandy Station on June 8, 1863, the largest cavalry engagement of the entire conflict. He limped for the rest of his life as the result of a ball lodged in his leg. The young officer was stationed in Danville for the remainder of the year and in 1864 gave up military life to resume his seat in the House of Delegates, serving there until the end of hostilities.

Within weeks of Appomattox, McKinney opened a law office in Farmville, a town he knew well from college days and home of two of his brothers. He soon qualified to practice law and five years later formed a partnership with Francis D. Irving. Almost from the moment this thirty-three-year-old veteran arrived in Farmville he was embroiled in politics as a staunch Conservative. More organizer and debater than orator, McKinney always was ready to whip the troops into shape and urge them onward against the foe. Whenever a carpetbagger, scalawag, or Readjuster was not Commonwealth's attorney for Prince Edward County, McKinney was. He held that office in the late 1860s until removed by federal authorities, regained the post for a few months in 1870, and served two somewhat longer terms in the 1880s. In 1872 he lost out in a race for Congress in the predominantly black Fourth District but three years later headed a fusion ticket that gained control of Farmville. That same year he ran for the House of Delegates and was defeated once again by the black-and-tan Republican machine.

Although McKinney experienced his share of setbacks, he nevertheless was earning the respect and gratitude of fellow Conservatives. As early as 1873 the Chatham *Tribune* suggested that McKinney would make a fine attorney general, and the Farmville *Commonwealth* agreed. McKinney was, the local editor noted, a lawyer, a veteran, and a gentleman of "high-toned and chivalrous character." These political balloons proved premature, but within a few years the Farmville lawyer would attract statewide attention.

Meanwhile, McKinney's personal affairs prospered. By 1880 his son, Robert Christian McKinney, was studying law and sharing quarters with the deputy clerk of courts in Farmville. McKinney lived alone nearby, probably at 408 Beech Street, the structure which became his home sometime during these years. Two days before Christmas 1884, Annie Clay Lyle, the thirty-eight-year-old daughter of a local physician, became the second Mrs. Philip W. McKinney. A tall, statuesque, but stern-appearing matron, she owned some property and soon joined her husband in real estate speculation, a pursuit which did not bring great riches but did provide considerable income.

In November 1887 the couple's only child, a daughter, Frankie Irving (named for McKinney's law partner), was born. At about this time, perhaps while the family was living in Richmond (1890–94), the Beech Street house, located not far from what is now Longwood College, experienced a very dramatic "Victorianization." What had been a standard story-and-a-half wooden structure with a typical central hallway became a whimsical two-and-one-half story, multigabled "cottage" encompassing seven spacious rooms, three large halls, and two smaller rooms, all embellished with gingerbread scrollwork, turrets, and an incredible ski-slide roofline.

During the 1880s McKinney made three bids for state office, the last of which proved successful. In 1881 he was nominated for attorney general on the ticket headed by John W. Daniel which was overwhelmed by the Readjusters. However, because a few thousand votes were thrown out, McKinney ran slightly ahead of the rest of the losing slate, a fact his supporters would emphasize in subsequent campaigns. Four years later McKinney enjoyed the backing of John S. Barbour, Democratic party chairman, for the governorship, but Fitzhugh Lee outpolled him on the first ballot and soon carried the day.

By 1889, when Democrats gathered at Richmond's First Regimental Armory for the largest convention they had ever staged, this son of Buckingham could no longer be denied. His rivals included Colonel Richard F. Bierne, editor of the *State,* a stout, compact man who had studied at Blacksburg, Randolph-Macon, and Leipzig; Congressman Charles T. O'Ferrall of Harrisonburg (whose turn would come four years later); and James Hoge Tyler, a farmer-businessman from the Southwest and the man who would succeed O'Ferrall. McKinney had nearly 600 votes on the first ballot and was so near a majority on the second that the nomination was his. Most of his original support came from a band of communities south of Richmond stretching across the state from the Tidewater to the mountains. James Hoge Tyler won the party's nomination for lieutenant governor and R. Taylor Scott for attorney general. The selection of Tyler, active in the Farmers' Assembly since it was organized in 1885, was an obvious nod to troubled agricultural interests in a state still 80 percent rural.

On the afternoon of August 16, 1889, McKinney left Richmond in triumph to be greeted in Farmville by more cheers, huzzahs, and fireworks. Five days later Republicans met in Norfolk and selected the aging but indomitable William Mahone as their candidate for governor. McKinney launched his campaign in Charlottesville on September 2 with an address in the courthouse which reflected his Reconstruction-born antagonisms toward Republicans and blacks. He opened with a scathing attack upon northern Republicans and their policies: "Nearly all of the [federal tax] revenue collected has been spent for the advantage of the North, and their cities have prospered and their agricultural districts have been improved. While the fields of the North have been made to smile and blossom, ours have become barren. . . . Has it been because of your climate, your men, your want of intelligence, your lack of industry? No, it has been because of the federal legislation ever since the war that has been against you." The tariff was the cause of these evils, McKinney argued. The North was rich, the South poor, all because of Republican programs. Following a few jocular jabs at the opposition ("a party with its head in the North, its tail in the South"), McKinney turned his attention to the black man: "You can't take him into your homes, introduce him to your daughters, or let him attend your schools and colleges. What would be the affect [sic] of sending twenty-five colored people to your grand university? Suppose you put Negroes in your academies or public schools, the result would be your schools would come to nothing. A cyclone would not sooner uproot the turrets of your university. Its halls of learning would become the lodging place of owls and bats." Black rule, he stressed, would stifle the state, and Albemarle, though less than 50 percent black, must think of the entire Commonwealth. During succeeding weeks McKinney traveled to all sections of the state, attending barbecues and rallies and delivering much the same message: maintain party unity, reject "outside" Republican interference, beware of Negro rule.

Despite the furor stirred up by Democratic editors, the outcome never was seriously in doubt. The Democrats controlled electoral machinery at the precinct level; and according to Nelson Blake (Mahone's biographer), the battle-scarred Republican welcomed the gubernatorial nomination as vindication of his leadership but realized he headed a divided, declining party. This election was typical of most held in Virginia during these years: early fireworks and enthusiasm which declined as the struggle became more and more one-sided (and less interesting).

On November 5 the *Dispatch* told readers of an ingenious scheme to broadcast election results. A large canvas would be erected in front of that newspaper's offices, and beginning at 7:30 P.M. Dr. William H. Taylor, city coroner, "by means of a powerful oxhydrogen calcium lantern" would display returns interspersed with cartoons "in all of which Billy Mahone will figure conspicuously, if not creditably." Local landscape scenes and photographic representations of Scripture would "vary the program and relieve monotony," rare public admission that Old Dominion election news could indeed be boring.

McKinney won by 50,000 votes. Mahone carried twenty-one counties—largely in the Tidewater–Black Belt region and in the far Southwest—and only one city, Williamsburg; McKinney's 5,346-vote margin in Richmond alone wiped out the slight advantage Republicans eked out in those scattered strongholds. The Democrats swept the General Assembly, gaining control of three-fourths of the Senate and seven-eighths of the House. This overwhelming victory was aided in some measure by disgruntled white Republicans who objected to Mahone's autocratic grip on party affairs and by blacks angered by his fight to keep John Mercer Langston, a prominent Negro educator, out of Congress.

The Virginia that had chosen Philip Watkins McKinney as its first citizen was a mix of the old and the new, still largely agricultural and rural in 1890 but certainly not the plantation realm of folklore. Railroads, industry, and public education were beginning to change the lives of the Old Dominion's 1,655,908 citizens, about one-third of them black and only 1 percent of foreign birth. In that year 290,965 pupils (94,117 black) attended school. In 1890, 445,473 males and 106,366 females over the age of ten were gainfully employed, largely in agriculture (over half of the males) or as domestic servants (64 percent of the females). Manufacturing, trade, transportation, fishing, and the professions did not loom large, none of these fields having more than 10 to 15 percent of all workers. Some 5,000 women were teachers, although a few hundred were musicians, government clerks, artists, doctors, actresses, authors, preachers, janitors, saloon keepers, and bartenders. Somewhere in the Old Dominion one lone female was an engineer, another was keeping a livery stable, and two more were earning their livings as a plasterer and a brick mason.

The total number of farms had increased during the 1880s from 118,517 to 127,600, most being between 100 and 500 acres in size. The decade had witnessed a dramatic increase in poultry and beef cattle and a marked drop in the number of swine and sheep. Corn, oats, wheat, hay, potatoes, apples, peaches, and tobacco continued to be important crops, although the 1890 tobacco harvest (48.5 million pounds) was about half that of 1880. Economic distress was focused in the declining tobacco belt; other, more diversified rural areas posted moderate economic gains during the decade. By way of contrast, urban Virginia was experiencing boom conditions. The number of manufacturing establishments remained virtually unchanged in the 1880s, but capitalization nearly tripled ($26.9 to $63.4 million) and wages rose from $7.4 to $19.6 million. Shipyards, tobacco factories, and flour mills (each turning out goods worth from $5 to $7 million each year) led the industrial parade, followed by ironworks and textile plants. Fifth in population among the states in 1860, the Old Dominion had fallen to fifteenth by 1890, although the number of inhabitants (despite the departure of West Virginia) increased slightly in those decades (from 1.6 to 1.65 million).

McKinney, resident of a small Southside community where tobacco and general agriculture were all important and veteran of a quarter century of interparty strife, did not have to pour over such statistics to formulate the goals of his administration. Nearly all were calculated to improve the state's economy and stifle any love affair between latent Readjusterism and emerging Populism, thus assuring continued Democratic ascendancy.

Since the 1889–90 legislative session began under his predecessor, McKinney did not consider its deliberations his immediate concern. He and his wife wisely used these weeks to ingratiate themselves with local society. In mid-January they attended a fancy-dress ball held at Belvidere Hall and two weeks later were honored guests at a colonial assembly staged by the Association for the Preservation of Virginia Antiquities. According to the *Dispatch,* this affair, "a dream-like picture" and a gathering of unusual splendor, was arranged to introduce the McKinneys to Richmond. Despite the governor's expressed wishes, the APVA was determined to have an inaugural ball of some sort, and this event served that purpose. On February 12, to the strains of a string band, the McKinneys held their first formal reception. But this social whirl was taking its toll. A few days later Mrs. McKinney complained to Mrs. Parke C. Bagby (her APVA hostess) that she was being overwhelmed by callers. Mrs. Bagby's subsequent invitation to join a cooking club elicited a polite refusal. There was so much company at the Executive Mansion, so many visitors. "[There is] almost always someone staying in the house," the new governor's wife declared. "I feel that my dear little girl is often neglected."

The remainder of 1890 was largely uneventful. The press kept a wary eye on Farmers' Alliance meetings throughout the state, the governor appeared at various ceremonial functions, and he and his family summered at Blue Ridge and Cold Sulphur springs. Just before returning to Richmond, McKinney granted an interview which would have warmed the heart of Henry W. Grady as he cited substantial progress in all parts of the Commonwealth. What was happening in Norfolk, Newport News, Roanoke, and other centers was "truly wonderful." Yet McKinney could not resist a boost for his native Buckingham ("no county in Virginia is more filled with minerals") and used the opportunity to heap praise upon the public school system. "The great trouble is the prejudice among us against mechanical pursuits," he observed, "but it is gradually wearing away. We have sent the hickory to the North to be worked into axe-handles then sent back for us to buy. Thus our money has all the time been going out."

That fall the Democrats swept to victory in the state's ten congressional districts, and the following year the party continued its winning ways, eliminating blacks from the General Assembly for the first time since Reconstruction and cutting Republican strength to a lone senator and two delegates. Shortly before the newly elected all-white legislature was gaveled into session, McKinney was able to announce that Virginia's vexatious public debt problems—the source of bitter controversy for more than two decades—were virtually settled. On November 20, 1891, the state's dailies proclaimed the good news that English creditors had agreed to surrender $23 million in old bonds in return for $19 million of a new issue.

In essence, the so-called Olcott Settlement came about because the state had to extricate itself from a worsening situation as quickly as possible. Bond-holders were granted interest payments over a much longer period—2 percent for ten years (during which the state presumably would get its finances in order), then 3 percent for the next ninety years, compared to 3 per cent for fifty years under the defunct Riddleberger plan. This new arrangement, re-cognizing a total debt of $25,081,242.50, hardly ended this complex litiga-tion but did push a very thorny issue into the background for good. Virginia authorities continued to do battle with a handful of disgruntled bondholders and with the state of West Virginia, which finally agreed in 1918 (under federal court order) to pay a proportionate share of the Old Dominion's ante-bellum debt.

On December 2, 1891, the legislators received McKinney's message, the first of two very detailed reports he would submit. Ever conscious of farm discontent, he stressed the need for economy in government, called for the creation of a railway commission, suggested ways to cut penitentiary costs, boasted of repairs made to the Capitol (wooden floors replaced by marble), and outlined measures designed to shift fiscal responsibility back to the local level. He also suggested that Commonwealth's attorneys receive salaries and not earn their income by a fee system which he thought encouraged litigation, urged appropriation of a "reasonable" sum for a state exhibit at the Chicago World's Fair, and, prompted by the death of a VMI cadet in a fistfight, demanded strict enforcement of prizefighting legislation. In a somewhat dif-ferent vein, McKinney noted that "a very general demand" existed for legally mandated racial segregation in railway coaches. The races now were separate in schools, churches, and hotels, he argued, so why not while traveling as well? Although this suggestion was not acted upon for a decade, it earned the governor a low place in the esteem of blacks.

However, it was Governor McKinney's proposal that judges, not the General Assembly, grant corporation charters which undoubtedly raised the most eyebrows. Judges, he stressed, had more opportunity to consider peti-tions and were in a better position to protect the rights of the public. By following this course, he instructed the lawmakers, "you will then also get rid of lobbyists who vex and annoy legislative bodies. You will have more time to devote to the consideration of such general legislation as may be necessary, and you will save thousands of dollars to the Treasury of the State." The last legislature, McKinney observed, spent three-fourths of its time on private bills, the rest on public matters, and this was unfair to taxpayers. He also cautioned lawmakers to make few laws: "Hasty legislation generally results in injudicious legislation, doing harm sometimes rather than good."

A short time later McKinney submitted a special message on oysters and shellfish, a matter in which he took intense interest. What prompted this concern was a crisis in the fishing industry and the governor's high hopes that reform could produce substantial state revenues. Rampant exploitation of Virginia waters during the 1880s had caused a dramatic decline in the oyster harvest, resulting in widespread unemployment in what had become a very lucrative enterprise. McKinney vetoed a fisheries bill passed early in 1890 and then proceeded to give the problem his personal attention. In September he toured the coast, an enjoyable outing marred only by a squall which broke up "a pleasant game of whist." A year later he again cruised about the same region with the governor of Maryland as his guest. Armed with this experience, McKinney proposed a survey to determine the extent of natural oyster beds, the leasing of barren estuarine bottoms to oyster "planters," the creation of a shellfish commission to regulate natural beds, and high taxes on equipment used in the oyster business. This effort, far more intense and systematic than any mounted by his predecessors, spurred the General Assembly into action, and in February 1892 McKinney signed a bill incorporating most of his ideas. This program had salutary effects, and although McKinney's hopes of huge revenues were not realized, an operation which had been costing the state money yielded net tax revenues of nearly $100,000 over the 1890–1902 period, a sizable gain indeed. McKinney's action won him high praise, especially since this reform came hot on the heels of the debt settlement. The Richmond *Dispatch* (February 24, 1892) proclaimed the latter to be "a great and honorable distinction." And resolution of the oyster question as well marked the McKinney regime "as one of the most memorable administrations within the modern history of Virginia."

Despite these triumphs, railroads, not oysters, were the key issue during the 1891–92 legislative session. Members of the Farmers' Alliance and many rank-and-file Democrats were determined to curb railroad power and had campaigned hard to elect men pledged to do just that. This drive climaxed nearly fifteen years of agitation begun by Grangers and now being fueled by rural distress, Alliance organization, and rebuffs suffered at the hands of skillful railroad lobbyists. In 1877 the General Assembly set up a weak, ineffective railroad commissioner who did little except collect data and issue annual reports. Attempts to broaden his powers got nowhere, and early in 1892 the reformers once more went down to defeat when a bill offered by R. C. Kent of Wythe County was sidetracked in favor of the Mason bill. This measure— the brainchild of Delegate John E. Mason of King George and Stafford counties and backed strongly by Tom Martin, Hal Flood, and others closely allied with railroad money—retained the one-man commission (not a three-member board with authority to fix rates as Kent had proposed) with slightly increased powers. Most important of all, the commissioner continued to receive his salary from the railroads, not the state. True regulation would have to await the creation of the State Corporation Commission under the 1902 constitution.

What role Governor McKinney played in this affair, if any, is not known. He was not an intimate member of the emerging Martin machine and, from all indications, would have gone along with the Kent bill if it had gotten through the General Assembly. In his 1891 message to the state's lawmakers the governor gave strong support to a three-man commission and pointed to alleged evils to be investigated. Historian Allen W. Moger sees McKinney as an "old-time" Democrat, and it is true he was a down-the-line party work-horse who reflected the conservative views of the ruling clique. Had it been otherwise he never would have been nominated or elected. On the other hand, he was not a well-to-do man with easy access to railroad executives, and his outlook was influenced by rural ties. He perceived the necessity of pacifying the farmers—a perception born of firsthand experience with Readjuster victories and knowledge as a small-town attorney of the rising tide of farm discontent evident throughout Virginia. His emphasis upon economy in government, sanctity of educational funds, creation of an effective railroad commission, elimination of lobbyists—all reveal that he was surprisingly in touch with his times and more willing than many leading Democrats to come to grips with the political threat posed by dwindling farm income.

Hardly had the railroad controversy subsided when the governor faced still other problems, among them plans for a State Library building, appointment of Virginia's representatives to the Chicago World's Fair, and preparations for a party conclave which would name delegates to the Democratic national convention. Then, five days before the faithful were to caucus on May 19, 1892, startling news arrived from Washington: Senator John Strode Barbour, former railroad president and architect of the Democratic party's resurgence from the depths of Readjusterism, was dead. Since Barbour's term did not expire until March 1895, it was up to McKinney to make an interim appointment. The press generally made Fitzhugh Lee the favorite, although Albemarle County residents put forth the name of Thomas Staples Martin, a Scottsville lawyer and veteran political operator who launched a very effective campaign for the post as soon as he learned of the senator's death.

Two months later the governor surprised almost everyone by selecting General Eppa Hunton of Fauquier County. Hunton, seventy years old, had retired from the House of Representatives in 1881 to be succeeded by Barbour, the man he now replaced. Although questioned at the time, Mc-Kinney's choice made good sense and conformed to his expressed view that any appointee should have substantial legislative experience, something neither Lee nor Martin possessed. Also, the selection of Hunton was a "safe" decision. McKinney's choice made no enemies and left open the possibility (remote as it was) that he himself might eventually get the job.

The final year of the McKinney administration, 1893, was by far the most exciting. In April the governor hosted a meeting of southern governors in Richmond, called to coordinate promotional efforts at the World's Fair. Seven chief executives were McKinney's guests. All agreed to prepare papers to be distributed at Chicago, but apparently only four men did so—South Carolina's Benjamin R. ("Pitchfork Ben") Tillman, McKinney, and the governors of Arkansas and Alabama. The Virginia booklet was, above all else, a blatant appeal for immigration to the state of "men who want homes for themselves and their families . . . good men . . . steady, industrious, law-abiding men."

In mid-September the governor, Mrs. McKinney, and sixteen guests journeyed westward to Chicago. While they were away, a simple assault in Roanoke developed into an explosion of racial violence that left seventeen dead and twenty-five wounded. On September 20 a black youth named Thomas Smith beat up a white country woman who had come to town for market day and stole $1.93 from her. Mrs. Henry Bishop was bruised and battered but by early afternoon was recovering nicely at a local saloon; however, her son, a Norfolk and Western foreman, soon was at the head of a mob, several thousand strong, which roamed the city for twenty hours. The enraged throng stormed the jail, lynched Smith and burned his body, staged an armed clash with the militia, and tried to murder Roanoke's mayor when he attempted to protect the youthful assailant and restore order. Although this tragedy began as a racial incident, hard times and tensions spawned by the panic of 1893 undoubtedly served to exacerbate antagonisms.

A grand jury indicted sixteen local residents. One man was fined $100 and sentenced to thirty days in jail; the others got lesser sentences or were found innocent. McKinney, much distressed and embarrassed because this affair occurred during his absence, subsequently told the General Assembly that the law must prevail throughout the Commonwealth at all times. Lynching for the "unspeakable crime" might have been justified during Reconstruction when courts were defective, he said, but that was no longer true. As blacks pointed out, however, McKinney did not take an unequivocal stand against lynching, then at the crest of its sordid popularity.

On the eve of the opening of the General Assembly on December 6, 1893, McKinney told reporters he had no plans to seek a Senate seat. He said it was not proper for him to campaign while governor, but if the lawmakers wished to consider him, they knew his record. The following day the *Dispatch* hailed McKinney's four years as "one of the most memorable administrations Virginia has ever had," singling out for high praise the debt settlement and the chief executive's scrupulous attention to detail. In his message to the General Assembly, McKinney reiterated several proposals made two years earlier and not acted upon (most of them economy measures) and issued a special appeal for additional funds for the State Normal School, noting that four colleges for males received a total of $125,000 each year and the Farm-ville institution for white women only $12,000. Lawmakers, he cautioned, should give the female mind "a fair chance." "Give our girls an education which will enable them to be independent, and you will elevate them above the low grade of work to which women have so often to resort."

The governor concluded his remarks (covering forty-three pages in the House *Journal*) with a summary of what he considered the most notable achievements of his administration. The debt was settled, state revenues were up nearly $500,000, and "not less than $150,000" had been saved by not calling special sessions. New revenues were flowing from Virginia's oyster grounds, which now had been properly surveyed. Lunatics had been taken from local jails and lodged in enlarged state asylums, there was a new student barracks at Blacksburg, and a fireproof state library and records depository soon would appear, $200,000 already having been appropriated for that pur-pose. Veterans' pensions had increased from $65,000 to $100,000 and the annuity to the Soldiers' Home from $10,000 to $30,000. At Old Point Com-fort U.S. military property valued at $281,000 and previously not taxed constituted a new source of state income, and $448,000 collected by federal agents during the Civil War was being returned to Virginians or to their heirs.

Since 1889, McKinney reported, 295 schoolhouses had been built, and educational outlays had increased by nearly $200,000. The number of pupils had increased by 11,523, and an additional 509 teachers had been employed. The Executive Mansion and the Capitol had been refurbished with paint, marble, and new carpets (all of these expenditures coming out of the contin-gency fund), and a balance of $3,000 for such purposes returned to the treasury. McKinney took special pride in what had been done at the peniten-tiary; a shoe factory, work farm, trades programs, and conditional pardons had cut costs at that institution substantially. During the past four years these reforms returned a profit of $120,000, and he predicted that an annual net income of $50,000 might be realized.

Like all politicians, the governor put the best possible interpretation upon his administration, yet he could point to undeniable progress and im-provement. Philip Watkins McKinney closed this glowing report of what he termed "four of the best years of my life" with sanguine hopes for the future of the Old Dominion.

Although legislators may have read his well-turned phrases with passing interest, their thoughts were elsewhere. Forty-eight hours later, after six hard-fought ballots, Tom Martin beat back Fitzhugh Lee and won a full six-year term in the U.S. Senate. A few days later the governor submitted a special message on taxation which pressed for a state income tax and proposed crea-tion of a five-man commission to review tax policies. Few, however, were listening. McKinney's days were numbered, and the public furor over Martin's victory overshadowed anything he might say or do.

On January 2, 1894, after the inauguration of Charles Triplett O'Ferrall, McKinney and his wife returned home to a tumultuous reception. All of Farmville's stores closed for the occasion, and the entire normal school student body was on hand to cheer them at the Opera House. Addresses by black and white friends revealed what McKinney's neighbors viewed as the real accomplishments of the past four years: a dignified, honest administration, settlement of the debt, interest in the welfare of all classes (expecially convicts, the insane, and other unfortunates), and increased funds for education and higher pensions for veterans—all accomplished without the imposition of new taxes. McKinney, deeply touched by this outpouring of emotion, uttered a few words of thanks, concluding that his only wish was to return to the practice of law and spend the rest of his days among those he knew and loved best.

That time turned out to be brief. In the early months of 1899 McKinney's health began to fail, and he died on March 1 after a short illness complicated by a bout with pneumonia. Two days later he was laid to rest in the Farmville Cemetery in the presence of a large crowd which included numerous state officials. McKinney's son, who died in 1918, and second wife, who died in 1936 at the age of ninety, also are buried there.

Philip Watkins McKinney was almost a model Virginia governor, or at least a model those eager to follow in his footsteps might do well to emulate. He was dignified, modest, reluctant to spend tax money for frivolous purposes, and seemingly concerned with the welfare of the less fortunate. McKinney rose to the Executive Mansion through dogged determination and unwillingness to accept defeat. As governor he displayed a scrupulous attention to detail and dared to venture into new areas such as tax and charter reform and revitalization of the seafood industry. He also displayed special interest in the education of women. Since McKinney left virtually no personal papers, one must interpret his thoughts, goals, and ideals from two extensive messages to the General Assembly and from the public record. The figure that emerges is that of a solid, small-town lawyer, a conscientious, careful administrator, and a pragmatic politician sobered by the party strife of the postwar decades.

Nearly every move he made was calculated to strengthen the Democratic party against all foes and, at almost any price, to avoid factionalism. This unswerving dedication, hand-in-hand with obvious personal overtures to those listening to the siren song of Populism, enabled the Democrats to ride out a stormy period. To Philip Watkins McKinney, who as chief executive talked of curbing the power of lobbyists and railroads, cutting government expenditures, and enacting a state income tax, belongs much of the credit for this outcome.

Often remembered only as "the man who beat Mahone," McKinney was, in fact, a sturdy, hardworking individual who, at times, could be surprisingly innovative and resilient, so long as such steps led to increased party unity, the cornerstone of his political philosophy. In the final analysis, he was a small-town politico whose integrity, values, attitudes, and social mores comported well with the needs of the Old Dominion in the early 1890s.

SOURCES

For the most part one must rely upon Richmond newspapers and Mc-Kinney's messages to the General Assembly for the story of his administration. Herbert Clarence Bradshaw's *History of Prince Edward County* (Richmond, 1955) provides pertinent information on both McKinney and Farmville. The most notable unpublished analyses of the period are two University of Virginia M.A. theses: Bernice Bryant Zuckerman, "Philip Watkins McKinney, Governor of Virginia, 1890–1894" (1967), and Richard J. Boudreau, "Two-Party Politics in Virginia, 1888–1896" (1974). Other unpublished materials include county records and census returns, the Henry De La Ware Flood Papers (Library of Congress), the Bagby Family Papers (Virginia Historical Society), and McKinney's Executive Papers (Virginia State Library). Mr. and Mrs. Emeric T. Noone, owners of what was once McKinney's home at 408 Beech Street, Farmville, kindly provided numerous details concerning his family life.

CHARLES T. O'FERRALL

"Gray Eagle" from the Valley

Minor T. Weisiger

Born near Brucetown in Frederick County, Virginia, on October 21, 1840, Charles Triplett ("Trip") O'Ferrall spent his youth in Morgan County, in the northern reaches of the Shenandoah Valley. His father, John O'Ferrall, a veteran of the War of 1812, ran a hotel in Berkeley Springs, situated only two miles from the Mason-Dixon line. John took as his second wife Barbara Green, the daughter of John Green, Methodist minister and doctor. They were the parents of the future governor. John O'Ferrall, who served several terms in the Virginia legislature and in 1851 was elected clerk of Morgan County, died suddenly in 1855, and the local judge considered his fifteen-year-old son sufficiently knowledgeable to fill his father's unexpired term. This obvious competence enabled him to win election to a full six-year term when only seventeen.

In October 1859, when John Brown seized the armory at Harper's Ferry, Trip joined a militia company which rushed to the scene, but he and his associates arrived too late for any action. When war began two years later, he joined the Confederate forces although Morgan County (which became part of West Virginia in 1863) was, in O'Ferrall's words, "Red-hot Union" in sentiment. Mustered in as a cavalry private, O'Ferrall served under the famed Turner Ashby until that officer's death in June 1862. By August of the same year he had advanced to the rank of major, in command of his own squadron. His unit was used primarily for picketing, scouting, and raiding forays in the Valley, but it also participated in Stonewall Jackson's famous Valley campaign and in the battle of Brandy Station, the largest cavalry engagement of the war. A courageous soldier, O'Ferrall was wounded eight times. His most serious wound came at the battle of Upperville in May 1863, when he was shot through the lungs and left for dead. He spent over a year recovering. While visiting his brother in Mississippi, he met and married a young widow, Annie McLain Hand, the daughter of a Confederate general. O'Ferrall resumed active service early in 1865 as a colonel in command of all cavalry forces in the Shenandoah Valley and continued in that position until Lee's surrender in April.

The twenty-five-year-old O'Ferrall and his wife then opened a hotel in Staunton, but innkeeping proved neither financially remunerative nor person-

CHARLES T. O'FERRALL

Governor of Virginia

1894–1898

ally congenial. In addition, the newly created state of West Virginia sought to have O'Ferrall extradited for wartime raids within its borders. Worried, the former cavalryman hurried to Richmond to see Governor Francis H. Pierpont, who was also a native of West Virginia. His strenuous intercession with federal authorities prevented O'Ferrall's arrest.

In the autumn of 1868 the young veteran entered the law department at Washington College in Lexington, where he defrayed the cost of his education by operating a small hotel. Obtaining his degree in August 1869, O'Ferrall began his law practice in the market town of Harrisonburg, located midway up the Valley. His political bent reasserted itself quickly, and he ran successfully for a seat in the House of Delegates in 1871. O'Ferrall was elected as an anti-Funder and while in the legislature fought against full debt repayment. Reelected in 1872 and ambitious for higher office, he ran unsuccessfully for Congress in the same year. When Ulysses S. Grant and the Republicans carried the state, O'Ferrall ceased opposition to the dominant Funder wing of the Conservative party, fearful such action would deliver the state government into Republican hands.

In 1874 the Funder-controlled General Assembly appointed the Harrisonburg lawyer to a six-year term as judge of the Rockingham County court; but, finding the monthly terms "onerous," he longed to "cast aside the judicial ermine" and dabbled in politics to relieve the tedium. At the 1877 state convention of the Conservative party, O'Ferrall served as deputy floor manager for Frederick W. M. Holliday of Winchester, who wrested the gubernatorial nomination from William Mahone and John W. Daniel. Though never a prominent Funder, O'Ferrall had by now joined forces with the debt-paying faction. For this reason he was not reappointed as judge by the 1879 legislature, solidly controlled by Readjusters.

Resuming law practice, O'Ferrall threw himself wholeheartedly into politics once more. A polished orator, well schooled in the rhetorical phrases and flourishes of the day, he became a popular speaker for Democratic candidates and in 1882 was prevailed upon to oppose John Paul, Readjuster congressman from the Seventh District, the largest congressional district in the state. O'Ferrall began with little hope of unseating the popular Paul, but when the ballots were counted, he trailed by only 200 votes out of some 24,000 cast. He contested the results and eventually was ordered seated. After this victory, O'Ferrall was reelected five times without major opposition, retaining the post until he resigned to assume the governorship in 1893.

O'Ferrall's ten-year career in the House was not especially memorable, but he was an able representative of the interests of his party and region. The only committee on which O'Ferrall served at length was the powerful Privileges and Elections Committee. Disputed returns were commonplace, and the committee generally decided appeals on the basis of which party controlled the House. O'Ferrall disliked these partisan maneuverings and on one occasion filibustered to delay Speaker Thomas B. ("Czar") Reed from unseating a Democrat in favor of a Republican. Reed prevailed, but the Virginian gained increased influence, becoming the second-ranking Democrat on the committee, behind his friend Charles F. Crisp of Georgia. When Crisp was chosen House speaker in 1891, with O'Ferrall as his floor leader, the Virginian became committee chairman.

A staunch supporter of President Grover Cleveland, O'Ferrall regularly supported low tariffs, which favored farming interests, and voted in favor of creating the Interstate Commerce Commission—yet condemned those "always ready to engage in idle clamor against railroad monopolies." He cautiously approved free coinage of silver, though he subsequently voted, at Cleveland's request, to repeal the Sherman Silver Purchase Act. In spite of the strict constructionist principles which he shared with most southern Democrats, he boldly advocated federal aid to education, believing that since the national government had freed the Negro, it should assist in his education. This seemingly benevolent attitude did not extend to the federal elections bill of 1890, popularly known as the Force Bill, which he and his southern brethren staunchly and successfully opposed.

Although O'Ferrall remained in Congress for a decade, his gaze was never completely deflected from Richmond and the Governor's Mansion. Unable to get the nomination in 1885 and 1889, he decided in 1893 to make an all-out effort which soon won the support of various Democratic leaders. By the time the state convention opened in Richmond in August he was the clear favorite. O'Ferrall's opponents were former state Senator James Hoge Tyler of Pulaski, an advocate of free silver, and A. S. Buford of Nelson County. By now O'Ferrall had abandoned his flirtation with the silver panacea and had begun to espouse a more conservative stand which favored a balanced, bimetallic, gold and silver currency. With the backing of the Democratic organization, he won an overwhelming first-ballot victory. Despite objections from prosilver forces, his bimetallist views were incorporated into the platform, which also advocated a graduated federal income tax, economy in government, and support of agriculture, schools, and road construction.

Arrayed against the Democrats were the Populists and their gubernatorial candidate, Edmund Cocke of Cumberland County, scion of an old Virginia family who ably articulated the grievances of disgruntled farmers. Hoping to put together a coalition of farmers, blacks, and Republicans, the Populist platform advocated free silver, state and federal income taxes, support for schools, and the repeal of the Anderson-McCormick election law, which kept the Democrats in power by sanctioning fraudulent election practices.

Though he despised the Populists and their doctrines, O'Ferrall realized their vote-getting potential and moved carefully, straddling the money issue whenever possible and even urging blacks to vote Democratic. Campaigning vigorously, he averaged a speech a day from September until the election. Yet the Populist threat proved illusory. O'Ferrall won by some 45,000 votes, a majority undoubtedly swelled by fraud. Other factors also helped O'Ferrall. The General Assembly was to choose a U.S. senator in December, and aspirants for that post—notably Thomas Staples Martin—worked diligently to elect Democrats of their choosing, thus boosting the turnout across the state. In addition, O'Ferrall and his allies were able to portray the Populists as extremists and cranks who would rule the state in alliance with Negroes and Republicans. Lastly, O'Ferrall was an attractive, energetic, and able candidate, with a long political career and many friends.

Fifty-three years old, Charles T. O'Ferrall could look back on almost forty years of public life. A self-made man, his ambition and energy had sustained him on both the battlefield and the courthouse green. Although he was not on intimate terms with state Democratic leaders, his star was clearly in the ascendant. A proven orator, a conciliator rather than an ideologue, the "Gray Eagle" (as he was known to admirers) confidently prepared to guide the Old Dominion through its next four years.

On the eve of his inauguration, O'Ferrall viewed a state politically secure but economically unsettled. Bank failures, industrial collapses, and a drain of American gold reserves were chiefly responsible for a nationwide panic and depression which began in 1893. Virginia had already begun to feel the effects of these national trends, and problems stemming from the state's economic plight would shortly beset the new O'Ferrall administration.

Since 1865 inaugural ceremonies had generally been kept to a dignified and parsimonious minimum, but O'Ferrall departed from this style. On New Year's Day, 1894, thousands of Virginians, along with numerous bands and militia units, packed Capitol Square to hear the first inaugural address since 1878. Although the new chief executive touched on a number of topics, he reserved his strongest words for the theme of law and order. Upset by accounts of unrest in other parts of the nation, O'Ferrall warned that in Virginia "there will be no temporizing, with law breakers or law defilers." This was meant to embrace both economic and racial troublemakers.

The first test was quick in coming. Virginia and Maryland had long shared a lucrative oyster fishery in the Chesapeake Bay. By the early 1890s constant dredging had exhausted the Maryland beds, and that state's watermen began frequent incursions into Virginia waters. In February 1894 Virginia authorities seized a Maryland vessel, Maryland's governor protested vehemently, and O'Ferrall moved to resolve the dispute, displaying both force and restraint. He proposed to the General Assembly that two new patrol boats be constructed, but he also suggested that both states should adopt reciprocal arrangements for the pursuit and capture of "oyster pirates." In addition, he called for a joint commission to work out boundary differences. O'Ferrall made a trip to Tangier Island to talk to Virginia watermen and later

met with Maryland's governor. All of this did much to calm the situation, and
O'Ferrall regarded its swift resolution as one of the top achievements of his
administration.

The oyster controversy brought to the fore two of the major themes of
O'Ferrall's first two years in office: a concern for Virginia's economic health
and a desire to preserve law and order within the state's borders. An economic
conservative, he believed that stable growth would depend on northern investment capital, an influx of immigrant artisans, laborers, and farmers, and a
well-connected system of roads and railroads. This represented no deviation
from the stances of previous governors, but O'Ferrall made up in enthusiasm
what he lacked in originality. Acting like a one-man chamber of commerce,
he missed no opportunity to extol Virginia's geography, people, products,
and heritage. Well-received, such remarks also proved well timed and politically advantageous.

For the first half of his term, O'Ferrall's economic decisions were politically astute. During the 1894 legislative session he vetoed several railroad
incorporation bills on the grounds that they were loosely worded and poorly
defined. This had the effect of soothing residual Populist sentiment against
railroad power, while at the same time not actually threatening potent companies such as the Norfolk and Western and the Chesapeake and Ohio. The
1896 session witnessed similar vetoes.

Cautious when dealing with railroads, O'Ferrall manifested no such reserve with strikers and labor unions. Echoing the opinions of most Virginians,
he heartily approved President Cleveland's use of troops to quell striking
employees of the Pullman Company in Chicago. Dealing with similar circumstances closer to home, O'Ferrall became the first Virginia governor to articulate the "right-to-work" philosophy that was to become firmly entrenched in
the state's political creed during the twentieth century. Briefly stated, this
stance maintains that no worker can be denied the right to work because of
strikes or compulsory unionization.

In May 1895 the governor dispatched troops to the Flat-Top region of
southwest Virginia, where a strike by coal miners was under way. Having
learned of the intention of West Virginia miners to march on Virginia, he
promptly ordered the Richmond Howitzers and other militia units to the
scene to protect nonstriking Virginia miners. In his opinion the West Virginia
miners were "cats paws" of the West Virginia mine operators, who had encouraged the strike to gain lower freight rates from the Norfolk and Western,
the railroad which served the region. Eager to view the situation firsthand,
and perhaps to enhance his visibility in the state press, O'Ferrall traveled to
the scene. He was convinced that Virginia mine operators were treating their
employees fairly and insisted that the principle involved was "the right of a
man to work without fear, intimidation or molestation." National and state
papers generally supported his vigorous response, but the independent-

minded and sometimes fiery editor of the Lynchburg *News,* young Carter Glass, criticized the governor as a tool of the mining companies. There is no evidence to substantiate or refute this charge, but O'Ferrall did feel constrained to defend his policy to the 1896 General Assembly as necessary, effective, and inexpensive.

In the summer of 1894 when several hundred men under the leadership of Jacob Coxey of Ohio marched on Washington to draw attention to the plight of the nation's jobless, O'Ferrall became apprehensive about their encampment outside Alexandria. For years nearby Rosslyn had been a center for racing and gambling, and the influx of Coxey's group exacerbated matters. O'Ferrall issued a proclamation ordering "Coxey's Army" to disperse, and within a few hours militia forces broke up the makeshift camp. A public made jittery by nationwide economic disturbances applauded O'Ferrall's action.

Somewhat surprisingly, the governor was equally swift in calling out troops to prevent lynchings, moves far less likely to elicit approval from the mass of the electorate. In 1894 he twice dispatched troops to save blacks from mob violence. The white press said little, but the Richmond *Planet,* the state's most influential black newspaper, praised O'Ferrall as a courageous statesman.

He was, in fact, more flexible in race relations than many of his predecessors had been or than some of his successors would be. O'Ferrall had grown up and lived in areas relatively free of racial tension; nevertheless, his contact with black leaders was cautious and discreet. He politely declined an invitation to address the Afro-American Press Association in September 1894 and six months later went to considerable lengths to explain his reception of a group of Massachusetts lawmakers at the Governor's Mansion, among them a black man, Joseph Teamoh. O'Ferrall insisted that he did not know of the Negro's presence beforehand and stated, "I draw the line on the negro at the social circle or anywhere else that suggests even a semblance of social equality." This response was a predictable one for the period, but there is reason to question its accuracy. John Mitchell, Jr., editor of the Richmond *Planet,* had also been invited to attend, suggesting that O'Ferrall knew Teamoh would be present.

In December 1895 the governor proposed a stiff antilynching statute to the 1896 General Assembly, urging the legislators to make counties or cities in which lynching occurred liable for fines up to $10,000 as well as the cost of paying the militia. To aid passage, a proviso imposing the death penalty for rape or attempted rape was attached, but nothing substantive would be done about the problem until 1928. A white supremacist Democrat, O'Ferrall was no liberal in race relations, but neither was he a blustering, race-baiting demagogue. Like most politicians, his concern for a people's welfare was closely intertwined with a concern for how their votes would be cast.

For the first half of his term, O'Ferrall remained a much-sought-after speaker. Stumping vigorously for Claude Swanson and other Democratic congressional candidates in the autumn of 1894, he blamed Republicans for current economic troubles. In almost every speech he also defended the Walton Act, which was drawing Republican fire as blatantly partisan and unfair. Passed by the General Assembly earlier in the year, it amended the 1884 Anderson-McCormick election law and gave the Democrats even tighter control of the electoral process. The new law instituted a secret ballot but made marking it absurdly complicated, opening the way for what historian Allen W. Moger has characterized as "irregularities . . . as unlimited as the ingenuity and expediency of politicians." In spite of such obvious flaws, O'Ferrall contended that the act gave greater protection to illiterate voters, virtually eliminated vote-buying, and was entirely proper in the light of past Republican disfranchisement of Democrats.

Although O'Ferrall continued to champion his party and its measures, many of his public appearances were devoted to eulogizing Virginia and the "Lost Cause" at monument dedications and encampments of Confederate veterans. His addresses always contained a dual theme: the matchless heroism, patriotism, and sacrifice of Virginia's people and its soldiers and—at the same time—reconciliation and loyalty to the Union. Yet O'Ferrall's gubernatorial routine was not all politics and speeches. His daily schedule was far from strenuous, and he was in his office only from 9:00 A.M. to 3:00 P.M., including lunch. He was assisted by his private secretary, Evan R. Chesterman, son of the editor of the influential and pro-Democratic Richmond *Dispatch,* William Dallas Chesterman. This proved a politic appointment, and O'Ferrall received extensive and favorable coverage from the *Dispatch* for much of his term.

The O'Ferrall family also made life in the Governor's Mansion agreeable. O'Ferrall's first wife died several years after their marriage, leaving two sons. He then married Jennie Knight, a daughter of Colonel William Knight of Richmond, in January 1881. She and O'Ferrall had four children, who, together with the offspring from her previous marriage, made for a large and lively family. They spent the bulk of each summer at either Allegheny Springs or Blue Springs, not far from O'Ferrall's boyhood home. The Commonwealth's first family entertained and socialized on a modest scale, holding the obligatory levees and attending larger functions in the Richmond social whirl.

At midpoint of his administration in December 1895, O'Ferrall could look back upon two eventful, though not especially controversial, years. He had responded promptly and forcefully when he believed Virginia's interests threatened, preserved law and order, and alienated few if any fellow Democrats. As a result, he remained generally popular with party and citizenry alike. Confident of the future, he made recommendations to the 1896 General Assembly that were extensive and ambitious in scope. He urged increased appropriations for schools, Confederate veterans, and the volunteer militia. O'Ferrall also outlined plans for new agencies, including establishment of a state weather service and creation of a commissioner of state banks, insurance companies, and savings and loan associations. He suggested that all insurance companies doing business in Virginia be required to deposit 5 percent of their capital stock in Virginia banks. Miscellaneous proposals included establishment of a black reformatory, rebuilding of the University of Virginia's Rotunda (which had recently burned), and financing of local road projects by counties. Although O'Ferrall's program was progressive in tone and admirable in its objectives, it was overly ambitious, and virtually none of it was adopted.

These setbacks were small in comparison with what awaited O'Ferrall later in 1896. A presidential race loomed on the horizon, and economic issues dominated the political realm. When the state's senior senator and titular leader of Virginia Democrats, John W. Daniel, embraced the silver cause, many followed his leadership. At the Democratic state convention in Staunton (which O'Ferrall did not attend) even Senator Thomas S. Martin, theretofore a fiscal conservative, endorsed free silver.

As a sound-money, probusiness conservative, O'Ferrall was appalled by these developments and by the Democrats' nomination of William Jennings Bryan for the presidency. In August 1896 a group of prominent Democrats who shared his views met in Richmond to plot an independent course of action. Besides O'Ferrall, these dissident "goldbugs" included Joseph Bryan, publisher of the Richmond *Times,* ex-Governors Fitzhugh Lee and William E. Cameron, William L. Royall, a prominent lawyer, and businessmen Basil Gordon and B. B. Munford. Affirming their commitment to economic orthodoxy, they officially adopted a platform which praised Jeffersonian Democracy, the gold standard, and the principles and actions of Grover Cleveland.

O'Ferrall, who subsequently explained his course in terms of respect for Republican nominee William McKinley, worked hard to defeat Bryan. He believed that party harmony would only be temporarily strained by the money question (which was true), but he miscalculated the effect of his stand on his career. The newspapers, including the once-friendly *Dispatch,* ripped into him, charging the "renegade" with hypocrisy and ingratitude. When O'Ferrall attempted to speak at a rally in September, he was greeted with catcalls and boos.

Silverites and goldbugs vociferously espoused their positions. William Jennings Bryan appeared in Richmond in September before the largest political rally ever held in the state, and the Richmond *Times* barraged readers with a stream of progold editorials. In November the Nebraskan won a 20,000-vote victory over McKinley in Virginia, though McKinley captured the White House. The gold Democratic ticket (Palmer-Buckner) received only 2,000 votes in the state. Corrupt tactics characterized the conduct of both the major parties. The more prosperous western and southwestern counties went Republican, with the depressed Southside going heavily for Bryan.

The Bryan victory in Virginia sealed O'Ferrall's political fate, rendering him a virtual lame duck for the remainder of his term.

In May 1897 Virginia voters were faced with a referendum on whether to call a constitutional convention. Convinced that the convention would be costly and was unnecessary, O'Ferrall opposed it and denounced demands for such constitutional "reforms" as restrictive railroad laws, compulsory road service, and emasculation of funding for the public school system. The convention was defeated by a wide margin, chiefly because both Democrats and Republicans feared the other side would control it, to their own detriment.

The Democratic state convention of that year was once again firmly controlled by silverites. James Hoge Tyler, O'Ferrall's principal rival in 1893 and now the clear favorite, was nominated by acclamation. The platform was a repeat of the Chicago platform, and the only row came over a proposal that U.S. senators be nominated by a popular primary vote instead of by legislative caucus. This move constituted a challenge to Senator Martin and his growing organization by more progressive elements of the party, including Congressman William A. Jones and future Governor Andrew J. Montague. The plan was narrowly beaten back, but the struggle offered a preview of future challenges to Martin's sway.

O'Ferrall was not present at the convention, but in September he made his opinions known. Refusing to support the convention slate, he lambasted the gathering for approving a carbon copy of the party's 1896 national platform. Insisting that he was not seeking notoriety, he then proceeded to attack Senator Daniel, the most popular man in the Virginia Democracy. This led to a bitter exchange in the press which opened old political wounds—monetary matters, who had supported Cleveland and who had not, in fact, who was telling the truth. In the process, O'Ferrall reversed his stand and agreed to support the party nominees. It was a strident and highly personal repartee, uncharacteristic of both men, and demonstrated how divisive the currency question could be.

The Tyler ticket was easily elected, though O'Ferrall's prophecy that silver was beginning to recede as an issue soon would be fulfilled. In December 1897 he sent his last official message, a bold package of old and new ideas, to the General Assembly. It included antilynching legislation, penalties for gambling and criminal assaults, expenditures for road construction, new taxes on oysters and fertilizers, and increased aid to Confederate veterans and widows, even at the expense of money for public schools and colleges. And, stung by the vote frauds of 1896, O'Ferrall advocated new election laws which constituted a repudiation of the Walton Act. These proposals were expensive, controversial, and consequently anathema to the Democratic leadership. Receiving no serious consideration, they proved the final disappointment of his term.

Upon leaving the Governor's Mansion, O'Ferrall settled in suburban

Richmond at a home he had purchased in Chesterfield County. He opened a law practice with Samuel Regester, but ill health and business troubles plagued the partnership and it was dissolved in 1904. Hoping to revive his slumping fortunes and vindicate his public career, in 1904 O'Ferrall published his autobiography, *Forty Years of Active Service*. It is a pleasant memoir, devoid of rancor and recrimination, and written with the fulsome self-praise and hindsight such works usually contain. Much emphasis is laid on his congressional years and relatively little on the more controversial and more recent gubernatorial term.

The completion of this work was followed all too quickly by O'Ferrall's death on September 22, 1905, in his sixty-fifth year. He had not been well for some time, owing partly to wounds received in the Civil War, and succumbed to nervous prostration and paralysis of the throat. In death he was honored and eulogized almost as a fallen hero. His body was carried in military procession to Richmond's Hollywood Cemetery upon the same caisson that had borne the coffin of Jefferson Davis twelve years before. Cannons fired salutes, and the caisson was followed by a riderless horse. Present at the grave were many allies and foes, including Senators Martin and Daniel. It was an impressive finale to a life of long public service, a career which only eight years before had ended abruptly and in near disgrace.

O'Ferrall clearly merited the praise showered upon him. He had served his state bravely on the battlefield, and his political record, although not devoid of controversy, was creditable as well. He had transformed his Valley district into a Democratic bastion, routed the Populist dragon, and shown himself to be an able, forceful, even flamboyant leader. Yet O'Ferrall's gubernatorial record was, on the whole, disappointing. An unpopular stand against free silver in 1896 neutralized his political effectiveness long before his term was over, and his proposals to the General Assembly were out of harmony with prevalent fiscal austerity and racial reactionism.

In large measure the reasons for O'Ferrall's failure can be found in the circumstances that had enabled him to capture the governorship. Seeking to fend off the Populist challenge, Virginia Democrats tapped the Gray Eagle because of his war record, longevity on the political scene, and seeming flexibility and moderation on the currency question and other major issues of the day. He won on the strength of these virtues, but both party and populace looked to others for leadership, notably the aging but still charismatic Daniel and the colorless but painstaking Martin. Clearly, O'Ferrall's political fate and that of his administration had depended on the extent to which he could retain the support of these political power brokers.

Only within this context can the impact of free silver on O'Ferrall's career be properly understood. Elected on a platform reflecting essentially moderate views on the money issue, he remained faithful to that stand, even as Daniel and Martin succumbed to the popular clamor for wholesale inflation. They changed; he did not. Cut adrift on this divisive question, he forfeited all influence in Virginia affairs. O'Ferrall's struggle for the gold standard in 1896 had been, in this respect, a battle which he could not win.

Why had the governor taken such an obstinate position? He had, after all, subordinated his anti-Funder debt views in the 1870s to the demands of party unity, and his congressional activities had reflected a considerable degree of flexibility as well. Nevertheless, there was always a vein of iron evident in O'Ferrall's personality. He had defied the jeers of Unionist neighbors at the outbreak of the Civil War to join the Confederate cause and demonstrated the same spirit in 1896. Once he defined his position on the currency question, which he regarded as one of fundamental importance, he stood by his guns, with disastrous results. Flying into the whirlwind of Bryanism, the Gray Eagle crashed to earth. Virginia was the poorer for the loss.

SOURCES

The O'Ferrall Executive Papers (Virginia State Library) are modest and deal primarily with the administrative matters. A smaller collection of O'Ferrall Papers at the College of William and Mary contains a few personal letters from his early years. There are several O'Ferrall letters at the Virginia Historical Society, and a few more concerning political patronage matters can be found in the Grover Cleveland Papers (Library of Congress).

The best source on O'Ferrall's career is his autobiography, *Forty Years of Active Service* (New York and Philadelphia, 1904). Also, see Richmond newspapers and these items: Charles T. O'Ferrall, "Lee's Birthday," *Southern Historical Society Papers* 19 (1891): 402–5; Charles T. O'Ferrall, "Election Contest—Noyes vs. Rockwell . . . Speech of Hon. Charles T. O'Ferrall of Virginia, in the House of Representatives, Friday, April 22, 1892," *Appendix to Congressional Record,* 52d Cong., 1st Sess., vol. 33, pt. 8, April 1892, pp. 234–43; and "O'Ferrall vs. Paul: Papers and Testimony in the Contested Election Case of C. T. O'Ferrall vs. John Paul, from the Seventh Congressional District of Virginia," 48th Cong., 1st Sess., *House Misc. Doc. No. 16* (Washington, D.C., 1884).

Useful secondary accounts include Charles E. Wynes, "Charles T. O'Ferrall and the Virginia Gubernatorial Election of 1893," *Virginia Magazine of History and Biography* 64 (1956): 437–53; William C. Woolridge, "The Sound and Fury of 1896: Virginia Democrats Face Free Silver," *Virginia Magazine of History and Biography* 75 (1967): 97–130; William DuBose Sheldon, *Populism in the Old Dominion: Virginia Farm Politics, 1885–1900* (Princeton, N.J., 1935); and Allen W. Moger, *Virginia: Bourbonism to Byrd, 1870–1925* (Charlottesville, 1968).

JAMES HOGE TYLER

Rebellious Regular

Thomas E. Gay, Jr.

Dame Fortune both smiled and frowned upon James Hoge Tyler. He inherited a proud name and substantial lands which in time gave him financial independence, had a large family of seven children and a happy domestic life, and enjoyed a long and successful career. Yet luck was not always on his side. His mother died at the time of his birth, and until the age of fifteen he was raised by her elderly parents in southwest Virginia. His budding political career was temporarily cut short by Readjusters (an experience which left lasting scars), and only the most fortuitous of circumstances gave him the governorship two decades later. Tyler's turn-of-the-century administration was filled with momentous events—the Spanish-American War, cries for reform and challenges to the emerging Martin machine, and a constitutional convention—but he was more spectator than participant.

James Hoge Tyler was born on August 11, 1846, at Blenheim, in Caroline County. Large landholdings and political privilege ran in the family, but he did not grow up among the patricians of eastern Virginia. When his mother died he was taken as a newborn infant to mountainous Pulaski County to live with her parents, the Hoges, an elderly Scotch-Irish couple. Well-established gentry, they accepted the infant as one of their own; even so, life was not easy. His grandmother died when he was ten, and his grandfather was crippled by paralysis shortly thereafter. As a result, young Tyler had to assume unusual responsibilities, at the same time keeping up with a program of private education administered at home.

When his grandfather died in 1861, James returned east to live with his father and soon enrolled in Minor's Academy in Albemarle County. In 1863 (although only sixteen) he enlisted in the Confederate infantry. Tall and mature beyond his years, Tyler was offered a commission but chose instead to serve as a private. The fledgling soldier saw considerable action in the Richmond-Petersburg area during the final months of the war but emerged unscathed, a more experienced and self-reliant individual. Tyler returned to Hayfield, the 1,000-acre Pulaski County estate that he had inherited from his grandparents, and plunged into a career as farmer, businessman, community leader, and, in time, politician. The farm was in deplorable shape, but Tyler soon restored a measure of order—making liberal provisions for the former

J. HOGE TYLER

Governor of Virginia

1898–1902

slaves which induced most of them to remain. In 1865 he met Sue Hammett of Montgomery County, crowning her the queen of love and beauty at a Christiansburg tournament, and three years later they were married. Of Scotch-Irish stock and a devout Presbyterian, a faith Tyler himself embraced at nineteen, she displayed an active interest in her husband's work and fortified his moral and spiritual convictions.

During these years Tyler concentrated on cattle production and soon had Hayfield out of debt. A true son of the New South, he was eager to develop not only the agricultural potential of the Virginia Southwest but its industrial and mining resources, too. Railroads, capital, and low taxes constituted key elements in this drive, and Tyler was determined to create a political milieu favorable to economic expansion of his region. The dynamic young farmer thus emerged as a dedicated community booster in the economic realm and a conservative in fiscal and political matters—stands which clashed head-on with William Mahone's railroad schemes and later with the Readjuster movement. Tyler opposed the Petersburg magnate's monopoly of transportation in the Southwest, favoring instead competition and direct ties to badly needed northern capital. Tyler's attitude toward the state debt issue was considerably more ambivalent. He was willing (at times) to suspend interest payments to avoid tax increases but refused to countenance repudiation, which might alienate capital and split the Conservative party.

An extrovert, witty in speech and ingratiating in manner, he liked people, and—for the most part—people liked him. After several terms as president of the Pulaski Farmers' Club, he spearheaded a movement in 1873 to organize agriculturalists throughout the Southwest, thus laying the groundwork for his reputation as the "farmer's friend." Tyler also launched a premature bid for the state Senate in the same year which quickly foundered. Undeterred, he remained active in political affairs. In 1876 he was a delegate to the Democratic national convention in St. Louis and the following year mounted a second (and successful) bid for a seat in the Virginia Senate. His opponent, W. A. French of Giles County, was also a Conservative, and the campaign focused on the state debt. Adroitly straddling the issue, Tyler criticized the unpopular Funding Act of 1871 but did not actually call for readjustment. Once in Richmond he voted with the debt-paying Funders, a stand which in 1879 led to his defeat at the hands of French, now an all-out Readjuster. Attempting to aid the farmers, Tyler used his Senate term to introduce measures that eventually banned the introduction of diseased cattle into Virginia, reduced government salaries, and cut taxes somewhat. But Tyler the businessman could not bring himself to back "forcible" readjustment of the debt, which might tarnish the state's honor and drive off northern capital. In short, his dilemma—one that would plague him throughout his career—was his dual role as farmer and businessman.

With the Readjusters in control of the state from 1879 to 1883, Tyler's political fortunes were at a low ebb. He was appalled by the Readjuster alliance with blacks and struggled to reinvigorate the temporarily demoralized Conservative machine (known after 1883 as the Democratic party). Meanwhile, the southwestern entrepreneur continued to prosper as a highly successful businessman-farmer. He quickly doubled his landholdings to over 2,000 acres and—with the discovery of coal on his property in the 1870s—began to play a significant role in the rebirth of the coal and iron industry in his region. His personal stake in the Belle Hampton Mines (named after two of his daughters) was estimated to be worth $100,000. Active in the founding of the Farmers' Assembly in 1885, he served on that group's executive committee and was appointed to the administrative boards of Hampden-Sydney College, the Virginia Agricultural and Mechanical Institute, and several church-affiliated organizations. With economic position and social standing secure, Tyler was ready for his initial bid for the governorship.

Forty-two years of age, in the prime of life, he had considerable cause for optimism in 1889. His health was excellent (he neither smoked nor drank), and he was personally and physically attractive. Six feet tall with black hair and brown eyes, he sported a fashionable moustache and goatee. Attuned to the value system of late-Victorian Virginia, Tyler was a man of deeply ingrained ethical and religious convictions who felt an abiding sense of loyalty to his state and his party. Further adding to his appeal, he possessed a distinguished family name and had served in the Confederate army.

In spite of these advantages, Tyler's drive for the Governor's Mansion fell far short of the mark. One of six contenders, he commanded only limited delegate strength at the Democratic convention, and the nod went instead to Farmville's Philip W. McKinney. Although hampered—as usual—by poor organization, Tyler still might have carried the day had he been willing to rally Virginia farmers, ripe for rebellion because of economic distress; but, fearful this might split the party, he rejected all suggestions to become their candidate. Nevertheless, the party leadership recognized his vote-getting potential among the farmers and, anxious to retain their loyalty, asked Tyler to accept the nomination for lieutenant governor. Tyler initially demurred, weighing the $600 salary against business and family responsibilities, but soon succumbed to the lure of politics. He worked hard in the ensuing campaign against Mahone and the Republicans, traveling 7,000 miles and making fifty speeches in forty-four counties. McKinney and Tyler swept the field in November, and the southwesterner shared in the glory of the triumph.

As lieutenant governor, Tyler performed routine duties and at McKinney's request served on the commission that finally resolved the debt issue. Yet he continued to long for the prestige of the Governor's Mansion. As the 1893 gubernatorial race approached, however, the Democratic organization swung into line behind Charles T. O'Ferrall, a conservative Valley congressman. Determined to avoid another defeat, Tyler attempted to enhance his cause by declaring support for free silver. He thus assumed a bold stand on a significant issue, but events soon demonstrated that boldness and audacity were not enough, for O'Ferrall easily won the nomination. Yet Tyler had identified himself with an increasingly popular issue. His day would come.

During the next four years Thomas S. Martin won a U.S. Senate seat and began to grasp the reins of power, and William Mahone died, providing yet more evidence of the end of a bitter and controversial era. Overshadowing these developments, the financial panic of 1893 brought economic distress to the entire nation. As a businessman, Tyler came through the hard times in good stead; and as a result of the depression, his political fortunes skyrocketed. The popular outcry for free silver, his pet demand in 1893, gained strength with every passing month, and Tyler's gubernatorial prospects blossomed accordingly. Virginia Democrats endorsed free silver in 1896 and delivered the state's electoral votes to William Jennings Bryan, developments which greatly enhanced Tyler's chances in 1897. Thoroughly identified with free silver, he benefited as well from the weakness of his opposition. His only serious rival was J. Taylor Ellyson, a Richmond businessman and chairman of the Democratic state committee throughout much of the 1890s. A conservative goldbug at heart, he quit the race shortly before the Democrats convened in Roanoke. Unopposed, Tyler won his party's gubernatorial nod by acclamation on his fifty-first birthday.

The battle for second spot on the ticket was much more interesting. Virginia Populists, in an effort to join forces with the Democrats, made only one nomination when they met in July, fielding Edmund S. Cocke, a native of Cumberland County, for lieutenant governor. Although Cocke showed surprising strength on the first ballot in Roanoke (trailing the leader by only 100 votes in a field of seven), the Democrats soon nominated Edward Echols, a conservative Martinite from Staunton. The next day, after an arduous five-hour struggle, Andrew Jackson Montague, a federal district attorney from Danville with liberal, anti-Martin leanings, was endorsed for attorney general.

Up to this point the Roanoke gathering represented, on balance, a victory for free silver, political reform, and opponents of Senator Martin. But when it came to the platform, the Martin forces refused to budge from the traditional strategy of emphasizing national concerns and playing down state issues. Delegates endorsed radical stands on free silver, a federal income tax, and trust regulation but failed to express their views concerning the need for honest elections in Virginia. When liberals attempted to commit the party to the nomination of U.S. senators by preferential primaries, the conservatives shouted them down. The "Bryanization" of the Virginia Democracy obviously had its limits. Free silver was one thing—the political "loaves and fishes" something else.

Although divided on the question of preferential primaries, Old Dominion Democrats stood solidly behind Tyler's gubernatorial candidacy, and he won easily. The Republicans offered only token opposition in the form of mercurial Patrick H. ("Little Pat") McCaull of Culpeper County—a veteran of the debt struggles of the previous decade. Maintaining party unity by stressing national issues, Tyler rolled to victory, 109,655 to 58,860. The Democrats also elected all of the state senators and 94 of 100 House members. Nevertheless, no one was quite certain whether these men were conservatives or reformers. As events would show, most were Martinites.

Tyler's inaugural address consisted largely of a generalized attack on federal economic policies, corporate influence in politics, high taxes, and bureaucratic waste of public funds. These were traditional agrarian complaints, and it was not surprising that the "farmer's friend" should voice them. By way of contrast (and perhaps as a concession to conservatives), he offered no specific suggestions for dealing with these problems at the state level. In short, the new governor hit all of the right chords in his effort to promote party harmony, but not very distinctly, and the result sounded more like commentary than a call to action.

Perhaps fortunately for Tyler, events in Cuba dominated the first months of 1898, and he soon was immersed in the problems of mobilization for the Spanish-American War. On April 25 Tyler issued a call for 3,000 volunteers which was answered by five times that number. The first units to depart were white, but a subsequent decision to federalize black militiamen under the command of their black officers met with some criticism, the influential Richmond *Dispatch* speaking out strongly in protest. Tyler declared that the officers, duly qualified, could not be removed solely on the basis of color. Rallying support for his stand, the governor consulted with Virginia's senators and congressmen and reported that they agreed with his position, although several of them later charged that their views had been misrepresented. Nevertheless, on June 29, 1898, two black battalions and their black officers were mustered into federal service as part of Virginia's second quota. On this issue, at least, Tyler had taken a stand based on principle instead of expediency—with positive results.

Official preoccupation with the war left little time for political intrigue in 1898, but antagonisms within the Old Dominion's Democratic hierarchy came to the fore during the following year when Martin's critics mounted a major effort to defeat him. On May 10, 1899, some eight hundred Democrats, representing almost every county and city, met in Richmond's Academy of Music to endorse election of U.S. senators by the people, not the state legislature. The organizers of this independent outburst (the "May Movement") were William A. Jones, First District congressman from Warsaw; Attorney General Montague; and William A. Anderson, a well-known Lexington lawyer. The gathering was marked by fiery and idealistic demands for a variety of reforms, but the central objective was obvious to all: the dissidents were determined to unseat Martin, and they believed that the people would support them if allowed to vote on the matter.

Popular opinion may well have favored the independents at the time of their Richmond meeting, but they squandered their opportunity by pursuing a wavering and vacillating course. They failed to nominate a candidate to oppose Martin, agreeing instead to petition the Democratic state central committee (which the senator controlled) to order nominations by preferential primary. On July 12, 1899, the committee rejected this proposal, predictably enough, whereupon Jones—the obvious choice to run against Martin—declared that he would not do so.

At this juncture, Governor Tyler made the most momentous political decision of his career. Although he had remained aloof from previous maneuvers against the senator, he announced that he himself would run against Martin. Just why is not entirely clear. Perhaps Tyler overestimated his popularity as a result of the landslide victory of 1897; perhaps key members of the fast-evaporating May Movement convinced him to play the role of sacrificial lamb. Motivated, it would appear, by a lethal amalgam of vaulting ambition and political naiveté, Tyler set off—as he had so often before—down the road to defeat. Without an effective organization, he attempted an almost single-handed fight against the powerful Martin machine. J. Taylor Ellyson, Tyler's adversary in 1897 and still party chairman, quickly engineered "snap" regional conventions that met and chose candidates for the upcoming General Assembly races before the governor knew what was happening. Ellyson, Henry D. ("Hal") Flood, and other loyal Martin lieutenants dispensed railroad money liberally and, to nail down victory, produced evidence that Tyler, as lieutenant governor, had supported Martin against Fitzhugh Lee in the controversial 1893 senatorial race. The embattled chief executive angrily denied this charge, but the damage had been done. Incensed by such tactics, Tyler refused to campaign any more. On September 29, 1899, the Democratic central committee met, endorsed Martin's legislative nominees, and rejected those favoring the governor. In December the General Assembly (103 to 27) gave Martin his second term in the U.S. Senate.

It would seem that Tyler had followed a very foolish course. He joined the anti-Martin movement too late, launched an ineffectual challenge, and quit in a peevish huff. Yet the governor had won a Pyrrhic victory of sorts since he compelled the Martin forces to resort to the underhanded tactics of 1893 once again, stirring up bitter memories in all parts of the Commonwealth. This, in turn, rekindled popular demands for reform in general and a constitutional convention in particular and also made the gubernatorial nomination of Montague somewhat easier in 1901, at the expense of Martin's handpicked candidate, Claude Swanson. And, when the senator sought reelection in 1905 he would face a party primary; as a result, he would have to give ground on a variety of issues in order to curry popular favor.

Rebuffed in his senatorial campaign, Tyler turned to state issues, and his message to the legislature in December 1899 constituted a wide-ranging agenda for reform. He demanded close supervision of trusts and corporations, suggesting that any corporation whose officers were guilty of vote buying should lose its charter and that those involved face criminal proceedings. Election returns, he stressed, must be fair and accurate. Tyler also recommended, not surprisingly, a statewide primary for federal senate races. Yet he singled out constitutional reform as the single most important item of business. The Underwood Constitution, he informed the lawmakers, was expensive, cumbersome, and Yankee-inspired and should be changed so as to "give us a simple, direct, and successful plan of government." He suggested that reform of the document could be accomplished through amendment, convention, or legislative joint committee. Fearful the Martinites might seize control of a constitutional convention, Tyler actually favored the joint committee approach, the least expensive method.

The governor had pointed to the need for revision of the Commonwealth's fundamental law, but after this initial gesture he exerted little influence on the movement leading to the Constitution of 1902. Determined to protect their remaining political rights, Republicans of both races opposed any change, as did various courthouse cliques and corporate executives who feared infringements on their privileges and prerogatives. The Martin organization was divided on the issue. The senator and Claude Swanson, his foremost lieutenant, instinctively opposed a convention, while organization stalwarts such as John W. Daniel, Hal Flood, and J. Taylor Ellyson favored it. This split allowed independent Democrats to exercise unusual influence. Drawing their support primarily from middle-class, urban-oriented professionals and businessmen, these dissidents emerged as the driving force in the crusade for constitutional change.

In March 1900 the General Assembly authorized a referendum, and two months later the Democratic state convention in Norfolk agreed—with the important reservations that no citizen (or his descendants) who had been eligible to vote in 1861 should be disfranchised and that the new constitution would be submitted to the people for ratification. On May 24, backed by nearly all leading newspapers, the constitutional convention won voter approval, 77,363 to 60,375. This outcome, sanctioned by less than a third of the electorate, was achieved largely in the cities; majorities in 52 of 100 counties rejected this proposal, 25 of them west of the Blue Ridge where blacks were few in number.

Seven months later a special session of the General Assembly determined that the convention would consist of 100 members, one from each House of Delegates district. In rather listless proceedings 88 Democrats and 12 Republicans were elected on May 23, 1901, 10 of the minority coming from the western part of the Old Dominion. Yet the group that convened in the House of Delegates on June 12 included some of the state's best minds: Senator Daniel, former Governor William E. Cameron, railroad attorney Alfred P. Thom, ex-Senator Eppa Hunton, Jr., Henry C. Stuart, R. Walton Moore, A. Caperton Braxton, William A. Anderson, elder statesman John Goode, and Carter Glass, the Lynchburg newsman who would play a key role in the deliberations that followed. The convention was composed of sixty-two lawyers, twenty-one farmers, and an assortment of merchants, ministers, and bankers. Independent-minded Democrats claimed a majority, but actual control was rendered uncertain by the presence of a number of individuals with no distinct ties to either camp within the party.

There was general agreement that the main purpose of this gathering was to end fraudulent manipulation of the black vote, and recent Supreme Court decisions concerning Negro political rights in the Deep South appeared to open the door to such provisions. Even so, no one was quite sure how it should be done. After prolonged and intense debate the suffrage article was finally adopted on April 4, 1902, by a vote of 67 to 28. It provided for the creation of two lists of voters, a "permanent" roll to be prepared before January 1, 1904, and another to be compiled and maintained after that date. The permanent list included Confederate and Union veterans and their sons, those who paid property taxes of $1.00 or more, individuals who could read and explain any part of the constitution, and illiterates who could give a "reasonable" explanation of constitutional provisions read to them by local officials. Registration was restricted to male citizens of the United States—at least twenty-one years of age—who could satisfy certain residency requirements. All voters except veterans had to pay a poll tax (originally $4.50) at least six months before any election in which they wished to participate.

These complex hurdles—complex for those who opposed the Democrats, simple enough for those who did not—quickly eliminated Republican opposition in most of Virginia, particularly in the predominantly black counties of the Southside and Tidewater. Indeed, these suffrage barriers reduced the electorate to such manageable proportions that the Martin organization and its successor, the Byrd machine, had things much their own way for the next half-century. Only stirrings outside the Old Dominion and demands created by World War II at last ended the long, lazy summer of conservative somnolence. In 1900 some 147 votes were cast by each 1,000 Virginians, but in the next three presidential elections voter participation plunged to about 67 per 1,000. Only in 1928 did returns equal those of 1888, despite a steadily increasing population and the addition of women to the electorate. The 1900 Democratic state convention had promised that no whites would be deprived of their votes, but the election returns bore eloquent testimony that this pledge had not been honored. Tens of thousands of illiterate, impoverished, or apathetic whites (along with the overwhelming majority of blacks) had been effectively excluded from the political process.

The second most important feature of the new constitution, the establishment of the State Corporation Commission, was the brainchild of A. Caperton Braxton. This tactful, astute lawyer-businessman from Staunton was neither an independent nor a machine man, but he knew what he wanted and finally prevailed. His goal was the creation of an agency to supervise all corporate activity within the Commonwealth. Especially wary of railroad influence in the convention, he conducted a very cautious campaign and eventually—with powerful public support—won most of the delegates to his side.

Under the new constitution the governor remained relatively weak, although he gained increased appointive power and the right to veto individual items in appropriations bills. The old county courts were replaced by circuit courts, a change which meant the demise of the traditional monthly court day, long a time for shopping, gossiping, carousing, and petty business deals. Elimination of the county judge also served to circumscribe the prerogatives of the semiautonomous courthouse cliques; henceforth—even more than in the past—true power would rest with the General Assembly and with those who controlled it, the leaders of the Democratic organization.

Having already violated the Democratic party's pledge not to disfranchise any white voters, at the urging of the Martin forces the convention broke yet another commitment by proclaiming the new constitution to be the law of the Commonwealth instead of submitting it to a popular vote. Disgruntled Republicans challenged this maneuver in the courts, but the federal judiciary upheld the convention's stand. John C. Underwood's Reconstruction-era handiwork was relegated to the dustbin of history, replaced by the Constitution of 1902, a curious blend of reaction and reform.

By the time the convention's work was done, James Hoge Tyler was a private citizen, having been succeeded in office by his attorney general, Andrew Jackson Montague. In January 1902 the Richmond *Times* struggled manfully to say something concrete about "Governor Tyler's Record." The best its editor could do—the *Dispatch* was silent on this matter—was to conclude that the ex-governor was scrupulously honest, enjoyed the respect and goodwill of most Virginians, and was a cordial gentleman who, as first citizen, always maintained close contact with the people. "We would say," the *Times* continued, "that the most prominent characteristic of Governor Tyler's administration has been kindness." This analysis also provides a clue to Tyler's fatal weakness: he was a "kindly" man who wanted to be liked more than he wanted to be a true leader who had to make decisions, enforce party discipline, and perhaps create enemies.

The ex-governor retired to his Radford estate where he spent the remaining twenty-four years of his life, busying himself with various enterprises and dabbling in politics. Clinging to his antimachine principles, Tyler never backed any gubernatorial candidate clearly in the Martin camp. He continued to cherish ambitions for high office, particularly for the federal Senate seat which had eluded him in 1899, but the knock of political opportunity never came; as a result the old-time silverite and "farmer's friend" gradually withdrew into the dignified obscurity of private life and personal affairs. He died in 1925 at the age of seventy-nine.

Viewed within the context of his times, James Hoge Tyler was an estimable man with excellent personal qualities who lacked the organizational skills and the conscienceless determination necessary for sustained success in Virginia politics. Although popular with the rural masses, he was strangely out of place in an era dominated by political rings, railroad money, and chicanery at the polls. As a result, he experienced far more setbacks than victories. Elevated to the governorship in 1897 because of a fortuitous association with free silver, he soon squandered his effectiveness in a futile clash with the machine that had permitted his election in the first place. A contradictory figure, he sought reform but remained at heart a Democratic regular, even though his party was controlled by men whose methods he abhorred. Tyler was ambitious, but never ruthless—at a time when only ruthlessness could have produced lasting results. In the final analysis he really was no threat to Senator Martin and of little use to Martin's foes.

SOURCES

The James Hoge Tyler Papers (7,000 items), discovered in 1967 at Halwick, are at the library of Virginia Polytechnic Institute and State University. Most of the material deals with his political career, 1890–1901.

A detailed bibliography can be found in Thomas E. Gay, Jr., "The Life and Political Career of J. Hoge Tyler, Governor of Virginia, 1898–1902" (Ph.D. diss., University of Virginia, 1969). See also Allen W. Moger's *Virginia: Bourbonism to Byrd, 1870–1925* (Charlottesville, 1968) and his articles: "The Origin of the Democratic Machine in Virginia," *Journal of Southern History* 8 (1942): 183–209; "The Rift in the Virginia Democracy in 1896," *Journal of Southern History* 4 (1938): 295–317; and "Virginia's Conservative Political Tradition," *South Atlantic Quarterly* 50 (July 1951): 318–29. In addition, see Raymond H. Pulley, *Old Virginia Restored: An Interpretation of the Progressive Impulse, 1870–1930* (Charlottesville, 1968); Herman Lionel Horn, "The Growth and Development of the Democratic Party in Virginia since 1890" (Ph.D. diss., Duke University, 1949); and George M. McFarland, "Extension of Democracy in Virginia, 1880–1895" (Ph.D. diss., Princeton University, 1934).

ANDREW JACKSON MONTAGUE

Governor of Virginia

1902–1906

ANDREW JACKSON MONTAGUE

Virginia's First Progressive

William Larsen

Only thirty-nine years of age at his inauguration, Andrew Jackson Montague was the first governor since the Civil War without Confederate service. He rose to power as a charismatic reformer, advocating good schools, good roads, democratization of government, and an end to political corruption. The crusade he helped lead can be described as the Virginia phase of the national Progressive movement.

Montague grew to manhood amid conservative, traditionalist influences in the Virginia Tidewater where his ancestors had lived since the seventeenth century. His father, Robert Latane Montague, elected lieutenant governor in 1859, was an early advocate of secession. Three years later, his wife, Gay Eubank Montague, having fled their Middlesex County home because of the war, gave birth to their second son in Campbell County on October 3, 1862. The name given the infant, Andrew Jackson, was that of an uncle recently slain in the conflict then raging. After the war, the family returned to Inglewood, a large frame house located on a bluff overlooking the Rappahannock River, where his father, an unrepentant rebel, managed a modest living as a farmer-lawyer and continued a minor political role as a Middlesex County legislator and judge.

Young Jack performed ordinary farm chores and in his quiet Tidewater environment became an avid reader. According to a notebook in which he listed his books, fiction dominated his early reading (especially sea tales and pirate adventures). At the age of nine, Jack began his formal education, attending schools in Middlesex and Williamsburg and also being tutored at home. He soon matured into a serious, sometimes moody young man with quick wit, a penchant for storytelling, and a volatile temper. Inwardly, he tended to be pessimistic and slightly introverted; outwardly, he was cheerful, gracious, and assertive. When full grown he stood five feet, ten inches and (though of large frame) in youth weighed only 150 pounds. His most prominent features were an oval face, a small, amiable mouth, a straight nose, clear blue eyes, and flaming red hair—altogether an appearance labeled handsome by early acquaintances.

Robert Montague died in 1880, and shortly thereafter Jack, then eighteen, enrolled in Richmond College, a Baptist institution located in Virginia's capital. The two years spent there developed his social and leadership capacities as well as his intellect. He helped edit the literary magazine, joined a social fraternity and a literary and debating society, and won top honors for his oratorical skills, selected by the society to be its commencement orator in 1882.

Following graduation, he became a private tutor for two years in Orange County where he instructed a half-dozen pupils in Latin, French, mathematics, and history. During these years Montague also developed a serious interest in Elizabeth Lyne Hoskins, daughter of a King and Queen County family. Six years younger than her future husband, Betsie had a gregarious, sparkling spontaneity which counterbalanced Montague's serious and somewhat shy disposition. But before marrying his fianceé, Jack was determined to be in a position to support her in proper style. Just three weeks after they were engaged in 1884, he enrolled in the law school of the University of Virginia. Though his classes were temporarily interrupted by the death of his invalid mother, he managed to complete his degree in July 1885. Three months later he established himself in the Southside town of Danville where he quickly developed a successful law practice. His oratorical prowess, first recognized at Richmond College, proved a powerful asset. After he successfully defended an accused murderer in 1888, Jack wrote Betsie, "I not only carried many of the people in the audience from laughter, to serious thought and then to tears. . . . The jury wept." Indeed, one of the jurors later announced that his next son would bear Montague's name.

In 1889 Montague obtained the prestigious position of local attorney for the Richmond and Danville Railroad (later part of the Southern Railway system). This gave him not only financial stability but contacts with other railroad lawyers around the state, a professional and political asset. On December 11, 1889, Jack and Betsie were finally married at her Tidewater home; a brief New York honeymoon followed. (They would have three children: Gay in 1891, Janet in 1895, and Robert Latane in 1897.) Even before marriage, Montague had launched his political career, becoming a local Democratic campaigner and an office seeker as well.

Though narrowly defeated in a race against Danville's incumbent Commonwealth's attorney in 1888, Montague persisted, and in 1892 his efforts were rewarded by appointment to the state Democratic executive committee. In the elections that year, he toured the state, extolling Cleveland's virtues and speaking in behalf of Claude A. Swanson, the youthful Democratic nominee for Congress. The following year he became U.S. district attorney for Western Virginia. Both his professional and political aspirations had been realized, and a public career of forty years' duration had begun. Throughout it all, the most persistent theme in Montague's public commentaries was his characterization of the Democratic party as the party of humanism and the Republican party as the party of materialism.

Privately, however, the emerging politician was disturbed by corruption within his own party, especially the influence of railroad lawyer-lobbyist Thomas S. Martin and his rise to the U.S. Senate. Yet in 1896, along with most Virginia Democrats, he joined Martin and the silver cause and supported its national champion, William Jennings Bryan. During the ensuing campaign, Montague delivered at least twenty speeches for Bryan and silver. Proclaiming the cause of silver to be the cause of the people, he avowed that "if standing for the rights of the people be anarchy then I am an anarchist." The conservative college student had traveled a long way, at least rhetorically.

It is impossible to determine Montague's private views on silver. Conceivably, he broke publicly with goldbug Grover Cleveland (and risked losing his job as district attorney) mainly to advance his political ambitions. In the spring of 1896 he had already consulted friends about running for attorney general of Virginia, and they had encouraged him to do so. Eventually, six candidates entered the race, all of them possessing acceptable silverite credentials.

At the 1897 Democratic state convention in Roanoke factional alignments took shape that would persist for two decades or more. Montague, clearly identified with those opposed to Martin, on the third ballot won a narrow victory in his race for the attorney general nomination. His strongest backing came from the Danville area, southwest Virginia (part of his circuit as district attorney), and Richmond. Montague easily defeated token Republican opposition in the general election. At the age of thirty-five, only twelve years out of law school, he had become the Old Dominion's preeminent lawyer, a tribute to his personal magnetism, abilities, and political acumen.

Meanwhile, the lines of division in Virginia politics were becoming ever more clearly defined. At Roanoke, Congressman William A. Jones introduced a resolution to establish the preferential primary method of nominating Democratic candidates for the U.S. Senate. Montague supported the move, obviously a rebuke to Martin, whose election by the Assembly four years earlier remained controversial. Agitation over the direct primary should be viewed as the first important catalyst producing a coterie of antimachine progressives within the Virginia Democratic party.

Martin and his allies managed to derail the primary proposal in 1897, but in 1899 the progressive element tried again, this time organizing a May conference of primary supporters. Montague took a prominent role in this "May Movement," but the Democratic state committee refused the conference's request for a primary, and Martin went on to win election a second time by vote of the legislature.

Another developing issue that united the progressives (and which attracted some machine men, too) was the simultaneous movement for a constitutional convention. This movement encompassed many objectives, including the reduction of governmental expenses, but its central aim was the elimination of Negro suffrage—thus striking, thought the progressives, at vote buying and other political corruption. Attorney General Montague ardently backed the movement, while Senator Martin maintained a passive silence. The voters narrowly approved calling a convention, and delegates were elected early in 1901.

Both the disfranchisement and primary reform movements were provoked by the same concern—corruption in politics. But it remains to be explained why Montague and others should articulate this reform impulse around 1900 instead of earlier or later. The answer lies mainly in shifting patterns of racial tension and antagonism. The turmoil of Reconstruction, Readjusterism, and Populism behind them (divisions among whites that could increase Negro political influence) and encouraged by recent U.S. Supreme Court decisions, Virginia whites now felt free to impose their racial settlement without threat of outside interference. Intraparty divisions thus became less dangerous, allowing progressive elements increased opportunity to plead their case.

Other turn-of-the-century factors also tended to increase political flexibility. Genuine economic prosperity brought a revival of collective self-confidence; the state proudly contributed men in 1898 to the war against Spain, an act of emotional catharsis from the lingering bitterness of the Civil War; and finally many young Virginians who had matured since Appomattox, free of any stigma attached to sectional origins, felt ready to play a part in the nation's councils.

In advocating disfranchisement in 1900 and 1901, Montague, as a practical politician, employed the typical demagogic litany of white supremacy. But he was not a racist of the "red-neck" stripe and, unlike some contemporaries, viewed disfranchisement as a temporary expedient. With improved education, he insisted, an enlightened and incorruptible Negro electorate would eventually develop. In the meantime, relieved from negrophobia, white Virginians could engage in healthy political division on issues of substance, which in turn would bring internal progress and enhance the state's importance in national politics.

On January 19, 1901, the ambitious attorney general announced that he would personally canvass the state in his quest for the gubernatorial nomination, appealing directly to the voters on specific issues; heretofore Democratic candidates had for the most part refrained from preconvention campaigning. Montague's innovation thus added another democratic dimension to Virginia progressivism. Alarmed by Montague's evident popularity, Martin and his cohorts rallied behind Congressman Swanson. Swanson and Montague had maintained an uneasy alliance from 1892 through the 1897 convention, but by 1900, Swanson clearly was identified with the Martin group.

As the 1901 campaign got under way, Montague unveiled a reform platform endorsing disfranchisement, good schools, good roads, and an employer's liability bill. When Senator Martin and several congressmen openly backed Swanson, Montague retaliated by accusing Martin of ring rule and political corruption. He also reiterated his call for a primary to guarantee that in the future no man would hold office against the will of the people.

Support for Montague initially came from educators, labor unions, and moralists distressed by political corruption. He charmed thousands more with his oratorical flourishes and personal charisma, and the press affectionately dubbed him "the Red Fox of Middlesex," a nickname earlier bestowed upon his father. Progressive Virginians viewed Montague as a man capable of returning Virginia's statesmanship to the elevated levels of the nostalgic past, and Montague deliberately evoked such historical pride. In preacher fashion, Montague the reformer waxed most eloquent when excoriating corrupt politics and machine rule. Speaking at Roanoke, he declared, "I would rather be defeated a thousand times by the 'bosses' than elected by them." At Richmond he struck a similar chord: "Indifference to dirty politics prolongs dirty politics . . . I wish every man and boy could come to look with horror upon the man who holds office against the wish of the people."

Montague and Swanson met in joint debate at Boydton on May 20 where Montague repeated his charge that Martin's organization exerted an unhealthy influence in Virginia affairs. The attorney general's crusading platform was so well attuned to the progressive mood of the day that Swanson swung belatedly to endorse primary reform and the employer's liability principle. But Montague had wider recognition than the congressman, and a groundswell of support developed as the various cities and counties (some of them using the primary method) selected convention delegates. Long before the Democrats met in August, Montague had cinched the nomination. The convention ratified the fait accompli, then went on to write a progressive platform endorsing the liability principles and adopting the primary method of nominating all future Democratic candidates for statewide offices.

In the fall election Montague defeated the Republican candidate, J. Hampton Hoge, by a three-to-two margin, narrower than the Democratic victory four years earlier. Two factors explain this difference: the bitter intraparty fight before the nomination and the uncertainties concerning disfranchisement aroused by the constitutional convention then in session. Soon after Montague's inauguration early in 1902 the constitutional convention concluded its deliberations. The new constitution included poll taxes and literacy tests as the method of restricting the suffrage. More clearly evincing the progressive spirit of the new century, the constitution also established the employer's liability principle and created a strong State Corporation Commission empowered to set railroad rates, assess corporate properties for tax purposes, and regulate and supervise business activities.

As Montague had hoped, the abatement of racial antagonisms following disfranchisement appears to have encouraged reform ferment in other directions. The best evidence of this political chemistry at work—and the governor's most important contribution to the reform spirit—was the rapid growth of the good schools movement. White illiteracy had increased in Virginia following the Civil War, and as late as 1900 Negro illiteracy remained at about 50 percent. Elementary schools typically met for only brief terms, few high schools existed, and compulsory education was unknown. Similar conditions prevailed across the South, sparking an educational crusade beginning about 1900; this crusade was labeled the Ogden movement in honor of Robert C. Ogden, its chief northern philanthropist and organizer.

Montague soon established contacts with Ogden and his local agents. Just three days after taking office, the new governor met in Richmond with a group of educators to discuss ways to arouse public interest in the plight of the schools. Thereafter, he spoke at scores of gatherings of educators and laymen in Virginia and elsewhere, advocating increased funding, longer terms, and better teacher training. Early in 1903 he startled a conference of Virginia school superintendents by subtly supporting the concept of compulsory education, a concept opposed by whites in counties with large Negro populations. That same year, at the governor's invitation, a general southern conference on education met in Richmond, adding still more impetus to the movement. By early 1904 Montague was able to report to the General Assembly some concrete progress—increased local funding, school consolidation, lengthened terms, and higher teachers' salaries.

In March 1904 Virginia's educational reformers created the statewide Co-operative Education Commission, with Governor Montague serving as chairman of its executive board. The commission endeavored to establish local branch leagues throughout the state. To this end, the group resolved at its first annual convention (December 1904) to ask the governor and Edwin A. Alderman, the president of the University of Virginia, to lead a statewide speaking campaign the following May with the objective of holding an "all-day meeting in every county" during that month. The May Campaign succeeded beyond expectations. Coinciding opportunely with the state's 1905 nomination struggles for the legislature and statewide offices, the movement elicited the support of politicians who had heretofore remained aloof or indifferent. Because Montague was clearly the crusade's political leader, Senator Martin viewed the whole business skeptically and at one time privately dismissed the good schools rhetoric as so much "hot air." But in 1905 Martin himself was running for reelection against Montague, so he, too, consented to make a few addresses at educational meetings.

Next to good schools, Governor Montague emphasized the need for good roads. By 1900 the state had a good railway network—but few paved highways. Construction and maintenance of roads remained a purely local affair. Both in his 1897 and 1901 campaigns Montague called for improved highways as a means of removing "a social and industrial blockade" to Virginia's progress. As governor, Montague performed essentially the same oratorical mission for the good roads movement as he did for good schools. From 1902 until 1905 he spoke at numerous good roads conventions throughout the Commonwealth, and organizations were intermittently formed on both the state and local levels. The governor also attended and spoke at conventions of the National Good Roads Association and served on the group's advisory committee.

In the first year of his governorship, Montague laid before the legislature a comprehensive highway program calling for creation of a state highway commission, financial aid to localities on a matching basis, state guarantees of local road bond issues, and the use of convict labor for road maintenance. In 1902 and 1903 the Assembly defeated most of the bills incorporating these ideas but did approve issuance of county road bonds. Frustrated by the legislature, Montague and others took the cause into the 1905 electoral arena, with results similar to those achieved by the education drive the same year. Just before leaving office early in 1906, the governor once again presented his highway program, with some modifications, to the newly elected Assembly. Two months after Montague's term ended, the legislature created the State Highway Commission and made state convict road gangs available to individual counties.

The growth of the good schools and good roads movements revealed Montague's adeptness as a statesman and reformer—his evangelical ability to arouse public opinion. On the stump he had no peer in Virginia. In these respects he closely resembled his progressive counterpart on the national level, President Theodore Roosevelt. Yet Montague displayed a strange attitude toward getting his programs enacted. He once told the delegate heading the fight to create a highway commission: "My position as Governor prevents my interceding with members of the legislature in behalf of any measure." He also had a stock reply whenever reporters asked him about legislative issues: "I do not think I should undertake to favor in advance bills which are likely to come before me for approval or disapproval."

Although the governor generally did not see fit to meddle in the legislative process, he had no compunction about urging friends of the primary to run in the 1903 legislative elections. Some were successful. One such ally introduced into the 1904 Assembly a bill to require the primary for all Democratic nominations. Versions of the bill passed both houses, but in conference a Martinite filibustered the measure to death in the waning hours of the session. Meanwhile, Montague endeavored to ensure that proprimary delegates were elected to the 1904 state Democratic convention. He had little apparent success except in Richmond, and Martin's forces dominated the convention. By now, however, the primary had become a permanent fixture, and the senator acknowledged that fact by personally introducing the motion adopted by the convention that reaffirmed the primary principle.

The stage was now set for the 1905 senatorial race between Martin and Montague. As early as 1902 Montague had determined to make the race, but not until mid-1904 had other progressives (including ex-Governor James Hoge Tyler and Congressman Jones) somewhat reluctantly withdrawn, leaving Montague as Martin's sole opponent. Both candidates entered the campaign with assets. The governor had proven electability, personal magenetism, and a reputation as a reformer. The senator had political organization, superior financial resources, and, most important of all, the advantage of incumbency.

Montague attempted to capitalize upon his progressive image by contrasting his vigorous endorsement of good schools, good roads, and the employer's liability principle with Martin's conservatism. Most of all, he stressed the issue of the primary itself, reminding voters in Virginia's first popular senatorial election that Martin had attempted to prevent adoption of the democratic process in which they were about to participate. On the national level, Montague advocated tariff reduction, railroad rate regulation, and elimination of business contributions to political parties. He characterized Martin as essentially a Republican in Democratic garb who favored business interests over popular rights. From the beginning, the governor also charged that Martin had failed to provide creative statesmanship for Virginia in the Senate, instead performing the prosaic duties of a "department-runner" or errand boy for his constituents. As for Martin's political organization, the governor lambasted it as a private government "of friends, by friends, and for friends."

Martin at first declined to attack Montague directly, instead defending himself as an effective, practical, hardworking senator. He soon came out for good schools, good roads, and the employer's liability doctrine on the national level. He managed to ignore the primary issue for several months before he admitted having opposed the reform in 1897; to minimize the political damage of this admission, however, he falsely claimed to have favored the primary since that time. As the campaign shifted into high gear, the vitriol flowed from both camps, and Martin labeled Montague's lambasts against his organization as "cry-baby talk of a machine to hide the only real machine that exists"—namely Montague's. The two once met in joint debate, and (according to most accounts) Martin surprisingly held his own against the man reputed to be his oratorical superior.

In the August balloting, Martin defeated Montague easily, garnering 56 percent of the total vote. The embittered governor privately blamed corruption, but it is doubtful that corruption alone explains the margin of victory. Basically, Montague lost because Martin adopted the governor's positions on all the popular issues of the day. Other factors contributing to the outcome included Montague's personal assaults on Martin's mundane statesmanship (which offended Virginia's gentlemanly electorate) and his inability to maintain unity within the anti-Martin camp, a definite failure of leadership. Ironically, disfranchisement also contributed to Montague's defeat. Virginia's voting population, white and black, had been halved after 1902, and in this reduced electorate Martin's cadre of loyal courthouse followers naturally exerted greater weight.

After 1905 the Martin machine virtually monopolized Virginia's politics, but this did not mean a return to political conservatism. Though defeated and outnumbered, the progressive clique, Montague among them, remained a reasonably coherent and articulate minority for years and continued to apply pressure. In a very real way, Montague won the war while losing his personal battle. Put another way, Martin and his organization—however slowly and reluctantly—gradually turned progressive after 1900, especially in the Wilson years. Montague and other Virginia progressives supported Wilson's prenomination candidacy in 1911 and 1912, while Martin's group did not. After 1913, however, both factions gave unstinting backing to Wilson's progressive program. Thus, with factional distinctions blurred, Swanson (appointed to the Senate upon the death of Daniel in 1910) and Martin would win reelection to the U.S. Senate without opposition; the machine appeared impregnable.

Montague's career after 1905 was anticlimatic. He taught law for a time at his alma mater, the University of Richmond, and in 1912 he ousted the incumbent to win election to the U.S. House of Representatives from the Richmond district. As congressman, he joined other Virginians in defending Wilson's progressive program, at times piloting minor pieces of legislation through the House. He hoped for appointment to the U.S. Supreme Court, but when his name was advanced by political allies in 1916, the opposition of Senators Martin and Swanson spiked whatever chances he may have had.

Montague remained in Congress for a quarter of a century, but he lacked influence after the Wilson years. A Wilsonian internationalist, he felt out of step during the Republican domination of the 1920s and was not in line for a committee chairmanship when the Democrats returned to power in 1930. He was, nevertheless, respected by colleagues for his lucid mind and courtly manner. In his last years, because of his position on the Judiciary Committee and his personal bearing, he acquired the appellation "Judge." Growing conservative with age, he gave Roosevelt's New Deal only limited support. He voted for the Social Security Act in 1935, but he opposed establishing the Works Progress Administration and the Tennessee Valley Authority, the latter on constitutional grounds. Several secondary accounts maintain that Montague, like most antimachine leaders, eventually made peace with the organization, but no evidence has been discovered to support this contention. When Martin died in 1919, Montague evidently remained silent. In the 1920s and early 1930s he avoided factional fights, but there is some indication that he was not highly regarded by the Byrd machine.

In 1936 Montague, now in failing health and running for a thirteenth term in Congress, faced his first significant opposition since 1912. Rallying his stored reserves of oratorical fire, he fought back and won a narrow victory. But the fight was too much for a man of seventy-five. The Red Fox of Middlesex died on January 24, 1937.

Few Virginia governors since the Civil War have had the breadth of cultivated learning, the largeness of vision, or the power of eloquence that Montague possessed. Throughout his life he retained a love of books; his intellectual interests encompased a wide diversity of subjects and earned him two honorary doctorates from American universities. An English acquaintance once commented to his wife, "Your husband's mind is like a well-ordered desk; he can reach up to any pigeonhole, and take down any subject he wants." This mind and these interests, combined with Montague's personal charm and magnetism, offered promise of a brilliant and productive career.

Thwarted in his highest ambition, Montague played a prominent role only as governor, performing creditably in promoting the crusades for schools, roads, and the senatorial primary. As a vigorous progressive, challenging the right of the dominant organization to govern the Commonwealth, he also rendered service vital to democracy itself—that of promoting political dissent. As a catalytic agent, he helped force the Martin machine to shift its ideological base—making it more representative and responsive to Virginia's needs.

To the end, Montague retained his idealism, sentiment, and scholarly bent. But he lost his enthusiasm and ambition. In the words of Colgate Darden, a congressional colleague, "Some of the fire and daring which according to all accounts so marked him in the early days had given way to a philosophical detachment and serenity which made him most attractive." Montague the elder statesman never found complete satisfaction in the House. When assured by friends that he had done his state honor through his performance there, he shook his head and declared: "No, the House is too large for a man to do anything. In the Senate it is different." "In his own heart," as Douglas Southall Freeman wrote, "he felt that circumstance, a subtle conspirator against man's wisest planning, had thwarted him. Perhaps it had . . . but it never could sour the sweetness of his spirit."

SOURCES

The best manuscript collections for the period are the Montague Papers (Virginia State Library); the William A. Jones Papers (University of Virginia); and the Henry D. Flood Papers (Library of Congress). Montague's daughter, Gay Montague Moore of Gloucester County, Virginia, possesses a collection of personal papers which are especially valuable for her father's early years.

For a full-length biography of Montague, see William Larsen, *Montague of Virginia: The Making of a Southern Progressive* (Baton Rouge,

La., 1965). A broader interpretation of Virginia's progressive movement is available in Raymond H. Pulley, *Old Virginia Restored: An Interpretation of the Progressive Impulse, 1870–1930* (Charlottesville, 1968). Allen W. Moger's *Virginia: From Bourbonism to Byrd, 1870–1925* (Charlottesville, 1968) is also very good for the Montague years.

CLAUDE A. SWANSON

Governor of Virginia

1906–1910

CLAUDE AUGUSTUS SWANSON

"Fully Concur and Cordially Co-operate"

Henry C. Ferrell, Jr.

Late in the afternoon of January 31, 1910, amid grit, machinery, and dusty timbers forming the lower level of the Governor's Mansion, tall, dark-eyed Claude Swanson, a few weeks shy of his forty-eighth birthday, instructed shorter, white-thatched William Hodges Mann in the art of obtaining a proper draw from the balky furnace that heated the drafty house. Pointing out gears and cables to his successor, Swanson demonstrated not only an inquisitive intelligence that penetrated to the heart of matters but also the simplicity that had adorned his governorship. A cynical observer might have noted the appropriateness of the scene, for Swanson had acquired a reputation as a master political wire-puller. Yet more than mere manipulation had been required of this Pittsylvania native to achieve the most effective gubernatorial record since the Civil War.

Born on March 31, 1862, the third son of John Muse and Catherine Pritchett Swanson, he entered a family whose forebears during the 1760s had settled in Pittsylvania County, invested in tobacco, and obtained considerable political influence. Raised a Methodist—a lifelong affiliation—he was educated at a private academy, attended Virginia Agricultural and Mechanical College, graduated from Randolph-Macon, and in 1886 received a law degree from the University of Virginia. During these years young Claude worked in the fields, taught school, clerked in nearby Danville, and edited a Democratic newspaper, the *Hanover and Caroline News*. He then practiced law in Chatham, maintaining and renewing acquaintances with local and state Democratic leaders. In the process, he developed a proficiency in the spoken word and a disciplined mind that permitted him to concentrate his angular, sinewy body upon vast amounts of work.

In 1892, at the age of thirty, Swanson won election to Congress from the Fifth Virginia District, composed of Danville and the counties of Pittsylvania, Henry, Franklin, Patrick, Floyd, Carroll, and Grayson. Times were hard, and from the outset he favored an active, concerned government which would aid and sustain the economic endeavors and ambitions of his constituency. During seven terms in the House of Representatives (1893–1906) his basic political stance was derived from party platforms forged in a highly partisan era. In the 1890s, he had to deal with well-organized Republican opposition,

Populists, Prohibitionists, and goldbug national Democrats. In order to survive, Swanson involved himself in the minutia of precinct politics. In 1896 he
endorsed Bryan and emerged as one of the foremost Virginia advocates of free
silver. Ideological adversaries, rather than engage Swanson and his popular
political opinions, accused him of being the epitome of a machine politician,
expedient to a fault; and within the decade, he encountered stiff Republican
opposition in two contested elections.

By 1898 Swanson had mastered the Democratic party within his district
and possessed extensive influence within the state party mechanism, thus
broadening his earlier relationships with Senator Thomas Martin. In 1899
the Southside politico angled for the 1901 Democratic gubernatorial nomination, but his close identification with Martin proved a crippling handicap.
Finally, in 1905 he gained the gubernatorial nomination in Virginia's first
statewide Democratic primary. Defeating Nottoway's William Hodges Mann
and Lieutenant Governor Joseph Willard, a northern Virginia millionaire, by
a clear majority, Swanson united the party to overcome the challenge of
Richmond Republican Lunsford Lewis. In the same year, Martin successfully
repulsed Governor Andrew Jackson Montague's ineffectual senatorial candidacy, and many believed that Martin's muscular machine had eased Swanson's way into the governorship. Such was not the case. Had Swanson faced
only one opponent in the gubernatorial primary his total vote would have
exceeded Martin's senatorial tally by at least 10,000.

Swanson assumed the governorship in 1906 with a specific set of goals.
These included state subsidies to local school districts, increased wages for
teachers, a longer school term, and a single, less expensive book list. Swanson
supported improved roads not only as a means of easier access to rural schools
but to alleviate the harshness of rural life. He proposed financing road improvements with local, state, and federal money. Swanson also favored white
immigration, and he hoped to encourage out-of-state investment. He argued
for lower rail rates from the mountains to the seaboard. Reflecting another of
his concerns, the governor directed the Department of Labor to produce
reliable labor statistics and useful drafts for labor legislation reform. Like all
chief executives of the time, Swanson wanted to increase Confederate pensions. As for patronage, he indicated that he would screen appointments,
making promises to no man; but all other things being equal, he would stand
by his friends. Overall, Swanson promised an "attentive and business-like
administration" that emphasized a concern for rural citizens.

Working to maximize his influence, Swanson appointed to his official
staff men who would obtain the greatest political return. Each appointee
received the rank of colonel, a valued cognomen that would attach to some
appointees for years. These aides were expected to attend the governor on
state occasions and to help him in the more practical work of lobbying the
legislature. His eighteen-member staff included—among others—a delegate

from the city of Richmond, a former mayor of Roanoke, the brother of an influential state senator from Newport News, a future state senator and lieutenant governor, a former state senator from Norfolk, an old college friend who had married a prominent southwestern Virginia woman, and a Petersburg lawyer who was the scion of an influential Southside family. In addition, two close friends—Chatham bank cashier Edwin S. Reid and Pannill Rucker of Martinsville—helped give the group an informal and open air; but Swanson typically considered all members close personal friends. Geographically, his staff represented Big Stone Gap across the lower third of the state to Norfolk and Cape Charles; only a few resided in the lower Valley or northern Virginia. He used these men to flatter and activate that marvelous but contrary body, the General Assembly of Virginia.

In an era when tradition limited federal involvement in social and economic affairs, General Assembly members collectively dominated state government, restraining governors and haphazardly harmonizing the divisive effects of localism. The bicameral body featured a 40-member Senate, peopled with self-assured suzerains from dozens of political enclaves who easily handled transitory governors. On the other hand, the House of Delegates was an exuberant group of 100 representatives, many of whom knew little of legislative decorum and consequently required firm handling by their speaker and senior members. For Swanson to succeed, he would have to court veteran senators; influence, if not control, finance committees of both houses; establish a working relationship with the House speaker; and maintain an effective network of alert legislative associates who would inform him of any untoward movements.

Swanson also was aided by various old friends. Beverly B. Munford, for example, formerly of Chatham and now a prominent member of the Richmond bar, helped open the doors of Richmond power brokers still suspicious of Swanson's earlier Bryanism. But beyond the bankers and lawyers, the mercantile barons and railroad presidents, were the "county" legislators who had grown to know and trust Claude Swanson. His openness and easy grace carried their sometimes barely articulate requests to fruition. To them he was simply "Claude" of the tobacco warehouses and country stores, of the heated August primaries and sweat-stained convention clashes. As their man, Swanson had won them many an improbable victory with his wit and wisdom.

The governor's beautiful wife, Elizabeth Deane Lyons Swanson, whom he had married in 1892, was also an asset. Her father and grandfather both served in state government; and now, during her husband's administration, she hosted President Theodore Roosevelt, William Jennings Bryan, and other notables and also played a prominent role at the 1907 Jamestown Tercentennial.

But Governor Swanson needed more to motivate the General Assembly than association with a benign U.S. senator, a handsome wife, kind feelings, and personal friendships. By cultivating an enlightened local self-interest that would translate into legislative majorities, he gave focus to ill-defined waves of reform enthusiasm. Concern over public education is a case in point. Partly as the result of the demands of Populists, church organizations, professional educators, and campaigns begun by Governor Montague, fifty-two different education bills crowded the legislative agenda in the 1906 session. But such legislative enthusiasm threatened disorder.

No Johnny-come-lately to educational concerns, Swanson waded into this sea of motions and amendments and selected as the "first great need of this state" the enhancement of public primary schools. There followed during the sessions of 1906 and 1908 an orderly series of legislative proposals. First came transformation of one-room school houses into more substantial structures; second, state subsidies to provide adequate salaries and a retirement system to stabilize the teaching profession; third, expanded summer institutes and the establishment at Harrisonburg and Fredericksburg of teacher-training institutions. The legislation to accomplish these goals was followed by the creation of traveling libraries, absorption of the College of William and Mary into the state system, a state-funded educational journal, procedures for rural high school construction, the beginnings of demonstration education, and stricter state regulation of school construction. While the legislature echoed with the huzzahs of victory, however, the state Board of Education, one of the most powerful in the nation, provided a potential barrier to lasting accomplishment.

The board, created by the 1902 constitution, was shaped by the Senate, which quadrennially elected three members from a list of college professors nominated by the trustees of the six public colleges. These professors joined ex officio colleagues—the governor, the attorney general, and the superintendent of public instruction, who chaired the board. Once constituted, the board elected two additional persons, a county and a city superintendent. In 1904, despite legislative requests and Montague's pleas, the board refused to adopt a single book list for public schools, instead allowing localities to select their own texts, presumably a more expensive method. The 1906 legislature purged the board and the new membership soon created a single book list for lower grades, to be extended in 1910 to high schools as well. Finally, in 1909, the board also combined a number of weaker districts into sixteen new districts to be staffed with full-time, competent superintendents. In many districts professionally trained superintendents replaced less able predecessors. Howls of protest arose, and not all of the appointments stuck.

Swanson influenced an intractable State Corporation Commission as well. Before 1906 the commission had reassessed railroad properties for tax purposes, nearly doubling revenue received by the state and localities. Yet the 1906 legislature discovered that this evaluation amounted to only one-third the federal government's estimate. In retaliation the General Assembly passed the Churchman Act, which demanded a flat 2-cents-a-mile passenger rate. The commission refused both the rate act and a petition by Swanson's attorney general for higher appraisals. The Virginia Court of Appeals sustained the commission. Meanwhile, in April 1907 the commission published a uniform freight schedule which erased intrastate sectional discrepancies. The commission also established a compromise passenger schedule which increased rates from 2 to 3½ cents a mile. The railroads protested, and in July 1907 a federal district court enjoined the commission's actions. This news brought Claude Swanson from vacation on Chincoteague Island, armed and primed for a fight.

Upon his return to Richmond, Swanson demanded that the commission publish its new rates, to be effective in October, censured the federal court for overstepping its bounds, and publicly speculated upon the necessity to convene a special session of the legislature. Stunned railroad officials telephoned Martin to restrain the governor and urge Congressman Henry D. Flood to quiet Swanson, who "has been trying to gain a little popularity . . . by very wild declarations." Swanson, in turn, assembled representatives of the major roads to his office and—in a twelve-hour session—convinced them to accept the commission's rate schedule until the Supreme Court might rule. Eventually the court ordered a new hearing before the commission, now graced by yet another Swanson appointee, William H. Rhea. The regulatory body published in 1909 a 2½-cent passenger fare and allowed sale of coupon books with 2-cents-a-mile fares. (Swanson personally preferred a popularly elected commission but was able to influence the agency so as to benefit citizens through higher corporate tax assessments and lower rail rates.)

These maneuvers required considerable political leverage, and Swanson, always the practical reformer, capitalized upon a wave of reformist public opinion. Utilizing his contacts with the legislature, he dissolved and formed new voting blocs as issues arose. The governor kept his inaugural vow "that the best result of legislation, the best administration of government, are obtained when the executive and legislature fully concur and cordially cooperate." But often the issue was not only what should be done but who should do it, as ideas and substances were frequently tied to individuals. In reorganizing the Board of Education to favor the single text list, for example, he removed Lynchburg's superintendent, E. C. ("Ned") Glass, a brother of Congressman Carter Glass, leaving the Glasses "pretty sore." At the same time the General Assembly nominated Senate clerk Joseph Button to head a newly created insurance commission, an adjunct to the Corporation Commission. The Corporation Commission, led by its Montague-appointed chairman, objected to the procedure, preferring to name its own candidate. Since Button had worked closely with Martin and Flood, factional passions mounted. The Virginia Court of Appeals upheld the legislature and forced Button upon the commission. On another occasion the legislature removed a judge who, in addition to having performed a slipshod fashion, had censured Swanson's use of state troops to prevent a lynching, sneering from the bench at the "boy soldiers." Following a legislative investigation Swanson also named a new state librarian and reorganized Eastern State Hospital, where "perfect disorder and chaos" reigned, but none of his appointments drew greater fire than that of William Rhea to the Corporation Commission.

Succeeding his neighbor Henry C. Stuart of southwestern Virginia, Rhea carried with him a reputation as a high-handed, partisan Democrat who had participated in the region's harsh and strife-ridden politics. Republicans and Martin Democrats criticized Rhea, but in a distraught joint session, replete with parliamentary ploys, the Assembly finally gave its approval, 87 to 46. Twenty-three Democrats in addition to the 23 minority party members bucked the governor. Once installed, Rhea proved competent and favored close state control of corporations. Swanson had followed an old Jacksonian principle he often quoted: "He never failed a friend," thereby repaying Rhea's past allegiance as well as recognizing the importance of southwestern Virginia's white votes in the future.

The imperatives of revitalizing a decrepit road system constituted another concern of the Swanson governorship. Although Virginia had earlier supported road and canal construction (as well as the development of railroads), by 1900 free public roads were in ill repair, and toll roads such as the Shenandoah Valley Turnpike were scarcely better. Democratic candidates had expended considerable rhetoric on the need for good roads, but it remained for Claude Swanson's administration to provide the leadership to turn proposals into macadam and concrete. To ensure his success he constructed a typical Swanson majority—a variety of interest groups who desired the same goal but for different reasons.

Conservative, corporation-oriented leaders—who might otherwise object to extensive state regulation of their economic interests—argued that not only the state but the federal government as well should assume the burden of the good roads issue. The president of the Norfolk and Western observed that railroads could no longer profitably provide feeder lines to every hamlet and inhabited cove. Public thoroughfares were the answer. City boosters in Petersburg, Danville, Roanoke, and elsewhere dreamed of "farm to market roads." Formed in Danville in 1905, the Virginia Good Roads Association became a network for lobbying activities. School enthusiasts recognized the need for better roads, but rural Virginians provided Swanson with his greatest support. Before his inauguration Governor-elect Swanson assembled representatives of these interests and, as in the case of school legislation, proceeded to construct a rational legislative agenda.

Of first priority was the creation of a centralized agency to coordinate and furnish professional advice to localities, and the 1906 legislature concurred by establishing a State Highway Commission. The legislature also broadened the powers of localities to issue road bonds and passed enabling legislation to employ convicts for road building, a move considered a reform at the time. In the autumn of 1907 Swanson and several influential legislators met in Richmond for a series of discussions to draft a "bill looking to direct appropriations of money from the state treasury" for road construction. Swanson insisted upon the New Jersey plan for road financing, that is, equal local and state financing. Just as he had used local pride to build schools, he now sought to use the same sentiment to build roads. Notably, the 1908 legislature appropriated $250,000 directly for road building, the first such expenditure in Virginia history.

Other progressive moves by the legislature received Swanson's encouragement. Responding to campaigns of church leaders and secular reformers who had organized the Virginia Conference of Charities and Corrections in Marion in 1900, the legislature established state welfare standards and increased funding for poor relief, child welfare, state prisons, mental patients, and epileptics. Swanson then cleared the way for a state Board of Charities and Corrections. Public health agencies were also overhauled. The Assembly strengthened pure drug laws and awarded to the Pharmacy Board powers of indictment of malefactors. A Food and Drug Commission with broader regulatory powers agreed with Swanson's instructions to the dairy commissioner to enforce standards in bakeries. A child labor law prohibited in most cases the employment of children under fourteen. And a new Board of Health worked to enforce new regulations. Earlier capital appropriations formalized these efforts by building new state hospitals and sanitoriums for tuberculars, the blind, the deaf, and the mute.

In these programs, a tendency to discriminate between black and white Virginians was evident. Many educational reformers held that blacks should receive only manual or technical training. Although Swanson and the 1906 legislature rejected proposals to fund school improvements on the basis of tax receipts paid by each race, they did allow local school boards to appropriate funds to each race as they deemed necessary. Salaries of black teachers were below those of white counterparts, but Virginia salary averages led most of the South. There is some evidence that black teachers were better prepared than whites. In Virginia, unlike other southern states, school terms for the races were equal, and the state eventually duplicated for black children the general educational system provided for whites, although fiscal discrimination continued. Of course, advances in road building, rural libraries, demonstration education, public health, industrial regulations, penal reform, and railroad rate reduction benefited black Virginians as well as white. Unlike his contemporary, Carter Glass, Swanson sought to avoid race as a political issue. He declined to join a proposed southern interstate racial commission because he feared that a congressional investigation might evolve from resultant publicity and stir anew racial tensions. "We have no Negro problem here," he declared; the franchise had been restricted, racial animosity had cooled, and Virginia had moved toward more prosperous times. As a man who had used black organizers and voters in the 1890s and had not favored the disfranchising Constitution of 1902, the governor paternalistically observed in 1907 that an equitable racial settlement "cannot be accomplished all at once, but only through years of patient, persistent, and patriotic endeavor." Thus Swanson carefully avoided irresponsible racial rhetoric. During his first two years in office no lynchings occurred; in the last two, however, mobs provoked by alleged sexual outrages victimized a black male and two white males. On at least two occasions his prompt action prevented further tragedies. Racial conditions, far from ideal during his governship, certainly were better than during the previous two decades.

Swanson considered government an instrument that should assure "individualism," placing "the man above the dollar." He and his agrarian friends sought to use government to maintain paths to capitalist opportunity when untoward circumstances and greedy special interests threatened to block the way. Swanson and his associates believed that government should sponsor education, road building, railroad regulation, and economic development. Open competition in the marketplace must be carefully guaranteed by government agencies. Swanson preferred such a middle way. On one side, "predatory wealth" struggled to "add to its ill-gotten gain by further government favors and perquisites." On the other, socialism strove to control government. If the former conquered, Swanson declared, "industrial slavery and the rule of a rich oligarchy" would follow. If the latter prevailed, the "lazy and improvident shall share the savings of the energetic and prudent."

As a Democrat who claimed Andrew Jackson as a model, Swanson often admitted among his confidents that "no man can change his mind any quicker than Claude Swanson" upon the reversal of political sentiment. However, an underlying theme in his politics aligned Swanson with those Virginians who aspired, who had not made their place in the world. His inclusive politics and personal merriment bewildered humorless young aristocrats and stern self-seekers such as Montague and Carter Glass. Resisting restrictionist ideologies, Swanson evaded for a decade the doctrinaire Prohibitionism of the Reverend James Cannon, Jr., but eventually ran with the "prohibitionist hounds." Even so, he observed that the "wet rabbits in the Virginia hills could grow very long claws." Should they return to the majority, he would run with them. In 1906, however, Swanson eagerly allied himself with Cannon's parallel interest in improving schools in the Old Dominion, thereby tying the hardworking Methodist to educational reform.

No convincing evidence exists that any one group or person dominated Swanson. Certainly he was not a "swashbuckling lieutenant" of Thomas Martin. Even Bryan, who had enchanted the young congressman with his "Cross of Gold" speech, could not always retain the loyalty of the mature politician who grew aghast at the well-intentioned Nebraskan's inflexible, factionalized brand of politics. Yet in 1908 Governor Swanson refused to follow Martin and Flood when they sought to neutralize Virginia sentiment for Bryan in order to curry favor with northeastern, old-line Democrats and thus gain funds to finance and control the Virginia Democratic party. Although occasionally a beneficiary of this largesse, Swanson sided with rural Virginians and renewed his affection for Bryan and his aggressive politics. So deep and powerful flowed the current in 1908 that anti-Bryan Speaker Richard Byrd failed to win election to the state Democratic convention, and Lynchburg voters for similar reasons turned away from senior U.S. Senator John W. Daniel. Upon this wave of resurgent Bryanism, Swanson became by 1910 the most popular leader in the state.

During Swanson's governorship continued economic growth provided funds for new state programs and agencies. In 1908 he argued that considerable stimulus for prosperity emanated from the agencies themselves, from expanded state expenditures, and from the wise laws enacted during his administration. When predominantly rural Virginia suffered from tight credit at harvesttime in 1907, at Swanson's request federal authorities placed additional funds in local banks to facilitate the marketing of crops. The governor never achieved the strict regulation of state banks he desired, but he did succeed in requiring quarterly statements from state agencies dealing with financial matters. In 1910, in his concluding message to the General Assembly, Swanson emphasized the need for an improved state accounting system and revision of an inequitable tax system. Swanson also reported that all but ten counties were in the process of taking advantge of state funding for road building, that hundreds of new schoolhouses were under construction, and that more than two hundred high schools were in various stages of planning and development. He stressed the need to strengthen the Board of Health, to develop a rational procedure for registration of deaths, to create juvenile courts, and to prevent stream pollution. At the beginning of his term he said he would be satisfied if, at its conclusion, he might witness "marked . . . moral, educational and material progress of my state." Then he should "have been fully compensated for a lifetime of earnest work and endeavor." Late in January 1910, Claude Swanson must have been a satisfied man as he conducted his successor about the Governor's Mansion.

Within weeks, Thomas Martin, apprehensive about his chances for re-election in the 1911 primary, convinced a reluctant Governor Mann to appoint Swanson to the vacancy in the U.S. Senate created by the death of John W. Daniel. Martin desired a popular running mate, and in the primary Martin and Swanson routed their respective opponents, William A. Jones and Carter Glass. Following the election of Woodrow Wilson to the presidency, both senators proved staunch supporters of Wilson's New Freedom. Swanson performed in the Senate as he had with the Virginia Assembly, seeking the middle ground or creating majorities through compromise. He cooperated with Wilson in obtaining tariff reduction, the graduated income tax, currency reform, antitrust legislation, rural credits, federally sponsored vocational education and demonstration work, and federally financed aid to public roads. An invaluable friend of the U.S. Navy, he served as chairman of the Senate Naval Affairs Committee during World War I. At the war's conclusion he struggled in vain as a member of the Foreign Relations Committee to realize Wilson's vision of peace through the League of Nations.

During the decade of the 1920s Swanson fended off a series of blows which might have felled a less resilient and resourceful person. In 1920 his wife died. (He married her widowed sister, Lulie Lyons Hall, in 1923.) Several close political associates also died, and the senator himself suffered from ill health. In the 1922 election Swanson faced a determined opponent in Governor Westmoreland Davis, but he restructured his political base and won a signal victory. In doing so, he introduced Harry Flood Byrd to the state as Democratic party chairman and recruited newly selected Senator Carter Glass into his political orbit.

Meanwhile, Swanson used his Senate seat to champion relief for farmers, good roads, the World Court, and reduced tariffs. As the ranking Democrat of the Senate Foreign Relations Committee he helped mold the party's foreign policy statements and served as a delegate to the Geneva Disarmament Conference in 1932. Swanson's refusal to endorse Harry Byrd's presidential campaign that year and his support for Franklin D. Roosevelt drove a wedge between Swanson and Byrd. Differences over the nature of government—together with Byrd's perpetuation of a long-term family antagonism toward the aging senator—finally led to Swanson's resignation from the Senate in order to avoid a primary fight with Byrd. But President-elect Roosevelt appointed Swanson to the post of secretary of the navy, where he used his persuasive talents to convince Congress to rebuild the neglected American fleet. Swanson's health finally failed, and he died at the federal government's Rapidan Camp in northern Virginia on July 7, 1939, at the age of seventy-seven.

Few Virginians since the Civil War have achieved as much as Claude Swanson. A confidant of presidents and ministers of state, he worked with unflagging energy to ameliorate the confusions and crises of his era through rational and carefully drawn government action. In the day-to-day activities of government, his confidence and humor made him a pleasant associate. He did not hate well, and in the final analysis, many a Virginian came to love Claude Swanson for that very reason.

SOURCES

Manuscript materials on Swanson should be evaluated carefully, since many reflect the bias of friend and foe. Important collections at the University of Virginia are the papers of Edwin A. Alderman, A. Caperton

Braxton, John W. Daniel, William A. Garrett, Donald P. Halsey, James Hay, William A. Jones, George S. Shackelford, and A. Francis Thomas. Other significant collections are the Henry D. Flood Papers (Library of Congress), the Tucker Family Papers (University of North Carolina), the Charles T. Lassiter and Francis R. Lassiter Papers (Duke University), and the J. Hoge Tyler Papers (Virginia Polytechnic Institute and State University). The Swanson Executive Papers (Virginia State Library) offer few insights, but those of Andrew Jackson Montague provide many.

Pertinent articles include Joseph D. Eggleston, Jr., "Claude Swanson: A Sketch," *Virginia Journal of Education* 1 (Oct. 1907): 1–3; Henry C. Ferrell, Jr., "Prohibition, Reform and Politics in Virginia, 1895–1916," *East Carolina College Publications in History,* 3 (1966): 175–242; Robert A. Hohner, "Prohibition and Virginia Politics: William Hodges Mann versus Henry St. George Tucker, 1909," *Virginia Magazine of History and Biography* 74 (1966): 88–107; George B. Keezel, "History of the Establishment of the State Teachers College at Harrisonburg," *The Virginia Teacher* 9 (May 1928): 130–40; and Robert T. Taylor, "The Jamestown Tercentennial Exposition of 1907," *Virginia Magazine of History and Biography* 65 (1957): 169–208.

Overly critical estimates of Swanson appear in such studies as Louis R. Harlan, *Separate and Unequal: Public School Campaigns and Racism in the Southern Seaboard States, 1901–1915* (Chapel Hill, N.C., 1958); William Larsen, *Montague of Virginia: The Making of a Southern Progressive* (Baton Rouge, La., 1965); and Allen W. Moger, *Virginia: Bourbonism to Byrd, 1870–1925* (Charlottesville, 1968). More balanced are Raymond H. Pulley, *Old Virginia Restored: An Interpretation of the Progressive Impulse, 1870–1930* (Charlottesville, 1968), and Jack Temple Kirby, *Westmoreland Davis: Virginia Planter-Politician, 1859–1942* (Charlottesville, 1968).

WILLIAM H. MANN

Governor of Virginia

1910–1914

WILLIAM HODGES MANN

Last of the Boys in Gray

William A. Rhodes

William Hodges Mann, the fourth son of John and Mary Hunter Bowers Mann, was born on July 30, 1843, in the sleepy village of Williamsburg, Virginia. The Mann family traced their Virginia roots to the seventeenth century and were active in local politics and Bruton Parish Church. When William Hodges Mann was only one week old his father died. In 1852 his mother remarried, and the family moved west to Brownsburg in Rockbridge County. There he continued his education at Brownsburg Academy, absorbing the stern Presbyterian morality and Prohibition sentiments that pervaded that institution. In 1857, at the age of fourteen, he decided to strike out on his own and moved to Petersburg to follow his brothers into the legal profession. During the next four years he worked as a court clerk's apprentice, studying law in his spare time.

When the Civil War broke out, Mann served with the Twelfth Virginia Infantry until a disabling injury forced him to seek other service. This included a position with the Confederate government, clerkships of courts in Nottoway and Dinwiddie counties, and a stint as a scout and spy for the Confederacy. After Appomattox, Mann passed his bar examinations and began to practice law in Nottoway County, where he was soon chosen Commonwealth's attorney, and in 1870 he became county judge. In the meantime Mann paid off debts he had accumulated and then married Sallie Fitzgerald, daughter of C. W. Fitzgerald, a successful Nottoway farmer. This marriage would be childless, but Petersburg (and later Nottoway) abounded in nephews close to their Uncle William. Mann's determination to pay off his debts illustrates the high standards he set for himself throughout his life: self-denial, discipline, hard work, and an ambition directed by a sense of right and duty to others and to self. In later life he joined the Presbyterian church and became an elder, though he was never a narrow sectarian. His records show that he often contributed to other denominations.

In 1874 the leaders of the Conservative party in the Fourth Congressional District, of which Nottoway was part, were searching for some means to defeat the radical Republicans, whose dominance was based upon the district's black voting majority. They decided not to nominate a candidate for Congress openly but to declare support for an independent Republican and at

the same time secretly prepare ballots for a Conservative, whose candidacy
would not be revealed until election day. The secret candidate was William
Hodges Mann, who had already begun what would be a long career as a
political orator and whose ability and lack of political enemies recommended
him for the post. Although the strategy failed, Mann continued to work for
the Conservative party and soon was embroiled in the Funder-Readjuster
conflict over the funding of the state's prewar debt. Forced to choose sides,
Mann initially played an active role in the Readjuster movement, working for
his Petersburg neighbor William Mahone in various capacities. Early in 1878
he was one of those appointed to inform the public of Readjuster progress and
to determine their course of action. But when the Readjusters decided to
create a completely separate political organization, Mann separated himself
from the movement. As he explained in a letter to Mahone, he believed that
the formation of a separate party posed a threat to white solidarity in the
Southside. In spite of his stand, Mann was reelected as judge of Nottoway
County by the Readjuster majority in the General Assembly of 1879–80.
When the Conservative Funders (who renamed themselves Democrats in
1883) regained control of the legislature, Mann was reelected once more in
1885. He thus survived the political turmoil of the Readjuster era in surprisingly good stead.

In the meantime, Mann's life was being affected by events outside the
political arena. In 1882 his wife of twelve years died in childbirth, and the
child, their first, was stillborn. In October 1885 Judge Mann married Etta
Donnan, daughter of Alexander Donnan, a leading attorney and banker in
Petersburg. The large Donnan family constituted one of the Southside's leading clans, and their influence would prove beneficial to Mann's career. Etta
Donnan Mann, a person of resolute character and strong religious faith,
would later write a chatty social history of her husband's gubernatorial administration, *Four Years in the Governor's Mansion of Virginia*. The new family
was soon— and unexpectedly—greatly expanded. The judge's brother, Edwin M. Mann of Petersburg and his wife died suddenly, leaving nine children, ranging in age from eleven months to nineteen years. Judge Mann and
his mother, who lived in Brownsburg, divided the children between them to
raise. The Manns also had a son of their own in 1886, but he died in 1889. A
second son, William Hodges Mann, Jr., was born shortly thereafter and lived
to follow his father into law and politics.

With such a family to support, Judge Mann devoted considerable attention to his economic interests, including a variety of business ventures in the
Southside, three local banks, and a profitable relationship with the Norfolk
and Western Railroad Company as local attorney and lobbyist. In addition he
managed a Nottoway County farm, where he applied the increasingly popular
principles of scientific agriculture. Emerging as an advocate of rural improvements, he worked through the Farmers' Council of Virginia and North Car-

olina to secure legislation favorable to agriculture—activities that presaged his major interests as governor. Desire to devote more attention to his legal practice and these other interests caused him to retire in 1891 from the judicial post he had filled for twenty-two years. To express their appreciation for his services, the citizens of Nottoway presented Mann with a gold-headed cane. This move also paved the way for more active participation in Virginia political life. In 1893 Thomas Staples Martin, victor in the contest for the U.S. Senate seat made vacant by the death of John S. Barbour, set about constructing the political organization with which William Hodges Mann would be associated for the remainder of his political career. The organization's effectiveness derived in large part from close alliance with the business interests, especially railroads. Money from the railroads helped sway votes on crucial issues, and this, plus the power of patronage, ensured the loyalty of local officials. Organization members were permitted considerable latitude. They might oppose one another in primary elections on the basis of personal ambition, regional differences, or even occasionally on emotional issues such as Prohibition. Senator Martin's able lieutenant was Delegate and later Congressman Henry D. ("Hal") Flood of Appomattox, whose political advice Mann frequently sought. Mann's business orientation, desire for white political unity, and ambition for political office quite naturally made him a loyal member of the Martin organization.

During the 1890s Mann continued to work for state and national Democratic candidates and also tried to advance his own political fortunes, but his attempts to win a seat on the state Supreme Court of Appeals in 1893–94 and the nomination for attorney general in 1897 were unsuccessful. Undeterred by these setbacks, Mann took advantage of a unique opportunity in 1899. As a result of a division among local Democrats, organization leaders asked him to run for the state Senate seat for Nottoway, Lunenburg, and Brunswick counties. Mann was somewhat reluctant to accept the offer, realizing that election would curtail his profitable activities as a railroad attorney; nevertheless, he felt he could restore party unity and was duly nominated by regular Democrats.

The contest between Mann and the anti-Martin (or independent) Democratic candidate, E. P. Buford, Commonwealth's attorney for Brunswick County, soon developed into one of the state's hottest races. When the votes were counted, Buford had carried Brunswick easily and Lunenburg narrowly, but Mann's large majority in Nottoway gave him the election. Buford's supporters cried fraud, and the theft of the Nottoway poll books three nights later suggested that Martin loyalists might indeed have padded Mann's majority. Mann apparently had no knowledge of this, and even Buford's supporters did not accuse the judge of complicity. Buford failed to contest the election, enabling William Hodges Mann to take his seat in the state Senate where he would build a record that provided the basis for his future gubernatorial campaigns. His senatorial career also added impetus to the drive to close saloons and the campaign for better educational facilities. Mann is best remembered for his contributions to these reforms.

When the General Assembly convened in December 1901, the new senator introduced what became known as the Mann liquor bill. It was actually an amendment to a revenue act that would have resulted in virtual Prohibition in rural areas. Since 1886 the sale of liquor had been regulated by local option. Voters in a city, town, or district could choose whether or not a distillery or saloon could operate in their area. The local judge, however, could rule against a would-be distiller or saloon keeper if he deemed the applicant's character deficient or the proposed place of business unsuitable. By 1900 nearly three-fourths of Virginia's magisterial districts were dry, but much liquor still flowed in dry territory—some from wet areas outside the district, some from illegal saloons within.

To combat the powerful forces of the liquor dealers, who were allied with the Martin organization, the Anti-Saloon League of Virginia was organized early in 1901. Largely a creation of Baptists and Methodists, the league developed a highly centralized organization dedicated to the goal of complete Prohibition. Mann had long been a foe of the liquor trade; as a judge he had refused to grant a single liquor license, and as a Presbyterian layman he was active in the Anti-Saloon League from its beginning.

Although Mann's bill died in committee, he reintroduced the same proposal in the 1902 session. The Anti-Saloon League, the Women's Christian Temperance Union, and the churches rallied behind it, and a steady stream of petitions urging passage flowed into the General Assembly from every section of the state. The bill, weakened somewhat in the Senate, finally won approval, and by January 1905 seventy of one hundred counties, as well as three cities, had no saloons. In the countryside, especially, the Mann Act was indeed drying up the Old Dominion.

The success of this legislation perhaps caused Mann to seek the Democratic nomination for governor in 1905. He did not enter the race until January 1905, a surprisingly late date in view of the strong candidacy of Claude A. Swanson, generally conceded to have the backing of the Martin organization. Yet Mann had the support of some friends in the organization, notably Hal Flood, and effective assistance from the Anti-Saloon League. Especially helpful was the effort by the state's best-known antiliquor crusader and Mann's personal friend, the Reverend James Cannon, Jr., president of the league and a Methodist minister serving as principal of Blackstone Female Institute, a church-related school in Mann's own Nottoway County.

Although Mann ran far behind Swanson in the primary, he had demonstrated the vote-getting potential of the antiliquor issue, and his showing indicated that the Democratic machine and its liquor interest allies would eventually have to face up to this problem. To Mann, it seemed that compromise—and, once again, preservation of party unity—was desirable. Even before Swanson was inaugurated, Mann wrote confidentially to his nephew and campaign manager James Mann that he had been given reason to believe that the organization would support him next time—in the 1909 gubernatorial race.

Before this contest, however, the state senator from Nottoway would achieve one of the most significant triumphs of his legislative career—the Mann High School Act. Until this measure became law, the state provided aid to colleges and universities and substantial funding to public primary schools, but there was no state-sponsored link between these two levels of education. In 1906 publicly supported high schools were rare; only 10 percent of the children of Virginia had an opportunity to take high school work, and only half of that number were actually doing so. The 1903 legislature had authorized the establishment of high schools but had provided no funds for this purpose. Mann then introduced a bill to appropriate up to $500 to any school district that would provide matching funds for support of public high schools. Reverend Mr. Cannon, interested in education as well as Prohibition, helped Mann prepare the bill, but this proposal and a similar measure introduced in the House failed to pass the General Assembly.

In May 1905 the Cooperative Education Association, a group of Virginia educators, sponsored a month-long deluge of propaganda for improved schooling known as the May Campaign. Meanwhile, Mann's unsuccessful primary campaign of that year also emphasized educational needs. With this groundwork established, high school bills closely resembling Mann's earlier proposal were introduced early in 1906. Mann sponsored such a measure in the Senate, and Eugene Ould, delegate from Campbell County, in the House. Ould's bill advanced more rapidly than Mann's. When it reached the Senate, Mann shepherded it through, though not without amendments. After the House concurred with these changes, the bill became law. This measure stimulated secondary education, and by the end of the 1908–9 school year the state had 345 high schools, nearly half of them four-year institutions. There were high schools in nearly every county, and some counties had one in every school district. Additional work was needed, but the efforts of Mann and Ould provided significant educational opportunities for the state's children.

In the meantime the liquor issue continued to spark controversy. In 1908 Mann cosponsored a bill, known as the Byrd-Mann bill, to enact out-and-out Prohibition in rural areas and to restrict further the legal liquor trade. Since this bill had Senator Martin's somewhat grudging support, the Prohibition forces and the Martin organization seemed to be moving toward a rapprochement. The gubernatorial primary of 1909 revealed the extent of this agreement. Martin had decided by late 1906 that a Mann candidacy might unite the Prohibition vote with railroad and banking interests that were already favorably inclined toward the Nottoway legislator. Martin's concern that

Mann might alienate the liquor interests seemed to have been eased by Mann's assurance (offered at the urging of Hal Flood) that he would not advocate statewide Prohibition. Mann and Flood then persuaded Cannon to convince the Anti-Saloon League to advocate local option rather than statewide Prohibition. Only after considerable soul-searching had Mann been able to convince himself that since public sentiment was not yet ready for complete Prohibition in all parts of the Commonwealth, "the cause" might best be advanced by having a "temperance man" in the Executive Mansion.

In opposition to Mann, the antiorganization faction of the party offered Henry ("Harry") St. George Tucker of Rockbridge County, who had served at various times as congressman, dean of the Washington and Lee University School of Law, president of the Jamestown Exposition, and president of the American Bar Association. Mann and Tucker presented similar platforms, each calling for good roads, better schools, more benefits for Confederate veterans, uniform taxation, and bank examinations. Tucker was a "wet" and Mann a "dry"; yet the only difference in their positions on liquor legislation was that Tucker promised to veto any bill for statewide Prohibition, whereas Mann would sign such a bill if the General Assembly submitting it had been elected on that specific issue. Both men indicated that they would favor a referendum on Prohibition.

The campaign was generally dull and uninspiring. Mann's declaration during debate that he would vote dry in a referendum on statewide Prohibition caused Martin concern, but he was able to persuade his proliquor allies to distinguish between what Mann would do voting as a citizen and what he would do in his official capacity as governor. Some organization stalwarts were unenthusiastic about Mann, but he managed to win, 39,281 to 34,203.

In the gubernatorial campaign that followed Mann exerted himself little and easily outpolled Republican William P. Kent of Wythe County, 70,760 to 40,357. Thus, William Hodges Mann—at the age of sixty-six—became the last of the Confederate veterans, the "boys in gray," to attain the governorship of the Old Dominion. He took the oath of office on February 1, 1910, with his fingers resting on the 125th Psalm: "They that trust in the Lord shall be as Mount Zion, which cannot be removed, but abideth forever." The coming four years would demand of Governor Mann much of the resolve expressed in the psalm.

The state that the former county judge would govern was, like the rest of the nation, undergoing considerable change, becoming more populous, more urban, and more prosperous. New state revenues enabled the Commonwealth to provide the additional services that progressive reformers were demanding. In the first decade of the twentieth century the state had expanded school facilities, upgraded prison and asylum conditions, limited child labor, regulated food and drugs, made some efforts at election law reform, reorganized its judicial system, and consolidated various administrative offices. Governor Mann and the General Assembly would have to determine if Virginia could fulfill these new obligations without some revision of the tax system. The question of Prohibition was also a likely issue, and farmers were demanding more aid as well.

Of all these matters, Prohibition had the greatest potential for stirring conflicting emotions. Throughout Mann's administration Prohibition forces tried unsuccessfully to secure passage of an enabling act to permit voters to petition for a referendum on statewide Prohibition. Under the proposed act, the governor would call a referendum if petitioned by one-fourth of the state's qualified voters. As governor, Mann continued to support local option and took no stand on the enabling act, but privately he was strongly opposed to the use of liquor, and throughout his administration the Governor's Mansion was dry. Mrs. Mann, herself an enthusiastic supporter of Prohibition, supplanted the usual libations with fruit punches. Mann's refusal openly to endorse the enabling act brought him criticism from some leaders of the Anti-Saloon League. But the governor would only privately urge Senator Martin to support the controversial measure as a means of preventing its numerous supporters from leaving the Democratic party. Not until 1914, however, did Martin and other organization leaders become convinced they had to support the enabling act. The possibility loomed, as Mann had prophesied, that Cannon would lead the Prohibition forces into an alliance with antiorganization Democrats. To prevent this, the organization passed the enabling act, though by this time Mann was a private citizen.

Governor Mann had stuck to his campaign pledges and had made no attempt to be a "Prohibition governor." Some said this was because the liquor interests, organization leaders, the Anti-Saloon League, and Mann made a political deal in 1909; yet agitation on the matter continued throughout his governorship. A more likely explanation is that Mann, at the start of his administration, sincerely believed in local option as the best policy for achieving effective Prohibition and maintaining Democratic unity. When he became convinced that an enabling act would better serve these ends, he resolved the discrepancy between platform and personal beliefs by remaining above the battle; he stood on his noncommittal campaign pledge, while privately urging Senator Martin to support the enabling act. Thus he attempted to reconcile his public pledge with his private beliefs as a Prohibitionist and a faithful organization Democrat.

Although the Prohibition battle captured headlines, agricultural problems and rural demands received a larger share of the governor's attention. The first such issue was raised by Westmoreland Davis, president of the Virginia State Farmers' Institute. Davis lobbied for state employment of convict labor to quarry and grind limestone for agricultural use. This proposal,

supported by farmers and agricultural journals, was opposed by lime manufacturers, railroads that might have to ship lime at low rates, and those who
regarded such an enterprise as "socialistic."

Although the lime bill failed in 1910, Governor Mann promised his
support in the 1912 legislature. First he persuaded the Norfolk and Western
Railway to lower its rates for agricultural lime. Then (to meet objections
regarding the constitutionality of the limestone-grinding proposal) Mann
drafted a substitute bill declaring its objective to be employment of convicts—
about which there was no question of the state's constitutional power—and
that the grinding of limestone and oyster shells was only incidental to the
employment of convicts. The substitute bill easily passed both houses with
only minor amendments.

The lime act successfully withstood court challenges, and other railroads
soon followed the lead of the Norfolk and Western in lowering their rates on
ground limestone. Mann had left office by the time the first convict-operated
lime-grinding plant began what proved to be a highly successful operation;
nevertheless, his role in the Old Dominion's effort to fill a need largely ignored
by private enterprise constituted a high-water mark of progressivism during
his administration.

Governor Mann's second major effort to aid agriculture focused on creation of a United Agricultural Board. Proposed in a special message to the
1910 General Assembly, the new agency would coordinate efforts in agricultural education then divided among the U.S. Department of Agriculture, the
Virginia Agricultural Experiment Station, Virginia Polytechnic Institute
(VPI), the state Board of Education, and the state Board of Agriculture.
Mann, an enthusiastic supporter of farm demonstration work, would head
the proposed board, limiting somewhat the powers of Commissioner of Agriculture George W. Koiner, who was less inclined to favor demonstration
programs.

The board bill passed the General Assembly, but only after some legislative maneuvering by the governor, and even then there was no funding until
1911. In the meantime Mann urged counties to appropriate funds for demonstration work to be matched by the state. The counties responded so enthusiastically that by January 1911 the board had to put a damper on requests
since they threatened to exceed any state appropriation for that purpose. In
1912 Mann succeeded in securing from the General Assembly an expansion
of demonstration work under the board. But this provoked opposition from
Commissioner Koiner and VPI President Paul B. Barringer, who wished to
preserve their remaining influence in agricultural education. Although the
legislature had removed both of these officials from membership on the
United Agricultural Board, Mann believed that demonstration work could
not be fully successful until more sympathetic individuals filled their positions. Consequently he engineered the resignation of Barringer as head of

VPI, replacing him with his own man, J. D. Eggleston, formerly state super-intendent of public instruction and an enthusiastic supporter of demonstration work. Mann was not successful in his efforts against Koiner. Although he campaigned actively for Koiner's opponent in the 1913 Democratic primary, Koiner was easily nominated and reelected.

Perhaps feeling that the United Agricultural Board had made too many enemies, Mann subsequently began transferring the responsibility for dem-onstration work from the board to VPI. Eggleston and the VPI faculty were enthusiastic about the proposed change, and when Mann made the recom-mendation to the 1914 General Assembly, the legislature agreed. Demonstra-tion work was now firmly established—after a Byzantine series of maneuvers; yet Governor Mann and the United Agricultural Board deserved a large measure of the credit.

Mann's efforts in behalf of lime production and demonstration farming yielded positive results, but he failed in another major area of concern—reform of the Commonwealth's tax system. The State Tax Commission (of which the governor was a member) urged that the state move toward equalization of the tax burden, primarily by closely supervising the assessment of real and per-sonal property. Although Mann requested prompt attention to the matter, the General Assembly was uninterested and nothing came of this effort.

The record of the Mann administration in the area of public welfare and social services was mixed. When Mann took office, some convicts were used on the roads, but most were working in the state penitentiary producing shoes under a contract with a Boston concern. The feeling was growing that it would be more profitable to the state, as well as beneficial to the health of the convicts, if they worked on the roads or ground lime. When a new, more profitable contract with the shoe company was negotiated, Governor Mann, the state highway commissioner, and the superintendent of the penitentiary apparently lent their support to a bill classifying "dangerous" convicts as factory workers. This approach still provided sufficient convicts for road maintenance, and the compromise proved so appealing that legislators op-posed to contract labor were easily outvoted. The Mann administration thus assured that Virginia would continue to have contracted convict labor for at least five more years—a dubious legacy.

The General Assembly continued the progress of the Montague and Swanson administrations in public health and welfare, providing increased powers and appropriations to the Board of Health and the Board of Charities and Corrections. Facilities were established for epileptics, delinquent girls, and the feebleminded; public health services were extended; and the hours of labor for women in certain fields were restricted. The governor himself re-vealed a growing awareness and understanding of public health and welfare, a subject to which he had devoted little attention as a legislator.

Mann's administration thus compiled an excellent record in agricultural reform and a generally creditable one with reference to social services. In later years his efforts in behalf of the farmers would be well remembered, but so would another, more dramatic episode of his term, one which quickly captured public attention. On March 14, 1912, Floyd Allen, leader of a mountain clan virtually a law unto themselves, was in Carroll County circuit court in Hillsville to hear the jury verdict on a charge of interfering with an officer of the law. Rumors abounded that Allen's family would not permit him to be convicted, and—to lend substance to the rumors—several of his kinsmen were in the crowded room, openly displaying rifles and revolvers. As soon as the jury returned the guilty verdict and the judge sentenced the fifty-year-old leader to one year in the penitentiary, Allen drew a revolver hidden inside his sweater. No one knows who fired first, but a fusillade of shots exploded from guns that appeared on all sides. The judge, the sheriff, the Commonwealth's attorney, one of the jurors, and a spectator were either killed instantly or died shortly afterward. Several others were wounded. The Allens then fled, some heading into the hills of the Blue Ridge and others, including Floyd Allen, who was badly wounded, taking refuge in the Hillsville Hotel. The clan leader and those with him were quickly apprehended and jailed in Roanoke, and by the end of March all but two of those implicated in the shooting were in custody. They finally were captured in Des Moines, Iowa, six months later.

Floyd Allen and his son, Claude Swanson Allen, subsequently were convicted of first-degree murder and sentenced to die in the electric chair on November 22, 1912; others involved received prison sentences. Governor Mann was soon besieged by pleas to commute the sentences, especially that of young Claude, to life imprisonment. Mann granted a series of reprieves, probably hoping that Floyd or Claude would confess to a conspiracy to murder Carroll County court officers; such a confession would have eliminated any doubt of the justice of the death penalties. But on March 6, 1913, when Mann announced his fourth reprieve, he set March 28 as the date for the executions.

Attorneys and a small group of sympathizers made one last attempt to save the condemned men on the evening of March 27 when Mann was in Philadelphia for a speaking engagement. They tried to persuade the lieutenant governor, J. Taylor Ellyson, that he was acting governor and could commute the sentences. The constitutional question thus raised caused the superintendent of the penitentiary to postpone the executions. Mann's son, told of the scheme by the attorney general, called his father at 3:00 A.M., and the governor hastily returned to Richmond, arriving in his office about noon. Mann then informed the superintendent of the penitentiary of his presence, and the electrocutions were carried out shortly after 1:30 P.M. Mann received much editorial praise around the nation for his dramatic return to the state and his decisive action. Thus he largely succeeded in erasing the appearance of indecision which the series of reprieves had created in some minds. Fate had worked through the Allen affair to assure that William Hodges Mann would be remembered as a strong and decisive governor.

Yet life at the Governor's Mansion was not all crises. As they prepared to leave, the Manns could look back on many happy experiences: automobile rides in the summer evenings, enjoyable trips to governors' conferences and serving as hosts to the group in 1912, a breakfast for President Taft, Mrs. Mann making grape jelly and juice from the Mansion's vineyards, and a lively round of dances, receptions, concerts, and lectures.

William Hodges Mann and his family settled in Petersburg, where they had many relatives. Unable to get a state or federal appointive position, Mann associated himself with his son's law practice in Richmond and Petersburg. He continued to strive for Prohibition and to support agricultural demonstration projects, applying many of the innovations developed through such work on his own extensive dairy farm. In addition, he pursued banking and business interests, provided valuable volunteer services during World War I, and continued to be an active Presbyterian layman. Having worked a full schedule all his life, Mann kept up this pace until his death on December 12, 1927. Characteristically, though he was eighty-four years old, Mann was at his law office desk in Petersburg when he suffered an apparent heart attack and died. He was buried in Blandford Cemetery, Petersburg. As he had wished, his tombstone bore the inscription, "Author and Patron of the Mann Bill and Patron of the High School Bill in the Senate of Virginia."

Nevertheless, his greatest achievement as governor was in the field of agriculture. Mann played an active role in initiating legislation to provide cheaper lime for farmers and in persuading railroads to haul that product at lower cost. Even more significant were his efforts to widen the scope of agricultural demonstration work. By transferring a great degree of responsibility for this effort to Virginia Polytechnic Institute, Mann assured the continued progress of scientific agriculture in the Old Dominion and the dissemination of this knowledge to farmers. The effects on the economy of the state, on the profitability of farming, and on the living conditions of rural Virginians would be difficult to estimate.

For a man in his late sixties Governor Mann displayed surprising drive and determination in striving for the improvement of agriculture. In other areas (notably tax reform and convict labor), however, he had been stymied either by unresponsive legislatures or by an inability to discern the need for change. William Hodges Mann was a Virginia gentlemen of the old school. As a Confederate soldier, county judge, progressive agriculturalist, state senator, and governor of the Commonwealth he had done his duty—as he saw it—faithfully and well.

SOURCES

The William Hodges Mann Papers (University of Virginia) include personal and business correspondence, diaries, ledgers, and newspaper clippings from the 1860s to 1927. Interviews with Mrs. Ann S. V. Mann, his daughter-in-law, and with James Mann, Jr., a grandnephew, were extremely helpful. Etta Donnan Mann's *Four Years in the Governor's Mansion of Virginia* (Richmond, 1937) provided additional insights, as did Richmond and Petersburg newspapers.

Published works on the first decades of the twentieth century include Jack Temple Kirby, *Westmoreland Davis: Virginia Planter-Politician, 1859–1942* (Charlottesville, 1968); Raymond H. Pulley, *Old Virginia Restored: An Interpretation of the Progressive Impulse, 1870–1930* (Charlottesville, 1968); and Allen W. Moger, *Virginia: Bourbonism to Byrd, 1870–1925* (Charlottesville, 1968). See also William H. Gaines, Jr., "The Connecting Link: The Expansion of Virginia's Public High Schools, 1900–1910," *Virginia Cavalcade* 5 (Winter 1955): 15–19; and Robert A. Hohner, "Prohibition and Virginia Politics: William Hodges Mann versus Henry St. George Tucker, 1909," *Virginia Magazine of History and Biography* 74 (1966): 81–107.

Helpful unpublished studies include Henry Clifton Ferrell, Jr., "Claude A. Swanson of Virginia" (Ph.D. diss., University of Virginia, 1964); and Burton I. Kaufman, "Henry DeLaWarr Flood: A Case Study of Organization Politics in an Era of Reform" (Ph.D. diss., Rice University, 1966).

HENRY CARTER STUART

A Patrician Facing Change

Charles E. Poston and Edward L. Henson, Jr.

Virginia counties west of the New River have been of only intermittent interest to the rest of the state. Southwest Virginia achieved importance in the 1850s when John B. Floyd was governor and received some attention during the Civil War because of its railroad and the mines at Saltville, but then the region was beset by residual violence, bypassed by industrialism, and largely ignored.

By the end of the nineteenth century the Stuarts were among the leading families in southwest Virginia. Their kinsmen included the Campbells, Smiths, Prestons, and Carters who had dominated the area from the days of the first settlement. Henry Carter Stuart was born at Wytheville on January 18, 1855. His well-to-do father, William Alexander Stuart, manufactured salt for the Confederacy while his uncle, James Ewell Brown ("Jeb") Stuart, was leading rebel cavalry against the Yankees. The Stuarts moved to Russell County in 1874, and young Henry received the bachelor of arts degree from Emory and Henry College, a local institution. The following year he attended the University of Virginia law school, although he apparently had no intention of pursuing law as a profession.

His father, an astute businessman who suffered during the depression of the 1870s, had varied financial interests which included the popular resort at White Sulphur Springs. Seeking to recoup the family's fortunes, he saw in his twenty-year-old son a mixture of dedication, intelligence, and obsession with the details of agriculture. As a result, he made Henry the general manager of his Russell County properties, a move which launched the future governor on the road to success.

Those who knew Henry Carter Stuart rarely failed to remark upon his encyclopedic mind and his scholarly interests. He became one of the most knowledgeable agriculturists in the United States, building an empire embracing the largest cattle operation east of the Mississippi River. It covered 6 percent of all the improved farmland in four southwest Virginia counties. This operation depended upon a large number of families who tended to specialize in certain skills that were passed on from one generation to another. Workers were expected to shun the temptations of towns and to avoid alcohol while on Stuart property. The necessities of life, as defined by Henry Carter

HENRY C. STUART

Governor of Virginia

1914–1918

Stuart, could be obtained in company stores in exchange for Stuart scrip. One visitor remarked that she had never understood the feudal system until she visited Elk Garden.

Elk Garden was the heart of the Stuart operation. The house was of majestic proportions, set among magnificent walnuts and boxwoods. The man who rode out from this place to supervise the seventy-eight square miles of Stuart lands was impressive by any standards. It is said that he remembered every head of cattle on the place and could recall the current weight of each. Well over six feet in height and physically imposing, he had tremendous reserve and dignity which inspired respect on the part of farm laborers and members of the Stuart family alike. It was said that no one ever uttered a word of profanity or told an off-color joke in his presence. A niece remarked, "No one in the family would have thought of doing anything that Uncle Henry did not approve of." Stuart was forty-one years old when he married his cousin Margaret Bruce Carter. Although she was a native of southwest Virginia, she seemed to prefer life in northern cities and in Europe. The couple's only child, Mary Fulton, apparently shared her mother's lack of enthusiasm for country living and rebelled against the Victorian standards which her father attempted to enforce, an exception to the pattern of familial obedience.

Succeeding in the economic realm, Stuart also was a member of the county electoral board and a trustee of the state mental hospital in Marion. In 1892 he began forty-one years of continuous service as a trustee of Emory and Henry College, and he also served on the board of visitors of the University of Virginia. Stuart helped to organize the Virginia State Fair and served as its first president. Throughout his life he was a leader in the affairs of the Methodist church. Not only a civic-minded farmer, Stuart was an aggressive businessman who presided over a bank and a coal company. He promoted the sale of beef and other agricultural products all over the world and entertained a cosmopolitan collection of business leaders at Elk Garden. Like Westmoreland Davis, another patrician destined to become governor, Stuart bridged the gap between agriculture and business. Unlike Davis, who was living at Manhattan's Waldorf Hotel when the depression of 1893 struck, Stuart absorbed the impact of that calamity as a full-time resident of rural Virginia. In that year Stuart actively supported Fitzhugh Lee in his bid to defeat Thomas Staples Martin in the race for the U.S. Senate. Martin's controversial victory generated the "May Movement" of 1899 to secure the popular election of senators. Stuart, already marked as an independent Democrat, joined fifty-one other prominent Virginians in signing a petition urging the selection of senators by popular vote.

Meanwhile, a commercial revolution was developing in southwest Virginia which threatened the region's traditional ruling class. Mine owners and railroad executives were challenging the prerogatives of the old-line agricultural patriarchs. Although Stuart could not have known that one day a mine operator would own Elk Garden, it was apparent that dependence upon planters and drovers was declining each year. Not surprisingly, Stuart became interested in a variety of progressive measures which would protect the farmer in a rapidly industrializing America. He had the farmer's traditional desire to nurture honesty and frugality in government and—as a scholarly man with broad social and business contacts—was touched by the currents of reformist thought then coursing through the nation. As an agriculturalist, he knew firsthand the need for railroad regulation; he had also experienced the inequities of the tax system, especially the disproportionate burden borne by real estate. As a patrician, he had reason to deplore the antecedents if not the quality of much of Virginia's leadership since the war. Stuart, in keeping with the conventional wisdom of the day, had also become convinced that the quality of Virginia government could be improved only by curtailing the black vote. When Virginia voters decided in 1900 to abandon the Reconstruction-born Underwood Constitution, Stuart, therefore, was a strong supporter of this move.

Although Russell County was a Republican stronghold, Stuart easily became a delegate to the 1901–2 constitutional convention. Perhaps Republican opposition did not develop because of his reputation for fairness in the registration of voters of both parties. At the convention he served on the vital suffrage committee that wrote the article virtually eliminating the black voter, and as a member of the finance committee he worked to transfer tax burdens from private citizens to corporations. Stuart was the logical choice as chairman of the agriculture committee, where he encouraged state involvement in the development and teaching of new agricultural techniques.

The future governor thus played a significant convention role and received some criticism as a result. Republicans assailed him and his Democratic colleagues for not honoring a preconvention pledge to submit the new constitution to popular vote, and the new literacy requirements aroused much opposition, especially in southwest Virginia where Negroes were few in number and thousands of uneducated whites were barred from the suffrage. Even so, Stuart derived political benefits from his work at the convention. Working closely with such prominent men as John W. Daniel and Carter Glass, Stuart forged valuable contacts, and his special efforts to see that southwest Virginia Republicans were not completely disfranchised enhanced his reputation for fairness. His contributions, especially with regard to suffrage, helped to develop his statewide image. Lastly, his understanding of the constitution he had helped to create would smooth his tenure as governor.

Virginia's new fundamental law required the creation of a State Corporation Commission, providing Stuart another opportunity for political advancement. Governor Andrew Jackson Montague was very cautious in selecting the new three-man commission. He believed that the individuals should be prominent, moderate, wealthy, and—above all—pose no threat to efforts to build his own political strength against Martin. The first four prospective appointees refused to serve, and Stuart became his fifth choice. He and his colleagues, Beverly Crump, a Richmond lawyer, and Henry Fairfax, a Loudoun County planter and engineer, all moderate men, were not expected to be forceful regulators. Disappointed in the governor's choices, some ardent supporters of corporate regulation doubted that Stuart and his associates could handle the complex tasks confronting them.

These apprehensions proved ill founded. The new commission was very successful in its campaign to rationalize the growth of corporations and integrate them into an orderly regulatory framework. Stuart, Crump, and Fairfax initiated hearings on railroad problems that resulted in classified and uniform freight rates. Other efforts led to a doubling of tax receipts from the corporate interests during the first year of the commission's existence. Not the least of the agency's accomplishments lay in convincing the consuming public that something was being done on their behalf.

As Stuart's term drew to a close in February 1908, hearings were held to determine the fitness of Judge William F. Rhea, a machine politician from Bristol, to take his place. Stuart himself testified against Rhea's appointment, bringing with him a copy of a letter he had written in response to illegal efforts by Rhea's supporters to alter voting results in Buchanan County. Stuart's letter included a high-minded appeal to dignity and fair play. Although this maneuver failed to prevent Rhea's confirmation, press reaction was, for the most part, very positive. Hailed by one editor as "this noblest Roman of them all," Stuart's stand won him support from independent Democrats as well as Martinites. His courageous Rhea testimony made him a minor celebrity and a contender for the gubernatorial nomination in 1909.

But the Martin organization had other ideas. Stuart threatened the chances of its candidate, William Hodges Mann, so he was induced to withdraw from the race—but with substantial compensation. Tradition supported by evidence indicates that a deal was made. Like some political Saint George, Stuart would be sent in 1910 to do battle with powerful Republican Congressman C. Bascom Slemp in Stuart's own Ninth District, with full Martin organization support. Should Stuart fail to unseat Slemp, then the way would be cleared for his election to the governorship in 1913.

Politics provided one of the few paths in southwest Virginia to upward social and economic mobility. Officeholding was as vital to status and livelihood as the ownership of land. Large, close-knit families living in single political subdivisions—together with fierce party loyalties transmitted from generation to generation—served to increase both political interest and the temptation toward electoral malfeasance. Even within this context, however, the 1910 congressional campaign in the Ninth District was distinctively exciting, expensive, and corrupt. Outside speakers, including Theodore Roosevelt, poured in to whip up already volatile crowds. Before the campaign ended the two parties spent a half-million dollars, much of it for monetary and spirituous inducements to influence voting. When the crowds listened to issues at all, they heard Stuart talk about the tariff and about his part in the disfranchisement of Virginia's blacks. Slemp countered with the mountain art of "poor-mouthing," contrasting the frugal life on his Turkey Cove farm with the splendors of Elk Garden. He neglected to mention 86,000 acres of coal land which his company reportedly controlled in Kentucky.

Stuart lost by 217 votes—a moral victory of sorts in a district Republicans usually carried by 2,000 votes. The campaign afforded Stuart additional statewide visibility as a heroic would-be dragon-slayer who had lost a close and hard-fought decision. Soon local organization leaders began to receive constituent pressure to support Stuart for the governorship in 1913. Stuart further cemented his deal with the Martin men when in 1911 he did not support independents Carter Glass and William A. Jones in their unsuccessful challenge to Martin and Claude Swanson for U.S. Senate seats.

Only the volatile issue of liquor, "wets" versus "drys," remained as a possible obstacle in Stuart's path. His problem involved a proposed enabling act calling for a statewide referendum on Prohibition. Although Stuart had always favored local option, he pledged if elected governor to sign the Prohibition measure if the General Assembly passed it. This promise was sufficient to make him acceptable to the Reverend James Cannon, Jr., leader of the Virginia Anti-Saloon League. Stuart subsequently kept his counsel, talked little, and projected an image of conciliation and fair-mindedness. When his good friend Henry St. George Tucker withdrew from the 1913 race, there was no longer a need for a Democratic primary. The demoralized Republican party failed to nominate a candidate, and Stuart became the only man since the Civil War to be nominated for and elected to the governorship of Virginia without opposition. Stuart's willingness to abandon his own preference for local option was both a measure of his desire to unify Virginia Democrats and an explanation for the absence of opposition. It also meant that the issue was relegated to the race for the attorney general from which the victorious John Garland Pollard emerged as a leader of those seeking statewide Prohibition.

Stuart took office early in 1914, and more than two thousand people attended the inaugural reception despite an outbreak of smallpox in Richmond. In one of her last public appearances before the onset of serious illness, Mrs. Stuart wore a white brocaded velvet gown with a lining of pink chiffon. The new governor and his wife were accompanied in the receiving line by his aunt, J. E. B. Stuart's widow for fifty years. It may be presumed that the Stuarts' vivacious daughter, Mary Fulton, mingled with other teenagers and may even have affected the "debutante slouch"—an aberration in posture fashionable at the time.

Inaugural festivities soon gave way to the ongoing battle over Prohibition. Had Stuart been less intent upon conciliating opposing Democratic factions, he might have been able to postpone the enabling act for a few more years. Still, momentum was with the Prohibitionists. The act, passed by the House two years before, had failed in the Senate by only eight votes. The Reverend Mr. Cannon, who had been pressing for Prohibition since the organization of the Anti-Saloon League in 1901, smelled victory and lobbied energetically and illegally on the very floors of the General Assembly, while his publications flooded the homes of voters. Since the Democratic organization numbered among its most ardent champions the liquor dealers of the state, getting the support of Martin and his followers was a crucial test of Cannon's political skill. The leader of the Anti-Saloon League had a fine appreciation of the organization's tendency to adopt as its own causes that had gathered popular support. Martin and his followers had accepted with good grace the introduction of local option, the first step toward a dry Virginia, and Cannon had every reason to believe that the organization would follow the trend of public opinion until his goal was reached.

A careful strategist, Cannon had extracted a promise from J. Taylor Ellyson, the new lieutenant governor, that he would vote for the enabling act should the vote in the Senate end in a tie. He also had Stuart's word that he would endorse the enabling act if it were approved by the legislature. The bill passed the House by an overwhelming four-to-one margin, but produced a tie vote in the upper chamber. Ellyson broke the deadlock in favor of the act, although "wets" contended he was constitutionally prohibited from doing so. They argued that the act affected revenue and must therefore be approved by a majority. Stuart, after accepting written briefs from both sides, declared the enabling act had been passed and (in accordance with his preelection pledge) gave it his approval. The way was at last opened for a referendum, and a popular vote was scheduled for September 22, 1914.

This was the signal for Cannon to bring the full force of his political steamroller to bear against local option advocates mustered behind Stuart's friend Henry St. George Tucker. A large sum of money for publicity purposes was funneled into Cannon's hands, much of it in the form of loans from country banks on notes bearing the cosignatures of local political leaders. Richard E. Byrd joined the lieutenant governor in public support of Cannon, while Attorney General Pollard emphasized the link between Wilsonian progressivism and statewide Prohibition. Prohibitionists apparently were able to convince some voters that a vote against the liquor interests was a blow against the Martin organization. As the day for the referendum approached, Cannon exuded genuine confidence. Four days before the voting, he predicted victory in every part of the state except Richmond, and the returns proved him right. When statewide Prohibition was adopted by a margin of 30,000 votes, Martin and his colleagues were solidly in the Prohibitionist camp, giving every impression that they had been there all the time.

Stuart had a brief skirmish with Cannon over the details of enforcement. The Mapp bill, which gave legislative effect to the referendum, provided for appointment of a commissioner of moral welfare to work under the supervision of the legislature—a slap at gubernatorial influence and prerogative. When Cannon approved a compromise giving the governor the right to remove this official, Stuart shelved his reservations and became a strong supporter of statewide Prohibition.

Stuart's administration thus coincided with the triumph of the crusade against "demon rum" in Virginia, and his term witnessed other, less dramatic victories for the progressive impulse as well. One of these involved tax reform, an issue to which the governor attached particular importance. Since virtually all property was taxed as a source of state revenue, local officials were tempted to manipulate the system so as to shift the burden of taxation away from their communities. Resulting inequities are illustrated by the fact that Carroll County assessed property at 12.5 percent of true value; Rockbridge, at 36.5 percent.

General Assembly debate resulted in two proposals. One recommended a permanent tax commission to equalize assessments. The other proposed a "segregation plan" under which some taxables would be dedicated to the state treasury and others would belong exclusively to localities—thereby reducing pressures for fraudulent or discriminatory assessments by local officials. After some vacillation, Stuart came out strongly for the segregation plan, and the General Assembly enacted the proposal into law. At the end of the 1916–17 fiscal year, tax officials attributed a revenue increase of $740,134 directly to the implementation of the new system. This tax reform was a source of great satisfaction to Stuart, who expressed the belief at the end of his administration that the change had "justified itself completely."

In addition to upgrading the Commonwealth's revenue structure, the governor also worked to improve its criminal justice system. He appointed a commission to revise the Code of Virginia and in 1914 vetoed a bill which would have authorized penitentiary officials to parole convicts who had served at least three years of their sentences. Believing that the power to parole was an executive prerogative, Stuart also used his influence to delete from the revised Code of Virginia a law permitting the penitentiary board to parole convicts who had completed half their sentences. As had been the case with Prohibition enforcement, the cattle-king governor from the Southwest was determined to preserve and enhance the powers of his office.

In liquor control, tax reform, and law code revision, therefore, Stuart buttressed his standing as a moderate progressive. Even as he compiled his record on these issues, however, developments were transpiring thousands of miles away that would first overshadow, then engulf, the progressive impulse in the entire United States as well as Virginia. The governor had been in office less than five months when Archduke Francis Ferdinand was shot by a tubercular college dropout in the streets of Sarajevo. This event tripped the switch on the complex diplomatic and military machinery that would drag most European nations into war in 1914—with the United States following in 1917.

Shortly after the sinking of the *Lusitania* in 1915, Stuart began to advocate the bolstering of the nation's defenses. When President Wilson asked for a declaration of war in April 1917, Virginia's governor endorsed the move and plunged into his wartime duties. Stuart took special pride when the Old Dominion led all other states in filling its draft quota, and he also demonstrated an ongoing concern for increasing the Commonwealth's food production. One of Stuart's first acts was to proclaim "Planting Day," encouraging gardening in yards and window boxes. At the end of the first month of war, he appointed a Council of Defense which immediately predicted a serious food shortage in Virginia. Responding to resulting public pressure, the Virginia Bankers Association extended $200,000 in loans to farmers so they could expand production.

Hardworking and energetic, the governor made substantive contributions to the war effort, but his activities also made him susceptible to the "superpatriotic" excesses of the day—with unfortunate consequences for civil liberties. The First World War was marked by bitter and unreasoning hatred of people and things associated in any way with Germany. Even in Virginia, where Germans had been among the earliest settlers, those with Germanic names were harassed by their neighbors. Alleged German spies were arrested in such unlikely places as Norton; two mountain boys were arrested less than thirty miles from Elk Garden and charged with conspiring to overthrow the U.S. government.

In this tense atmosphere Professor Leon Whipple, director of the School of Journalism at the University of Virginia, explained his pacifism in a speech at Sweet Briar College, arguing that war could not "make the world safe for democracy" or destroy autocracy. Governor Stuart was greatly disturbed, and as a result, President Edwin A. Alderman of the University of Virginia asked the board of visitors to dismiss Whipple. (Apparently no one recalled Thomas Jefferson's famous injunction to "tolerate any error.") Stuart's role in this affair was perhaps the least creditable aspect of his wartime administration. In general, however, his record was much better than this episode would indicate, especially in regard to the economic and racial turmoil which World War I brought to the traditionally staid, straitlaced, and conservative Old Dominion.

Even before America's official entry into the conflict, industries supplying weapons and other equipment to the belligerent nations mushroomed in Virginia. After the United States joined the fighting, troops and supplies were shipped to Europe from Old Dominion ports; munitions works and other factories were hastily constructed in the Tidewater area, attracting large numbers of people of diverse backgrounds. One did not have to share Stuart's rural background to be appalled by the disorderly—frequently violent—conditions which arose.

In one instance, Governor Stuart ended illegal betting at the Jamestown Jockey Club by dispatching twenty special officers from western Virginia to the scene, but the situation at Hopewell was more difficult. Problems began when the Du Pont Company built a large munitions plant in this small country town just south of Richmond. Fed by war contracts, the new plant flourished, and Hopewell grew in a short time to a town of twenty thousand. Governmental machinery buckled under the strain, and new inhabitants, taking advantage of the anonymity afforded by a strange town, patronized the gin mills and brothels that soon flourished. In the middle of June 1915 Stuart sent L. R. Driver, an Ashland newspaper editor and former Internal Revenue agent, to investigate conditions in this new Gomorrah. He was robbed in his hotel room during his first night in Hopewell.

As the situation worsened, Attorney General Pollard asked that additional investigators be sent to the disorderly city. On August 2 the entire Hopewell police force was relieved of its duties and replaced by Du Pont security forces. The chief of police was charged with extortion, and a grand jury indicted 150 people within a fortnight. As the crackdown continued, the governor and his advisers decided further action was needed. Tentative plans were made for hiring detectives with state funds, and a patrol was established on a lonely stretch of highway between Hopewell and Petersburg where travelers had been molested. Stuart asked the Du Pont Company to construct a badly needed jail with the hope of reimbursement from the next General Assembly. Offering rewards for the capture of highwaymen, bootleggers, and gamblers, he also sent in a special prosecutor to share the burdens of the local Commonwealth's attorney. Toward the end of September 1915 the governor's chief of detectives reported a worsening of conditions, but this pessimism may have been caused by fatigue. It is true that one still encountered men in Hopewell with names such as "Oklahoma Harry" and "Mexican John" with pistols stuck in their belts. An outsider might also be shocked by the enthusiasm with which prominent citizens patronized a prostitution ring led by one "Bo Peep." Nevertheless, the county judge was quoted as being pleased with the improvements.

When three-quarters of the town of Hopewell was destroyed by fire on December 9, 1915, Stuart declared martial law and sent in the militia. A short time later the Mecklenburg Infantry was ordered to raid a "blind tiger," an establishment in which the dispenser of liquor was concealed from his customers. In the excitement a militia private plunged his bayonet into a Russian subject named Schake, and the troubles in Hopewell temporarily reached international proportions. The excitement that attended this incident gradually subsided.

Dealing firmly and effectively with the Hopewell situation, Stuart reaffirmed his commitment to law and order, a commitment also challenged by rising racial tensions. The increased demand for war matériel (coupled with the virtual cessation of immigration) soon created a nationwide labor shortage. Labor recruiting agencies in cities such as Richmond helped to facilitate the movement of blacks from Virginia to better-paying jobs in the North. Using newly passed legislation, Governor Stuart intervened personally to make examples of two agents who were trying to lure Du Pont workers from Hopewell to Pennsylvania. The black migration created large congregations of transient blacks at transportation centers, alarming some white citizens.

The labor shortage also gave blacks new affluence resented by many whites. These feelings, creating near hysteria in the Richmond area, greatly increased racial tension, and persistent rumors that German agents were stirring up racial unrest added another dimension to the situation. Yet there were Virginians who believed that the discriminatory treatment to which blacks had been subjected was a far greater stimulus to movement than the promise of material rewards. They argued that an amelioration of segregation practices and a just application of laws to all races would slow down the loss of valuable Virginians.

One of Governor Stuart's contributions to racial harmony lay in his determination to prevent lynchings and mob violence, and he dispatched militia all over the state to protect the rights of prisoners. Not until midway through the last full year of his administration did a masked mob succeed in taking a man from jail and hanging him. This Northumberland County outrage was the only incident of its sort during Stuart's tenure.

After four years in the Governor's Mansion—years of moderate reform, wartime mobilization, and social turmoil—Stuart completed his term early in 1918. He then accepted President Wilson's appointment to the War Industries Board, where he served as chairman of the Agriculture Advisory Committee. In 1920 he declined Wilson's invitation to serve on the Interstate Commerce Commission. Stuart went back to Elk Garden alone. His wife, who had been ill during most of his administration, died in 1920. In his mid-sixties, he had begun to suffer from the infirmities of age. A heart condition, which he had resolutely chosen to ignore, became worse. He also suffered from diabetes, but the self-discipline that marked the rest of his life did not extend to food. Special dietary products were ordered from Richmond, but a nephew observed that Uncle Henry ate them while he was waiting for dinner to be served.

In spite of ill health, Stuart again rode out over his outlying farms. Chauffeur-driven automobiles drove up to Elk Garden bearing meat-packing executives, their families, and their French maids. Stuart maintained his political contacts and in 1921 served as president of the Pay-As-You-Go Association which was instrumental in defeating a proposal to sell highway construction bonds. He also gave active support to Harry F. Byrd in his bid for the governorship in 1925. His business life was relieved by frequent trips abroad, which he made in the company of a nurse.

Stuart became ill in May 1933, and physicians abandoned hope for recovery after the middle of July. A final turn for the worse came on the morning of July 24. During the last hours of his life the former governor regained consciousness long enough to say to anxious relatives: "I realize that I am quite ill. . . . I don't want the word to go out that I am on my death bed." He died peacefully during that long summer afternoon.

Stuart's death was mourned throughout the state and especially in southwest Virginia where he enjoyed a special relationship with people of all ages, often regaling listeners with an endless supply of mountain stories and eminently repeatable aphorisms. A master of understatement, a gift much appreciated by mountain people, Stuart once prefaced some public remarks on calf prices with, "I deal a little in cattle myself." People remembered the special chairs provided at public occasions to support his massive frame. Some recalled his church work; others, the Olympic-type games he held at Elk Garden for small boys when he was in his mid-seventies. To most of his neighbors he was a man whose demeanor inspired respect and who was, in the words of his niece, "elegant, erudite, and charming."

Stuart always disliked the "hail fellow well met" role that the quest for public office demanded. Politics were to him a sideshow rather than the main event. Stuart was, above all else, a farmer and a very good one. The adroitly handled expansion of his estate and the efficient management of his large and complex operation attested to superb organizing skill and firm leadership. Perhaps it was a sense of duty, an adherence to the planter ideal, or even a middle-aged urge to make his life "count" which caused Stuart to venture into the mainstream of Virginia politics. He took with him the experience, abilities, and prejudices of a mountain patrician.

Like his contemporary Theodore Roosevelt, Stuart had an almost religious desire to see order prevail; his determination to guard the prerogatives of the executive branch apparently stemmed from the same obsession. Accustomed to administrative complexities, he had no difficulty in dealing with the bureaucratic imperatives of wartime governorship. Experience with taxation and railroad freight rates made it possible for him to make lasting contributions in both fields. One might expect years of running a virtually autonomous operation to breed a degree of imperiousness, but Stuart showed considerable flexibility—even to the point of changing his mind completely, as he did with regard to tax segregation, statewide Prohibition, and his attitude toward the Martin organization. If Stuart's background and temperament precluded more conspicuous involvement in the progressive cause, his reasoned flexibility, basic sympathy with many progressive goals, and ability to work with opposing factions made him a good choice for the governorship in a time of change.

SOURCES

Stuart's Executive Papers (Virginia State Library) and the James Hay Papers (University of Virginia) are helpful in understanding the governor's career. An interview with Cecil Glovier of Lebanon, Virginia, provided insights into Stuart's agricultural operations. Interviews with Mrs. Harry C. Stuart, a niece by marriage, and William A. Stuart, a grand-nephew, were invaluable in portraying Stuart's personality, especially in his later years.

These books and articles provide indispensable background: Allen W. Moger's *Virginia: Bourbonism to Byrd, 1870–1925* (Charlottesville, 1968); Andrew Buni's *The Negro in Virginia Politics, 1902–1965* (Charlottesville, 1967); Ralph Clipman McDanel's *The Virginia Constitutional Convention of 1901–1902* (Baltimore, 1928); Henry C. Ferrell's "Prohibition, Reform, and Politics in Virginia, 1895–1916," *East Carolina Publications in History* 3 (1960): 175–242; and Guy B. Hathorn's "Congressional Campaign in the Fighting Ninth," *Virginia Magazine of History and Biography* 66 (1958): 337–44.

A comprehensive bibliography may be found in Charles E. Poston's "Henry Carter Stuart in Virginia Politics, 1855–1933" (M.A. thesis, University of Virginia, 1969).

WESTMORELAND DAVIS

Governor of Virginia

1918–1922

WESTMORELAND DAVIS

Progressive Insurgent

Jack Temple Kirby

Westmoreland Davis was a genteel maverick of brief public career and lasting significance to the agricultural, political, and administrative history of the Commonwealth. The scion of planting families of Virginia, South Carolina, and Mississippi, he was born aboard a sailing ship on the North Atlantic as his parents made their annual voyage to Liverpool in August 1859. Ten months later Morley Davis was left fatherless when "a pestilence" swept through Hinds County, Mississippi, taking Thomas Gordon Davis and Westmoreland's older brother and sister. Virginia-born Annie Morriss Davis and her infant son went to live with her brother in Richmond, where they endured the Civil War and its aftermath. In the meantime, after some years of apparent mismanagement, five plantations in Hinds and Yazoo counties were sold for pittances. Frustrated belle Annie later complained of "many bitter years of poverty and destitution."

Despite these reverses she reared Morley Davis well amid the cream of Old Dominion society. After studying at a private school in Hanover County, he won a state cadetship to the Virginia Military Institute and (at the tender age of fourteen) went off to Lexington. Before graduation at seventeen in June 1877, young Davis had become a Sigma Nu, a skilled debater, and company co-commander of cadets. Returning to Richmond, he found social success as the youngest captain of the city's historic Company C of the Virginia Volunteers, and after a year of postgraduate study at the University of Virginia he enrolled as a law student at Columbia University. For three years he studied and slept in a garret and clerked in a New York law office.

His reward was meteoric success. Upon graduation in 1887 Davis began practice with an established firm in the new Equitable Building on Broadway. In a short time he was a partner, dealing primarily in corporate matters. In 1892 his financial well-being was magnified several times over by marriage to Marguerite Inman, a petite, cultured daughter of Georgia–New York planter and cotton broker William H. Inman. In both Davis and his southern-born wife the gentry tradition of quiet and secure wealth was strong. They wore expensive but tasteful clothes, lived well but not ostentatiously. Nonetheless both were children of the neo-Gothic, brownstone Victorian era. They spent their first married year at the prestigious Waldorf Hotel, then moved twenty-five miles north of Manhattan to an estate in the Tuxedo district of Orange County. Early in 1901 Marguerite, who was four feet eleven inches tall and weighed only about 105 pounds, appeared on the cover of *Rider and Driver,* a sophisticated equestrian magazine. A year later a photograph in the New York *Press* showed the couple, mounted and in hunting togs, leaping over an ivied stone wall somewhere in Orange: Marguerite, the picture of gentility, and Davis, stouter than his VMI portrait and wearing side-whiskers.

Their marriage was a sound bond of love and mutual respect; there were no children, but Marguerite idolized her older companion, and Davis seems to have always played the role of fond guardian. Between the couple, however, there existed a fundamental difference in personalities. Mrs. Davis loved society and the less serious life. He, having "gotten ahead," was never able to ease his pace; constant and deliberate work was now a way of life. And retirement from the law and from New York at age forty-four in 1903 did not imply a change of character. Purchasing Morven Park, a colonial-era plantation near Leesburg, Virginia, the couple became members of the Loudoun Hunt Club, but Davis did not become a full-time country gentleman. Instead, he transformed Morven Park into a productive dairy farm, voraciously consuming the literature and spirit of agricultural reform—or "progressive farming" as it was called. He planted alfalfa and purchased purebred stock for his textbook-model farm. He diversified and rotated crops, limed and heavily fertilized fields, stored ensilage in new concrete silos, and built modern barns with gravity-filled manure bins. Within four years the heaviest labor was done, and Davis restlessly gravitated toward other activities.

Late in 1907 he cofounded and became first vice-president of the Virginia Dairymen's Association, a lobby designed to transform the Old Dominion into a Wisconsin of the South and to win state legislation protecting dairymen from dairy substitutes. Two years later he became president of the Virginia State Farmers' Institute, a small but prestigious group of about two hundred middling-to-wealthy farmers interested in progressive farming. The institute, like similar organizations in other states, held annual meetings where professors and successful farmers lectured on such topics as red clover, Percheron horses, and beekeeping. After Davis became president the educational sessions continued, but the new leader converted the sedentary society into a determined lobby. He created a legislative committee with himself as chairman, contacted key legislators, and in 1910 began to press for a comprehensive program of agricultural reform which was in the main implemented within a half-dozen years.

In January 1910 Davis and the Farmers' Institute presented their first legislative package to the General Assembly—with less than encouraging results. But two years later they achieved passage of a bill to establish state-owned fertilizer plants and an innocuous-appearing "ice cream act" discriminating against confections made from dried or condensed dairy products. According to the act, ice cream not comprised chiefly of fresh milk had to display a large label stating the fact.

Davis and the institute achieved their greatest success in 1914. Organizational work in the 1913 elections led to formation of a nonpartisan legislative farm bloc known as the Agricultural Conference, giving added weight to Davis's lobbying efforts. The most important of the institute-sponsored bills created a legislative reference bureau—a Davis-inspired copy of a Wisconsin institution. Operating independently from the State Library under its own director, the bureau was a device to aid farmer-legislators who lacked legal training. A peculiarly progressive synthesis, it sought both to return the machine-dominated General Assembly to the people and to utilize the services of experts in a complex world. The 1914 Assembly also passed a law penalizing owners of dogs that destroyed farm animals and crops, increased appropriations for rural roads and schools, created farmer cooperatives (facilitating the work of the new Virginia Farmers' Educational and Cooperative Union), and permitted individual farmers (in addition to middlemen and cooperatives) to buy fertilizer in bulk.

The institute and the Agricultural Conference won further success in the 1916 session, the last before the progressive farming movement ran its course and was stifled by war. First, a commission merchants law, designed to protect farmers from fraud by registration and bonding of agricultural produce middlemen, was passed. Then, after nearly a quarter century of lobbying by Senator Eugene C. Massie, the General Assembly adopted the Torrens system of land registration, a simple, low-cost method of recording and transferring land.

Creation of state-owned fertilizer plants in 1912 was an especially brutal fight. Taking a cue from Illinois where convicts ground lime and railroads transported the product at a low rate, in January 1910 the Farmers' Institute petitioned the General Assembly for a reproduction of the Illinois plan. Despite opposition from the Richmond lobby of the National Lime Manufacturers' Association, a limestone bill easily passed the House of Delegates. It was blocked, however, in the Senate. A battle of interest groups ensued with Davis excoriating his opponents in classic Progressive-era language as a nefarious "trust" and an "arrogant and insolent body of alien and mercenary manufacturers." The lime manufacturers maintained that the stymied bill was "socialistic" and unconstitutional in that it would place the state in competition with private enterprise.

In the meantime Davis broke whatever ties he may have held with the laissez-faire past. An interested partisan, he found ideological justification for his course during a visit to the University of Wisconsin in 1911 where he absorbed the ideas of liberal economics professor John R. Commons, toured the university's famed College of Agriculture, and imbibed hearty drafts of La

Follette progressivism. Davis seemed most taken with the broader implications of the "Wisconsin Idea"—that a state university had an obligation to
taxpaying supporters to spread its expertise throughout the entire state. From
Wisconsin, Davis exhorted Virginians to "abandon [their] economics [of]
austere individualism . . . and set in motion the benign methods of *aided*
individualism, which offer opportunity . . . in all the walks of life. England,
Ireland, France, Germany and the Progressive Northwestern states have
blazed the way; we have but to profit by their experience and example."
Citizen-farmers, he stressed, must learn to use the machinery of government
for their (and presumably the public's) self-interest, just as industrialists and
railwaymen had for decades. What maverick Davis proposed was not particularly novel, but it was rather shocking nonetheless to Old Dominion tradi-
tionalists. As the lime debate neared its climax, Davis obtained an additional
forum in 1912 by purchasing the *Southern Planter,* a monthly agricultural
paper. What had been a nonpartisan journal became under Davis a strident
advocate for his views and eventually a political organ as well.

With the warm support of Governor William H. Mann, the legislature
finally authorized two lime plants early in 1912, but the struggle was not
over. Of nine railroads operating in the state, only two agreed to a low freight
rate, and lime manufacturers petitioned the state Supreme Court of Appeals
to declare the act unconstitutional. Not until January 1914 did the judges
validate the legislation; the first plant finally began operations in mid-1915.
This victory seemed a turning point in the agricultural history of the Old
Dominion. "Lime, Legumes, And Then Anything You Want To Grow" was
the *Southern Planter*'s "watchword of progress and the new civilization to
be." Virginia's farm problems were, of course, not solved, but a most productive six-year campaign was concluded—accompanied by the most important
ideological departure since the creation of the Corporation Commission at the
turn of the century. And, in the process, Westmoreland Davis had contracted
an incurable case of political fever.

In his mid-fifties, Davis, by virtue of his energy and devotion to work,
probably deserved the position of leadership he so ardently desired; yet one
must appreciate his personality—and the importance of financial security to
the fulfillment of his ambitions. At his death in 1942 the value of Davis's
tangible and intangible property—that is, Morven Park, other real estate, and
stocks and bonds (including those of the *Southern Planter*)—was estimated at
$697,000. The personal wealth of Marguerite Davis and her sister, Willie
Lee Inman (who lived with the Davises), was much greater: with intangibles,
Miss Inman alone was worth more than $1 million in 1931, and Marguerite
had at least a comparable fortune. Davis managed their holdings, and the
Inman money and his own kept him constantly involved in correspondence
and travels. Nevertheless, wealth had its rewards.

The family lived in the showplace of northern Virginia, and there was no shortage of funds to finance Marguerite's architectural landscape projects and Davis's agricultural experiments. Marguerite's gowns came from Paris; they owned a veritable stable of automobiles; and in 1925 they acquired a yacht. Called the *Virginian,* it sported a blue ensign with the initial "D" and was used primarily on long vacations from Morven Park down the Potomac to Miss Inman's property in Florida. Davis could never bear so much relaxation and sold the *Virginian* in 1929 for $16,500. Life at Morven Park combined the easier temperament of Marguerite and the drive of Westmoreland—on a grand scale. The balls and luncheons they hosted became a tradition which lasted well into the 1930s. At a 1928 luncheon for local farmers the fare included fifty-five turkeys, twelve boiled hams, fifty gallons of ice cream, fifty gallons of coffee, and fifty gallons of oysters. Twenty waiters served; a seven-piece band entertained. Whiskey and beer appeared at these galas after the repeal of Prohibition.

As an economic enterprise Morven Park was a model of businesslike farm efficiency and served also as a testing station for crops and procedures recommended in the *Southern Planter.* For four decades, however, the chief enterprise was livestock breeding. The Guernsey herd remained the backbone of the farm, but Davis prudently shifted his investment from draft horses to race horses during the twenties. By the mid-thirties he had become one of the Saratoga track's major suppliers; five colts brought $7,000 in 1936. During the thirties he also invested heavily—with commensurate profits—in poultry.

There was the aura of the antebellum planter and his domain at Morven Park, but Davis was thoroughly "modern" and diversified. He learned economy, efficiency, and scientific management from the Yankees and employed these new techniques to revive the agrarian tradition of his ancestors. As evidenced by occasional emotional outbursts during his public career, beneath the disciplined surface there was a very human Westmoreland Davis. Normally reserved, self-righteous, and somewhat Victorian in his personal relations, among close friends and associates he was warm, considerate, and witty. For much of his life nearly everyone around him was his junior—his wife included. They remember him as kindly and paternal. With close contemporaries, though, he seems to have been jovial, even garrulous. The *Southern Planter* offices soon became his base of operations, and no matter where he happened to be—in Europe, New York, Virginia, Georgia, or Florida—Davis demanded a precise flow of communications. On one occasion, unable to reach his secretary by long-distance telephone during business hours, he delivered a sharp rebuke and required her to submit a three-paragraph explanation of her failure to answer.

On the subject of his record of public service, Davis was almost paranoid, fearful that posterity would forget him and suspicious that the press was systematically awarding his accomplishments to others. The limestone-grinding act, the legislative reference bureau, and his later gubernatorial accomplishments were monuments he rightfully insisted upon for himself. Thus in his personal papers and in the *Southern Planter* this concern for proper credit appears time and again. These fears focused on the dominant Democratic political organization. Mere mention of Senator Thomas S. Martin and, later, Harry Flood Byrd would raise Davis's eyebrows, and a favorable remark about the Byrd administration (1926–30) would send him into near paroxysms. At the age of eighty, in the centennial edition of the *Southern Planter,* he offered this self-serving assessment of his journalistic efforts: "The *Southern Planter* has at times been criticized for its inquiries into governmental matters and its boldness in exposing inefficiency, wastefullness, and misfeasance in public office, but *invariably* this criticism has come from those whose abuses of public trust the paper was striving to abolish. A policeman is never popular with a burglar."

But while an impatient, contentious, and vigorous man of many affairs, Davis was also a reading and reflective man. For practical uses he consumed technical matter on farming, business, and government, but he also found time to read the novels of Winston Churchill and, later, Margaret Mitchell's *Gone with the Wind.* A conspicuous section of his library contained the works of the Ohio progressive writer, Frederick C. Howe. Much like Howe, Davis left a lucrative corporate law practice to shout against the trusts. There the parallel ends, for unlike the Ohioan, Davis was primarily a man of action. An intelligent, sensitive being, he needed intellectual justification for his course, but impulse to act usually preceded sanctification of motive. Intellectualized self-interest probably best characterizes the twists and turns of his public career. In short, the Lord of Morven, the captain of the *Planter* bridge, and the wizard of economy and efficiency was a humanly fallible if extraordinary member of the species. Yet despite many mistakes, perhaps that is the worst that might be said of him, for he was utterly sincere and his self-interest often corresponded to the public good.

Under normal circumstances Davis's ambition to be governor (becoming obvious as early as 1914) would have been frustrated. Despite his family background he was a relative newcomer to the Commonwealth who would have to contend with "Yankee carpetbagger" charges. Further, Virginia politics was run by the Democratic organization's "Big Four"—U.S. Senators Thomas Staples Martin, Jr., and Claude A. Swanson, Congressman Henry D. Flood, and House of Delegates Speaker (1908–12) Richard E. Byrd. Westmoreland Davis had not served any political apprenticeship, and although he had worked well with organization Governor Mann, his looming candidacy was considered an outside challenge by the Martin organization. Virginia's small, conservative, white electorate was generally satisfied with its honest, quiet, and lackluster rule; yet Martin and his men were resilient enough to respond to popular issues such as the progressive agriculture program of Davis and the Farmers' Institute.

But it was Prohibition, not farming, that gave Davis his chance. After years of agitation, in 1910 the Virginia Anti-Saloon League, led by brilliant Methodist cleric James Cannon, Jr., began demanding statewide Prohibition. When efforts to secure a popular referendum on Prohibition were rebuffed in the legislature, Cannon threatened in 1914 to hitch his considerable popular strength to the rising star of young independent John Garland Pollard, an ardent "dry" and candidate-apparent for the 1917 gubernatorial nomination. Martin and Flood then came around, mercilessly cracked the whip over state senators, and produced a tie vote on a Prohibition referendum enabling bill. The tie was broken in Cannon's favor by Lieutenant Governor J. Taylor Ellyson, aging Confederate veteran, Martin henchman, inveterate imbiber, and now the organization's dry candidate for governor. Later in the year Virginia's voters endorsed Prohibition, which became the law of the Commonwealth late in 1916.

Into this near-comical situation stepped Davis, who made the 1917 contest one of the few three-cornered affairs in the state's postbellum history. With organization support behind Ellyson and most independents backing Pollard, Davis would have had no chance had he not declared himself in 1914 opposed to Prohibition. An unemotional Episcopalian who, ironically enough, abstained from alcoholic beverages, Davis announced that he favored local option. In Progressive-era parlance this made him a "wet" in a race with two "drys." Such was the irony that would make a wet, inexperienced, independent Democrat the governor of a dry and machine-controlled state. Davis received fewer than half of nearly 90,000 votes cast. Ellyson and Pollard split the rest, and the split elected Davis. Divided Prohibitionists and shocked organization men observed his inauguration on February 1, 1918, with dismay and hostility.

The Davis governorship was marked by backbiting partisanship and interminable battles between the executive and legislature. To make matters worse, Lieutenant Governor B. Frank Buchanan, Attorney General John R. Saunders, and all other elected state administrators were Martin men. Yet Davis was successful in establishing a record as a progressive "business governor." The appellation "business" meant not that he reverted to the corporate lawyer role, but that Davis was obsessed with economy and efficiency in government, with centralizing and systematizing admistration after the industrial-corporate model which he admired.

When Davis was inaugurated, there were approximately ninety administrative agencies, only about fifty appointed directly by the executive and nearly half of this number requiring Senate confirmation. Most individual agencies, after appointment, selected their own chairmen. Davis felt that "the affairs of the state should be conducted as those of a business concern," with all departments answerable directly to the executive, who would be "in effect the state manager." For his tenure, however, Davis had to content himself with taking advantage of existing executive prerogatives and building toward his ideal.

Davis's most lasting contribution was the creation of the executive budget system—a nonpartisan measure endorsed by the General Assembly early in the 1918 session. Until 1920, when the new budgeting system became effective, the biennial, sixty-day legislative session was the scene of frantic budget making for the coming fiscal biennium. Appropriations bills were characterized by local jealousies and an inefficiency which militated against the broader interest. Davis believed that the techniques of scientific, rational management which he had learned in New York and carried to agriculture were applicable to such matters.

The new system, which centralized state budgeting in the hands of the governor, worked this way. Biennially, in the fall of odd-numbered years, all state agency heads would submit estimates of operating expenses for the next two years. The state auditor likewise presented an estimate of money needed for appropriations by the incoming General Assembly. All reports were to show the current financial situation and explain increases or decreases relative to previous appropriations. The governor, with a reasonably accurate balance sheet for the entire state in hand, would then conduct his own survey of state needs, prepare an overall budget and requests for appropriations, and present his findings to the legislature. The executive budget measure authorized the General Assembly to alter amounts of individual items; but, except in emergencies, it could not consider new items or totally eliminate any proposed. The gradual undoing of Virginia's overwhelming legislative supremacy and bureaucratic tangle had begun.

The 1918 legislative session also witnessed Davis's first effort to create a state central purchasing agency. Thwarted by a hostile Senate, he persevered until authorization finally was granted in 1920. Prior to the Davis administration each of the ninety-odd agencies and institutions of the state had made its own purchases, frequently with small or no invoice discounts. Now, wherever practicable, mass purchases would be engineered by the central purchasing administrator, whose salary and office expenses were soon more than offset by proven savings.

Broader than the economy and efficiency theme were penitentiary reforms Davis carried out toward the end of his administration. Public criticism of guard brutality and living conditions in the main prison at Richmond became common as early as 1919. But the governor's participation in the controversy dated from a disagreement early in 1920. The Board of Charities and Corrections had recommended new punishment rules for the penitentiary and the hiring of a full-time resident physician in place of a part-time doctor. The penitentiary board, some of whose members Davis had appointed, dallied, then refused to act on the full-time physican suggestion. The incumbent doctor, it appeared, simply did not wish to give up either his private practice or his prison position. Davis, embarrassed by the recalcitrance of his own supporters, decided to act decisively.

Late in March 1920, he dismissed three penitentiary board members and replaced them with "reliable" men. Over the next two years sweeping reforms, both humanitarian and businesslike, were effected. The new full-time physician, with the aid of state and federal health officers, battled venereal diseases and instituted health record-keeping. Dispensaries and prison hospitals were renovated, screens installed in windows, toilets added, and better lighting and bedding provided. Virginia Polytechnic Institute experts expanded the progressive agriculture movement into state penal facilities. The penitentiary guard was militarized, retrained, and given new command. Traditional striped garb was abandoned in favor of "prison brown" uniforms. So far as possible the races were separated—culminating a "reform" movement begun years before throughout the South by white progressives. Davis also ordered the systematization of prison accounting and (in order to make procedures comport better with the executive budgeting system) departmentalized the penal administration.

Perhaps the most important of the governor's prison reforms was the institution of state-use industries. For decades Virginia had indulged in the notorious practice of leasing its convicts to private businesses, where they were worked mercilessly. The 1918 and 1920 General Assemblies voted to end leases in favor of a state-use industrial system, but the penitentiary board did not act until Davis reconstructed it. Soon prisoner-staffed shops were producing guard uniforms and shoes, public school furniture, and small metal products. A printing office was also opened under Davis's new prison Industrial Department. And after Davis left office, as existing contracts expired, the leasing system came to an end.

From the outset of his administration, Davis decided to build his own organization and do battle with the machine, rather than seek conciliation and reward from the Martin group. Where possible he replaced Martin and Cannon associates with his planter colleagues and "wet" urban followers. Untouchable and unfriendly state bureaucrats were punished with executive harassment and stationary salaries. Although Davis pretended to respect the popular decision on Prohibition, in actuality he worked to undermine the "noble experiment." Chief targets were Prohibition department head J. Sidney Peters, Methodist minister and principal Cannon lieutenant, and the department's $50,000 enforcement appropriation. An attempt in 1918 to reduce this fund failed, but public alarm at violence accompanying agent activity in 1919 led to success early in 1920. The Assembly agreed to reduce the department's appropriation and to replace Peters with an alienated organization man who had become a Davis follower.

Davis's rising star corresponded to the nadir of the old Martin constellation. The national preparedness controversy of 1915–16 and America's subsequent entry into the European war sapped the energies of organization leaders Martin, Swanson, and Flood—all of whom chaired critical congressional committees. "The reins of leadership," R. E. Byrd sadly observed, "are lying on the ground." Davis boldly attempted to seize them. Martin's death in November 1919 presented a golden opportunity. Among many the governor might have appointed to fill the vacancy, Carter Glass seemed a brilliant choice. Not only had the old insurgent achieved national stature as Wilsonian fiscal policymaker in the House and as secretary of the treasury, but his elevation to the Senate removed a sure rival of Davis himself. Davis obviously assumed that Glass would become his ally in the 1922 primary battle against Senator Swanson.

But Davis's fortunes rapidly declined. In the 1921 gubernatorial primary he backed the wrong candidate. Kindly, professorial Henry St. George Tucker, perennial office seeker, had publicly denounced both Prohibition and woman's suffrage when the state and nation were committed to both—and when women in Virginia were about to vote in their first state election! Consequently it was not surprising that Tucker was crushed by his organization opponent, E. Lee Trinkle. In the six months between Trinkle's inauguration and the senatorial primary, the new state regime ousted all vulnerable Davis appointees. Meanwhile, Carter Glass, wearied of factional battles and eager for peace and security, was wooed into neutrality, then outright membership in the machine, by irresistable Claude Swanson.

Although the organization stood almost leaderless (Flood died in 1921), the local courthouse-clique foundation remained firm, along with traditional allegiances and habits. Then suddenly a new generation of leaders appeared. From the Valley area young state Senator Harry Flood Byrd (son of Richard E. Byrd and nephew of Henry D. Flood) galvanized the Seventh District against Tucker and Davis and began building strong personal ties with organization men in the Southwest and Southside. From Tucker's own Lexington another state senator (and future U.S. senator), A. Willis Robertson, joined hands with Byrd. And in Alexandria, Commonwealth's Attorney Howard Worth Smith helped organize northern Virginia. All this, with the addition of the revered person of incumbent candidate Swanson, sent Davis down to ignominious defeat in August 1922.

From his political oblivion Davis watched the rise of Harry Flood Byrd as the machine's new master. As governor during the late twenties, Byrd brought to a grand conclusion Davis's work of systematizing the state government. Yet Davis remained on the outside. Indignant and cantankerous throughout, he bitterly opposed the Byrd organization and became one of the state's most ardent New Dealers in the thirties. Frustrated in a variety of attempts to overthrow Byrd, Davis in one of his last public acts proposed in 1938 the elimination of poll taxes, hoping that a broadened electorate might vote his way. Davis was in good health on his eighty-third birthday in 1942, but a week later he was suddenly stricken at home and died quietly at the Johns Hopkins hospital in Baltimore on September 2.

Quick, deliberate, and precise, this versatile man had achieved striking success in three careers before his sixty-third birthday, then built a legend (perhaps a fourth career) upon his tenacious opposition to Byrd. Always a pragmatist, he adapted readily to the changing scene about him. He was ever abreast of his times, occasionally far ahead of them.

In essence, the life of Westmoreland Davis was a microcosm of the industrial and scientific revolutions of his day. In a southern context Davis mirrored, perhaps epitomized, the transition in one man's lifetime from a relatively primitive order to the highly complex, systematized world of the twentieth century. Since Davis belonged neither to the masses nor the national leadership elite but to society's middle-level "doers," his sensitivity to the mathematical rhythm of material progress and his impulse to apply this precision to public affairs helps explain a great deal about his era. Imaginative, dynamic men, fascinated by throbbing engines and sophisticated techniques, applied the methodology of the machine age to society and government and never lost hope of reconciling man's nobler institutions with his practical inventions. Virginia had such a figure in Davis. Political ineptitude and bad luck abruptly ended his political career. In another state with another political system he might have served well for another decade or more.

SOURCES

The Westmoreland Davis Papers (University of Virginia), a collection of 140 boxes, comprise the basic source for this essay. Included are voluminous collections of newspaper clippings, publications by the Virginia State Farmers' Institute and other groups with which Davis was associated, files of his *Southern Planter,* and considerable gubernatorial correspondence. Nevertheless, the Davis Executive Papers (Virginia State Library) remain valuable for routine administrative matters.

See also Allen W. Moger's *Virginia: Bourbonism to Byrd, 1870–1925* (Charlottesville, 1968); Raymond H. Pulley's *Old Virginia Restored: An Interpretation of the Progressive Impulse, 1870–1930* (Charlottesville, 1968); Robert A. Hohner's "Bishop Cannon's Apprenticeship in Temperance Politics, 1901–1918," *Journal of Southern History* 34 (1968): 33–49, and his doctoral dissertation, "Prohibition and Virginia Politics, 1900–1916," (Duke University, 1965); and Henry C. Ferrell's dissertation biography of Claude A. Swanson (University of Virginia, 1964).

A detailed biography is found in Jack Temple Kirby, *Westmoreland Davis: Virginia Planter-Politician, 1859–1942* (Charlottesville, 1968).

E. LEE TRINKLE

Governor of Virginia

1922–1926

E. LEE TRINKLE

Prelude to Byrd

L. Stanley Willis

The years between the death of Thomas S. Martin in 1919 and the election of Harry F. Byrd as governor in 1925 were significant ones for the Virginia Democratic organization. Facing many challenges during this vacuum of leadership, the machine anxiously awaited the emergence of a new "boss." The governorship of E. Lee Trinkle served as the battleground, and among the victims was Trinkle himself.

Elbert Lee Trinkle was born in Wytheville on March 12, 1876, the youngest of three sons. Great-grandson of German Lutherans who had migrated from Pennsylvania before the Revolution, Trinkle had a comfortable childhood. His father, a distinguished Civil War veteran and a pillar of the local Presbyterian church, died in 1883, leaving a sizable landed estate. Young Lee, well educated in local private schools, at an early age demonstrated a propensity for oratory. In 1892 he entered Hampden-Sydney College and, after graduation, studied law at the University of Virginia. He was first in his class at Hampden-Sydney, belonged to Sigma Chi Alpha fraternity, won numerous medals for debating and oratory, and was manager of several athletic and literary activities. At Virginia he won first prize in the moot court competition in 1897–98 and was voted most influential man at the university by the student body.

When the twenty-two-year-old fledgling lawyer returned to Wytheville, his forte was pleading before a jury. Of average height, with long arms and a deep, heavy chest, Trinkle was, in the vernacular of the time, "prosperous looking." Wavy black hair parted stylishly in the middle topped his large head. Square jaws and broad brow encompassed his oval eyes, large, straight nose, and full mouth. An attractive figure, he was completely at ease before an audience or jury. He never spoke too long and was adept at the colloquial allusion so loved by his mountain brethren. Neither a deep nor an original thinker, he was, instead, an accomplished speaker undisturbed by legal or political abstraction. As a successful attorney and businessman, Trinkle added to the family landholdings. A booster and a joiner, he belonged to a wide range of professional and service organizations which, for him, served several purposes. A gregarious man who loved fellowship, Trinkle also understood the political advantage of wide acquaintanceship.

In 1898, the year that Trinkle began to practice law, the Ninth District was torn by a bitter congressional race that saw Judge William F. Rhea of Bristol defeat his Republican opponent. Four years later Rhea faced an old Mahone follower, Colonel Campbell Slemp of Wise County. When Democratic election officials allegedly adjusted the vote, Slemp challenged the returns, and the state Board of Canvassers awarded him the victory. For the next two decades, Campbell Slemp and his son C. Bascom controlled the Ninth. Bascom Slemp, one of Virginia's most astute politicians and a brilliant organizer who succeeded to the House on his father's death in 1907, extended his organization into every precinct and made precinct leaders see that new Republicans were registered and that every Republican's poll tax was paid. To redeem the Ninth from this efficient organization became one of the fondest dreams of Virginia Democrats. Money and talent poured in each election year, and whoever contested Slemp was assured of wide public recognition.

Trinkle, deeply involved in these efforts, served as Wythe County Democratic chairman at a time when it was alleged that fully one-fourth of the county's vote was for sale. In 1910 he had his first real opportunity for wide exposure during a congressional campaign which featured the "Battle of the Giants" between Bascom Slemp and Henry Carter Stuart of Russell County, owner of the largest cattle ranch east of the Mississippi and the district's leading Democrat. Stuart's real goal was the Governor's Mansion, and it was widely acknowledged that he was contesting Slemp so as to build a statewide image. Trinkle toured the hustings with Stuart, and although Stuart lost a close contest marked by intense bitterness and extraordinary corruption, Trinkle proved a popular and effective speaker. From that time on he was much in demand during every district campaign.

Trinkle's first chance for elective office came in 1915 when the local state senator did not stand for reelection. Two Democrats, one of whom was Trinkle's cousin, were anxious to fill the seat, but party leaders looked for a compromise candidate who would not be resented by either man. Trinkle was the choice of Wytheville Democrats, and when presented to the district convention at Pearisburg, he was nominated by acclamation. Unopposed by the Republicans, he was elected in November. Trinkle, who served in the next four sessions of the legislature, consistently spoke out on three issues—Prohibition, woman suffrage, and the ongoing effort to equalize educational opportunities for women. These stands cast him as a member of a small progressive wing of organization legislators. Normally, his legislative activities would have been quickly forgotten. Fate stepped in, however, and made him the organization's gubernatorial choice in 1921.

Prohibition was a major issue in Virginia throughout the first quarter of the twentieth century. Led by James Cannon, Jr., a Southside Methodist minister, the Anti-Saloon League posed a major threat to the organization by 1910. Resisting its demands for a time, the organization finally embraced the

league after 1912 and supported a successful referendum on statewide Prohibition in 1914. In 1916 the legislature was faced with the task of implement-
ing that decision. The league wanted the state Prohibition commissioner
elected by the legislature, but Governor Henry Carter Stuart preferred an
official directly responsible to him. In a major speech, Trinkle staked out a
position independent of both the dry forces and the organization. He supported an amendment to place the commissioner under the attorney general's
office with the attorney general as ex officio head. Stressing that utilization of
existing administrative machinery would be cheaper and more efficient, Trinkle put himself in the progressive camp. His proposal, however, was unacceptable to the machine because Attorney General John Garland Pollard, an
organization nemesis and probable gubernatorial candidate in 1917, as ex
officio head of the Prohibition commission, would be constantly in the public
eye. The league's wishes were eventually sustained, but Trinkle's willingness
to support the more efficient approach demonstrated an emphasis on principle
and an independence of action continued throughout his political life.

Trinkle also captured the spotlight on two other issues during the same
session—woman suffrage and the coordinate college question. Although suffrage played a minor role in the 1916 Assembly, it would soon be of major
concern. At the 1916 session Trinkle established himself as a champion of
the movement, serving as patron of Richmond suffragists—a group that included Mrs. Mary Munford, Ellen Glasgow, Mary Johnston, and Mrs. Lila
Meade Valentine—when they appeared before a crowded joint meeting of the
Committees on Privileges and Elections. The matter was not debated in the
Senate, and a proposed joint resolution to submit the question to a referendum
was defeated in the House, 40 to 52. A 27-vote increase since 1912, this
indicated growing support. Trinkle made political capital from his stand, even
though it put him at odds with a majority of the organization.

His position in the coordinate college debate was less supportive of female equality. The movement to establish a women's college in conjunction
with the University of Virginia began in 1910 and had widespread support.
Privately, Martin and other organization leaders endorsed the move, but
alumni opposition was strong, and little headway had been made by 1916.
During the debate, Trinkle came out squarely in opposition. Even though his
stand alienated the same women he had worked with on suffrage, his position
was consistent with concepts of democratic progressivism demonstrated earlier. He argued that a coordinate college would be expensive and would serve
primarily the interests of 200 or 300 well-to-do women. Trinkle contended
that the four normal schools established in 1908 were not being properly
supported and warned that if the legislature did not heed the public cry for
better public schools, a day of reckoning would come. The bill was defeated,
but alumni pressure, not principle, was responsible.

Well before the session ended, western newspapers were predicting that the Wytheville legislator would run for Congress. Until a week before the Ninth District Democratic convention, Trinkle, citing personal and political reasons, insisted he would not. However, at the convention, "red, perspiring and trembling with emotion," he accepted a draft. Trinkle knew his chances of defeating Slemp were slim. Since poll taxes had to be paid six months before election, it was too late to qualify more voters. Facing a 3,000 or 4,000 Republican majority, Trinkle decided to emphasize a few simple issues and try to force Slemp to commit a critical mistake.

The campaign was dull in spite of Trinkle's energetic effort. Slemp, one of the South's leading Republicans, was more interested in the national election of 1916 and served as head of the speaker's bureau for the GOP presidential campaign. Operating from a "safe" seat, his primary concern was personal political power, not congressional activity. His goal was a cabinet post, an honor sought and denied three times. Slemp did not open his campaign until September 25, after which he made only a few token speeches and collected his usual majority on election day. But Trinkle, too, had won—although in a different way. He had made the good fight and met and campaigned with all of the state's leading Democrats who had flocked to the Ninth. He had spent time and money in the effort and (good businessman that he was) understood that he had made an investment in his future.

Trinkle went back to Richmond for the Assembly session in 1918 and again in August 1919 to a special session called to vote matching state funds for a large federal road-building subsidy. At both of these sessions and again in 1920, the Wytheville senator adhered to voting patterns established in 1916. He solidly backed the equal suffrage drive, now endorsed by President Wilson in a switch to advanced progressive tenets. He continued to support Prohibition, although there is evidence that the organization now regarded Cannon and the dry forces as less important than they had been. More generally, Trinkle voted with the progressive wing of the organization, favoring bills for a motion picture censorship board and supporting increased allocations for roads, schools, and tuberculosis care.

More important for Trinkle's future, however, was the death of Thomas Staples Martin in November 1919. For the organization, Martin's death came at an inopportune time. Virginia's congressmen, nearly all of whom held important committee chairmanships, had been busy with pressures generated by World War I. They had let political fences go unmended, and in 1917 a political maverick, Westmoreland Davis, won the Democratic gubernatorial nomination and was subsequently elected. Attempting to forge his own organization, Davis filled Martin's senate seat with Carter Glass, the old Lynchburg independent. He then persuaded Henry St. George Tucker, another independent who had not held elective office since 1896, to run for governor. In addition, most politicians were aware that Davis planned to contest Claude Swanson's Senate seat in 1922.

Trinkle was quickly affected by these events. Although eager to be governor, he had established no real claim to the office. He was only forty-five years old, had served in the state Senate only five years, and lacked political seasoning and public familiarity generally possessed by aspirants. Furthermore, he had taken positions on political questions counter to those of organization members. Under normal circumstances he would not have received much backing in any bid for the Executive Mansion. But times were not normal. Neither Claude Swanson nor Congressman Henry D. ("Hal") Flood, nominal leaders of the party, was in a position to lead. Swanson's major concern was the challenge by Davis; Flood, as chairman of the House Foreign Affairs Committee, had been confined to Washington and was not wholly in touch with state affairs. Nevertheless, Flood, a superb organizer, appreciated the seriousness of the situation. His first impulse was to enter the primary against Tucker, his kinsman. It was not until December 1920 that he decided not to run. Other potential candidates surfaced and for one reason or another declined to make the race. Evidence also indicates that the organization considered letting Tucker run unopposed and tried unsuccessfully to compromise with him. Then in mid-December 1920 the Roanoke *Times,* which seemingly always had a pipeline to organization thinking, reported that Trinkle would become a candidate. Accurately assessing the dynamics of the situation, the *Times* noted that Trinkle could get the support of the organization, equal suffrage forces, and dry voters. Furthermore, with eight months remaining until the primary, an energetic campaigner could accomplish much.

When Trinkle announced on December 30 that he would run, office-holders reneged on earlier promises to Tucker and fell into line behind the organization. One of those who quickly pledged support to Trinkle was Harry Flood Byrd of Winchester, another young man actively building a political base and head of Swanson's campaign in the Seventh District. Since the gubernatorial primary and the Senate race were viewed as a joint effort to mend organization fences, Byrd also worked in Trinkle's behalf. Strong in his own district and in the Southwest generally, Trinkle astutely extended his influence into eastern cities where Tucker reportedly commanded great strength among the "wets." In Newport News, Trinkle enjoyed the support of Homer L. Ferguson, president of the Newport News Shipbuilding Company and a political power. More important, however, were Trinkle's Norfolk contacts, who included James Mann, Jr., former Governor Mann's nephew and a prominent attorney and businessman, and one of Mann's law partners, General W. W. Sale, adjutant general under Governors Mann and Stuart, who served as Trinkle's overall campaign manager.

Tucker's platform, emphasizing "progressive economy and productive efficiency," endorsed most of the progressive programs advocated by Governor Davis. Realizing these positions would appear to conflict with his known opposition to Prohibition and woman suffrage, Tucker attempted to give his slogan, "Back to the Constitution," a positive tone as "a call to the service of the future—to the ideals of constitutional government promulgated by our forefathers as a basis of progress." In short, he believed that the federal government had usurped many powers properly belonging to the states; he would accept responsibility for necessary services at the state level to keep them from being absorbed by the national bureaucracy. This brittle intellectual opposition to the currents of twentieth-century reform, coupled with his age (sixty-eight) made Tucker vulnerable to attack.

In contrast, Trinkle took no hard and fast positions. He geared his campaign instead toward establishing himself as a vigorous, young, progressive businessman who would somehow run the state like a well-managed corporation. He was careful to temper his relative youth and inexperience by pointing out that his progressive outlook was safely consonant with the larger principles shared by all Virginians—i.e., there would be no tax increase.

In a dull campaign that finally degenerated into a highly partisan attack on Tucker's record, only one issue emerged—the public roads question, which had virtually no effect on the outcome. Both Tucker and Trinkle favored an expanded road-building program, but both initially opposed a bond issue to support such a project. However, in a move that would prove most important, Trinkle in May 1921 softened his antibond stance and took the position that the people should make the decision by their choices to the Assembly. Organization leaders, including Hal Flood and Harry Byrd, were quick to object. Forcefully opposed to any hint of a bond issue, they directed their arguments toward the farmer, who would be left in the mud, they said, while out-of-state motorists whizzed by on hard-surfaced arterial roads. Furthermore, they contended that bond issues would violate the Jeffersonian dictum of not saddling future generations with debt.

Meanwhile, the 1921 primary campaign focused increasingly on Tucker's record, particularly on his controversial opposition to Prohibition and woman suffrage. In contrast, Trinkle's record on Prohibition drew Anti-Saloon League support, and he stood to profit from ratification of the Nineteenth Amendment which gave women their first opportunity to vote in a Virginia gubernatorial primary. Then, with less than two weeks remaining, the attack on Tucker's alleged party disloyalty intensified. Organization spokesmen accused Tucker of having bolted the party in 1896 when he resigned his congressional seat in protest against the adoption of free silver by the national party. Tucker tried to defend himself, but the charges came too late for adequate answer. When the returns began to come in on August 2, it quickly became apparent that Trinkle had won. Of 151,098 votes cast, Trinkle received 86,812 or 57.4 percent. His margin came almost totally from the Fifth, Sixth, and Ninth Districts.

Meantime, the Republicans met in Norfolk and nominated Colonel Henry Watkins Anderson of Dinwiddie County, a highly successful corporate lawyer and a man anxious to build a viable Republican party in the state. The Republican platform was progressive and "antimachine," with planks endorsing a businesslike administration, better educational facilities, and better roads. It called as well for repeal of the poll tax and reform of election laws to remove the machinery from the hands of Democratic election officials. In protest against the exclusion of nearly all Negro delegates from the convention, black Republicans met in Richmond on Labor Day and nominated a slate of black candidates headed by John Mitchell, Jr., editor of the Richmond *Planet*. Their platform attacked the Republican party for deserting its historic principles and denied that the Negro had any desire to destroy cordial relations existing between the races in Virginia.

Capitalizing on the race issue, Trinkle, speaking in Dickenson County in late September, gave the campaign a decidedly negative tone. He charged the Harding administration with creating "hard times," attacked the Republican Reconstruction record, called the Republican plank to repeal the poll tax a sop to the black voter, and voiced fears that full Negro enfranchisement could set state progress back a half century. Thus, the race bogey, in spite of Anderson's protests, became *the* issue. The fully enfranchised Negro, Democrats claimed, would hold the balance of political power. The abolition of the poll tax would "lead to promiscuous voting of the Negro" and constitute a distinct threat to white supremacy.

The outcome was never in doubt. On election day Trinkle garnered 65 percent of 213,000 votes cast. Mitchell received slightly over 5,000 votes. Anderson had tried to keep the campaign on a higher plane, but the Democracy impaled him on the race issue.

As Lee Trinkle assumed the governorship, at least two things were apparent to him: he had an opportunity to assume control of the relatively leaderless state Democratic party, and his chances of doing so were linked to a successful program of public road construction.

Virginia's roads were abominable. Little progress had been made in actual construction of a modern system, but much of the groundwork had been laid. A State Highway Commission had been created in 1906, primarily to administer funds allocated to localities on a matching basis. In 1918 the Assembly had designated a 3,800-mile arterial system to be constructed and maintained by the state, allocated matching funds for a federal subsidy provided in 1916, and increased the state commission from three to five members. Property and automobile license taxes were raised to provide additional road revenues, and the constitution was amended to provide authority for the issuance of state bonds for road construction.

The question of bonds, the only real issue in Trinkle's primary fight, now became the crucial issue of his administration. Flood, Byrd, and most of the Democratic leadership opposed bonds. Some sincerely believed that bonded indebtedness violated Jeffersonian principles and the lessons of history. Others felt that rural folk would get short shrift from the arterial approach, and a few came from areas which already had good roads. For some the target was highway commissioner George Coleman, a bond advocate who, they felt, had too much power. Coleman, his Virginia adherents, and bond spokesmen across the nation countered by pointing out the business and social benefits to be derived from rapid construction of a modern transportation network.

In his inaugural address, delivered on a slushy February day, Trinkle proposed a reorganization of the Highway Commission, a major plank in his primary platform. Emphasizing the theme of governmental efficiency, he declared that modern road building required both technical skills and managerial ability, a rare combination for one man to possess. Calling for a division of duties, he recommended that the highway commissioner be a businessman appointed by and responsible to the governor, with authority to appoint his own subordinates.

What Trinkle did not say was more important. His position on the bond issue had been formulated well before his inauguration. He would work with organization stalwarts to reorganize the Highway Commission and eliminate Coleman. Once this was accomplished, Trinkle, after carefully lining up support, would propose a bond issue hedged with enough safeguards to make it palatable. Success could launch the state on a viable road-building program, something the governor sincerely desired. Further, it would eliminate the possibility of a deep party split and go far toward establishing Trinkle as a dominant leader in the Democracy.

Unhappily for Trinkle, the plan proved too complex. As the session began, Harry Byrd, rapidly gaining recognition as a major political figure, introduced a bill to reorganize the Highway Commission and then pushed through a Senate resolution to investigate Coleman's conduct. When Coleman's friend and fellow bond advocate C. O'Connor Goolrick of Fredericksburg countered with a bill of his own, a legislative fight broke out. Resulting animosities were so intense that Trinkle had to abandon his cautious, Byzantine plan to bring a bond issue out of the 1922 session. Instead he determined upon a more dramatic gesture.

On February 22, in a speech to the Norfolk Woodrow Wilson Foundation, the governor openly advocated a bond issue. Following that, he forcefully lobbied for the $12 million bond issue that had been recommended by the Virginia Good Roads Association. The bill passed the Senate by two votes, but when it was amended in the House to provide for a bond referendum in the 1922 general election, legislative maneuvering by Byrd in the Senate killed it. Trinkle was disappointed and understandably bitter. Although probably correct in assuming that popular sentiment was on his side, he underestimated organization opposition and relied too heavily on his own ability to overcome that resistance. Trinkle did not know it, but having lost this fight, his administration was doomed to failure.

The bond people were clamoring for an extra session—a proposal to which the organization was increasingly opposed; all citizens were demanding more and better roads, and failure to find a solution would jeopardize the governor's political future. After stumping the state testing opinion, Trinkle on October 11, 1922, unveiled a $20 million bond plan to be financed by a two-cent per gallon gasoline tax. Two weeks later Lewis Epes of Nottoway, with the support of Byrd, countered with a pay-as-you-go plan based on a three-cent gasoline tax. The Epes plan was a compromise. It avoided both long-term indebtedness and the necessity to increase the property tax, while incorporating Trinkle's original idea that cities, whose residents owned most of the automobiles, would finance the major part of the road construction program through gasoline tax payments.

In the ensuing six weeks Trinkle shifted position. On December 23 he called a special session to meet on February 28, 1923, to provide emergency funds for road construction. Desiring, as always, a united party, Trinkle was reluctant to make the all-out fight necessary for success. Faced with the toughness and political superiority of Byrd and other organization leaders, the governor gave up. He accepted the compromise and worked for the possible, which also would maintain party accord and organization control. At the opening of the special session, Trinkle came out in favor of a $50 million, seven-year building program based on present sources of revenue. Bond advocates countered with a $50 million bond measure. After a month of unproductive debate, the Assembly decided to submit the question to the voters. Independent of the proposed bond issue, the session also imposed Virginia's first gasoline tax, which was designed to provide funds for the 1923 construction program.

Harry Byrd, chief strategist of the pay-as-you-go forces, wrote the organizational plan for the campaign that ensued. He created a tight chain of command reaching into the precincts, urged that poll taxes be paid before the May deadline, and got Trinkle and other state leaders to release state officials to work against the probond sentiment. In spite of rain-soaked roads, considered a plus for bond advocates, they lost 127,187 to 81,220. The only substantial probond vote came from cities and the tier of Allegheny counties located west of the Valley. The Valley was unanimously antibond, indicating the area's satisfaction with a relatively good highway system. Upper Piedmont and Southside returns suggested that organization arguments against higher taxes and bonded debt appealed strongly to the innate conservatism of rural voters. The results represented a mandate for the pay-as-you-go program, and the 1924 Assembly made the temporary fuel tax the permanent basis for future highway construction.

The referendum was a turning point in the careers of Lee Trinkle and
Harry Byrd. Byrd was more resolute, better organized, and won. Trinkle
appeared to vacillate, finding an open party fight both personally and politically distasteful. Byrd emerged as the strongest political leader in the state,
and "pay-as-you-go," the Byrd shibboleth, became the guiding policy of Virginia government for decades to come.

While no evidence exists to suggest an organization conspiracy against
Trinkle, in a very real sense he was a political stalking-horse through most of
his administration. In one way or another the governor served as a foil
for Harry Byrd's emerging leadership. As Byrd's political star ascended,
Trinkle's declined. Although Swanson and other organization stalwarts appreciated Trinkle's efforts in stemming the independent tide in 1921, a recur-
rent rumor in late 1922 that Trinkle would contest Carter Glass for the
Senate in 1924 tempered Swanson's gratitude. This trial balloon was quickly
deflated, but the affair bound Glass to the organization still tighter and damaged Trinkle's ties with the leadership.

In late 1923, as the bond referendum fight was coming to a climax,
Trinkle announced that the treasury faced a deficit, necessitating a cut in
appropriations. In response to rumors of a property tax increase, Byrd quickly
advised the governor that a general increase would endanger pay-as-you-go
and might result in a political rebellion serious enough to return the state to
Republicanism. When the 1924 legislative session began, Trinkle announced
a deficit of over $1 million and argued that programs begun in the prosperous
heyday of Stuart and Davis could no longer be funded during depressed
times. Within ten days, Byrd and most of the state press attacked the Trinkle
deficit. The governor assured his friends that there was no serious break
between him and Byrd, but it was clear that Byrd had decided that pay-as-
you-go applied not only to road financing but to the entire economic structure
of the state. Although it pained him to do so, Trinkle subsequently contacted
Byrd on all important economic questions. The transition was complete.
Harry Byrd had seized the reins of power.

The rest of Trinkle's administration was a personal and political disaster.
He broke his elbow in September 1924 while on the Fish Commission yacht,
and his brother Clarence's economic difficulties forced liquidation of much of
the family's landed interests. In 1925 a series of near scandals produced a
constant stream of criticism. The most notable misconduct involved the commissioner of the Department of Game and Inland Fisheries, W. McDonald
Lee of Irvington, who had held the same post under both Mann and Stuart.
In February 1924 antiorganization forces charged that Lee had used the
commission's yacht, the *Commodore Maury,* for private parties involving liquor and young ladies of questionable moral character. An investigation revealed evidence of Lee's indiscretion, but the investigative committee divided
along political lines, with the majority exonerating Lee. Trinkle deliberated

for two months before siding with the majority and was severely criticized for taking too much time in rendering a decision. Private correspondence reveals that Trinkle's procrastination resulted from loyalty to friends, even when that loyalty was politically damaging.

Trinkle played little part in the gubernatorial campaign of 1925 between Harry Byrd and G. Walter Mapp, but one event in the lame-duck period before Byrd's inauguration revealed Trinkle's pique. The governor became incensed at the Norfolk dinner while listening to Byrd talk about his plan to improve the state. Trinkle "fairly exploded" and in his own remarks implicitly challenged Byrd to make a better showing at the end of his term.

Lee Trinkle was only fifty years old when he left Richmond. Reentering the business world as the first vice-president of the Shenandoah Life Insurance Company of Roanoke, he remained the active, enthusiastic man he had always been. The range of his nonpolitical, nonbusiness activities continued to be impressive. Within a few years he was one of the state's grand old men, and few public occasions were complete without his presence. Trinkle addressed high school and college commencements by the dozen, was a regular speaker at booster banquets, served on the board of trustees of Hollins College, and was a fund raiser for all manner of good causes. It was a rich, rewarding life, and Trinkle enjoyed it fully.

Politically, Trinkle was an active supporter of Democratic candidates at all levels. Nevertheless, Byrd did not seek his advice, and over the years Trinkle gradually moved into the anti-Byrd camp. He was the best known political leader to oppose John Garland Pollard, an old antiorganization stalwart and Byrd's choice for the gubernatorial nomination in 1929. Trinkle was also rumored to be a candidate against Glass for the Senate in 1930, incurring Glass's eternal enmity for not publicly disavowing the rumor.

Although the ex-governor remained abreast of state politics, his real interest in the 1930s was public education. Pollard appointed him chairman of the state Board of Education in 1930, and Trinkle retained the post until his death in 1939. As chairman, he was active in bringing education policy under centralized control. More important, perhaps, was his work as a propagandist. One of the state's most desirable, able, and available public speakers, he instructed audiences across the Commonwealth about the need to spend more for public education. He also advocated substantial expenditures for public welfare, a position which placed him even further outside the conservative circle of organization leadership. In keeping with the increasingly liberal bent of his thought, the ex-governor was a strong supporter of Franklin D. Roosevelt's New Deal programs, a stand which drove yet another wedge between himself and Byrd. And Trinkle often was in contact with those who opposed Byrd and Glass, particularly during the governorship of James Price.

Lee Trinkle experienced personal embarrassment during the last stage of his career. In September 1939 the public learned that the Shenandoah Life

Insurance Company was being investigated by a federal monopoly subcommittee; testimony revealed loose business practices involving personal loans to company officers. Trinkle claimed vaguely that the attack was politically motivated, but both his salary and his authority were reduced. Two months later, after presiding over a meeting of the state Board of Education, he suffered a heart attack and died.

Lee Trinkle lived a useful life. Had he not been elected governor, the course of Virginia history probably would have varied little—if any. Yet, because he was elected and became widely known and loved, Virginia was the better for it. He brought to politics, to service, and to life itself energy and dignity that deserved the esteem and affection of his state.

SOURCES

The Trinkle Executive Papers are at the Virginia State Library. Since no Trinkle personal papers apparently exist, one must rely on those of his contemporaries. Particularly important are the Tucker Family Papers (University of North Carolina); the Carter Glass Papers, Martin A. Hutchinson Papers, and Charles Harkrader Papers (all at the University of Virginia); and the Henry D. Flood Papers (Library of Congress). Other important collections include the Buford-Strange Family Papers (University of Virginia) and the C. Bascom Slemp Scrapbooks (Southwest Virginia Historical Museum, Big Stone Gap).

Particularly helpful were these daily newspapers: Richmond *News Leader,* Richmond *Times-Dispatch,* Roanoke *Times,* and Bristol *Herald-Courier.* Several volumes of clippings owned by the governor's son, James Trinkle of Roanoke, were graciously lent to the author for an extended period.

A full bibliography is available in Lee Stanley Willis, "E. Lee Trinkle and the Virginia Democracy, 1876–1939" (Ph.D. diss., University of Virginia, 1968).

HARRY F. BYRD

Leadership and Reform

Robert T. Hawkes, Jr.

Harry Flood Byrd directed the most significant gubernatorial term in post–Civil War Virginia. His unique political strength and ability to imprint his philosophies on state government through a major reorganization made his term one of achievement, change, and lasting impact. As governor, Byrd demonstrated that he could perform as effectively in public office as he had in private business and as a Democratic party organizer.

Born June 10, 1887, Byrd was a direct descendant of the William Byrds of colonial fame. His father, Richard E. Byrd, served as speaker in the Virginia House of Delegates, and an uncle, Henry D. ("Hal") Flood, was a congressman and leader in the Martin organization. The oldest of three sons, named Tom, Dick, and Harry in reverse order, Byrd grew up in Winchester where he absorbed the individualistic ethic of the Shenandoah Valley. Although intelligent and alert, Byrd was not a good student and clearly preferred an active outdoor life. The near bankruptcy in 1902 of his father's small daily newspaper, the Winchester *Evening Star,* gave the fifteen-year-old boy a chance to prove himself as a businessman and newspaper publisher. It also gave him an opportunity eventually to fulfill one of his dreams—restoring the Byrd family to the economic, political, and social prominence it had held in colonial Virginia. Through careful attention to detail, strictest economies, and hard work, Byrd managed to keep the presses rolling, pay off creditors, and within several years earn a profit.

In 1906 the young publisher took a second job as manager of the local Bell Telephone Company. His earnings enabled him to lease apple orchards, then buy them and also land on which to start new ones. Byrd was destined to become one of the world's largest and most successful apple producers. Energetic and enterprising, in 1907 he organized the Martinsburg (W. Va.) *Evening Journal* and the next year accepted the presidency of the Valley Turnpike Company which owned and operated the highway between Winchester and Staunton. He built and operated a cold storage facility for apples, expanded his orchards, and invested in stocks and bonds. By the time he became governor, Byrd was independently wealthy, but all his life he continued to take an active interest in his enterprises, especially apples, often supervising the work in the orchards himself.

HARRY F. BYRD

Governor of Virginia

1926–1930

Lack of formal education gave Byrd a narrow outlook. His own practical background convinced him that anyone applying industry and thrift could succeed. First of all a businessman, he brought business expertise to every political issue, as well as firm conviction that the role of government should be limited, leaving the citizen as free as possible in the marketplace.

After assisting his father in several elections, Byrd ran successfully for the Winchester City Council in 1908. Seven years later he was elected to the state Senate to represent the city of Winchester and Frederick and Shenandoah counties. In this first campaign for a state office, he sounded the perennial theme of his long career by calling for greater efficiency and economy in government. Although Byrd was favored to defeat his Republican opponent, he conducted a careful, systematic campaign, consulting with local political leaders, initiating an alphabetical card system on voters, and speaking at informal meetings and gatherings, which he preferred to rallies and public speeches. Byrd acted as if he were the underdog and took nothing for granted. Total effort and thoroughness, when most candidates would have rested on predictable margins of victory, became a Byrd habit. He won by a large margin. As a state senator, Byrd watched and learned from Democratic organization colleagues. He rarely made public speeches, delivering not one on the Senate floor for seven years. He was appointed to the Roads and Internal Navigation Committee and to the Finance Committee, and highways and finance would remain major interests throughout his Richmond career.

During these same years Byrd acquired a family. In 1913 he married a local girl, Anne Douglas Beverley, also from a famous Virginia family. Their first child, Harry F. Byrd, Jr., was born the next year. A daughter, Westwood, and two more sons, Beverley and Richard, completed the household. Mrs. Byrd, affectionately called "Sittie," suffered poor health and did not enjoy public life. A gracious hostess, she entertained often but, like her husband, preferred quiet, informal gatherings.

Meanwhile, Byrd's political prospects soared. Between 1919 and 1921 the Democratic organization lost its old guard leadership: U.S. Senator Thomas S. Martin died in 1919, state chairman Rorer A. James two years later, and Byrd's uncle, Hal Flood, shortly thereafter. Senator Swanson was facing a challenge from Governor Westmoreland Davis, newly appointed Senator Glass was not yet considered part of the organization, and Governor-elect E. Lee Trinkle had had little opportunity to demonstrate leadership qualities. Byrd, on the other hand, as state senator had demonstrated unusual finesse in judging political situations and in working with others; he had solid contacts with publishers throughout the Commonwealth and was particularly popular among rural editors in the Valley and the Southside. As state fuel administrator during World War I, he had gotten to know many businessmen and local government officials, and in January 1922 he became Democratic party chairman.

Byrd inherited over $3,000 in old campaign debts but quickly set out to rebuild the organization. He gave careful attention to all details, great and small, replenished the campaign chest, distributed funds to area chairmen, and made certain that Democrats paid their poll taxes. In effect, Byrd was shaping the powerful and loyal organization that would serve him well for four decades. The young party chairman made many trips to southwest Virginia where Democrats hoped to capture the congressional seat long held by Republicans and in the process created a close working relationship with Everett R. ("Ebbie") Combs, clerk of the Russell County court and chairman of the Ninth District Democratic committee. Combs, an unassuming, tireless, experienced politician, would serve Byrd faithfully in subsequent years as state comptroller, chairman of the state Compensation Board, political lieutenant, and confidant. Every Democratic congressional candidate in the state was elected, including George C. Peery in the Ninth District, and Senator Swanson easily turned back the Davis challenge. Virginia had a solidly Democratic delegation for the first time since 1902, and the organization had a strong new leader.

The statewide highway bond referendum in 1923 presented Byrd a second major opportunity to exercise leadership. Public pressure for improved and paved primary roads had mushroomed into a good roads movement, and by 1923 most southern states, including North Carolina, were using bonded indebtedness to construct highways rapidly. Although Byrd had supported local road bond issues, by 1920 he was opposed to bonds as a means to build Virginia's highway system. He realized the funds gained would be used largely to create a state primary system; the Valley, which already had relatively good primary roads, needed instead to improve its feeder or secondary roads.

Byrd first tried unsuccessfully to blunt a call for a special session on this matter; then, when members convened, he proposed a pay-as-you-go system to be funded by a three-cent per gallon gasoline tax. Byrd believed the tax would raise sufficient revenue to build the desired system over the next ten years without indebtedness and without paying interest. His opponents favored a $50 million bond issue. Both sides, fearing legislative defeat, turned to a November referendum to decide the question.

The campaign that followed was a lively one. Competing groups marshaled every means at their disposal, and, as in earlier campaigns, Byrd quickly developed a statewide organization to oppose bonds. He urged the governor to spend all available maintenance funds to get the roads in good shape before the referendum. In August, Byrd held the first of many annual picnics in his apple orchards, inviting political allies to what was to become a regular gathering of Virginia's leadership. Although a heavy rain threatened to keep antibond farmers away from the polls, the bond issue was defeated by a substantial margin. Voters clearly endorsed Byrd's pay-as-you-go system and confirmed him as leader of the Democratic organization. The referendum results also revealed a pattern that would characterize many subsequent elections. The Byrd forces produced their largest turnout in rural areas, primarily the Valley and southern areas of the state. Byrd would continue to look to the countryside for future victories.

On November 23, 1924, when Byrd formally announced his candidacy for governor, few were surprised. He pledged to give the state a progressive, businesslike, efficient administration, with a balanced budget and a highway system constructed on a pay-as-you-go basis. For the most part, however, Byrd ran on his ten-year record as a state senator and avoided presenting detailed position statements. His opponent in the Democratic primary was G. Walter Mapp, former Accomac County state senator, who was best known as a leader of Prohibition forces. Clearly the underdog, Mapp announced his candidacy early, but his appeal was diminished by declining public interest in the Prohibition issue and by Byrd's perfect voting record in support of Prohibition. Mapp had the unofficial support of the still powerful Anti-Saloon League, but this group did not endorse him openly since it could not quarrel with Byrd's record. With the organization and its "courthouse rings" performing perfectly, Byrd won easy victories in the primary and general elections.

The young man who mounted the platform to deliver his inaugural address on February 1, 1926, did not look like a traditional Virginia governor. Only thirty-eight, he was robust and almost six feet tall, weighing 180 pounds. He had blue eyes, brown curly hair, a ruddy complexion, and a boyish, round face accentuating his youth. His address was the first to reach the state's citizens by radio and the first to be broadcast by loudspeakers to the crowd. Byrd had learned how to deliver his message, but a high, raspy voice made him a poor public speaker.

The new governor outlined a major reform program, calling for extensive reorganization of state government to incorporate the business principles of efficiency and economy and to make the governor the real executive head with authority to match responsibility. He asked for the consolidation of many bureaus and departments into a streamlined, corporationlike structure, and requested creation of a citizens' commission to propose constitutional amendments to implement reorganization. He promised to reform the fee system by which local government officials were compensated, to build a pay-as-you-go highway system, and to reform taxes so as to attract business and industry. He also proposed a national campaign to publicize the state's growth potential.

Byrd outlined his specific programs in major addresses to the General Assembly on the following two days. The first message contained a far-reaching tax reform package. Byrd recommended that real estate and tangible personal property taxes go to local governments. By allowing each city or county to assess property as it wished, Byrd's "tax segregation" plan eliminated the regional inequities of state assessment. He proposed that the tax on capital used in industry be reduced, that industrial and farm machinery be subject to local taxation only, and that the tax on bonds, notes, and other evidences of debt be cut. The governor thus established a "hands-off" approach to local matters that he would continue throughout his administration. Separation of state and local taxation permitted the courthouse rings to manage their finances as they wished, a step that guaranteed future political support.

On the second day Byrd astounded lawmakers with another address outlining the major goal of his administration: a reorganization and streamlining of the state's cumbersome bureaucracy. Most importantly, he insisted that the governor be given real executive power, reducing the number of elected statewide officials from eight to three: the governor, the lieutenant governor, and the attorney general. The others would be appointed by the governor and confirmed by the Senate. He suggested that additional state officers currently elected by the General Assembly such as the commissioner of motor vehicles and the commissioner of insurance also be appointed by the governor and confirmed by the Senate. Byrd reminded the legislature that many safeguards against executive abuse of power would still exist and requested that none of these changes be made effective during his term of office. The new governor proposed consolidation of many bureaus, departments, boards, and commissions into eight to ten departments, adoption of a uniform accounting system, and payment of all moneys collected to the state treasury, except the funds for highway construction and maintenance. He also requested a $15,000 appropriation to hire an outside firm of "business experts," free from political influence or personal considerations, to suggest further reorganization and economies. Byrd's program was not a new idea. Other states, especially in the South, were adopting similar measures under the leadership of business-progressive politicians, and Byrd was pursuing reforms that his immediate predecessors had been unable to push through the traditionally conservative state legislature.

Most political observers predicted that Byrd's legislative proposals would be accepted by the General Assembly, and with few exceptions they were. A short-ballot amendment, which reduced the number of elected state officers to three, was modified in the House so that previously elected officials would be confirmed by both houses, and then the measure quickly passed. Another Byrd amendment which reduced the lame-duck period of the outgoing governor by changing the inauguration date to one week after the opening of the General Assembly session also found ready acceptance. The legislators appropriated $25,000 to hire an out-of-state firm to survey Virginia government; meanwhile, they created a new Department of Conservation and Development and abolished the commissions it replaced. The administration's tax recommendations won nearly unanimous approval. A statewide uniform accounting system was adopted and the fee system reformed. Byrd's recommendation for an increase in the gasoline tax from 3 to 4 cents per gallon to ensure the success of the pay-as-you-go highway system was accepted, along with an additional ½ cent per gallon tax for localities.

During the session, Delegate G. Alvin Massenberg of Elizabeth City County introduced a bill requiring separate seating for the races at public gatherings. The bill was the result of publicity concerning racially integrated concerts and meetings at black Hampton Institute. The Massenberg bill passed, and Byrd allowed it to become law without his signature. The measure thus became the capstone of Virginia's "Jim Crow" system. Although Byrd supported racial segregation, he preferred to avoid the race issue and did not refer to race in public addresses.

The impact of the governor's leadership on the 1926 session was amazing. No other governor had enjoyed as much success with the legislature. Every recommendation was accepted with overwhelming support, often including the small Republican minority. The House of Delegates adjourned without a single bill left on its calendar; and neither house found it necessary to stop the clock to complete business. Byrd successfully enacted a complete reform package that had been defeated year after year under other governors.

Two developments soon threatened, however, to diminish his success. When the General Assembly increased the gasoline tax 1½ cents per gallon, most gasoline dealers increased their own prices another ½ cent per gallon, and the public became alarmed. The governor then blamed the gasoline companies for raising prices, accused them of monopolistic tendencies, and called on President Coolidge to investigate pricing practices in Virginia. Although the Federal Trade Commission found no evidence of monopolistic practices, Byrd won praise as a champion of the people, leaving the gasoline companies as the culprits responsible for the price increase.

Soon after the legislature increased taxes on the gross incomes of public service corporations, the Chesapeake and Potomac Telephone Company of Virginia applied to the State Corporation Commission for higher rates amounting to $772,000 per year. Under state law, the company could implement new rates while appealing through the court system if its request was denied. When Byrd learned that the commission would not grant the full increase, he threatened to call a special session to change the law if the company put new rates into effect while appealing. This led to an agreement by the telephone company to institute only the smaller increase granted by the commission while the appeal was in court. (The company later lost its appeal.) These episodes enhanced Byrd's public image as a fighter for consumer rights, but, in truth, he was much more interested in protecting his highway and tax reform programs.

Maintaining momentum, Byrd announced in May that he had hired the New York Bureau of Municipal Research to conduct a survey of Virginia government. This private firm had reportedly recommended reforms cutting $600,000 from Tennessee's annual budget of approximately $15 million. The governor named thirty-eight prominent Virginians to a citizens' committee to receive the bureau report and to make recommendations to the legislature. Byrd insisted this method was less costly and just as effective as a constitutional convention. Furthermore, the committee assured popular support for the bureau's work, and since it was composed primarily of Byrd faithful, he could influence its work. This was but another example of political skill that enabled Byrd to succeed where others had failed. Whatever recommendations came to the General Assembly would have the backing of the bureau's experts, the governor, and a committee of prominent citizens.

This "businessman's committee," as it came to be known, was headed by William T. Reed, president of Larus and Brother Tobacco Company of Richmond and one of Byrd's closest personal friends and advisers. Other prominent members included state Senator and publisher George B. Keezell of Harrisonburg; John Garland Pollard, former attorney general and dean of the School of Citizenship and Government at the College of William and Mary; Robert H. Angell, president of the Shenandoah Life Insurance Company of Roanoke and state chairman of the Republican party; Homer L. Ferguson, president of the Newport News Drydock and Shipbuilding Company; and Douglas Southall Freeman, editor of the Richmond *News Leader*. The Reed committee received the New York survey in January 1927 and soon issued a report to the governor. Accepting most of the bureau's work, the committee recommended that a hodgepodge of agencies be combined into eleven major departments. Both bureau and committee agreed that twenty-eight of eighty state agencies could be abolished and their functions transferred elsewhere, and both concurred on the need to centralize state financial functions in one office.

Most of the reorganization could be effected without constitutional revision, but some changes required amendments. Byrd had already named a seven-member commission to study these matters. Chaired by Judge Robert R. Prentis, president of the Virginia Supreme Court of Appeals, the commission held public sessions throughout the state and on February 16, 1927, proposed fifty material changes to the Virginia constitution and thirty-one minor changes. Among the more important were reduction of state residence requirements for voting from two years to one and reduction of the period for paying poll taxes from three years to two. Other significant changes authorized counties to adopt optional forms of government, provided for the selection of school superintendents by local school boards and not by the state Department of Education, and limited state bond issues to 1 percent of the assessed value of all land in the state. The commission endorsed all of Byrd's pending amendments, including the short ballot.

Byrd called a special session for March 16, 1927, to act on the reorganization reports. In his opening remarks the governor announced that new fiscal methods had already turned an inherited budget deficit of $1.3 million into an unappropriated state surplus of $358,000. With minor exceptions, he endorsed the Reed and Prentis reports. The reorganization package passed both houses with few changes and not a single opposing vote. The proposed amendments were accepted with only minor opposition. Since the U.S. Supreme Court had just ruled against exclusively white primary elections, the legislature retained the three-year poll tax requirement. The special session quickly completed its work and adjourned, and primary elections for the state legislature five months later revealed that Byrd would continue to have a friendly General Assembly.

The governor had used his first two years to initiate reorganization of state government. During his last two years, Byrd would complete the reorganization, consolidate his gains, and assure that his political philosophy and leadership would extend far beyond his term in office.

His opening address to the 1928 General Assembly, a review of administration achievements, emphasized business efficiency and fiscal responsibility, tax reduction, and a balanced budget, the trademarks of his career. Byrd's second message looked to future benefits to be accrued from reorganization. He recommended a number of tax cuts specifically designed to attract new residents, new business, and new industry. Byrd asserted that these reductions would stimulate economic growth, increase state tax revenues, and allow larger state appropriations as well as more tax reductions. The governor presented a budget, approved by the Assembly, which included a reduction in state administrative costs and left an unappropriated surplus as a "margin of safety." At Byrd's request, the legislature appropriated $1 million to complete land acquisition for the Shenandoah National Park, matching the amount raised by a private campaign he had directed.

Unfortunately, education at all levels received little attention during Byrd's administration. A commission established by the 1927 special session to study Virginia's educational system recommended a uniform statewide accounting system for schools, better salaries for teachers, strengthening of compulsory attendance laws, and the election rather than appointment of school boards. Commission members also urged that money for education be generously increased since Virginia ranked near the bottom in most national surveys of state educational appropriations. Byrd endorsed modest increases in appropriations, but he offered little support for the commission's other recommendations. He opposed a suggestion to drop VMI as a state school and to create a chancellor of higher education, believing these proposals were simply unacceptable to Virginians. Clearly, political considerations outweighed Byrd's drive for economy, and, lacking administration support, most of the recommendations were ignored by the legislature.

Byrd's reaction to the New York bureau's report on county government is the most telling indictment of his economy-minded but politically conscious administration. Although the bureau completed its county government report by January 1927, Byrd did not submit it to the special session. The report was very critical of county government and the fee system for payment of local officials, observing that the system encouraged favoritism, nepotism, and little fiscal accountability. The bureau concluded that Virginia county governments in general had a "scattered, disjointed, and irresponsible type of organization" which was "grossly political, careless, wasteful, and thoroughly inefficient." The governor did everything that he could to suppress the report, recommending only one change in county operations to the legislature: that banks be required to pay interest on county deposits. The governor dared not risk alienating the courthouse rings forming the base of his political organization. The knife of economy and efficiency stopped at the political bone.

In 1928 over half of Virginia's population lived in rural areas, and more than a third were employed directly in agriculture. Byrd's themes of economy and efficiency and his tax segregation program remained extremely popular among rural people, who expected and got few government services. These folk provided the solid majorities for Byrd's organization that overcame opposition in urban areas. Yet this rural backbone of machine support was not enjoying the businessman's prosperity of the 1920s. During Byrd's term of office the number of owner-operated farms declined faster and tenancy increased more rapidly than during the depression years that followed. Yet the governor's program contained no relief for the agricultural population of the state, only tax reforms benefiting businessmen and investors. By 1928 it was clear that Virginia would continue to enjoy relatively low taxes at the price of very limited services and poor local government.

Despite the governor's inclination to avoid racial issues, one of the strongest measures recommended to the 1928 legislature was a bill to make lynching a specific state offense to be prosecuted by the attorney general. Furthermore, the bill authorized the governor to spend whatever sums were necessary to apprehend the participants in lynching. This bill was the result of two lynchings, one in Virginia in 1926 and one just across the border in Kentucky in 1927. Byrd had learned unofficially not only that the black Virginia victim was innocent, but that local officials were unwilling to bring those guilty to justice. Byrd's bill, a particularly stringent proposal, was passed by the General Assembly, and no known lynching has occurred in Virginia since then.

The 1928 General Assembly enacted every major recommendation of the governor with a minimum of opposition and reendorsed the proposed constitutional amendments relating to reorganization as the second stage of the amending process. At Byrd's request, a special public referendum on the amendments was set for June 19, well ahead of primary elections in August and the presidential election in November. He did not want his reorganization to be an issue in those elections.

Immediately after the 1928 session adjourned, Byrd turned his full attention to the referendum. Realizing that his biggest problem was voter apathy, he used state money, personal contacts, newspaper ads, and a tour of the state to whip up support. What little organized opposition there was came from the Virginia Education Association, whose teachers opposed the selection of school superintendents by local school boards and feared that tax segregation could result in a reduction of school funds. In general, educators resented Byrd's lack of support for education. The small Virginia Ku Klux Klan made its first entry in statewide politics to oppose the amendments on the grounds that they gave too much power to the governor. The Klan resented Byrd's antilynch law and his lack of public support for the Massenberg racial segregation law. Individuals who spoke against the amendments included G. Walter Mapp, Byrd's 1925 gubernatorial opponent, and Congressman Joseph T. Deal of Norfolk. Yet most voters and most of the state's newspapers supported the amendments.

The referendum vote was extremely small and the outcome close, but all amendments were adopted, thanks to solid proamendment majorities in rural areas. This victory essentially completed the most massive reshaping of state government in Virginia history. The extent of the change Byrd brought to state government and the degree of harmony and success he enjoyed with the legislature and the public are unparalleled in the annals of the Commonwealth. His stamp on Virginia life and politics was to outlast his own long career.

Although Byrd's reorganization plan was secure, he now faced a serious political challenge. The presidential candidacy of wet, Catholic Al Smith in 1928 divided Virginia Democrats and allowed Herbert Hoover to sweep to victory, carrying three Virginia congressional seats into the Republican column. That success augured well for a coalition of anti-Smith Democrats and Republicans who wished to smash Byrd's organization in the gubernatorial election of 1929. Unruffled, Byrd settled on John Garland Pollard as the candidate who could best unite the Democrats and continue his "Program of Progress." With all the resources of the organization behind him, Pollard rolled to an easy victory in the November election.

Byrd left office with an unappropriated budget surplus of over $4 million, instead of the deficit he found upon entering it. His administration had attracted national attention, five governors had visited Virginia to review his achievements, and Byrd had accepted invitations to speak in eight states. The entire legislature of Arkansas visited Virginia and subsequently adopted a similar program.

But the astounding success had come at a price. Byrd had rejected some

New York bureau recommendations for reasons of political expediency, and the rhetoric of efficiency and economy often exceeded the realities of accomplishment. The new finance department never came under unified administrative control, nor did the new conservation and development department. The Department of Public Welfare continued to consist of several independent boards. More importantly, very little had been done for the rural population. Heavy gasoline taxes and poor roads continued to cut into farm income. By 1930 over $93 million had been expended on the state highway system, but it was still incomplete. Wasteful county governments soon gobbled up savings brought by tax segregation. Although Virginia had the largest per capita wealth among ex-Confederate states, only one ranked below Virginia in education appropriations in proportion to wealth.

Byrd had established himself as unquestioned leader of the dominant Democratic organization. Changes in the fee system under his successor actually reduced the independence of local officials and served to ensure the loyalty of courthouse rings to the organization. Henceforth locally elected officials who performed certain state functions would be increasingly dependent on salaries set in Richmond. This laid the foundation for the system formalized and administered a few years later under the powerful state Compensation Board, usually composed of trusted Byrd lieutenants such as Combs. Circuit judges selected by Byrd associates wielded their extensive local appointive power so as to favor Byrd's political, economic, and social philosophy. Finally, a small electorate and traditional apathy among rural dwellers accustomed to leaving most political activity to their "betters" facilitated control by the organization and thus ultimately by Byrd himself.

When John Pollard was inaugurated on January 15, 1930, Byrd was out of office for the first time since 1916. Still a young man (forty-two), he claimed only a desire to return to his apple orchards and beloved Shenandoah Valley. His businesses continued profitable, and in 1929 he had purchased a country manor, Rosemont, on the edge of Berryville in Clarke County. It was to Rosemont that he moved his family from the Governor's Mansion.

While out of office, Byrd worked through close associates to ensure that programs he had inaugurated were preserved. With the advent of the depression, which neither he nor Pollard foresaw, Byrd's advice was clear: tighten the purse strings and avoid deficit spending. As the economic crisis worsened, Byrd proposed that the state take over county road systems to relieve hard-pressed localities dependent on real estate taxes. The General Assembly obeyed.

Although Byrd denied any interest in political office, he probably decided even before he left the Governor's Mansion to enter the U.S. Senate whenever he could. Some thought he might be the Democratic presidential nominee in 1932, and a campaign headquarters appeared in Richmond early that year. Although Byrd approved and encouraged this move, he remained officially inactive and cautious. The Virginia delegation went to the national convention pledged to Byrd, but his hopes were dashed when another favorite son, John Nance Garner of Texas, threw his support to Franklin D. Roosevelt, who easily defeated Hoover in November. There was much speculation that Byrd, Glass, or Swanson would be offered a cabinet post in the new administration. The president-elect offered the treasury post to Glass, who declined, citing advanced age and poor health. In truth, he was apprehensive about Roosevelt's fiscal positions. Glass then asked Roosevelt to offer a position to Swanson, so that Byrd could join him in the Senate. Swanson, realizing Byrd might mount a successful bid for his Senate seat in 1934, accepted the position of secretary of the navy. Very bitter about being pushed aside, he refused to resign early so that Byrd, Pollard's appointee, could enter the Senate ahead of his newly elected colleagues and gain seniority.

On March 4, 1933, Byrd took the oath of office as the junior senator from Virginia. There he would remain for six consecutive terms, the longest such service in Virginia history. As a U.S. senator he consistently applied the philosophy of government that he had developed as a young man. Government should be limited and simple. It should provide a laissez-faire atmosphere where citizens could, through initiative and hard work, acquire property and enjoy the benefits of their labor. Byrd believed government had a very limited role in providing social services and should never spend beyond its revenues. Limited government, pay-as-you-go, and free enterprise remained the themes of his Senate career.

For over four decades, Byrd was Virginia's preeminent public figure. His organization dominated Virginia's political life as long as he lived. Only James H. Price rose to the Governor's Mansion during Byrd's lifetime without his personal support. Byrd and his organization managed to turn back challenge after challenge through the same time-tested methods he developed as a young party chairman and as governor. His political skill and popularity enabled his organization to survive into the post–World War II era when urbanization, migration, increased incomes and literacy, and mass communications were changing the face of Virginia.

Byrd's gubernatorial administration remained as the high-water mark of progressive, reform state government in Virginia, but as time passed, his organization and the government it directed lost its flexibility and progressive stance. Changes were badly needed by the time Governor Mills E. Godwin, Jr., in his term as a Democrat, undertook the second massive reform effort of this century. Byrd himself led the resistance to change as his organization became less and less tolerant of would-be reformers, and those on the outside were kept out. The Democratic organization, aged and hardened in attitude, would not be able to retain its grip on Virginia beyond its leader's lifetime.

In 1965, seventy-eight years old and in poor health, Byrd resigned from the Senate, thus ending a remarkable political career. His oldest son, Harry

F. Byrd, Jr., was appointed to complete his term. The elder Byrd died less than a year later at Rosemont of a malignant brain tumor. His death marked not only the end of a statesman but the end of an era.

SOURCES

Pertinent manuscript collections are the Harry Flood Byrd Papers (University of Virginia), the Byrd Executive Papers (Virginia State Library), and the Reed Family Papers (Virginia Historical Society). Editorials published in the Winchester *Evening Star* reveal Byrd's position on public issues. Significant contemporary articles include one by Byrd, "Virginia through the Eyes of Her Governor," *Scribner's Magazine,* June 1928, pp. 682–89, and Virginius Dabney's "Americans We Like," *Nation,* June 6, 1928, pp. 632–34.

Perceptive unpublished studies include S. Walker Blanton, Jr., "Virginia in the 1920's: An Economic and Social Profile" (Ph.D. diss., University of Virginia, 1969); Ronald E. Shibley, "G. Walter Mapp: Politics and Prohibition in Virginia, 1873–1941" (M.A. thesis, University of Virginia, 1966); and J. Brent Tarter, "Freshman Senator Harry F. Byrd, 1933–1934" (M.A. thesis, University of Virginia, 1972).

Especially helpful articles are Henry C. Ferrell, Jr., "The Role of Virginia Democratic Party Factionalism in the Rise of Harry Flood Byrd, 1917–1923," *East Carolina College Publications in History* 2 (1965): 146–66; Joseph A. Fry, "Senior Advisor to the Democratic 'Organization': William Thomas Reed and Virginia Politics, 1925–1934," *Virginia Magazine of History and Biography* 85 (1977), 445–69; and George B. Tindall, "Business Progressivism: Southern Politics in the Twenties," *South Atlantic Quarterly* 62 (Winter 1963), 92–106.

See also Andrew Buni, *The Negro in Virginia Politics, 1902–1965* (Charlottesville, 1967); Allen W. Moger, *Virginia: Bourbonism to Byrd, 1870–1925* (Charlottesville, 1968); and J. Harvie Wilkinson III, *Harry Byrd and the Changing Face of Virginia Politics, 1945–1966* (Charlottesville, 1968).

For a detailed bibliography, see Robert T. Hawkes, Jr., "The Career of Harry Flood Byrd, Sr., to 1933" (Ph.D. diss., University of Virginia, 1975).

JOHN GARLAND POLLARD

A Progressive in the Byrd Machine

John S. Hopewell

Inauguration Day, January 15, 1930, was cold and dreary, with intermittent rain showers. At the Capitol the rain-soaked procession stopped long enough for John Garland Pollard to take the oath of office under an umbrella just as a downpour flooded the reviewing stand and a clutch of hardy spectators. Chuckling amiably, he remarked that it was "a proper kind of day for ducks and Baptists." Then Pollard went into the crowded House of Delegates where he delivered his inaugural address. He could not have known that the dreariness of that January day appropriately marked the beginning of a depression-plagued administration.

Pollard's journey toward the governor's chair began fifty-eight years earlier in King and Queen County. His father, John Pollard, was a Baptist preacher, and the family lived in Baltimore for a time before moving to Richmond where Pollard grew up on Church Hill. He was a frail, sickly child who spent most of his time reading or listening carefully to the Sunday sermon so that, standing on the kitchen stool, he could repeat it to the family cook. At sixteen, he entered Richmond College, where he became a member of the debating society and editor of the student newspaper. A bout with typhoid fever prevented his graduation, but he continued his education at Columbian College (now George Washington University) in Washington, D.C., where he studied law and supported himself by working at the Smithsonian Institution.

Receiving his degree in 1893, at the age of twenty-two, Pollard joined his uncle, Henry Robinson Pollard, in law practice in Richmond. Young Pollard was soon active in the Democratic party, supporting William Jennings Bryan and, like his uncle, identifying himself with the anti-Martin forces. Mingling with politically and socially influential people, Pollard quickly became a bank director, owner of real estate, and, briefly, a newspaper publisher. Handsome and good-natured, Pollard was of medium build with a commanding head, a firm, jutting jaw, and prematurely gray hair. His eyes and mouth always seemed ready to break into a smile that conveyed his well-developed sense of humor. At the age of twenty-seven he married Grace Phillips, a quiet, shy Portsmouth woman who endured his jokes and constant dabbling in politics. Between 1898 and 1906 four children were born to the couple, three of whom lived to maturity.

JOHN GARLAND POLLARD

Governor of Virginia

1930–1934

In 1901 Pollard won a seat in the state constitutional convention. Only thirty years old and the second youngest delegate, he displayed both idealism and fighting spirit when he proposed that the constitution's preamble—a relic from the American Revolution—be amended to delete the word "Christian" in its admonition to all citizens to practice "forbearance toward one another." No other minor proposal caused quite so much controversy, and the convention eventually defeated the amendment. On the question of eliminating Negro voting, the essential reason for the convention, Pollard shifted position without explanation and joined with fifteen other Democrats and twelve Republicans to vote against the entire suffrage provision. Doubtless he feared the law would not be administered fairly, thereby inviting fraud.

In the decade after the constitutional convention, Pollard expanded his law practice and began publication of the biennial *Pollard's Code of Virginia,* a detailed legal commentary that soon became an indispensable aid to most lawyers in the state. In addition he was elected president of the Children's Home Society of Virginia, which found homes for orphans and neglected children, a position he held for twenty years.

And through it all, Pollard continued to fight the Martin political machine. The climax came in 1911 when he vigorously campaigned for Congressmen Carter Glass and William A. Jones in their unsuccessful attempt to unseat Martin and Senator Claude A. Swanson in a double primary campaign. Then Pollard turned his attention to the presidential ambitions of Virginia-born Woodrow Wilson, the reform governor of New Jersey. Pollard helped organize the Virginians for Wilson Club, in spite of opposition by Martin and Swanson; with Wilson's victory, Virginia progressives hoped independent Democrats would receive presidential patronage, but Wilson disappointed them by giving all political appointments to Martin's friends.

In spite of these setbacks, the progressives decided to field candidates in the 1913 primary, and Pollard declared his candidacy for attorney general in a field of three, two of whom had machine ties. He called for reform of election laws, increased support for public education, and abolition of the fee system of compensation for public officials. With incumbent S. W. Williams and challenger S. G. Cumming splitting the machine vote, Pollard was able to build a solid base among progressive Democrats. In addition, his lifelong advocacy of Prohibition attracted those eager to make Virginia dry. This combination gave him a narrow victory in the August primary, the first for the antimachine group in a statewide election since 1901. Pollard won easily in November, along with Governor Henry C. Stuart and Lieutenant Governor J. Taylor Ellyson.

Pollard's triumph propelled him into the presidency of the Progressive Virginia Democratic League that convened in Richmond in February 1914 to urge adoption of the initiative, referendum, presidential primary, workmen's compensation, and other progressive reforms. The legislature, preoccupied with the question of Prohibition, ignored these proposals. Pressure for Prohibition had gradually built to irresistible proportions as a result of the efforts of the Reverend James Cannon, Jr., of the Anti-Saloon League of Virginia. Cannon pressured the machine to permit a public referendum on Prohibition. At first Martin refused to budge, and cooperation between Cannon and Pollard seemed possible. Then Martin acquiesced, and the enabling act for the referendum received legislative approval, passing in the Senate only with the tie-breaking vote of Lieutenant Governor Ellyson, a machine wheelhorse. Pollard threw himself in the Prohibition referendum campaign, traveling about the state at his own expense, and his speeches helped to make the Prohibition campaign a success. With a heavy turnout of voters, Virginia went dry by a large majority in September 1914.

Attorney General Pollard successfully concluded the suit against West Virginia for payment of the pre–Civil War state debt and regained possession of Martha Washington's will from J. Pierpont Morgan's estate, but his most controversial and dramatic action was a crackdown on long-established havens of gambling and vice in Norfolk, Hopewell, and Colonial Beach. Although the results were temporary, these activities kept Pollard in the public eye, making him a prime contender for higher office, and in 1915 he announced his candidacy for governor. The next day, Lieutenant Governor Ellyson entered the race, and four months later they were joined by Westmoreland Davis, influential publisher of the *Southern Planter*. Ellyson, a Confederate veteran, had been chairman of the state Democratic committee for more than twenty-five years and was a faithful member of Martin's machine. Although he made many friends with his tie-breaking vote for Prohibition, his well-known affinity for alcohol distressed his Baptist brethren. Davis, on the other hand, was personally dry but politically wet. He soon developed a surprisingly strong coalition of businessmen, farmers, wets, progressives, and independents. Ellyson claimed the support of the Martin machine, Cannon's Anti-Saloon League Prohibitionists, and the conservative business elements, making Pollard's task extremely difficult. Although the three candidates seemed to have similar platforms, their differences on Prohibition soon became the major issue.

Afraid that Ellyson and Pollard would split the dry vote, thereby allowing the wet Davis to win, Cannon endorsed Ellyson and encouraged his dry friends to desert Pollard. Cannon later admitted this had been "a mistake in judgment," but it goaded Pollard into vigorous activity; as the election approached, he claimed pledges of support from 34,000 registered voters. Yet Ellyson had the firm allegiance of Martin's machine; Davis, the support of the progressives. Bereft of a firm base, Pollard was further hampered by poor coverage of his campaign in Cannon's newpaper, *The Virginian,* which refused to mention his name or even carry his advertisements. The final blow was an eleven-column attack in the paper accusing Pollard of shirking Prohibition by not accepting Cannon's leadership. The effect was devastating. Fiercely loyal Anti-Saloon League members deserted Pollard for Ellyson, while independent and progressive voters, deciding Pollard's cause was hopeless, flocked to Davis in order to defeat Ellyson. Davis won the 1917 primary with a 44 percent plurality, gaining 39,318 votes to Ellyson's 27,811. Pollard came in third with 22,436.

The defeat was a disastrous blow. At the age of forty-six, Pollard faced a crisis. Involvement in politics had ruined his law practice, and he was unable to get a federal appointment. But the war in Europe offered new opportunities for service and adventure, and when the Young Men's Christian Association asked for volunteers to work among the troops, Pollard immediately answered the call and was sent overseas in January 1918. To sustain morale he traveled about the muddy French countryside giving talks about the nature of the war, writing letters for injured soldiers, and doing similar jobs. This wartime experience seems to have mellowed Pollard, making him more realistic, less given to flights of fancy, and more concerned with practical solutions to difficult problems. Nevertheless, for a man of his many proven talents, the eighteen months in France were probably misspent.

Upon his return in the summer of 1919, Pollard took several interim positions in Washington, including a short term on the Federal Trade Commission. Then in the autumn of 1921 he accepted an appointment as professor of constitutional law and history at the College of William and Mary and poured his energy into his classes and a variety of extracurricular activities. Now fifty-one years old, stout but handsome, he had a patriarchal look with his white hair and black-rimmed glasses worn low on his nose. Genial humor sparked his lectures. Generous with his time and resources, he taught evening classes in nearby towns and Sunday school in the local Baptist church and served as chairman of the area's Democratic committee and as mayor of Williamsburg.

Gradually Pollard returned to public service and political activity at the state level. The era of machine-progressive battles was over, having ended with the deaths of older politicians such as Martin and several of his foes and friends. Pollard's support for E. Lee Trinkle in 1921 and for Claude A. Swanson in 1922 indicated a desire to forget factional disputes. Appointed by Governor Trinkle as a member of the Commission on Simplification and Economy in Government, Pollard went to work with determined effort, making a yearlong study of state and local tax laws and producing a report critical of the Commonwealth's tax structure.

In 1926 newly elected Governor Harry F. Byrd consulted Pollard about taxation and other matters. Originally skeptical of Byrd, Pollard was particularly pleased when the governor appeared receptive to his report. Byrd's success in pushing a comprehensive reform package through the General Assembly filled Pollard with "hope for early progress" and calmed his earlier fears about Byrd's machine background. The governor cemented the old progressive's new allegiance by appointing him to an important advisory commission to assist the New York consulting firm hired to revamp Virginia's state government. Pollard worked energetically, but his support of the controversial constitutional amendments that resulted from the commission's work was more highly valued by Byrd. The proposals called for a variety of changes, including the short ballot, tax segregation, reorganization of the bureaucracy, and several less controversial items. When opposition surfaced in the eastern part of the state, Byrd asked Pollard for help; his seven speeches in Tidewater communities, in Byrd's opinion, ensured the narrow victory of all the amendments in the referendum.

Not only did Pollard aid Byrd in the referendum fight, he also stood firm when many of his fellow Baptists deserted the national Democratic party because of the presidential nomination of Governor Alfred E. Smith of New York. Although a dry Baptist, Pollard accepted Smith, a wet Catholic, because he believed that Smith could not weaken Prohibition if the people supported it; furthermore, Pollard resented the injection of the religious issue into the contest. Faithful to the party and to himself in this crisis, he actively supported Smith and thereby made himself politically indispensable to Byrd and his organization.

Pollard's stand brought him into yet another head-to-head battle with his old nemesis, James Cannon, Jr., now a Methodist bishop. Rallying his dry sympathizers, Cannon organized Anti-Smith Democrats into a significant third force that challenged Democratic loyalists for control of the state. The new coalition even offered Pollard support in the 1929 gubernatorial election if he would cease supporting Smith. Viewing this move as an immediate threat to Byrd's program, Pollard refused the offer and continued his speeches. But the Anti-Smith Democrats made an impressive showing. Herbert Hoover carried the Old Dominion, temporarily fracturing the solid South and electing three Republican congressmen from Virginia. Virginia Democrats were stunned, and many believed that Byrd's leadership and party control of the state were in danger. Some Anti-Smith leaders, especially Cannon, appeared ready to carry the intraparty battle into the 1929 gubernatorial race. Judging the uproar to be nothing more than popular dissatisfaction with national party policy, Byrd counseled patience and forgiveness toward the rank and file who deserted Smith, but he adamantly refused to treat with Cannon or allow him to dictate the candidates or the platform for 1929.

Republican margins in the Tidewater in 1928 suggested that the nominee ought to be an eastern man, and politics required that he be progressive and dry, but not a pawn of either the Byrd organization or the Anti-Saloon League. Given these political realities, Pollard was the most suitable candidate, and Byrd offered to support him. Pollard cautioned that if elected, he would be his own man, propose his own program, and remain independent of machine ties. With these stipulations understood, Pollard accepted the offer and announced his candidacy for governor. Two other candidates also joined the campaign: G. Walter Mapp, Byrd's opponent in 1925, and Rosewell Page of Hanover County. Mapp, from the Eastern Shore, hoped that his long association with Prohibition and sponsorship of the state's first Prohibition law would win disenchanted Democrats to his side. Ironically, his close association with Cannon was a severe liability, as was his opposition to Byrd's reform program. No one outside Hanover County took Page seriously.

Pollard based his campaign on endorsement of Byrd's program and never wavered from it, promising to lead the way to further progress, particularly in education, industrial development, and governmental efficiency. Mapp's hopes were dashed when Cannon urged friends to repudiate Byrd by avoiding the primary. As a result Pollard won an overwhelming 76 percent of the vote in the August contest. Two months earlier a convention of Anti-Smith Democrats, with camp-meeting fervor, nominated a professor of psychology at Washington and Lee University, William Moseley Brown, for governor. Brown had little political experience, but Virginia Republicans also nominated him, thus presenting for the second time in a year a united front to loyal Democrats.

At the same time, however, damaging allegations about Bishop Cannon's financial dealings began appearing in national newspapers, and in succeeding months revelations about numerous questionable transactions during the presidential campaign continued to discredit him and the Anti-Smith Democratic leadership. Brown's campaign was also weakened by a growing rift between the Anti-Smith group that wanted to stress national issues and Republicans eager to mount an attack on Byrd and local issues, especially the short ballot. Midway through the campaign, Brown shifted to local issues, increasing his criticism of Byrd and the Democratic party of Virginia. This was a fatal decision, pitting the coalition squarely against a very popular program. Brown's campaign quickly fell apart, his downfall triggered by the revelation that, despite vigorous condemnation of the short ballot in 1929, he had supported the measure and voted for it in the referendum of 1928. Pollard gained a 70,000-vote margin over Brown, picking up 63 percent of the total vote. He credited victory to the popularity of Byrd's administration and recognition by voters that Brown's campaign was based on spurious issues. The election of 1929 did more than defeat the coalition of Anti-Smith Democrats and Republicans. By successfully beating this challenge, Byrd consolidated the party behind his leadership. Even Pollard, one of the last antimachine progressives, had been won over.

Taking office after his cold and rainy inauguration in January 1930, Pollard faced problems of unanticipated magnitude. The collapse on the New York Stock Exchange triggered a series of economic crises that immediately affected Virginia, reducing state revenues and restricting state services outlined in Byrd's final budget. Nevertheless, Pollard attempted to maintain the momentum of reform. Although Byrd had completed a thorough governmental reorganization, changed the ballot, increased highway construction, and reformed tax laws, he had not tackled the problems of education, the seafood industry, agriculture, and local government. To all these, Pollard now turned his attention.

Pollard firmly believed that the counties were poorly organized and administered by a stubborn clique of fee officers whose inflated salaries resulted from fines and tax revenues they collected. The governor hoped to overhaul and improve county administration in the same way that Byrd had reformed state government. Although fee officers opposed creation of the Commission to Study Local Government, it quickly won Assembly approval, and its report, adopted by the 1932 session, provided for the present-day county manager and county administrator forms of government. The power of fee officials was greatly reduced, although counties were not required to adopt the reforms.

In other areas, despite opposition and legislative maneuvering, some traceable directly to Byrd in Winchester, Pollard had moderate success. His recommendations for improving the oyster industry were accepted, including a proposal to establish a Fisheries Commission to study the matter. Another recommendation led to the creation of a Commission to Study Election Laws that accepted Pollard's suggestions to limit primary election expenses, end bloc payment of poll taxes, and eliminate the "scratch" method of voting (crossing out all names except that of the preferred candidate).

The results of the 1930 session were satisfactory to both Pollard and Byrd. Passage of a workmen's compensation act and establishment of commissions on county government, election law reform, and fisheries represented substantial accomplishments. But there were failures as well, notably when fee officials blocked proposals to streamline administration. Although newspaper editorials generally praised the governor, Pollard's success with the legislature owed much to Byrd. Inexperienced in political arm-twisting and lacking a personal power base in the General Assembly, Pollard had to rely on Byrd's friends to implement his program. Often they changed it to suit their own views.

Pollard's respect and admiration for Byrd naturally made him turn to the former governor for advice and support. In any case, Byrd was deeply involved in the day-to-day operations of state government, recommending people for responsible positions, criticizing his opponents, and rewarding his friends. In fact, Byrd regularly received extensive written reports from high officials in the executive branch of government, particularly E. R. Combs, the comptroller, and C. H. Morrissette, the tax commissioner. By deferring to Byrd so often, Pollard helped to enhance the image of the former governor as a miracle worker. Byrd, in turn, voiced approval of Pollard, praising his successor whenever possible. Each had great respect for the other's abilities. Their letters, cordial but never familiar, began "Dear Governor," and ended with a full signature—evidencing restraint and mutual admiration.

As the spring of 1930 turned to summer, one of the most severe droughts of the century parched the state. The tobacco crop was cut in half and other farm produce stunted. Cattle suffered as well, and sale of unfattened stock sent prices plummeting. Pollard attempted to head off agricultural catastrophe by appointing Byrd chairman of the State Drought Relief Committee. With President Hoover opposed to federal assistance, the immediate remedy was to use the highway department as an unemployment relief agency. Winter snows eventually broke the dry spell, but diminished farm incomes reduced wages and tax revenues all over the state. The drought of 1930 probably had a greater effect on Virginia than the stock market crash of the previous year.

Pollard's troubles were compounded by a strike in September 1930 at the Dan River Mills in Danville. Declining profits caused increased work loads that workers refused to accept. When organizers for the United Textile Workers of America were fired and wages were cut 10 percent, the workers walked out and set up picket lines. To avoid a repetition of the bloody, violent strikes by textile workers in North Carolina in 1929, Pollard offered to mediate. The union accepted, but management refused to treat with the union or any of its representatives. Violence soon erupted, and Pollard reluctantly called out the National Guard to preserve order and protect property. With the Guard keeping the peace and the mills operating with nonunion personnel, the strike finally collapsed in January 1931. Pollard had dealt the union movement in the South a severe setback.

By mid-1931 farm income was less than two-thirds of the previous year; tobacco and wool prices were down 60 percent and corn 26 percent; industrial output had fallen 17 percent; the unemployed were estimated to number about 50,000. No longer was there a state treasury surplus, but a deficit that might cause political repercussions. Byrd, in correspondence with Pollard and others, insisted that the legislature not be given an excuse to tinker with the tax structure. He counseled against any increase in personal or corporate income taxes that might hurt Virginia in gaining new residents or industries. When confronted in August 1931 with the choice of a conditional appropriation for capital improvements in education or a balanced budget, Pollard swallowed hard, omitted the appropriation, and balanced the budget. It was a hint of things to come.

The threat of increased unemployment caused Pollard to appoint an Unemployment Relief Committee headed by Byrd's good friend and confidant William T. Reed, who accepted the position "to keep the state out of trouble." Reed surveyed the state and discovered somewhat less unemployment than feared. An advisory group without authority, Reed's committee asked for voluntary compliance from businesses for a new building program and a five-day work week. At best, the proposals were half measures because Reed and Byrd opposed expensive work relief programs.

Saddled with declining revenues and unable (because of recent constitutional amendments) to issue bonds except in an emergency, Pollard faced the choice of raising taxes to maintain existing programs or cutting spending. Fearing indiscriminate slashes by the General Assembly might weaken the educational program or the highway construction schedule and thereby increase unemployment, Pollard fought to avoid a deficit that might raise questions about the effectiveness of Byrd's financial reforms. At Byrd's suggestion, he sought a middle ground of retaining state services and personnel by cutting appropriations across the board. The result was a plan whereby the General Assembly would require the governor to withhold appropriations, including funds for salaries, unless Comptroller Combs, one of Byrd's lieutenants, could verify that sufficient funds were on hand to avoid a deficit. Buffeted by economic forces over which he had no control, the governor gave up his right to direct the state's financial affairs.

Pollard's principal message to the legislators in 1932 urged enactment of a series of financial proposals that continued the program begun by Byrd, modified only by the watchwords "curtail expenses; increase no taxes." Pollard's major recommendation was a salary cut of 10 percent for all state employees, including schoolteachers, a move designed to save about $1 million in state and local expenditures. Pollard proposed that the General Assembly give him the power to reduce salaries (except those of legislators and judges) and to restore them later if possible. To set an example, he volunteered to cut his own salary by 10 percent. In a separate message Pollard recommended continued reform of county government, overhaul of the fee system, and congressional redistricting. His proposals were immediately supported by Byrd, who declared that if the legislators followed the governor's advice, Virginia would benefit more quickly than any other state when prosperity returned. Byrd's imprimatur would be a decisive factor in the success of the governor's program when it reached legislative committees.

Nevertheless, an unexpected fight occurred over the large amount of money designated for road building. Tidewater delegates questioned whether 40 percent of the budget should go for highways when schools, hospitals, and other important services needed attention. They proposed to divert some of the money from highways to education. Pollard immediately opposed the idea, arguing that highway construction performed the double function of attracting industry and providing jobs. When Byrd jumped in to call the proposal "the greatest blunder Virginia could make," it was doomed. This development, of course, did not prevent schools closing because of insufficient funds. Smarting from this criticism, Byrd suggested to Pollard that the state assume the responsibility for construction and maintenance of all county roads, thereby allowing local officials to divert funds to schools or to reduce taxes. With Byrd's support, this proposal passed both houses by wide margins. The Byrd Road Act, as it was named, turned out to be a successful compromise, but the former governor was embarrassed by critical newspaper editorials questioning who was running the state.

A major disappointment for Pollard was the General Assembly's failure to act responsibly in redistricting the state after the loss of a congressional district in the census of 1930. A disgusted Pollard eventually allowed a bill creating a huge, disproportionate district running from Harper's Ferry to Cumberland County to become law without his signature. The redistricting plan was promptly ruled unconstitutional, forcing representatives to run at large in 1932. Another disappointment was the Assembly's failure to act on sweeping recommendations of the Fisheries Commission.

Yet with acceptance of his budget, Pollard was generally pleased with the session. The Assembly had authorized him to reduce appropriations if revenues did not match expenditures. Most important of all, the lawmakers had not increased taxes or changed any of the basic tenets of his administration. Nevertheless, Byrd was responsible for most of the governor's success. The Winchester conservative effectively represented the political and economic creed of those who dominated Virginia's Democratic party.

As the depression continued, unemployment in Virginia averaged 100,000 per month, peaking at 145,000 (19 percent of the work force) in July 1932. State revenues slumped 32 percent from the 1929 level; the price of farm products was down 18 percent; tax delinquencies mounted to 20 percent in some counties. State income soon dipped below the most pessimistic estimates. Consequently, in June 1932 Pollard ordered the inevitable 10 percent reduction in appropriations. Similar cuts followed in December and in June 1933, the third reduction sharply criticized by administration officials, particularly members of the State Corporation Commission who feared a fatal curtailment of services.

Fortunately, the sting of the final cut was mitigated somewhat by optimism generated by Franklin D. Roosevelt's New Deal. The election of Roosevelt also changed the complexion of Old Dominion politics. The appointment of Senator Claude A. Swanson as secretary of the navy left a vacancy that Pollard promptly filled with Byrd. The Senate seat strengthened Byrd's control over the Virginia Democratic party still more by providing him with a national platform and greater patronage power.

Nevertheless, Byrd's early months in the Senate were not entirely successful because he misjudged public sentiment on Prohibition. Moving toward repeal, Congress approved the Twenty-first Amendment in February 1933 and sent it to the states for ratification. The new Congress which convened in March soon legalized 3.2 percent beer. Byrd's vote against beer sparked widespread criticism that surprised the new senator and his ally in the Governor's Mansion. Meanwhile, pressure mounted for a special session of the General Assembly, a session Byrd and Pollard did not want. First suggested to consider unemployment relief, the idea was rejected by Pollard. In April, however, 3.2 beer began flowing freely in surrounding states and the District of Columbia, and tax dollars jingled into their treasuries. This double temptation could not be long resisted. Pollard still personally supported the ideal of Prohibition, but by the spring of 1933 he admitted that it was no longer politically viable. It was obvious that the state desperately needed new sources of revenue, and each day support for both repeal and beer increased.

The approach of the Democratic primary also accelerated the anti-Prohibition drive. Byrd's handpicked choice for governor, George C. Peery of Tazewell, after a period of indecisiveness, staked out a claim for the dry wing of the party. Antiorganization candidates Joseph T. Deal of Norfolk and Worth Smith of Louisa began advocating repeal and soon picked up popular support. In addition, a wet, antiorganization delegate from Fredericksburg, C. O'Connor Goolrick, was testing the political winds to determine whether he should run against Byrd in the primary for the unexpired senatorial term. The Prohibition issue, once again, threatened organization control.

With state after state endorsing repeal and with beer being sold openly, albeit illegally, in Richmond restaurants, something had to be done. Conferring in Richmond with Pollard and some friends, Byrd decided that strategic retreat was prudent, primarily to avoid endangering Peery's candidacy, and agreed to a special session. Pollard, however, remained unconvinced that a special session was necessary, and he did not wish to appear to be acting on Byrd's instructions. Letters, telegrams, and newpaper editorials did not move him, and he was soon cut loose by former allies, his own administration, and members of Byrd's organization. Depicted in a cartoon in the Richmond *Times-Dispatch* as Horatius at the bridge singlehandedly fighting back the wet forces, Pollard was an isolated man. By a two-thirds vote the legislature could call itself into session. At Byrd's request, state Senator William M. Tuck of Halifax County telegraphed each member and followed the telegram with a telephone call to tell the member that Byrd was in sympathy with the movement. Armed with favorable replies, Tuck confronted Pollard, who accepted his defeat with characteristic good humor: "If the boys want to come here and sweat in August, I will be here to sweat with them."

When the special session convened, approval of beer was assured. Following the governor's recommendation, the Assembly legalized beer and taxed it at the rate of a penny a bottle. The handling of the repeal amendment was also swift and positive. The legislature established a two-part public referendum, one to elect delegates to a constitutional convention to consider the amendment, the other to pose the choice between state Prohibition or some plan for liquor control. The referendum in October resulted in a resounding victory for repeal of national and state Prohibition by a 63 percent majority.

The convention gathered in Richmond a few weeks later, heard a short speech by Pollard, promptly ratified the Twenty-first Amendment, and then went home. Shortly thereafter a fifteen-man Commission on Liquor Control drafted legislation to establish a state monopoly on the distribution and sale of hard liquor in Virginia. The General Assembly of 1934 enacted the report into law.

With visible relief, in January 1934 Pollard relinquished his responsibilities to Peery, the easy victor in the primary and general elections. The depression and its economic and human crises had worn him down; simple worry had worked its inevitable damage. Fortunately for Pollard, Byrd had been a source of strength rather than an adversary. In his final message to the legislature, Pollard defended the philosophy of balanced budgets and stable taxes that had guided his administration. Pointing with pride to the low discount rate paid on Virginia's bonds, he insisted that fiscal conservatism, a low public debt, and a constant tax rate would restore prosperity.

Pollard's personal life, saddened by the death of his wife in 1931, changed for the better before he left office. In July 1933, to the surprise of even members of his family, the governor married his executive secretary, Violet E. MacDougall. Pollard derived additional satisfaction from his work in founding the Virginia Museum of Fine Arts. Accepting the challenge of philanthropist John Barton Payne to match his offer of $100,000 to found a museum, Pollard quickly raised the money. As president of the museum's board of directors, he continued his interest in the institution for the rest of his life.

Leaving the Governor's Mansion, Pollard moved to Washington, D.C., where he became chairman of the Board of Veterans Appeals—a post that President Roosevelt offered him until something more suitable developed. The president never found anything more "suitable," however, and Pollard chafed at the monotony of his bureaucratic work. Eventually time ran out on him. Never robust, his health began to decline, and he died on April 28, 1937.

Throughout his career, Pollard had a curious relationship with the dominant faction of the Virginia Democratic party. First a foe and then a friend, Pollard was never an insider, and sometimes Byrd's friends worked against him behind his back. Members of the organization eventually accepted him but rarely took him into their confidence, perhaps doubting the sincerity of his conversion. Furthermore, he was basically a political theoretician rather than a political animal. His old-fashioned idea of public service as a contribution to the public good set him apart from most politicians of a power-hungry and patronage-hungry era.

Pollard did not play for diversion; sheer idleness or unconstructive leisure was almost sinful to him. His sense of humor was dotted with gentle, corny jokes and frequent puns. He was a cautious man, choosing to be moderate and conservative, not daring. Yet he was a man of genuine ability, keen intellect, and humane sentiments who earned the respect and affection of those who knew him. Glass called him "one of the finest men who ever lived," and Byrd referred to him as "one of the most beloved friends I ever had."

Pollard intended to follow Byrd's successful term with positive achievements of his own, but funds for many worthwhile programs were cut to conform to Byrd's standard of fiscal conservatism. State officialdom all but ignored the human suffering created by the depression, focusing instead on the necessity of balanced budgets. Pollard's permanent legacy as governor must rest on his proposals for county government, fisheries, liquor control, and the Virginia Museum of Fine Arts, all of them solid contributions to the Commonwealth.

The record might have been more lustrous had Pollard not been eclipsed by Harry Byrd; but by the same token, it was Byrd who ended Pollard's political seclusion at William and Mary and made him his successor. While governor, Pollard occasionally would pat his large abdomen and remark that he "got that by swallowing the Byrd machine." Figuratively, at least, there was a sizable kernel of truth in the jest. Nevertheless, by compromising and working with the Byrd organization, he was able to achieve reforms that he had long advocated. As governor, he was highly effective in working with the legislature, particularly when his efforts were supplemented by Byrd's influence. Although the lawmakers occasionally changed some of Pollard's bills from his original intent and language, his record was still—on the whole— quite impressive. Viewed from this perspective, one might argue that he achieved a small triumph over the machine.

SOURCES

The John Garland Pollard Papers (College of William and Mary) contain personal letters, speeches, and scrapbooks. The Pollard Executive Papers (Virginia State Library) include materials relating to his administration. The Harry Flood Byrd Papers and the Carter Glass Papers (both at the University of Virginia) and the Reed Family Papers (Virginia Historical Society) provide additional insights.

Pollard's political career is fully recounted in John S. Hopewell, "An Outsider Looking In: John Garland Pollard and Machine Politics in Twentieth Century Virginia" (Ph.D. diss., University of Virginia, 1976), while economic conditions of the period are examined in Ronald Lynton Heinemann, "Depression and New Deal in Virginia" (Ph.D. diss., University of Virginia, 1968). Helpful published accounts include Virginius Dabney, *Dry Messiah: The Life of Bishop Cannon* (New York, 1949), and Raymond H. Pulley: *Old Virginia Restored: An Interpretation of the Progressive Impulse, 1870–1930* (Charlottesville, 1968). See also Alvin L. Hall, "Virginia Back in the Fold: The Gubernatorial Campaign and Election of 1929," *Virginia Magazine of History and Biography* 73 (1965): 280–302.

GEORGE C. PEERY

Byrd Regular and Depression Governor

Joseph A. Fry

The emergence of a new generation of party leaders was crucial to Harry F. Byrd's rise to power. As a charter member of the Byrd organization, George Campbell Perry personified this new Democratic elite—loyal, self-effacing, and conservative. Not merely representative, Peery also contributed significantly to the evolution of the organization and to Byrd's career. His dramatic victory in the Ninth Congressional District in 1922 augmented Byrd's growing reputation as a political organizer, and his overwhelming triumph in the Democratic gubernatorial primary of 1933 sealed Byrd's unquestioned control over the party. As governor from 1934 through 1938, Peery provided steady, conservative leadership that continued Byrd's philosophy and programs, reinforced Byrd's opposition to the New Deal, and allowed the new senator the freedom to shift much of his attention to national affairs.

Of Scotch-Irish descent, Peery was born in Cedar Bluff, a Tazewell County hamlet, in 1873. His father, James Peery, had served the Confederacy as a surgeon with Derrick's Battalion. While attending local schools, George worked on his father's farm, clerked in the family store, and at the age of sixteen did clerical chores in the Tazewell County clerk's office. His father's successful medical practice enabled him to enroll in Emory and Henry College in the depression-ridden 1890s. An able, hard-driving student, Peery demonstrated diverse abilities by winning medals in oratory and science.

Following graduation in 1894 he became principal of Tazewell High School but resigned two years later to enter the Washington and Lee University School of Law. Taking his studies seriously, he maintained a ninety-plus average and earned his degree in one year. After practicing law in Tazewell for two years, Peery crossed the mountains to Wise. Although he expected a short stay, legal work with several coal and land companies went well, and he soon built the largest house in town, a structure of nearly twenty rooms. In 1907 he married Nancy Bane Gillespie, the daughter of Albert P. Gillespie, a prominent Tazewell attorney. From this long, happy marriage came three children. Although Peery concentrated on his legal career in Wise, he gained valuable experience in public life and earned the respect of prominent local Democrats, many of whom later emerged as staunch supporters.

GEORGE C. PEERY

Governor of Virginia

1934–1938

In 1915 Peery returned to Tazewell as executor of Albert Gillespie's estate and soon joined Gillespie's former law partners, A. C. Buchanan and Archibald C. Chapman, to form the firm of Chapman, Peery, and Buchanan. In 1916 he was chosen as state Democratic elector-at-large on the Wilson-Marshall ticket; four years later he was tapped as both a delegate to the party's national convention and as chairman of the Ninth District Democratic committee.

Modest and retiring, Peery elicited the confidence of his political peers, and his penchant for meticulous and effective organization endeared him to both Democratic workers and candidates. By the eve of the 1921 gubernatorial election he had constructed what some considered the "best organization" in district history. E. Lee Trinkle confirmed this evaluation by becoming the first Democrat to carry the Ninth in twenty years.

The "Fighting Ninth," composed of the city of Bristol and the thirteen mountainous counties of southwestern Virginia, was a Republican stronghold. The man most responsible for Grand Old Party dominance after 1900 was C. Bascom Slemp. First as campaign manager for his father, Campbell Slemp, and thereafter on his own behalf, the "Sage of Turkey Cove" had skillfully marshaled Republican forces and scratched out hard-fought victories in each congressional election from 1902 through 1920.

Encouraged by Peery's effective organization, Trinkle's impressive showing, and Republican economic difficulties on the national level, local Democrats enthusiastically prepared to battle the formidable Slemp in 1922. After a preconvention "conference of active Democrats" had selected Peery as their candidate, nearly six hundred delegates trooped into Bristol on March 21, 1922, for the official convention. John W. Flannagan nominated Peery and set the convention's tone. The people, he said, had voted for "prosperity, plenty and a full dinner pail," but got "hell, Harding and hard times." Amidst a rollicking atmosphere of handkerchief-waving, newly enfranchised women and hat-throwing men, Peery was nominated by acclamation. In ensuing weeks, Peery and Everett Randolph ("Ebbie") Combs, his campaign manager and soon-to-be chief of staff of the Byrd organization, compiled lists of Democrats who had not paid their poll taxes. These lists were forwarded to Bristol where party leaders "looked after" the delinquent taxes, prodding party members to register and, on occasion, even dispatching registrars to their homes. In mid-October Combs smugly and accurately estimated that "we will qualify between two thousand and twenty-five hundred more new voters than they will. Things look mighty good."

Even with these prodigious efforts, the Ninth District Democrats required outside aid. Harry Byrd, then thirty-five, new chairman of the Democratic state central committee, sent state auditors to monitor Republican poll tax payments and later convinced Governor Trinkle to postpone a potentially divisive special session of the legislature until after the November elections.

Byrd provided his most critical contribution, however, by funneling badly needed funds into the district. He personally contributed over $1,000 and also tapped sources ranging from wealthy party supporters in Richmond to Democratic officeholders and state employees. Byrd also became the first state chairman in memory to campaign in the Ninth.

What had promised to be an extremely close contest became a rout when Bascom Slemp unexpectedly refused to seek reelection. John Hassinger, the Republican nominee and a state senator from Abingdon, was no match for Peery, who, despite his low-key manner, was a markedly superior speaker and a more energetic campaigner, traveling to all corners of the far-flung district. Emphasizing that he was one of the Southwest's native "mountain boys" (in contrast to the Pennsylvania-born Hassinger), Peery concentrated on the economic problems that had engulfed the nation under Harding. This cumulative effort yielded a resounding victory, Peery defeating Hassinger by more than 2,900 votes. Republican power in the Ninth was broken; and, like Henry Carter Stuart and E. Lee Trinkle before him, George Peery would discover that the road to the Governor's Mansion began in the rugged campaign trails of the Southwest.

The key to traveling this road without mishap was Peery's close identification with Harry Byrd, an association which over the next fifteen years proved mutually beneficial. Peery's victory significantly enhanced Byrd's political position; more importantly, by initiating lasting friendships with Peery and Combs, Byrd had begun the formation of his own personal organization. In congratulating Peery, Byrd observed prophetically, "I predict for you a wonderful career in Congress, and political honors in the future much greater than that of being a Congressman."

A large, rawboned man standing nearly six feet two inches tall, the new congressman cut an impressive figure. At forty-nine Peery's hair was silvering, and his heavy brow and thin mouth framed a sharply chiseled but handsome face. In personal encounters Peery was initially shy, but most acquaintances discovered his boyish smile disguised a genuine "warmth of manner." Often belittled by political opponents as "Silent George," Peery was never boisterous and consistently listened more than he talked. However, once he was on the platform, his dignified appearance, deep, resonant voice, and subtle, cutting wit surprised many an adversary and impressed numerous audiences. Strongly attached to the mountains of southwest Virginia, Peery found outdoor recreation satisfying and relaxing. Congressional teas were "a little difficult" and could not compare with riding horses, hunting birds, or pitching horseshoes. Prudent and cautious in his approach to problems, Peery displayed courage and resolution in supporting his views. As a "Bust Head dirt farmer" observed in 1933, "You take the Peery's and sometimes they can be as stubborn and sot in their ways as anything, especially when they are right."

With the aid of Byrd, Combs, and the smoothly functioning district organization, Peery spearheaded successful reelection campaigns in 1924 and 1926. Although he failed to sponsor any noteworthy legislation during three congressional terms, he did advance a conservative economic and political philosophy much attuned to that of Governor Byrd. Peery frequently deplored the plight of farmers; however, his proposed solutions to the agricultural depression looked back to the Populists rather than ahead to the New Deal. Instead of wholesale purchase of surplus crops by the federal government, he recommended the reduction of taxes, freight rates, and tariffs. Peery sounded much like Byrd himself in endorsing the pay-as-you-go approach to public finance. While debating alternative methods of financing road construction, he declared, "we are getting a splendid highway system in Virginia, and we are doing it without resorting to bond issue." He declined to seek reelection in 1928 and ended his congressional career in March 1929.

Peery attempted to squelch rumors that he might run for governor by stating in January 1928 that he favored Benjamin F. Buchanan, a Marion native and the organization's tentative choice. However, Herbert Hoover's 1928 success in Virginia (especially in Tidewater) forced Democratic regulars to turn to an eastern man who favored Prohibition but was not too closely tied to the organization. After surveying the field, Byrd tapped John Garland Pollard, former attorney general and professor of government at the College of William and Mary.

This did not, however, end speculation, and on March 26, 1929, Peery declared: "in hope of promoting harmony in the party . . . I do not expect to become a candidate in the approaching primary." He then joined organization leaders in backing Pollard. Virginia's Democratic press roundly applauded Peery's "patriotic" decision not to risk a sectional split in the party. The Petersburg *Progress-Index* predicted that he had put "himself in a strong position as a candidate . . . four years hence." The Richmond *News Leader* agreed that he was "already being looked on by many as the Democratic gubernatorial nominee in 1933."

These predictions proved accurate. Following Pollard's election in November, Governor Byrd immediately rewarded Peery's loyalty with an appointment to the State Corporation Commission; but his ultimate reward would come four years later. Not since E. Lee Trinkle had southwestern Virginia supplied the state's chief executive. It was logical that the organization would look to that region in 1933, and it was equally logical that George Peery would be the choice. Byrd and Peery were virtually of one mind on economic and political policy; moreover, Peery had demonstrated the ability to attract popular support and had exhibited unquestioned loyalty by postponing his gubernatorial aspirations. His credentials were flawless.

Peery's performance in 1933 was of vital interest to the Byrd organization. Initially Byrd supporters agonized over the widening rift between the "old guard" led by Senator Claude A. Swanson and new-generation men led by Byrd. By early 1933 disagreements over federal patronage and Byrd's ill-concealed desire for Swanson's Senate seat had become the main points of contention. But Swanson avoided a direct confrontation by accepting Franklin Roosevelt's offer to be secretary of the navy, and Governor Pollard then dutifully appointed Byrd to serve the remainder of his term. Always wary, the new senator still feared that a weak showing by Peery might generate opposition to his election to a full term in 1934.

In January 1933 Byrd decided that Peery should delay his formal campaign at least until mid-March. In the interim, Byrd and Combs would, in Combs's words, "immediately commit as many local political leaders to Peery as possible." After this solicitous cultivation of courthouse rings, Peery opened his campaign on April 6 by endorsing the Byrd reforms, which included the short ballot, tax segregation, consolidation of government machinery, and pay-as-you-go road construction. He also called for increased aid to education, reduction in the automobile license tax, abolition of the fee system wherever possible, and continuation of a balanced budget, which would bring "an earlier return to prosperity."

Public demand for a reduction of prevailing utility rates unexpectedly produced the first important issue of the campaign. In response to a number of protests, the State Corporation Commission had authorized Allen J. Saville, a prominent Richmond civil engineer, to evaluate the rates of the Virginia Electric and Power Company, the Virginia Public Service Company, and the Appalachian Electric Power Company. The companies themselves were to help finance the investigation. The ensuing controversy quickly enveloped Peery, chairman of the Corporation Commission when the investigation was authorized. Much of the furor originated with T. Ralph Jones of Norfolk, the most vocal member of the League of Virginia Municipalities and a rival candidate for governor. Jones and the league objected to financial involvement of the power companies in the investigation, and Jones denounced both Peery and Saville as decidedly "pro-power and utility."

Apprehensive over these charges, Byrd moved to defuse the situation. He convinced Governor Pollard to provide state funds for the investigation and thereby cut all ties to the power companies. Following Byrd's counsel, Peery refused comment prior to announcing his platform on April 6. He then recommended a prompt valuation of utility company properties as the basis for subsequent rate determination and advocated giving the Corporation Commission the power to amend rates temporarily. Much to the relief of the Byrd-Peery camp, this potentially explosive issue faded from view after Jones withdrew from the race on April 29.

Joseph T. Deal and W. Worth Smith now became Peery's opposition. Deal, a Norfolk businessman, had represented Virginia's Second District in Congress from 1921 through 1929. Smith, who (according to the *Times-*

Dispatch) was one of Louisa County's "most eminent possum hunters," had served in the state Senate since 1924. Both men proclaimed themselves New Dealers and harshly castigated Peery for his association with the Byrd "machine." Deal was especially vehement in his antiorganization stand, demanding the repeal of the short ballot and tax segregation, which he characterized as transparent devices to "perpetuate" organization control. Defeating Peery, Deal proclaimed, would be the key to ridding Virginia of Byrd's "officeholders trust."

Peery, proud of his organization ties, quickly pointed out that both of his opponents previously had supported the allegedly evil machine and dismissed Deal's demand for the decentralization of state government as "reactionary." Peery and Byrd had greater difficulty establishing a viable position on Prohibition repeal. The two men had personally and politically favored Prohibition for years, and both of them underestimated the strength of repeal sentiment. Moveover, with the 1928 Democratic split still quite vivid, the organization sought to avoid alienating "drys." Byrd advised dodging the Prohibition issue as long as possible, and Peery adopted this strategy. He supported repeal of the Eighteenth Amendment, but his policy for Virginia was equivocal. Taking no personal stand, he promised to abide by the wishes of the General Assembly or a popular referendum. When pressure for a special session of the Assembly mounted, the organization sought to get back in step with the electorate. On June 27, 1933, both Peery and Byrd announced support for a special session to legalize the sale of beer and to establish procedures for acting upon the Eighteenth Amendment and Virginia's antiliquor laws. Byrd then pressured reluctant Governor Pollard into permitting a special session, and the bogey of Prohibition was eliminated from the campaign.

Despite the vehement, at times abusive attacks of his opponents, Peery campaigned with a "dignity and poise" born of his own personality and the confidence of organization support. Organization tactics had so effectively disposed of troublesome issues that the *Times-Dispatch* dismissed the campaign as "colorless" and "listless." Still, as the August 1 primary date approached, organization insiders fretted over the "size of [Peery's] majority." Their anxiety was unwarranted. Peery carried eight of the state's nine congressional districts and polled 116,837 votes to Deal's 40,268 and Smith's 32,518. The transfer of power within the Democratic organization was complete. With the real contest finished, Peery and the organization virtually ignored the Republicans. Fred McWane, a Lynchburg manufacturer and the Republican candidate, repeatedly challenged Peery to debate; and other GOP representatives scored Peery and the "machine" for "Tammany Hall policies" and inconsistency. Peery's response was to take a leisurely fishing trip and meet with Governor Pollard to discuss the approaching administrative transition. After a relaxed, one-month campaign, Peery easily defeated McWane, 122,820 to 40,377.

Those in Richmond for Peery's inaugural on January 17, 1934, were greeted by glistening sun and a sharp, chill wind. After the usual formalities, including six bands playing "Happy Days Are Here Again," Peery sounded the dominant theme of his administration: "The one outstanding lesson that has come to all during these critical days is the need for thrift and economy in all lines of endeavor. . . . We need economy in government today, as we have never needed it before." Having run on the Byrd-Pollard record, Peery interpreted his victory as an endorsement of their conservative policies. Not a reactionary opposing all progress, he believed that the cost of progress had to be confined within a balanced budget. "Financial insecurity on the part of the state," he lectured, could not promote the permanent "social security" of the people.

Peery's initial encounter with the General Assembly was stormy. In the special referendum of October 3, 1933, Virginia had voted to repeal both the Eighteenth Amendment and the state Prohibition law, thereby necessitating revision of Virginia liquor laws. Peery recommended a three-man board to issue licenses for the sale of beer and wine, purchase liquors, and establish state-operated liquor stores. This plan made the liquor business a state monopoly limited to carryout sales. The opposition favored private liquor licensing and sale of liquor by the drink with meals in restaurants and hotels; they argued that Virginia's tourist trade demanded these innovative steps. Although Peery yielded to the popular demand for repeal, he resolutely defended temperance. "The object of the law," he pronounced, should be "to promote temperance and outlaw the bootlegger and racketeer." Successfully resisting pressure for liquor by the drink and private licensing, he also secured an amendment making the buyer of moonshine as guilty as the seller. By June 1938 the three-man Alcoholic Beverage Control Board had established 187 state stores, bootlegging had declined significantly, and the state was realizing a substantial profit from this monopoly. Observers agreed that Peery had staffed the board with excellent appointments and that the new system was working well.

Disagreement over liquor paled by comparison to the reception accorded Peery's request for increased taxes to fund public education. In his final message Governor Pollard had recommended that the state spend approximately $6 million for public schools over the upcoming biennium, but Peery said this would not fund normal eight-month sessions and called for an additional $1 million for each of these years. To retire a projected $2 million deficit by the end of the same period the state would have to balance its budget and hope for increased revenues. Simultaneous aid to public schools and a balanced budget necessitated tax increases. Peery's tax package would increase rates on personal incomes, utility companies' incomes, and inheritances and would levy new taxes on motion picture tickets and Virginia corporation dividends.

Even though Peery sought to offset these increases with a $1.8 million reduction in auto license fees, he encountered stiff opposition. The press was virtually unanimous in its condemnation. William A. Garrett, eighty-year-old chairman of the Senate Finance Committee, led the antitax forces in the General Assembly. Garrett blandly dismissed Peery's proposal as a "school teachers' salary program" and vowed that it would "never pass the Senate." As this "major revolt" swelled, rumors circulated that Byrd opposed Peery's program. Byrd had been initially ambivalent; but after talking with Peery and Combs, he advised an associate that "he should support whatever George Peery advocates, and I intend to do the same." Byrd then made a special trip to Richmond, meeting with the governor and various legislators. Byrd urged Peery to compromise, especially on taxing corporation dividends. Through personal conferences with organization stalwarts, the senator prepared the Assembly leadership for this move. Byrd also countered the vehement press attacks upon Peery by ordering his two papers, the Winchester *Evening Star* and the Harrisonburg *News-Record,* to insert "several editorials strongly supporting Governor Peery in his efforts for balanced budgets."

Byrd's actions were important, but Peery's were decisive. Skillfully employing the powers of his office and working privately through Combs and T. McCall Frazier, Virginia's motor vehicle commissioner, he unrelentingly pressured individual legislators. Publicly, he dramatized the issue in a speech before a joint session of the Assembly. After stressing that the tax increases were earmarked only for education, he explained that his proposed reduction in the auto license tax was greater than the cumulative additions in other areas. He then compromised slightly by eliminating taxes upon motion picture tickets and corporation dividends and assuaged urban opposition by altering the school plan to provide greater aid for cities and more populous counties. As the session ground toward a close, administration spokesmen prodded holdouts by threatening that rejection of Peery's program might necessitate a sales tax. Finally, and perhaps most importantly, Peery delayed signing the alcohol control bill with its substantial patronage features, using it as a lever to swing recalcitrant assemblymen into line. When these combined efforts produced lopsided victories in both houses of the Assembly, even Peery's most strident critics conceded that he had "routed" the opposition. A mixture of bitterness and near admiration characterized the *News Leader's* final comment on Peery's actions: "The use of force by an administration is common enough, but rarely since 1923 . . . has executive force been used with such full-armored, naive audacity."

The 1934 General Assembly enacted one other significant, though much less controversial, measure—revoking the right of the fee-paid justice of the peace to try cases and replacing him with a salaried official, the trial justice. (Biased decisions had become so prevalent that Virginians commonly referred to the initials "J.P." as "Judgment for the Plaintiff.") The 1934 Trial Justice

Act and a second, more comprehensive measure in 1936 established court-appointed trial justices in every county. The trial justice became the principal judicial officer on the local level, and the system has since evolved into the district court. As a practicing attorney, Peery took special pride in this reform, and shortly before his death he characterized it as one of his administration's most outstanding achievements.

The conclusion of the legislative session brought Peery no respite, for neither he nor the legislature had dealt meaningfully with the social and economic disarray wrought by the Great Depression. Because of its rural character and relatively balanced economy, Virginia had fared better than many states, and economic conditions had steadily improved since 1932; however, recovery was far from complete. The unemployed still numbered over 125,000. From July 1934 through June 1935 Virginia's relief rolls averaged 208,626, and not until 1937 would the Old Dominion regain its 1930 level of prosperity.

The depression's ongoing rigors heightened the importance of federal aid. Soon after Peery took office, Harry Hopkins, administrator of the Federal Emergency Relief Administration (FERA), threatened to terminate Virginia's relief funds. Hopkins was "very disappointed" that the state had appropriated no funds for direct relief; one of his assistants explained that Virginia had "not carried her fair share" and should provide more money "if she [expected] more from the federal government." Extensive appropriations for direct relief were anathema to Peery and the organization. Although sympathetic to the plight of the unemployed, Peery, like Byrd, gave greater priority to maintaining the state's financial integrity and allegedly to preserving individual character. From Peery's conservative and elitist perspective, large relief allocations ensured both deficit spending and diminished individual initiative. Peery would tolerate no deficit spending in Richmond. However, he adamantly contended that if Washington were to indulge in such "folly," Virginia should receive its "share" of federal bounty. Byrd agreed. Seeking to avert the threatened termination of funds, Byrd arranged a conference with Hopkins which produced an assurance that Virginia would have access to approximately $6 million through February 1935. Hopkins periodically renewed his demands, but they remained only threats as he consistently capitulated to the political power of Senators Glass and Byrd. This uncertain situation continued essentially unchanged until the summer of 1935 when Roosevelt began phasing out the FERA.

As the 1936 session of the General Assembly approached, pressure for greater state appropriations increased. From 1933 through 1935 the FERA had poured over $26 million into Virginia and paid over 90 percent of the state's relief bill. Without this aid, the state would have to assume greater responsibility. Public school spokesmen were also demanding larger appropriations. Former Governor E. Lee Trinkle, chairman of the state Board of

Education, joined the Virginia Education Association in championing a program requiring an additional $7 million. More funds were also needed for highway construction and maintenance and the new unemployment insurance and old-age pension programs created by the Social Security Act of 1935.

Peery's first recommendation to the 1936 General Assembly emphasized his resolve to hold the line against spending: "Virginia has reaped substantial benefits from the sound financial policies followed in the past and should not be led by insistent demands for increased appropriations to abandon the policy that expenses must not exceed income." While opposing new taxes, he proposed, nevertheless, an additional $347,935 for public schools, $2 million for direct relief, and approximately $8 million for roads. Turning to social security, he recommended the adoption of a state unemployment insurance plan since failure to do so would cost Virginia workers millions of dollars in benefits. On the other hand, estimating the annual costs of an old-age pension plan at $2 million to $11 million, he suggested that this matter be postponed for further study.

The General Assembly followed Peery's suggestions with only one exception—it rejected the unemployment insurance plan. An unidentified state senator succinctly summarized the 1936 session from the administration's perspective: "We met, we didn't raise taxes, we balanced the budget, and we adjourned, and it took courage to resist the demands for new projects that would have left a huge deficit." Others, of a more liberal ilk, pointed to the defeat of unemployment insurance, old-age pensions, an eight-hour labor law for women, probation and jail reform measures, and an antinepotism bill and concluded that this had been the most "reactionary Assembly" since 1920. Several factors explain the defeat of the administration-sponsored unemployment insurance plan. Many states' rights legislators balked at "dictation" from Washington, and forceful lobbying by the Virginia Manufacturers Association shoved others into the negative column. Although nominally in favor of the bill, Peery demonstrated none of the drive that had forced his proposals through the Assembly in 1934. The Roanoke *Times* decried the "startling lack of leadership," and other critics charged that the governor had "laid down" on the bill.

In the months that followed, Peery refused to call a special session to enact the plan. He contended that states without unemployment laws would command a sufficient majority in Congress to extend the December 31, 1936, deadline for parallel state legislation. However, Maryland, Pennsylvania, and New Jersey dashed Peery's hopes by indicating they would adopt the required laws. But before capitulating, the governor made certain that a majority of the assemblymen favored the proposed plan and would confine their action to the bill and others he might submit. By soliciting this dual pledge, Peery eliminated the possibility of funding a special session that would again reject the plan or meddle in other matters. Amid grumblings about "Huey

Long" tactics, the Assembly met on December 14 and enacted the unemployment insurance plan, which provided for a State Unemployment Compensation Commission to supervise collection of required taxes from the state's employers. By January 1938 when benefit payments began, the commission had also established an employment service with thirty-three offices throughout the state.

Meanwhile, labor unrest created new problems for Peery. After the passage of the Wagner Act and the rise of the Congress of Industrial Organizations (CIO), labor activity in 1937 reached new heights of intensity throughout the country. In Virginia there were fifty strikes involving 18,743 workers, both high marks for the decade. The most serious strike occurred at the Industrial Rayon Corporation plant in Covington.

Union activities at Covington were part of a concerted CIO campaign to organize the southern textile industry. After enrolling nearly 80 percent of the plant's 1,000 workers, union representatives initiated negotiations in late February 1937. Among their demands were an end to discrimination against union members, a substantial wage increase, and recognition of the Synthetic Yarn Federation of America (CIO) as the sole representative for collective bargaining. Talks soon reached an impasse. Suddenly, at 11:30 P.M. on March 29, the workers initiated Virginia's first major sit-down strike. The company promptly closed the plant, but nearly 400 sit-downers refused to leave. There was no violence. Instead a surprisingly amiable atmosphere prevailed. Union members agreed to clean the machinery, and management consented to keep the plant cafeteria open for their use. But this unnatural spirit of cooperation lasted only a few days.

Property-conscious Virginians, appalled at the newest labor tactic, considered the sit-down a blatantly illegal seizure of company property. Although Peery agreed, he decided against any hasty attempt to evict the strikers. He contended that initial responsibility for the protection of private property rested with local authorities, and his policy of purposeful procrastination paid dividends on April 7 when the rayon workers voluntarily evacuated the plant and established traditional picket lines outside the plant gate. After a three-month battle of attrition, Industrial Rayon challenged the picket line on July 7. Two buses and twenty cars of returning workers clashed with between 400 and 500 strikers. Although the strikers overturned two cars and numerous fistfights ensued, no one was seriously injured. Peery's reaction contrasted sharply with his reserved response of three months before. Operating on the theory that "strikes are legal, but any man who wishes to return to work certainly has the privilege and right" to do so, he quickly dispatched 25 state policemen to the scene. On July 9 the state troopers escorted 50 workers into the plant; by the thirteenth, 500 workers were back on the job; a month later 850 men were operating the plant at 75 percent capacity. The strike was broken.

Charges arose that the state police had acted as strikebreakers by convoying persons "not in the employ of the Industrial Rayon Corporation" when the strike began. Peery truthfully responded that he had been advised that the groups escorted by the police were all former employees. More fundamentally, Peery, like most Americans, had a narrow view of the strike as a weapon in industrial disputes and was uncomfortable with the concept of an enforced closed shop. This, together with his perceived obligation to maintain peace and order, dictated that the governor's practical policy would favor management.

On January 12, 1938, Peery made his final appearance before the General Assembly. Undoubtedly speaking for many predecessors, he declared, "I sincerely thank every friend who had any part in bringing to me the greatest honor of my life. No nobler mission can come to any man than that of serving as Governor of this Commonwealth." Several days later, as he started for Tazewell and a "long rest," observers noted that "his eyes were moist, his voice husky." Peery had carefully perpetuated Harry Byrd's reform program and his conservative economic and political philosophies. He had also presided over several significant innovations including adoption of the alcoholic beverage control plan, passage of unemployment insurance, enactment of the trial justice system, and appropriation of Virginia's first funds for direct relief. Like Governors Byrd and Pollard, Peery had pursued a policy of stringent economy. With the aid of increased revenues from the state liquor monopoly and returning prosperity, he converted the 1934 deficit of over $2 million into a projected surplus of over $5 million in 1938. Moreover, Virginia's bonded indebtedness had decreased from $20,009,535 to $16,866,455.

In evaluating his governorship, editorials emphasized such terms as "prudence," "caution," "courage," "candor," "integrity," and "conservatism." Writing in 1936, Westmoreland Davis, one of the organization's most strident critics, zeroed in on yet another trait. He acknowledged that Virginia bonds were "selling at a premium" but contended that it had been "accomplished through neglect of the state of its duty to its citizens." Liberal critics did not have to look far to substantiate this charge. In 1935 twenty-nine states furnished relief aid to the aged, the blind, dependent children, and the unemployed. Fifteen states aided two of these groups. Virginia helped only dependent children. In his 1936 budget recommendations Peery granted 80 percent ($8 million) of the additional funds requested by the highway department and 5 percent ($350,000) of the new allocations requested by the Department of Education. Virginia's 1937 expenditures revealed a similar pattern: 35.86 percent for roads, 11.19 percent for education, and 6.19 percent for welfare. This unbending conservatism and devotion to pay-as-you-go had led both Peery and the organization to sacrifice human priorities at the altar of fiscal orthodoxy.

His gubernatorial term completed, Peery returned to southwest Virginia.

He resumed his law practice, raised livestock, and served on the boards of
trustees for both Hollins College and Washington and Lee University. He
rendered his final public service as a delegate to the constitutional convention
of May 1945, which abolished the poll tax and registration requirements for
persons in the armed forces. After a period of declining health, George Campbell Peery died on October 1, 1952, and was buried in Maplewood Cemetery
in Tazewell.

At first glance, Peery seems to have epitomized the typical Byrd organization member—quiet, unassuming, colorless, little more than an inter-
changeable part. He was certainly one of the most representative members of
the organization, and his career clearly demonstrated the loyalty, patience,
and ability necessary to rise through its ranks. However, a low-key, undramatic style should not obscure significant contributions to Byrd's rise or
Peery's central role in the evolution of the organization. His victory in the
1922 congressional election launched Byrd on his way, and his victory in the
1933 gubernatorial primary secured Byrd's control of the party. Peery's gubernatorial term was an especially crucial one for Virginia and the organization.
His steady, dependable leadership allowed the Byrd forces to regroup and
consolidate control after the crisis of 1928–29, and it simultaneously enabled
Senator Byrd to assume a more national posture. Lastly, Peery's term coincided with the century's most serious economic crisis. His response mirrored
that of the organization, and his administration embodied the philosophical
tenets that have dominated twentieth-century Virginia government: efficiency, pay-as-you-go, suspicion of national spending, and hostility to the
growing federal bureaucracy. In sum, Peery was both a highly representative
figure and a substantial contributor to Virginia political history from 1920
through 1938.

SOURCES

Although Peery left no private papers, scattered Peery letters and other
essential materials are available in the papers of Harry Flood Byrd,
Everett Randolph Combs, and Carter Glass (all at the University of
Virginia); the Reed Family Papers (Virginia Historical Society); and the
Peery Executive Papers (Virginia State Library).

For background, see Ronald L. Heinemann's "Depression and New
Deal in Virginia" (Ph.D. diss., University of Virginia, 1968) and Robert
M. Hunter's "Virginia and the New Deal," in John Braeman, Robert H.
Bremner, and David Brody, eds., *The New Deal: The State and Local
Levels* 2 (Columbus, Ohio, 1975).

Principal secondary accounts of Peery's career include Joseph A.
Fry, "George Campbell Peery: Conservative Son of Old Virginia" (M.A.
thesis, University of Virginia, 1970); Fry and Brent Tarter, "The Re-
demption of the Fighting Ninth: The 1922 Congressional Election in the
Ninth District of Virginia and the Origins of the Byrd Organization,"
South Atlantic Quarterly 77 (Summer 1978): 352–70; Fry, "The Orga-

nization in Control: George Campbell Peery, Governor of Virginia, 1934–1938," *Virginia Magazine of History and Biography* 82 (1974): 306–30; and Fry, "Rayon, Riot, and Repression: The Covington Sit-Down Strike of 1937," *Virginia Magazine of History and Biography* 84 (1976): 3–18.

JAMES H. PRICE

Governor of Virginia

1938–1942

JAMES HUBERT PRICE

New Dealer in the Old Dominion

Alvin L. Hall

James Hubert Price was an anomaly in twentieth-century Virginia politics. He became governor without the initial blessing of Senator Harry F. Byrd during a period when Byrd's control of state politics was virtually unchallenged. Price proposed one of the most progressive and far-reaching legislative programs of the first half of the century; yet, despite immense personal popularity, his program became embroiled in complex political crosscurrents, and he accomplished virtually none of his goals.

Price was born at Organ Cave in Greenbrier County, West Virginia, on September 7, 1878, the oldest son of Charles and Nancy Price. Since 1748 the Price family had been small independent farmers in the region. Price attended local schools and in 1897 left to continue his education in the state that he would eventually govern. Price studied accounting at Dunsmore's Business College in Staunton for a year, graduating as a master of accounts. Prevented by modest circumstances and family responsibilities from going on to law school, he remained at Dunsmore's for ten years as a teacher and as private secretary to the school's founder and president. Price also opened an accounting office and acquired other business interests in Staunton. His long-deferred dream was finally realized in 1907 when he entered law school at Washington and Lee University—just before his thirtieth birthday. He was an excellent student, and despite his age, he also made his mark on extracurricular life as president of his graduating class and an active member of social and legal fraternities.

After graduation in 1909, Price returned to Staunton as an ambitious lawyer-businessman but quickly realized that Richmond held more opportunity. He moved to the capital in 1910, established a private practice in civil and corporate law, and soon was on the boards of directors of several banks and a large real estate firm. Price also served in the National Guard, attaining the rank of captain before resigning in 1913. He met his future wife, Lillian Martin of Stuart, Virginia, during the First World War while she was in Richmond with her father, Dr. Richard Martin, a prominent physician and a member of the House of Delegates from Patrick County. They were married on October 2, 1918. Price was one month past his fortieth birthday, fifteen years older than his bride. The union produced two children, James Hubert, Jr., and Lillian Martin Price.

During these years Price began another association that was as important to his career as law. He joined the Masons while in Staunton and subsequently became a Shriner, reaching the apogee of his Shrine career in 1927 when he was appointed Imperial Recorder, a position he held until his death. This office placed him in charge of financial affairs for the national organization and provided a network of friendships to complement those already established in the state. Price was an elder of Ginter Park Presbyterian Church and for many years taught a Bible class at Westminster Church. He was also active in various humanitarian endeavors. Some, such as his service to the Masonic Foundation, the Shriners' Hospitals for Crippled Children, and the Masonic Relief Foundation, were related to his fraternal activities. Others included his association with both the Richmond and Virginia Workers for the Blind.

Price was a handsome man. By the time he launched his political career, his black hair was sufficiently gray at the temples to suggest maturity. His face was dominated by deep-set, thoughtful, brown eyes surmounted by heavy, bushy brows. The total impression was one of seriousness, quiet dignity, and warmth. He gained weight with age but never became portly. He usually wore a conservative dark gray or blue suit, double-breasted after the fashion of the day, and his lapel frequently held a pin denoting his fraternal affiliation.

Of many adjectives available, "dignified" best describes both the person and manner of James Price. Despite his humble birth, his secretary of twenty years concluded that Price "was always the personification of gentleman to the manor born," which is to say, he was everything Virginia demanded of its politicians. Price was also modest. After his election as governor, Price refused to use the title except on the most formal state occasions. Associates who called him frequently were greeted with, "Hello, this is Jim Price, down at the governor's office," instead of the expected, "This is Governor Price." He had a phenomenal memory for names and faces. It was said that he knew some ten thousand Virginians by first name, and he could put the name with the face when the occasion called for it. Although this ability proved an invaluable asset to Price the politician, it stemmed from a genuine interest in people.

And, Price was ambitious. While still a student at Washington and Lee, he told at least one classmate of his desire to be governor. Shortly after his arrival in Richmond, moreover, he remarked to a future congressman from that city that his main ambition was to serve the state as governor. After several years on the Richmond Democratic committee, Price was elected to one of the city's five seats in the House of Delegates. In his first contest he ran second in a nine-man race. Price served seven consecutive terms in the Virginia lower house (1916–30) and by the early 1920s had advanced to the forefront of that body's leadership. He was chairman of the Committee on

Courts of Justice and ranked second on several others. Price also served as chairman of the Democratic caucus for three terms and as chairman of the State Auditing Committee. This record is hardly that of one not in the good graces of the dominant Democratic organization.

It is not clear just when Price's relationship with Harry Byrd began to deteriorate. The earliest indication came in 1926 when Thomas W. Ozlin defeated Price for speaker of the House—a development viewed by the press as another step in Byrd's consolidation of power. During the special legislative session of 1927 Price favored most of Byrd's reform package but had strong and vocal reservations about the short ballot reducing the number of elected officials to three—governor, lieutenant governor, and attorney general. Price was among those who considered this a dangerous and undue centralization of power. This streak of independence made it difficult for organization leaders to predict what Price would do in any given situation, a trait viewed with suspicion.

During Byrd's gubernatorial term Price was mentioned as a possible candidate for attorney general or lieutenant governor, but he discounted such talk, noting it would require great personal and financial sacrifice. Political events of 1928 and 1929, however, made such sacrifices less necessary. Following Republican Herbert Hoover's presidential victory in Virginia in 1928, leaders of the Democratic organization needed men such as Price to restore their control. Price had remained loyal to national Democratic nominee Alfred E. Smith in 1928, but his personal qualifications would appeal to the predominately Protestant and Prohibitionist Democrats who had supported Hoover. Moreover, his opposition to the short ballot would win friends among those not strongly attached to the organization, and his residence in Richmond would be attractive in heavily populated eastern counties. Finally, Price had just been appointed Imperial Recorder of the Shrine, a fact reflecting his personal popularity. It is no wonder the leadership sanctioned his bid to be lieutenant governor in 1929. In the ensuing campaign he established himself as a force to be reckoned with—a man of independent mind with an immense personal following. He led all candidates, defeating his Republican opponent by 184,536 votes to 103,758. He also polled 15,234 more votes than John Garland Pollard, the gubernatorial choice.

Price's position as lieutenant governor increased his public exposure and gave him new contacts in state government. It also increased his estrangement from Byrd. Although the Great Depression was not so severe in Virginia as in the rest of the nation, the Old Dominion did face a crisis of considerable proportions. When Governor Pollard failed to take bold action, Price called for stronger measures, including a special session of the General Assembly to set up a limited work relief program to reduce unemployment in rural areas. This would be accomplished by issuing certificates of indebtedness so that counties could continue building roads during winter months. This not only was contrary to the state constitution but also challenged one of Harry Byrd's most cherished ideas—pay-as-you-go financing of highway construction. Furthermore, the lieutenant governor attracted the attention of antiorganization Democrats; Westmoreland Davis, for example, was thought to be backing Price for the gubernatorial nomination in 1933. Since he still hoped Byrd would support him, Price was cool to such overtures. The presidential election of 1932 and the gubernatorial contest that followed ended this hope.

In the election of 1932 Price fervently embraced Franklin D. Roosevelt, speaking often in his behalf; and when FDR won, Price shared some of his popularity among the electorate. This did not, however, enhance his gubernatorial prospects. George C. Peery was clearly the organization's choice, so Price announced that he would run again for lieutenant governor. Several reasons have been advanced to explain Price's decision, but the simple fact is that he was unacceptable to Harry Byrd. Price usually had supported the policies of the dominant faction, but his occasional independence had aroused Byrd's suspicions. As in 1929, Price was unopposed in the primary and defeated his Republican opponent in the general election. He also led the canvass again, polling more votes than any other candidate, including Harry Byrd.

To this point, Price had been a model of obedience to the practices of the organization, if not to every facet of its philosophy. He soon realized, however, there was little chance that its leaders would ever willingly endorse his candidacy for governor. Thus, after years of deferring to their wishes, he decided to circumvent their opposition by appealing to the rank and file of the party. In 1934 Price launched a schedule of speaking engagements endorsing New Deal policies that left little doubt of his intentions. By the fall of that year, organization leaders were concerned enough by this challenge to seek an alternative: Thomas G. Burch, congressman from Virginia's Fifth District, a man of unquestioned loyalty who had virtually no following outside his district. To prevent his friends within the machine from committing themselves too early, Price on July 22, 1935, issued a simple statement that he would "be a candidate for nomination for governor in the 1937 Democratic primary." Organization leaders greeted this news with silence.

On the other hand, Price received enthusiastic backing from the antiorganization faction, men such as John W. Flannagan, Charles Harkrader, Martin Hutchinson, Norman Hamilton, Westmoreland Davis, and E. Lee Trinkle. Indeed, his candidacy became the focal point of opposition to Byrd and Glass. Byrd's silence and their support seemed to be the prelude to a Democratic party showdown. Throughout 1935 and 1936 support for Price grew within as well as without the organization. He received a warm welcome when he visited Washington to seek commitments from the congressional delegation and Virginians in the administration. Many local court clerks, the heart of the organization, supported him—as did members of the state legislature. One state senator, an associate of Byrd, declared, "We will string along with Harry Byrd in anything he wants, but we'd like to see him accept Jim Price as the organization's candidate."

Several events in 1936 encouraged Price. When the General Assembly failed to pass legislation making Virginians eligible for social security, there was an angry reaction among the working classes and the aged. This gave Price a prime campaign issue. During the Democratic state convention that summer, two pro-Price demonstrations erupted that the leadership could not halt. Since Byrd and Glass otherwise seemed firmly in control, these demonstrations took on additional significance. According to the Virginia Beach *News,* they "reflected the overwhelming sentiment of the rank and file of Virginia voters."

Confronted with this situation, Democratic leaders took the first step toward accommodation. In response to press statements that a bitter campaign might injure Byrd, the Winchester *Star,* Byrd's paper, offered an olive branch, noting that the prospect of a knockdown, drag-out fight was remote. The question was not one of machine versus antimachine but one of issues: pay-as-you-go state financing, improvement of schools, reorganization of the state government, and lower taxes. The implication was clear—any candidate who would pledge himself to these things would have, if not the organization's blessing, at least its acquiescence. Although the editor of the *Star* did not say so, the leaders also wanted a commitment that certain officials, especially Everett R. Combs, would be reappointed since they were vital to Byrd's continued control of state politics.

The 1936 elections provided the final blow to organization opposition. In the Democratic primaries in the Second, Third, and Ninth Congressional Districts candidates who supported both the New Deal and Price won over organization-backed opponents. Their margins of victory in the general election, combined with the results of the presidential election, indicated that the organization had definitely lost support on national issues.

Only one obstacle remained between Price and endorsement by Virginia's political leaders. He removed this barrier in a letter to two Richmond Democrats on December 22, 1936. It confirmed his commitment to "sound and conservative fiscal policy" and "efficiency in State government." Although Price remained silent concerning reappointment of key officials, he had provided the leaders a face-saving device. Within forty-eight hours virtually every major state official, all loyal organization men, had jumped on the "Christmas Eve bandwagon" and endorsed Price. Byrd, not among them, would go no further then to deny any "desire whatsoever to exert a personal influence over political affairs in Virginia" and to call Price "a gentleman of high character and great personal popularity, who holds the esteem and confidence of his friends in all walks of life." His statement that Price was "a candidate without opposition" was taken to mean that the organization was resigned to Price. Thomas Burch subsequently withdrew from the race.

Price's public statement provided the excuse for this headlong rush to support him, but it was hardly the real reason: the organization had no other choice. The leaders could resist and risk probable defeat, or they could accept Price and work to keep the organization intact by maintaining control over key positions. Neither course was especially palatable, but the second was preferable to the first. Some interpreted this decision as a sign of weakness, but Byrd was still very much in control. Confronted with a threat, the organization had once again demonstrated flexibility.

With all factions of Virginia's Democratic party united behind him, Price issued no platform and spoke only of general objectives. A specific stand on any issue might alienate supporters. The only excitement in this otherwise colorless campaign was the last-minute challenge by Vivian Page of Norfolk. Page acted because of an alleged breach of neutrality in the race for lieutenant governor, not out of any hope of victory. Price won the primary, polling 166,319 votes to Page's 26,955, and went on to defeat Republican J. Powell Royal of Tazewell in an equally bland race. In the Democratic primary Price not only carried every congressional district but also polled a majority in every county and independent city. In the general election Royal carried Carroll and Grayson counties.

Observers at the time and students of Virginia politics since have been tempted to interpret Price's victory as a great defeat for the Byrd organization. A few even looked to a day when a Price machine would supplant Byrd's. Neither conclusion was valid. Price's election was a great personal triumph rather than a defeat for Byrd. This is underscored by election of a lieutenant governor and attorney general with solid organization credentials. The organization was clearly in control. As for building a machine of his own, Price was not interested. Shortly after his election he wrote to an acquaintance that "my friends have felt for some time that I should accept the governorship as the capstone of my political career, and just between you and me, I think I have had just about enough of it."

Price's inaugural address seemed to augur well for the future, both for his legislative program and his relationship with the organization. He called for a government that was "more comprehensive" than an "agency for direct-ing . . . public fiscal policies," one concerned with "cultural and spiritual values" and with "the interests of that group of . . . people who are never the beneficiaries of special representatives." He was in "hearty sympathy with the present trend of government toward humanitarian ideals" and believed that "those . . . called to public service should unselfishly devote their time and talents to the welfare of the people. . . . Public service should be the control-ling consideration. One should . . . divorce oneself from active participation in political contests and controversies and . . . impartially discharge the duties of his office for the benefit of all the people." This was a much broader philosophy of government than the one normally associated with Virginia in the twentieth century.

Price also outlined specific legislative goals: passage of old-age assistance legislation that would conform to the federal Social Security Act and additional funds for public education to increase teachers' salaries, establish a sound teacher retirement system, and provide free textbooks. In keeping with the commitment to a balanced budget, funds to pay for these items and others would come from increased government efficiency, budget adjustments, and federal grants. In a more controversial proposal, Price suggested reducing the poll tax and redistricting the General Assembly. Reaction was overwhelmingly favorable. Even Senator Byrd characterized his remarks as "admirable in . . . tone." He noted that there might be "some disagreement . . . as to details, but the whole tenor . . . was extremely fine." With Price pledged to fiscal conservatism, there seemed to be no obstacle to continued cooperation between the new governor and the organization.

The early accomplishments of the 1938 General Assembly not only appeared to live up to this initial promise but also revealed Price to be an executive of considerable ability. An old-age assistance plan won easy approval; the embarrassment of being the only state outside the social security system was too great. The major question was how to finance the new program and also raise teachers' salaries. By canceling or postponing some $1,200,000 in capital outlays and by transfering an additional $525,000 from the Confederate widows' pension fund to the general old-age account, Price provided sufficient funds to assist teachers as well as the elderly. Additional achievements included approval of a forty-eight-hour work week for women and a law making Virginia cities and counties eligible for federal funds for slum clearance and urban development. Price played an active role in the passage of these measures. Such executive skills—together with his progressive philosophy—seemed to bode well.

Then he fired E. R. Combs and destroyed any hope of a good working relationship with the organization. As chairman of the State Compensation Commission, Combs was the key to Byrd's control of state politics. The commission determined the salaries of scores of local officials representing the state's authority and also fixed annual allowances for office expenses and the salaries of subordinates. This power was effective in assuring loyalty. Price received pressure from all sides concerning reappointment of Combs; even Byrd himself sent a personal request in behalf of his friend and lieutenant. Price ignored the request and appointed Le Roy Hodges, a former associate of Westmoreland Davis.

Some observers saw this as a declaration of war, but such an interpretation was too extreme. A full attack would have required replacing many organization appointees. Price retained far more people than he fired, and those he did replace were succeeded by technicians like Hodges, an economist with considerable knowledge of old-age assistance. This essentially apolitical approach guided Price's other appointments. Nevertheless, political motivation cannot be completely discounted. Price sympathized with those who wished to weaken Byrd; under pressure from antiorganization advisers, he yielded and fired Combs. But once he had taken the initial step he lacked the motivation or temperament, perhaps both, to carry the battle to its conclusion. On the other hand, organization leaders had both motivation and the temperament. Price's action against Combs was a threat to their control, and they were alarmed. Several efforts were made to limit the governor's freedom to name a successor to Combs, but he won this battle and retained the right to appoint the chairman of the Compensation Commission in the manner he saw fit. His margin of victory was so narrow, however, that there was little cause to celebrate. Price still needed organization support in both houses to enact a program.

In the final analysis, the first General Assembly session must be judged a success. It produced several significant pieces of legislation, not the least of which was the Old Age Pension Act. Price played a major role, and his leadership was adjudged moderate, "a just balance between over conservatism and the rashness of adventure that lies beyond the bounds of sane liberalism," said the Richmond *News Leader*. The same newspaper also noted that the governor and organization men saw eye-to-eye on nine-tenths of the legislation. Unfortunately for Price, the area of disagreement involved those very things which kept the Byrd organization alive, and his activities during the intervening biennium gave its leaders even more cause for concern.

The efforts of President Franklin Roosevelt to "purge" certain southern senators during the primaries of 1938 are well known. Although neither of Virginia's senators was scheduled for reelection, with Price's help he tried to discipline them as well. At the height of the purges, Charles Harkrader announced that the endorsement of Price would be necessary before any ambitious Virginian could hope to land an important federal job. Since Harry Byrd feared that control of patronage might be used against him, this statement provided further cause for opposing Price. The governor's role in the early stages of the so-called Roberts affair is unclear, but by its conclusion he was clearly antagonistic to Byrd. John Flannagan, the Ninth District's colorful congressman, had suggested Floyd Roberts, a Bristol jurist, to fill a newly created seat on the federal District Court for Western Virginia. When Roosevelt ignored candidates put forward by Byrd and Glass, the senators immediately declared Roberts "utterly and personally offensive." Hearings before the Senate Judiciary Committee represented a dramatic confrontation: Price and former Governors Davis and Trinkle appearing for Judge Roberts; Glass and Byrd in opposition, with Glass presenting the principal argument. Face flushed and eyes blazing, he spoke of a conspiracy involving the president and the governor of Virginia to humiliate Virginia's senators. During this tirade Price could only sit silently, but he later denied the charges with such quiet dignity that his response evoked widespread favorable comment. In the end, Glass, Byrd, and senatorial courtesy prevailed, and Roosevelt, Price, and independent Democracy in Virginia lost. Price's role was relatively minor, but the patronage fight exacerbated relations between the governor and organization leaders. More importantly, it cost Price much of the public support crucial to his earlier success. Virginians had not looked favorably on the "court packing" or the purges, and they saw the Roberts matter in the same light. The results would become clear during the 1940 General Assembly.

In the meantime, Price proved himself an effective administrator as he went about the daily business of being governor. Changes in the finance division resulted in increased collection of delinquent taxes at considerable reduction in cost. He added research and long-range planning to the task of assembling and digesting budget requirements and drafting the omnibus budget bill. Price thus continued the tradition of businesslike administration established by Westmoreland Davis and Harry Byrd.

Despite this record, Price faced criticism from friends and foes alike. His early supporters wanted an all-out attack against Byrd's organization, but with the exception of firing Combs and backing Roberts, Price showed no inclination to build a personal political force and refused all entreaties to do so. The antis soon became disillusioned. Even Martin Hutchinson, perhaps the man closest to Price, finally admitted, "I wish that he were a more gifted and aggressive man." They expected too much of Price; such a role was beyond the scope of his personal philosophy and political aspirations.

The General Assembly of 1940 was a complete debacle for James Price. As a result, posterity has judged his administration a failure. Closer scrutiny indicates that he was not personally responsible. The real culprit was factionalism within Virginia's Democratic party. In 1940 the antiorganization group pressed to end domination by the Byrd oligarchy, and the organization fought back. Price's legislative program got caught in the middle.

Price outlined his goals in an opening address and a budget message, both stressing improvements in education. Administrative reorganization came close behind, followed by other recommendations, some controversial, others standard fare. To cover increased costs of education and general welfare, he proposed adjustments in existing taxes and new taxes on beer, wines, and liquor. The implication of these two messages was clear. Price accepted the need to provide better services to the people. When it became necessary to find additional funds to support these programs, he proposed equalizing existing levies and imposing new taxes where they would be least burdensome. He was a fiscal conservative within the truest meaning of the words. Although it was frequently charged otherwise, the similarities between Governor Price and Senator Byrd in fiscal affairs were far greater than were their differences.

To enact his legislative program, Price would have to repair his relationship with the organization. Men with impeccable machine credentials filled every office in both houses, and E. R. Combs had returned to a position of power as clerk of the Senate. Byrd's men were in complete control, yet Price continued to antagonize them. His third major message of the session contained recommendations for consolidation of some administrative departments and abolition of others. Up to this point, his suggestions had been received favorably, but the legislators were not prepared for such far-reaching changes. Initially they charged it was too late in the session to introduce such complex matters. These attacks obscured more partisan fears that these proposals would affect state patronage. His recommendations for the highway and conservation departments threatened two extremely lucrative sources of patronage and would displace individuals favorably disposed to the dominant faction. A second event which created problems for Price was a published report that he would lead efforts in Virginia to secure a third-term nomination for Roosevelt. Price denied such rumors, but many legislators believed them and thus found an additional excuse to oppose his program. Price's entire legislative package soon was in deep trouble.

Some proposals, including the reorganization plan, died silently in committee. Others, such as increased aid to public education, were amended to cost far more than the governor wanted. This forced Price either to veto bills he had proposed or condone an unbalanced budget. Price also was accused of paying extravagant salaries to his appointees. The collective result was the defeat of much of his legislative program. Douglas Southall Freeman characterized it as "one of the best prepared and most complete legislative dockets ever laid before a Virginia legislature!" Yet of Price's major proposals, only a bill to raise the minimum teacher's salary and the revenue measures to fund it were passed.

Price must share the blame for this debacle. He made a serious error in submitting his reorganization plan so late. Moreover, when his legislative program got into deep trouble, he refused to fight back. He declined suggestions that he address a joint session, probably because it would involve the very kind of political fight he found distasteful. Only after the session was over did he issue a statement in which he charged that "a great deal of important and constructive legislation was delayed and killed in committee or otherwise by thinly disguised political activity."

If Price must accept some responsibility, Byrd adherents in the Assembly must take the lion's share. They set out deliberately to embarrass and discredit the governor so as to eliminate any threat to their dominance of state politics. Despite his record, Price was the public symbol of independent Democrats, and the first step to destroy the antiorganization movement was to humiliate

Price. At the same time, Byrd loyalists could take revenge for the governor's personal actions against the organization's power structure. In both aims, the organization's leaders succeeded beyond their dreams. After 1940 Price was a defeated man. He continued to function admirably under trying circumstances, but he clearly wanted one thing—out.

After the close of the 1940 General Assembly an increasing amount of Price's time was devoted to leading a large state in a nation preparing for war. Price initially shared the general feeling that World War II was a European affair, but the German blitzkrieg in the spring and summer of 1940 quickly dispelled such illusions. Because the legislature was not in session, Price found sufficient authority in his executive powers to meet the situation. Displaying strong moral leadership, Price effectively discussed important matters over a statewide radio network in "fireside" chats that revealed a flair for oratory not evident in his purely political addresses. Only one day after President Roosevelt appointed the National Advisory Commission on Defense to guide the national defense effort, Price created the Virginia Defense Council for the same purpose—the first state council in the country. To meet Virginia's most crucial problem—housing for workers at major defense installations in Tidewater, northern Virginia, and the Southwest—Price also formed a series of regional councils.

As he moved to set up machinery to administer the Selective Service Act, Price insisted that at least one black person be appointed to each local draft board, especially "in districts in which there was a large Negro population." He appointed the president of St. Paul's Polytechnic Institute, an all-black school, to the State Defense Council. Price was adhering to policies made in Washington, but as the first governor in the nation to insist that black people be given the opportunity to participate in national defense, he displayed no small amount of courage and personal commitment, particularly for a southern governor.

Through it all, Price reminded Virginians that his basic responsibility was to "maintain sound political, social and economic progress in the Old Dominion during the emergency period." Only in this way could the spirit and morale of the people be maintained. He combined this concern for the present with an equally deep concern for the future. To avoid serious postwar economic dislocations, he developed a six-year capital improvement budget for Virginia and revealed it a full year before the United States entered the war.

Despite the defense emergency, the political process continued. By the early spring of 1940 there were noticeable efforts to restore harmony within Virginia's Democratic party, efforts not limited to one side or the other. The state convention commended the records of all concerned and named both Byrd and Price as delegates to the Chicago national convention; nevertheless, the harmony was not complete. In Chicago, Price supported FDR's bid for a third term, while Byrd opposed it. This led to at least one unpleasant scene when Price carried an unofficial banner in the Roosevelt demonstration.

The newly discovered harmony carried over into the gubernatorial campaign of 1941. Colgate Darden, the organization's choice, received support from both factions of the Democratic party. Price remained noncommital, however, citing the defense crisis. In reality, he hoped that such a stance might gain a commitment from Darden to retain many of his appointees. The gesture was futile. Darden won easily without needing to commit himself. Nonetheless, after the election, Price did everything in his power to ease the transition for his successor.

The last two months of Price's administration were eclipsed by the attack on Pearl Harbor and other events that made domestic political squabbles seem insignificant. When the General Assembly met in 1942, Price and his successor canceled traditional festivities. In this setting, the outgoing chief executive rendered his final accounting to the people of Virginia. He gave primary attention to humanitarian programs and additional support for education enacted during his four years. But he also called for completion of the "unfinished business" of his term. Price's last official act was submission of the largest biennial budget in history, with total expenditures of more than $200 million. But he also announced the largest surplus in history, more than $13 million with a projected increase to $16 million by 1944. In a state that measured success by the size of the budgetary surplus passed on to succeeding administrations, this was of no small significance.

One week later, James H. Price returned to private life, disillusioned with politics and eager to resume fraternal work. "Politics is one of the most cruel and relentless influences," Price wrote less than two weeks after Darden's inauguration. Yet he was convinced that history would ultimately vindicate him: "I have the satisfaction of having given to the people of Virginia four of the best years of my life, and I believe that when the permanent record is finally made up . . . it will show many substantial advancements." Price did not have to wait long. Douglas Freeman had already labeled his program one of the best on record. The General Assembly of 1942 gave this claim credence by adopting virtually every portion of the program Price had introduced in 1940.

Price spent the remaining years of his life in pursuits that had dominated most of his adult years, devoting considerable time to his position as Imperial Recorder of the Shrine and combining service in that post with service to the public at large. He became a "dollar-a-year man" in the effort to sell war bonds, using his many fraternal contacts to good advantage. Unfortunately, he did not have long to enjoy the private life that meant so much to him. James Price died on November 22, 1943, at the age of sixty-five, after suffering a massive cerebral hemorrhage.

In a glowing eulogy, the editor of the Richmond *Times-Dispatch* listed five things for which Price's term should be remembered—emphasis on education, attention to humanitarian measures, a scientific approach to public questions, preparation of the state for war, and an ability to acquire federal grants to build public buildings. The editor concluded that Price's "gubernatorial administration should be considered one of the most constructive in modern Virginia history." While the achievements were significant, this overstated the case. James Price was a good man who wanted nothing more than to give his adopted state good government. His program went beyond that. However, in the final analysis, he failed to accomplish most of his aims. This was at once his fault and the fault of both his political opponents and his political friends.

Price's chief personal and political failure was an ambivalence toward the dominant Democratic faction. For most of his career, he was a reasonably good organization man. When the leaders would not support him for governor, he decided to run on his own and to accept antiorganization support. Once elected, he struck several blows at the machine's foundation but failed to follow through with more decisive action. He removed a few men from important offices but replaced them with nonpoliticians. Price was not a fighter, and he refused to use wise distribution of the patronage at his disposal to break the grip of the organization.

Antiorganization Democrats knew what was needed to accomplish the governor's program, yet they were so concerned with crushing the Byrd machine that they pressured Price to do things that hurt his administration. When they realized their efforts had failed, most of the antis made peace with the organization to salvage their own careers. On the other hand, leaders of the organization, determined to maintain control, lost sight of their primary function as elected representatives. They charged Price with building his own machine without hard evidence to support their contention. Yet, since he was the public symbol of those trying to build a rival power, they humiliated him and destroyed his program so as to undermine this opposition. Price was caught up in this struggle for power, but he failed to appreciate that partisan political activity, distasteful as it might be, was frequently the only way to govern effectively. This high-mindedness was his greatest strength as a man, but it was also his greatest weakness as governor. Since James Price was unwilling to use the political weapons at his disposal, he lost, but the real losers were the people of the Old Dominion.

SOURCES

The most important single source of material on Price's life and career is a set of twenty-one folio-sized scrapbooks containing newspaper clippings (1927–42), currently on loan to the author from James Hubert Price, Jr., of Sarasota, Florida. The material is arranged chronologically by subject. The James Hubert Price Papers (Washington and Lee University) cover the same period but contain little information on Price's career. The Price Executive Papers (Virginia State Library) are massive but provide little data concerning political affairs. A collection of Price Correspondence, 1940–41 (Virginia State Library), is separate from the Executive Papers and contains interesting material on the campaign of 1941. The William T. Reed Papers (Virginia Historical Society) provide insights into Harry F. Byrd's opinion of Price, while the Martin Hutchinson Papers (University of Virginia) contain much information on antiorganization activities in the 1930s. The R. Walton Moore Papers (Franklin Delano Roosevelt Library, Hyde Park) are valuable for information on Price's relationship to national politics, and the Franklin Delano Roosevelt Papers at the same repository contain important correspondence between Price and the president. The author also had the benefit of several interviews and a great deal of correspondence with Price's political and business associates.

For a full bibliography, see Alvin L. Hall, "James H. Price and Virginia Politics, 1878–1943" (Ph.D. diss., University of Virginia, 1970).

COLGATE W. DARDEN, JR.

The Noblest Roman of Them All

Stuart I. Rochester and Jonathan J. Wolfe

The Old Dominion, like the nation at large, was at something of a cross-roads in 1941; the times called for an individual of strength and moderation, a man who could both compel action and maintain a workable consensus. Virginia was fortunate to have at so critical a juncture a leader of uncommon qualifications and ability. Colgate Whitehead Darden, Jr., belonged to the fabled "lost generation" that came of age during World War I. Where some were shattered by that experience, Darden was nourished by it. Being a product of war and the politics of accommodation that marked his ascendancy in the interwar years, he was ideally suited for the tests of the early forties. Not surprisingly, he became one of Virginia's most popular and successful governors.

Darden was born on February 11, 1897, near Marle Hill, Southampton County, the eldest of three children. His father, a North Carolinian with Virginia ancestry dating to 1635, had married Katherine Pretlow, the daughter of a well-to-do Southampton landowner. Darden spent his early years on the family farm, acquiring his mother's love of reading. Formal education came in the public schools of nearby Franklin, where at the age of fourteen he was already developing skills as a public speaker and attracting notice as an ambitious and talented youth. From Franklin he proceeded to Charlottesville and its venerable university, but so circumscribed had been his boyhood orbit that he remembered the 150-mile trip as "going to the ends of the earth." Darden joined the Jefferson Debating Society, participated gamely if awkwardly in athletics, and enjoyed close contact with professors from his West Lawn residence. But the backwoods public school boy felt vaguely out of place, intimidated by social and academic pressures, and when World War I beckoned, he dropped out—departing abruptly in 1916 after two checkered years.

Like many of his contemporaries, Colgate was moved by both sympathy for the Allied cause and the lure of adventure. Seeking a noncombatant role so long as America remained aloof from the fray, Darden enlisted in the French Ambulance Corps, joining a celebrated contingent that would include John Dos Passos, E. E. Cummings, and Malcolm Cowley. In his first major assignment, in the infernal trenches at Verdun, the young volunteer lost his

COLGATE W. DARDEN, JR.

Governor of Virginia

1942–1946

illusions. In the fighting that followed, at Champagne and the Ardennes Forest, he nearly lost his life. Unrelenting action brought on fatigue and illness, resulting in pneumonia. Forced to return home, Darden was given a discharge and the Croix de Guerre for valor. With the United States warming to the war, he enlisted in the Naval Aviation Corps. After becoming a pilot, Darden resigned and joined the U.S. Marine Corps, transferring to Miami, Florida, as a flight instructor. Requesting combat service after the American intervention, Darden was sent to Dunkirk. There, a second time, he narrowly escaped death. A Marine Corps bomber he was flying crashed into an ammunition dump on takeoff, killing his copilot, Medal of Honor holder Ralph W. Talbot, and landing Darden in the hospital with a broken back and skull fractures.

His health restored after a lengthy recuperation, Darden enrolled in Columbia University Law School and returned to Charlottesville during summer sessions to complete his B.A. degree. In this dual endeavor he supported himself by tutoring, working in the library, and doing odd jobs. In 1923 Columbia awarded him a coveted Carnegie Fellowship in International Law, enabling him to study for a year at Christ Church College, Oxford. The stay in England convinced Darden that he was not an academic—the exacting work of research and writing held little appeal to his activist spirit—but he found the practice of law exciting. In 1924, upon his return to the Old Dominion, he settled in Norfolk and entered law practice with former state Senator James S. Barron.

While a Columbia student in 1920 he met Constance du Pont, the Delaware heiress, whom he married in 1927. The couple established themselves in Norfolk, but they also became active in the life of Franklin, where they farmed land at Beechwood, which had been in Darden's mother's family for five generations. Darden and his wife shared lively interests ranging from music and art to astronomy and lent their energies and resources to an array of community organizations, including the Boy Scouts (to which they eventually gave 220 acres at Beechwood), the Norfolk Orchestral Association, and the Norfolk Community Concert Association. Colgate was a prominent member of the American Legion and became a Shriner in 1930 after fourteen years as a Mason; Connie did charity work for the Episcopal church. They were a devoted couple, their lives enriched by three children—two sons and a daughter.

If the twenties were building years for Darden the lawyer and family man, they were also budding years for Darden the politician. Early on he cast his lot with the dominant Democratic organization headed by Harry Flood Byrd, supporting him in the 1925 gubernatorial race. Darden fitted well with Byrd's personal following. All were young, essentially conservative in outlook, and possessed a polished respectability and genteel manner that belied their hard-nosed politics. Darden joined them on the hustings in 1928, dutifully campaigning for presidential nominee Al Smith, a wet Roman Catholic whom Virginia Democrats backed reluctantly. In 1929 Darden won his first term in the Virginia House of Delegates where he established himself as a staunch friend of public education. In 1932, as the depression sharply reduced state revenues and threatened to close several county school systems, Darden was exercised enough to challenge the organization's "pay-as-you-go" fiscal policy; he introduced a bill that would have diverted moneys from the inviolable highway fund to keep schools open. Although the measure was overwhelmingly defeated, this would not be the last time that the party stalwart would show a maverick streak in the name of social responsibility.

That autumn Darden captured the Second District congressional seat, riding to victory on the Democratic tide generated by the depression. Helpful, too, was the Southsider's home-district popularity and good reputation, enhanced by his upstart challenge to Byrd fiscal policy at a time when liberalism was acquiring growing respectability in the Old Dominion. In the crucible of the depression, Darden was emerging as a patrician reformer—a man of wealth and conservative proclivities, but inclined to support an expanded suffrage, civil service reform, and fair labor practices. His mild progressivism accompanied by allegiance to traditional rural values well suited his constituents, a mix of hinterland farmers and urban workers, and they returned him to Washington in 1934.

Despite his emergence as an independent-minded congressman, Darden continued to be closely identified with the Byrd machine. But with the organization increasingly undermined by New Deal–style Democrats, Darden found his support steadily eroding until by 1936 he faced a serious challenge in his quest for a third term. The threat came from Norman R. Hamilton, editor of the Portsmouth *Star* and a veteran Democrat who had served as collector of customs for the port of Norfolk under Woodrow Wilson. He had lost that patronage post when Republicans regained the presidency, and he expected its return when Roosevelt won. Senators Byrd and Glass, however, found Hamilton unsatisfactory and blocked his appointment. Hamilton perceived an opportunity in Roosevelt's growing popularity. Accordingly, he attacked Darden's shaky base among New Dealers, portraying him as an obsequious puppet to Byrd and Glass and playing up father-in-law Irénée du Pont's leadership in the conservative American Liberty League. The strategy worked, despite Darden's progressive record and avowed backing of FDR. The organization carried rural voters for the incumbent, but New Deal–infused urban Democrats of Norfolk and Newport News outnumbered them. Darden's star seemed to fall as quickly as it had risen.

Determined to bounce back from defeat, Darden spent the next two years broadening his political base by bolstering his standing with both organization members and independents. A chance invitation afforded him an unexpected opportunity. When the U.S. Navy decided to name a new destroyer the *Ralph W. Talbot* after Darden's friend and fellow aviator, Talbot's mother invited him to attend the christening. Newspaper coverage of the event, particularly in the Second District, a stronghold of the navy and ship-building, spotlighted Darden's war record and won him new devotees, especially among powerful veterans' groups.

The 1938 Second District campaign was a repeat of the 1936 contest, but even more acrimonious. Darden campaigned in his customary high-minded fashion, affable and dignified, leaving the mudslinging and manipulation of party machinery to William L. ("Billy") Prieur, Norfolk Court clerk and Byrd stalwart. Hamilton's backers revived their erroneous charges that Darden had been FDR's enemy in 1936, and the organization responded with a race-baiting pamphlet suggesting that Hamilton harbored "improper" attitudes toward Negroes and that a vote for Hamilton meant "niggers will be teaching your children soon." (Darden apparently did not know of the offensive pamphlet before its release. Nevertheless, it remained a source of embarrassment in later years.) Hamilton, saddled also with defending Roosevelt's controversial effort to "pack" the Supreme Court, lost by less than 2,000 votes.

Colgate Darden returned to Congress gratified by his comeback but faced with a troubling dilemma. The term away from the House had nullified his seniority. To serve long enough to achieve a position of influence would require many more election contests. On the other hand, the unsettled political situation in Virginia, with Byrd and New Deal Democrats locked in a protracted struggle, could make him a compromise choice for the governorship. He passed his third congressional term creditably, performing his responsibilities on the naval affairs subcommittee while simultaneously cultivating political friendships wider than required for reelection to Congress. He helped John Flannagan, an independent, gear up for a tough race in the Ninth Congressional District, contributing campaign funds and speaking on Flannagan's behalf in the mountainous Southwest. He crisscrossed the Commonwealth in behalf of Roosevelt's third-term effort, in dramatic contrast to Harry Byrd, who resolutely opposed FDR's bid. Generous support of Flannagan and approval of Roosevelt enhanced Darden's standing with the anti-Byrd faction headed by incumbent Governor James Price. Darden was emerging as the only important organization member whom anti-Byrd liberals could countenance as Price's successor.

While welcoming their friendship, Darden was careful to keep his organization ties intact. He believed most Byrd followers could understand his support of a Democrat running for national office, especially the popular Roosevelt. He remained close with Billy Prieur, who arranged for him to address the Virginia court clerks' convention in 1940, a timely concentration of county organization leaders. Darden flew to the Hot Springs, Virginia, meeting directly from Panama, where he had conducted a well-publicized

House committee inspection of Canal defenses. He impressed the clerks with a knowledgeable, hard-hitting speech on preparedness that strengthened his standing with organization pros. His diligence was paying off handsomely. In the 1940 House election he ran unopposed, rolling up 29,788 votes, nearly as many as the total cast for him and Hamilton in the bitter contests of 1936 and 1938.

Judging the time right, Darden formally announced his candidacy for the governorship on December 21, 1940. Two antiorganization candidates, both Price men, were already in the race—Hundson Cary, an energetic but aging Henrico County state senator, and state Senator Vivian Page of Norfolk, who had run against Price in 1937 as an organization member but then defected and turned bitterly upon Byrd. Additionally, other organization men maneuvered on the sidelines. The most formidable contender, William M. Tuck, decided to seek the post of lieutenant governor, postponing his ambitions for four years. By spring only two Byrd men were active candidates—Darden and Ashton Dovell, an attorney from Williamsburg and a well-regarded member of the General Assembly.

With New Deal liberalism losing steam in the Old Dominion and the Byrd machine enjoying a revival, Cary and Page were not serious contenders. But Dovell was a formidable opponent. His organization credentials were solid, and his declared platform—poll tax abolition, government reform, and a strengthened state executive—seemed designed to attract the same Price-affiliated liberals that Darden had assiduously courted. Darden, however, had stolen the march. John Flannagan repaid his earlier debt and rallied the Ninth District to Darden's banner. Darden arranged a confidential truce with Price, assuring Price intermediary Donald Stant that if elected he planned no wholesale purge of Price supporters or dismantling of Price programs. Beyond that Darden would make no specific commitments, saying only that he sought a harmonious transition. The outgoing governor seemed satisfied and, to the dismay of anti-Byrd liberals, refused to endorse Cary or Page or the talked-about candidacy of the even more liberal Le Roy Hodges, the compensation commissioner Price had appointed to replace Byrd stalwart Everett R. ("Ebbie") Combs. Price refused to be swayed by the late-blooming progressivism of Dovell; and Dovell, finding liberals in both the Southwest and the Northern Neck quietly but firmly aligned with Darden, withdrew from the race on May 3.

Soon the Price camp dropped its reserve and demonstrated openly in Darden's behalf. Former Governor Westmoreland Davis, a respected independent Democrat and longtime Price ally, announced his support; and on July 12 Price, though for the record maintaining a studied neutrality, invited Darden (alone of Democratic primary candidates) to accompany him to a review of the Eighty-eighth Brigade of the Virginia National Guard. The next day Old Dominion newspapers featured photographs of the two on the reviewing stand.

For his part, Darden stumped the state in a small Chevrolet, at every stop burnishing his image as an enlightened and responsible moderate—sympathetic to needed domestic reform, but cautious about excessive spending and alert to the worsening international crisis and its local repercussions. He stressed the need for preparedness and called for a state government deeply involved in civil defense.

The outcome of the Democratic primary was predictable: Cary 12,793, Page, 19,526, Darden, 105,655. The general election was pure anticlimax. Darden literally napped through it, confined to home for an extended recuperation following a mid-September appendectomy. His Republican opponent, Benjamin Muse, onetime Democrat and state senator from Dinwiddie County, ran chiefly to preserve the two-party system; he publicly announced that with war impending, he did not intend to challenge the Democratic nominee in any manner likely to cause hard feelings. Rounding out the field were Socialist Hilliard Bernstein and Communist Alice Burke.

Colgate Darden became governor of Virginia by 99,120 votes to Muse's 21,783. Less than 2,000 voted for the fringe candidates. What went unspoken but was generally recognized was the overnight restoration of the Virginia Democratic party. The new governor, a Byrd adherent with uncommon latitude within that organization, carried with him an acceptance shaded from grudging to grateful among Price's liberal followers. In his person the organization accommodated itself to independent and anti-Byrd Democrats, ending a decade of rancorous feuding.

Few men had come to the Governor's Mansion with so broad or illustrious a background. Although only forty-four years old, Darden had lived a full measure of adventure and success. War hero, Oxford scholar, Du Pont in-law, prominent lawyer, and successful politician—he had ranged easily from battlefield to classroom to campaign platform, his low-keyed competence and genial personality winning friends without incurring enemies. He was, in short, an ideal choice around whom Virginians of different persuasions could confidently close ranks in the hectic winter of 1941–42.

From the outset Darden infused his administration with crackling energy. The inaugural ceremony, on an overcast Tuesday six weeks after Pearl Harbor, was appropriately austere. Darden's address, terse and grim with Churchillian overtones, lasted only twelve minutes. Two hours later he was at work in the Governor's Mansion. Unlike the old-school politicians still common in Virginia in the forties, Darden set little store by oratory and ceremony, preferring to speak directly and briefly and declining many of the perquisites of his position. To conserve tires and gasoline he had the official limousine put in storage for the duration of the war and used a car from the motor pool when necessary. He daily jogged the block from the mansion to his executive chambers. When walking did not suffice, he frequently rode public buses and streetcars. A curiously private man despite his outgoing public demeanor, he relished being able to walk through downtown Richmond without being recognized.

During the November-January interregnum he consulted regularly with the outgoing Price camp, keeping enough holdovers (nine out of nineteen department heads) to satisfy the liberal wing of the party and retain Price's friendship. At the same time he assembled an able staff from among his own supporters and Byrd men who had served prior to Price's administration, placing them in key positions and assuring renewed organization dominance. Symbolic of the shift of power was the return of Byrd's chief lieutenant, Ebbie Combs, as both chairman of the Compensation Commission and secretary of the Senate, twin posts from which he had direct lines to all segments of the organization—from Byrd and Darden to the legislature and the lowliest county official.

Darden was adroit at exploiting the instrumentalities of the Byrd organization and his own enormous personal prestige to work his will on the General Assembly. He alternately courted and prodded legislators, skillfully using both carrot and stick—respecting the Assembly's procedures and traditions and careful to consult its leaders, but delivering forceful messages and expecting prompt action. He was an effective governor not only because he wielded tremendous power through his command of a refurbished organization but because legislators genuinely liked him and respected his intelligence and earnestness. He gave them direction and purpose, and it did not hurt his efforts that he counted among his most enthusiastic backers a select circle of Assembly notables—men like Thomas B. Stanley, the new speaker of the House of Delegates; G. Alvin Massenburg, a prominent member of the House and future speaker; and state Senator Aubrey G. Weaver, a Darden protégé widely viewed as a future governor.

Among Darden's most valued liaisons with the legislature was his lieutenant governor, William Munford Tuck, a South Boston politico who, Darden would say, "knew every constable in Virginia and doggone near every policeman." Tuck also knew the organization inside out and could deliver votes at the drop of a hat. He was only a few months younger than Darden and like him a former marine. There similarities ended. The lieutenant governor was a blustery, earthy, Rabelaisian figure. His inelegant swagger and stout build contrasted sharply with Darden's handsome, aristocratic carriage and trim, six-foot frame. Tuck's capacity for all-night politicking while consuming immense quantities of tobacco and liquor was legendary, whereas Darden preferred to retire in the evening to classical music. Although coveting the top spot himself, Tuck served Darden well as a consummate legislative manager, and the two became great friends.

Darden's one impolitic move was appointing John Hopkins Hall, a Byrd regular not highly regarded even within the organization, to replace Thomas Morton as commissioner of labor (Hall had served in that post under former Governor George Peery). By June 1942 Hall had fired a quarter of Morton's staff, all Price men, and had compelled seven other employees to resign. Darden, sensitive to charges of spoilsmanship, held closed hearings into Hall's conduct that resulted in a severe public rebuke and the rehiring of three Price appointees. The governor's solicitude for the workers and his willingness to restrain an organization stalwart were applauded by liberals and welcomed by Byrd men embarrassed by Hall's indiscretion. Darden had managed to turn even a blunder to advantage.

The new administration's brisk energy and political virtuosity would have amounted to merely a triumph of style had not Darden possessed clear goals. Necessarily, defense concerns were paramount. Price had made a good start on preparedness, establishing the nation's first state advisory body to facilitate mobilization at the local level. The new realities after Pearl Harbor, however, required additional action. Accordingly, during his first week in office Darden reorganized Virginia's civil defense system, dissolving the volunteer council and its regional affiliates and placing civil defense authority directly in the hands of the governor. In practice, many of the council's personnel and programs were retained, but new laws assigned responsibility to locally elected and appointed officials who, in turn, reported to the governor, thus placing the full instrumentalities of the state behind the civilian defense effort.

The menace of war weighed heavily on Darden. He pledged not to leave the state at any time, since he wished to be on hand personally to direct state forces if the Commonwealth were attacked. Such fears were far from unfounded. The governor knew of German offensive capabilities from his experience on the House naval affairs subcommittee. Virginia, with its exposed Atlantic coast, offered myriad places for the clandestine landing of spies and saboteurs. There would have to be plans for fire control, first aid, casualty evacuation, and emergency police; for all these contingencies Virginia was made ready under Darden's wartime stewardship. Darden expected the war to be long and grueling. His solemn inaugural message reminded the Commonwealth's citizens that nondefense construction projects and plans for improved public services, to a large extent, would have to be deferred for the duration of the conflict. But he was too dynamic an executive to suspend the reform agenda altogether. He outlined some nineteen proposals he intended to present to the legislature and pressed these with the same determination with which he pursued civil defense matters.

High on the list of domestic goals, a concern inherited from his predecessor Price, was penal reform. The case of Odell Waller, a black sharecropper convicted of killing his white landlord, caused Darden great anguish early in his administration. Waller's attorneys petitioned for a commutation based on contradictory evidence and a botched sheriff's investigation. Pressure from liberal groups and his own abiding concern for justice led Darden to grant a stay of execution, but in the end he refused to overrule the courts. Waller went to the electric chair on July 2, 1942. This experience reinforced Darden's belief that placing commutation power in an unencumbered board would be fairer to the convicts and free the governor from an agonizing burden. He persuaded the General Assembly to create a Pardon and Parole Board that would be granted commutation power. For first offenders, Darden had a prison farm built in Southampton County. To eliminate inconsistencies in the pay of law enforcement officers—sheriffs and city sergeants were being compensated through a fee system, based on arrests made and legal papers served—he had the state take over the payroll; it would provide two-thirds of the salaries, the localities the remainder, with half of all fines collected reverting to the state. Finally, Darden oversaw the creation of a full-time Board of Corrections. Headed by Major Rice M. Youell, warden of the state penitentiary in Richmond, the board instituted new inspection procedures and closed several deteriorated facilities, significantly upgrading prisons throughout Virginia.

Darden turned next to education, an area in which Virginia ranked very low nationally. Almost every locality needed qualified instructors, with the state's chronic teacher shortage compounded by the draft and high-paying wartime jobs. To combat the personnel problem, Darden prevailed on the General Assembly to increase the state contribution toward teacher salaries from $610 annually per teacher in 1941 to $660 in 1943 and $1,050 by 1945; additionally, meeting a long-standing grievance, the state instituted a sound retirement system. In all, education expenditures rose from $31 million for 1940–42 to $38 million for 1942–44.

Darden's commitment to public education was unflagging. Not satisfied with mere budgetary increases, he appointed a commission headed by George H. Denny, a Virginian who had retired as president of the University of Alabama, to examine the deficiencies in Virginia's educational system and recommend changes. Denny's group spotlighted weaknesses in vocational education and small rural school districts. Darden brought these findings before a special session of the General Assembly in 1945, wringing from the legislators, among other concessions, expanded funds for school busing in outlying areas and a million dollars for audiovisual aids (the largest appropriation for such materials anywhere in the nation). The Denny Commission also identified problem areas in higher education. Darden responded with supplemental appropriations for the Medical College of Virginia, Virginia Polytechnic Institute, the Virginia State College for Negroes, and $3 million for a massive building program at the University of Virginia.

Teacher shortages were indicative of staffing problems throughout state government. The draft and lure of higher pay in private defense jobs drained qualified personnel from every department—the police force, highway department, and Alcoholic Beverage Control Board all reported huge manpower losses. Working closely with the legislature, Darden took a series of steps to prevent a breakdown in government services: women were recruited to perform light maintenance tasks in various departments, a merit system and pension plan were installed, and, most importantly, pay for lower-salaried workers was boosted considerably through a wartime bonus bill.

One of Darden's toughest fights was securing a limit on interest rates that finance companies could charge on small personal loans. When the General Assembly proposed to investigate unconscionably high rates and questionable collection practices, the companies hired a slick lobbyist, W. H. Cardwell, to protect their interests. Cardwell's smugness so angered Darden that he took command of the probe, eventually succeeding in lowering the interest ceiling on small loans from 42 percent to 18 percent and requiring fuller disclosure of terms and rates to potential borrowers.

To the wonderment of anti-Byrd skeptics, the Southsider had seemingly evolved into a full-fledged liberal, bringing to fruition many of the initiatives mounted by James Price's New Deal-oriented administration. Besides path-breaking penal and educational reforms and an attack on unscrupulous loan practices, Darden had commissioned a study of medical aid for the indigent, broadened workmen's compensation, and recommended the creation of a pollution control board to monitor waste treatment plants. Breasting criticism from rural elements, he supported a legislative redistricting bill favorable to urban areas. Altogether, even with the constraints posed by war, Darden presided over one of the most ameliorative legislative programs in Virginia history.

Still, there remained a shadow of the guarded conservative. Throughout his career, Darden had moved freely between liberal and conservative camps, by turns expansive or tightfisted depending on issue and circumstances. If the enterprising progressive seemed more in evidence in Richmond, nonetheless the Southside organization man would occasionally surface as well. For all the trappings of reform, on several key issues Darden remained true to his hinterland roots and organization obligations.

Retiring the state debt was the ultimate dream of every organization Democrat. It was a cherished hope, too, of broad conservative interests throughout the state, regardless of party. With Virginia's treasury brimming from inflated wartime taxes, a sufficient surplus had accumulated by midsummer 1942 to permit Darden to liquidate the debt. Summoning a special session of the legislature in September 1942, he announced a plan to invest the surplus in U.S. war bonds. The investment, he explained, would create a sinking fund that could be used to pay off the state obligations; at war's end, the bonds and the indebtedness would both be retired. In one stroke Darden had thus performed an act of both patriotic devotion and fiscal stringency. Byrd partisans and conservatives everywhere heartily approved.

Darden's organization loyalty was spotty, but he could be counted on in a pinch, as when the Virginia Democratic party divided over endorsing Roosevelt for a fourth term. In 1944, seeking to revive the floundering anti-Byrd movement, a group of liberals formed the Committee of One Hundred to back FDR. It fell to Darden, as titular head of the party, to coordinate the organization's response. Perceiving a possibly serious threat to the organization and disturbed by Vice-President Henry A. Wallace's socialist inclinations, Darden flawlessly steered the Byrd forces through the party convention at Roanoke, denying the One Hundred even a voice on the floor. Virginia delegates were uninstructed concerning a presidential candidate and were specifically prohibited from voting to renominate Wallace. A grateful Byrd wired the governor his appreciation.

In matters of race relations Darden was equivocal at best. He had never been a strident racist, even if his name was associated with the unfortunate race-baiting pamphlet in the 1938 congressional campaign. He quietly refused to enforce Jim Crow bus-seating laws during World War II, reasoning that short tempers would flare among both blacks and whites if blacks were crowded to the rear of conveyances. He gave aid to Negro colleges and attempted, unsuccessfully, to place Negroes at state hospitals where they could receive medical training without having to leave the state. He responded calmly to the near hysteria gripping Richmond in July 1943 when homicidal blacks were rumored to be about to attack whites with ice picks. Still, for all the gestures of good will, Darden skirted the issue of racial reform. Political expediency and organization fealty led him to take positions and tacitly support practices that he found personally abhorrent. He refused to follow the lead of Richmond *Times-Dispatch* editor Virginius Dabney and sponsor legislation formally repealing unworkable streetcar segregation laws. He was on record against the poll tax, viewing it as undemocratic and irrelevant to good citizenship. He preferred a literacy requirement for whites and blacks, regarding education as the prerequisite for responsible voting. But he permitted only Virginia servicemen on active duty to be exempted from poll taxes. Given the tenor of the times, Darden's racial record was not a bad one, but nonetheless it was a disappointment to moderates like Dabney.

Critics would charge that Darden was merely a genteel reformer, preoccupied with education and character-building reforms to the neglect of more thoroughgoing social reconstruction. Allegiance to the organization and his own residual conservatism, as well as wartime constraints, did at times prevent him from acting boldly and imaginatively. Nevertheless, if his liberalism had a mugwumpish quality, the record he left was indisputably progressive, one which addressed a broad spectrum of needs with both compassion and intelligence. Moreover, Darden's overriding conviction—that social progress could come about only incrementally, not through miracle programs but through the education process and the sound and prudent exercise of government—would be vindicated by subsequent events.

As Darden's term came to a close early in 1946, he was still a relatively young man, not yet fifty, in the prime of a political career that was, by all calculations, still cresting. Byrd had gradually been relinquishing leadership of the organization to his lieutenants and had tapped the outgoing governor as his heir apparent. Darden, too, was the overwhelming choice of the party to succeed the ailing Carter Glass in the U.S. Senate. His course seemed set—he would wear the mantle of party chief while returning to a prestigious seat in the Congress. But Darden demurred. He told Byrd he did not want to spend the rest of his life "wrestling over appointments." He rejected the Glass seat because he wanted to devote more time to his maturing family and believed that Washington held too many distractions. No doubt, too, Darden was tired of compromising differences with the organization and saw an opportunity to cut his ties cleanly and gracefully. In political retirement he could speak more freely, pursue a wider range of public and private interests, and involve himself more directly in his favorite cause, education.

Thus the indefatigable Southsider embarked on yet another chapter in a storied career. During the next twenty years he would add to his already considerable achievements a remarkable record of public service as educator and senior statesman. He finished out 1946 as chancellor of the College of William and Mary. There followed a twelve-year term as president of the University of Virginia, a brief stint as delegate to the United Nations, several advisory assignments in the Eisenhower administration, and membership on numerous corporate and civic boards of directors.

The University of Virginia post was offered to Darden early in 1947, upon the retirement of John Lloyd Newcomb. He accepted without hesitation, though his statehouse friends, he recalled, thought he had "gone off his rocker" in passing up the U.S. Senate for academia. His purpose was to restore the university to Jefferson's original concept, the capstone of public education in the state. He remembered his own souring experience as a freshman in Charlottesville and was determined to make the university a more accessible and comfortable place for public school students. To that end he encouraged such students to enroll and oversaw development of a student union complex and campus dormitories that would offset the elitist tendencies of the fraternity system. At the same time that he was democratizing the university, he used his influence with the legislature to secure substantial funds to upgrade the faculty and institute new programs, including a graduate school in business administration. He left Charlottesville in 1959 having managed to expand enrollments and raise academic standards. An appreciative faculty, which initially regarded him as an interloper, gave him the university's highest honor, the Thomas Jefferson Award, citing "wise leadership and administrative guidance worthy of the tradition of its great founder."

Darden gave graciously of his time and fortune in these postgovernor years. Unbeknownst to the public, he turned back his salary each year as president of the university. He donated land to facilitate the construction of Clinch Valley College in the disadvantaged southwest sector of the state. His work for President Eisenhower—studying foreign aid programs, advising the National Security Council, serving on a Commission on National Goals for the 1960s—interrupted his schedule and forced him on occasion to take an extended leave from Charlottesville. When his younger son, Pierre, was killed in a sailing accident in the fall of 1959, Darden plunged into another commitment, agreeing to chair a study group for the Southern Regional Education Board.

No sooner would Darden return home for a rest than he would be summoned for yet another assignment. In 1960 Governor Lindsay Almond asked him to serve on the state Board of Education. In 1963 Governor Albertis Harrison drafted him to reopen the public schools in Prince Edward County that had been closed four years to avoid court-ordered integration; the job "damn near killed him," but he succeeded with a characteristic blend of grit and diplomacy. He was a perennial volunteer. In his seventies, he was persuaded by Governor Mills Godwin to work on the Commission to Revise the Virginia Constitution. His efforts resulted in an amendment guaranteeing every Virginia child the opportunity for a sound education.

In October 1978, Darden, now eighty-one, returned to Charlottesville to deliver a convocation address. It was a muted message, expressing a concern over excessive government intervention and reckless spending and calling for self-discipline, moral strength, and the rediscovery of fundamental principles. Darden's conservatism had ripened with age. Yet even in his disappointment at mankind's slow progress, he was undespairing, declaring that "the noble ends toward which men have toiled for countless centuries continue to beckon and we can succeed if we do not lose heart." He told his young audience that "a certain sustained tension is part and parcel of university life and the absence of it, not its presence, bodes ill. When ferment dies away an educational institution starts to wither and die. So it is much better that university officials grow weary and depart than that student bodies and faculties grow quiet."

Darden's protean politics and rich, full life embodied that healthy tension. The Southside country boy became a world-traveled statesman. The machine politician transcended the courthouse and county rings to become an unaligned champion of good government. The conservative vied with the progressive to produce an often enigmatic but always searching public servant. Darden, at the age of eighty-four, died suddenly of heart failure on June 9, 1981, ten days after he had made a brief speech at the state Democratic convention nominating Lieutenant Governor Charles S. Robb for top spot on the party ticket and pleading for unity: "We can't do it by lying in ambush and shooting each other." Statesman, educator, farmer, politician, philanthropist—Colgate Darden was not unlike Jefferson in his multifaceted talents and singled-minded dedication. Benjamin Muse, his Republican opponent in the 1941 gubernatorial contest, referring to the generation of men that led Virginia through the turbulent thirties and forties, called him "the noblest Roman of them all. He never hesitated to follow his convictions." Even the creeping resignation of his twilight years could not alter that judgment nor dim the brilliance of Darden's service to the Commonwealth.

SOURCES

Students of Darden should begin with his executive papers (Virginia State Library). Other essential collections include the Price Executive Papers (Virginia State Library) and the papers of Virginius Dabney and Martin A. Hutchinson (both at the University of Virginia). The papers of the Virginia World War II History Commission (Virginia State Library) contain several useful items, particularly in Section B, "Reports from Localities."

The Richmond *Times-Dispatch* conveys shifting political currents in wartime Virginia. Helpful for demographic purposes are publications of the Virginia Bureau of Population and Economic Research.

Guy Friddell's *Colgate Darden: Conversations with Guy Friddell* (Charlottesville, 1978) provides lively insight into both the man and the politician. The most comprehensive examination of Darden's political career and governorship is Jonathan J. Wolfe's "Virginia in World War II" (Ph.D. diss., University of Virginia, 1971). The career of Darden's colorful lieutenant governor is described in William B. Crawley, Jr.'s *Bill Tuck: A Political Life in Harry Byrd's Virginia* (Charlottesville, 1978). Two books by Marvin W. Schlegel illuminate the impact of World War II on the Old Dominion—*Conscripted City: Norfolk in World War II* (Norfolk, 1951) and *Virginia on Guard: Civilian Defense and the State Militia in the Second World War* (Richmond, 1949).

WILLIAM M. TUCK

Governor of Virginia

1946–1950

WILLIAM MUNFORD TUCK

The Organization's Rustic *Rara Avis*

William B. Crawley, Jr.

Shortly before William Munford ("Bill") Tuck was sworn in as governor in January 1946, he received a sobering message from Senator Harry F. Byrd: "I think you, the organization and the Democratic party are faced with four very momentous years. We must recognize the fact that there is quite an evolution in progress in all public matters. People are restless and complaining. . . . The whole world is very unsettled." The senator proved to be prescient, to a much greater extent than even he could have anticipated. The Byrd organization's domination of state politics notwithstanding, the Tuck administration was destined to be one of the most controversial of the Byrd era. It was, moreover, one of the most intriguing: Tuck's political philosophy fitted the organization mold perfectly; his unabashed, freewheeling personality did not.

Born on September 28, 1896, in Halifax County, Tuck grew up on the farm his family had owned for three generations. His childhood as one of nine children was, in the main, fairly typical: arduous labor in the tobacco fields from spring through fall, relieved occasionally by hunting, fishing, horseback riding, and other rustic pastimes. There were two influences on the young Tuck, however, which made his early years somewhat different. First, the Tuck family had long been involved in politics; Bill's grandfather and father had both been active in local public affairs, and his father had served in the Virginia House of Delegates for three sessions. Second, there was an emphasis upon education unusual for turn-of-the-century rural Virginia. In the absence of public schools Bill's father, Robert James Tuck, had a small school constructed on his farm for the purpose of educating neighborhood children. There Bill Tuck's formal education began. As an adolescent, he also spent one year at a private training school, but when military discipline failed to convert him into a scholar, he was sent to William and Mary Academy, a secondary school which he attended for two years before enrolling in the College of William and Mary. As a collegian he was more interested in sports (track and football) and politics than studies, and he left William and Mary after two years to become, ironically, a teacher-principal in Northumberland County. By then, however, the United States had entered World War I, and Tuck, looking forward to a more suitable (or at least more exciting) career, enlisted in the Marines after only one year as an educator. His military service was brief, foreshortened by the signing of the Armistice before he even got to Europe. By the time of his discharge in July 1919, Tuck had decided to enroll in the Washington and Lee School of Law. Two years later, degree in hand, he set up practice in South Boston.

Given his inclinations, it was not surprising that the young attorney soon sought public office. In 1923 he outpolled two opponents to win one of two Halifax seats in the House of Delegates. Twice reelected with ease, he seemed headed for a lengthy political career when he abruptly announced in 1929 that he would not seek another term. The reason, he explained, was that as a result of his marriage the previous year to Eva Lovelace Dillard, a charming South Boston widow, family and financial considerations demanded that he devote more time to his law practice. His retirement, however, was short-lived; when his successor in the House died in 1930, Tuck was easily persuaded to replace him. The following year, he was elected to the state Senate, where he remained for ten years.

From the outset Tuck gave his full support to Harry Byrd, both as governor and senator. Yet much of Tuck's work in behalf of the organization was carried out surreptitiously. In 1933, for example, at Byrd's suggestion, he personally contacted every member of the legislature, importuning them to petition a reluctant Governor Pollard to call a special session to deal with the question of Prohibition. As provided by state law, when two-thirds of the legislators made such a request, the governor was obliged to convene the Assembly. The Assembly met and set up the machinery for a referendum on repeal (overwhelmingly approved), thus robbing antiorganization forces of an issue and facilitating the election of organization candidate George C. Peery to succeed Pollard.

Only in his initial attitude toward the New Deal did Tuck diverge from the established Byrd line. Reflecting the sentiments of his predominantly rural constituents who were benefiting from such New Deal innovations as the Agricultural Adjustment Act, Tuck was more favorably disposed toward the Roosevelt administration at the outset than was Byrd. In the state Senate he voted for measures permitting Virginia to participate in various New Deal programs, notably those involving unemployment compensation and the conservation of natural resources. In the 1936 presidential election, while Byrd studiously refrained from endorsing Roosevelt, Tuck campaigned for the president. Eventually, though, Tuck soured on the New Deal and joined Byrd in strident opposition, in 1938 denouncing "this wild orgy of spending."

All in all, Tuck emerged as one of Byrd's most loyal adherents, though the two men were not personally close. Throughout the 1920s and 1930s he delivered heavy organization majorities in his Southside bailiwick. His standing within the organization was evidenced by his elevation to the powerful position of leader of the Democratic caucus in the state Senate, enabling him to direct much of the opposition to the policies of antiorganization Governor James H. Price, who had succeeded Peery.

By 1941 Tuck was widely viewed as a leading contender in the gubernatorial contest of that year. In addition to his record of unflagging organization support for almost two decades, Tuck possessed other valuable political assets, the most notable of which was his uniquely engaging personality. Expansive of girth and of behavior, he was variously described as "salty, jovial, paunchy, . . . blimplike in his physical contours" and as "garrulous, blustery, earthy [and] stout as a tobacco hogshead." The Richmond *News Leader* pictured him as having "the comfortable appearance of a man who has just dined on a dozen pork chops" and noted that he was "known to chew tobacco, drink whiskey and play a wicked hand of poker. . . . His vocabulary began where the resources of Mark Twain left off." In Virginia, a state where the demeanor of public officials was traditionally as conservative as their political philosophy, Tuck proved to be a refreshing, if sometimes shocking, anomaly.

Though Tuck's unabashed behavior was usually an asset in attracting votes, it may well have been a liability in 1941. The organization over which Harry Byrd presided was a reflection of the senator's own reserved, unobtrusive style, and the patriarch apparently was leery of Tuck's flamboyance. For whatever reason, it soon became clear that Congressman Colgate Darden was Byrd's choice for governor. However disappointed he may have been, Tuck dutifully agreed to run for lieutenant governor—to create, in effect, an organization ticket which swept to easy victories in the primary and general elections. Taking office shortly after the United States entered World War II, the two dissimilar men—Governor Darden, erudite and urbane, and Lieutenant Governor Tuck, ever the country boy—worked harmoniously in leading wartime Virginia and in the process formed a lasting personal and political friendship.

The lieutenant governorship, traditionally a lackluster office, turned out to be a boon to Tuck's political career. The diligence with which he presided over the state Senate earned him respect from some who had been inclined earlier to view him, in the words of J. Harvie Wilkinson III, as a "playboy and clown who could never be trusted with the responsibility of high office." He continued all the while to demonstrate undeniable political acumen, notably in leading the campaign for passage of a referendum on calling a limited constitutional convention to facilitate voting by Virginians serving in the military. The so-called soldier-vote issue had become a serious annoyance to the organization, and Tuck's role in settling the matter did not go unappreciated. "I turned to him time after time for advice and help," Darden later recalled, "and he was no end of assistance to me." Most important of all, Tuck's service as lieutenant governor vastly increased his statewide visibility. Governor Darden, believing that with the war going on he should stay close to Richmond, dispatched Tuck with inordinate frequency to serve as the Commonwealth's official representative throughout Virginia and beyond.

As the Darden administration neared its end, several political facts became apparent. First, the antiorganization forces were now enfeebled, disunited, and without effective leadership. Second, and conversely, the Byrd organization had grown in strength during the popular Darden administration and was approaching the peak of its power. Third, Tuck, as lieutenant governor, had emerged as an organization leader possessing a considerable personal following. By 1945 Tuck believed, with good reason, that he had earned organization endorsement for the governorship. Still, Byrd held back, apparently preferring either state Senator John S. Battle or House of Delegates Speaker Thomas B. Stanley. The memory of the senator's snub in the previous contest heightened the anxiety of Tuck and his supporters. "We all have the feeling," one of them confided to the lieutenant governor, "that frantic efforts are being made to find a reasonable excuse for calling you in and asking you to stand aside again." Tuck's own brother was more succinct: "They are beginning to say, 'For God's sake, he isn't going to [let] Harry Byrd sidetrack him again, is he?' "

Eventually Tuck, who had gotten the feeling that he was, as he put it, "just about to be smothered in the closet," decided to announce his candidacy, even without Byrd's prior blessing. The key to that decision lay in his knowledge that he had the support of his friend Governor Darden. Some years later Darden recalled a lengthy conference with Byrd on the matter: "What it boiled down to was this. He [Byrd] was uneasy about Bill. And I told Harry that, no matter how he felt, I just had to be for Bill. . . . There is little doubt that if I had given any ground, Harry would have . . . set Bill aside." Once he realized that Tuck was determined to run and that Darden was going to support him, Byrd (as was his wont) accepted the situation rather than risk an internecine fight—which, in this case, might have been ruinous to the organization, given the immense prestige of Darden and the wide popularity of Tuck.

The securing of Byrd's support, however reluctantly it may have been given, was tantamount to election. After a tedious primary campaign, Tuck easily defeated Roanoke attorney Moss Plunkett, a frequent office seeker viewed rather skeptically even by fellow antis; with a mere 7.8 percent of the adult population taking part, Tuck won by a margin of two to one. In the general election three months later, the result was similar, Tuck defeating the Republican challenger, state Senator Floyd S. Landreth of Galax, 112,355 to 52,386—a total constituting a miniscule 9.4 percent of the Commonwealth's adult population.

The torpor of the electorate in 1945 was partly the result of absorption in war-ending developments in the Pacific, but it was mainly attributable to the stultifying power of the Byrd organization. At the time of Tuck's inauguration in January 1946, it controlled both U.S. Senate seats, all but one congressional seat, the vast majority of the General Assembly, and virtually all local offices. Yet, despite this dominance, Tuck was beset with difficulties from the very beginning. Many of the problems were not of his own making. It was simply Tuck's lot to arrive at the governorship as the nation was entering what historian Eric Goldman has aptly labeled "the crucial decade"; he was consequently forced to deal with a number of social, economic, and political problems that had been postponed—and in some cases exacerbated—by World War II.

Most notable were those relating to organized labor. Virginia, a predominantly rural state, was not extensively unionized and, with the exception of a celebrated strike at the Danville cotton mills in the early 1930s, labor-management relations had usually been amicable. But once the wartime restrictions were removed, labor and management both endeavored (often obstinately) to exact gains; the result was a plethora of regional and national strikes that alienated much of the nonunion public. It was thus in an atmosphere of hostility toward organized labor that the Tuck administration began. The 1946 session of the General Assembly passed legislation placing limits on strike activity and restricting the right of state employees to unionize. During that same session Tuck became directly involved in a labor dispute when he intervened in a ferry strike in the Hampton Roads area. Having failed to effect a settlement, the governor got legislative authorization to seize and operate the facilities. Eventually, in 1948, the state purchased the company and incorporated it into the highway system.

It was also during Tuck's first months in office that the controversial "Vepco affair" erupted. This imbroglio began with an announcement by the International Brotherhood of Electrical Workers (AFL) that a strike against the Virginia Electric and Power Company would commence on April 1, 1946, unless its demands, notably a wage increase of 17½ cents per hour, were met by that date. Such a strike would have curtailed power to some 1.7 million persons, well over half the state's population. With the dispute still unsettled and only ten days remaining before the strike deadline, Tuck endeavored to arrange a conference for mediation. That effort failed because of union unwillingness to attend.

Displaying the forthrightness which was to become the hallmark of his governorship, Tuck announced that he would "take full responsibility" in the face of the emergency. "I shall not sit idly by and do nothing," he proclaimed. Privately he excoriated the union leaders for their recalcitrance and for what he deemed an appalling callousness toward the public. "I'll be damned if they're going to cut the lights out in Virginia," he roared, according to one aide. "It's just like sticking a gun in your back. And they'll not get away with it as long as I'm governor." Meanwhile, the governor and a handful of his closest aides devised a stratagem to avert the threatened blackout.

Central to the plan was an obscure statute long on the books, but unused and generally unknown, establishing a so-called unorganized militia in addition to the regular militia or National Guard; such a unit hypothetically consisted of all able-bodied males between the ages of sixteen and fifty-five and could be summoned by the governor if needed. Tuck revealed nothing of his plan to the public, saying only that if the threatened strike was not called off, he might have to take what he called "drastic" action.

At precisely nine o'clock on the morning of March 29, two days before the walkout was to occur, Vepco facilities across the state were entered by uniformed members of the Virginia State Guard (a surviving wartime agency designed to replace the called-up National Guard). The guardsmen summarily presented startled Vepco employees with papers that read: "You are hereby notified that you have been drafted by the commander-in-chief of the land and naval forces of Virginia, the Honorable William M. Tuck, Governor of Virginia, into the service of the Commonwealth to execute the law which requires the Virginia Electric and Power Company to provide electric service to the people of Virginia customarily served by it." An accompanying order stipulated that the new draftees would be granted a "temporary suspension . . . of active military duties" until the strike deadline arrived, at which time they would automatically go on active duty. Further, lest the new recruits take their orders lightly, they were informed that they were thenceforth "subject to the military law of Virginia, and for disobedience to orders . . . are subject to such lawful punishment as a court martial may direct."

The bold maneuver produced front-page headlines across the country and brought a deluge of telegrams into the governor's office. A Virginia CIO spokesmen blasted the move as "the most sinister, damnable and unprincipled act to date coming from the high command of Byrdism," while AFL President William Green, claiming that Tuck was "enslaving labor," informed the governor that he planned to call on President Truman to intervene. Most of the unionist-militiamen themselves appeared to accept the draft with equanimity or even with humor, but not everyone was so complaisant: one irate telephone caller to the Governor's Mansion identified himself as a navy man and exclaimed, "I'm just back from Germany where I've been fighting the same kind of dictator that Tuck is trying to be. We got rid of Hitler and we'll get rid of Tuck. . . . [W]e're coming down there and clean up the Mansion." That and similar threats prompted the state police, unbeknownst to Tuck, to assign special plainclothesmen to protect him.

Antiorganization Democrats seized the incident as an opportunity to chastise Tuck in particular and the Byrd machine in general. Richmond attorney Martin Hutchinson (who would unsuccessfully challenge Byrd for the Senate the same year) commented that it was "not a very pretty or pleasant picture we have here in Virginia with the state militia billeted in the capital city." Tuck's erstwhile gubernatorial opponent Moss Plunkett was more succinct: "Governor Tuck has gone wild." Editorial opinion across the state generally lauded the governor's ploy, except in the Norfolk-Newport News area, where unionism was relatively strong.

As it turned out, the draft maneuver never went into its ultimate phase. Some twenty-six hours before the walkout deadline, the IBEW agreed to call off the strike and resume contract negotiations; after two weeks of bargaining, a new contract was signed between Vepco and the union. Settlement of the dispute mooted such questions as the constitutionality of Tuck's action, punishment of unionists who refused to work, paying the salaries of those who did work, and disposition of the profits made by Vepco while under state operation. Yet some results of the episode were clear. The draft earned Tuck the undying enmity of organized labor—at least of its leadership, if not the rank and file. Conversely, it won him the lasting admiration of most nonunion Virginians, who, largely unconcerned with the equities involved, saw the draft only as an audacious move that preserved their electrical power. For Tuck the incident was especially significant since it helped win him the confidence of previously skeptical Harry Byrd; moreover, it may well have bolstered his own confidence, helping him to escape the shadow of his predecessor, Colgate Darden, with whom he feared invidious comparisons. After the Vepco affair there may have been those who doubted Tuck's judgment or his discretion, but none who questioned his mettle. "From then on," he later recalled, "I was *governor!*"

Continued labor disturbances, especially in the coal fields of southwest Virginia, led to a widespread clamor for union restrictions. Tuck, in response to that demand, called a special legislative session for January 1947; though the session was summoned, ostensibly, to deal with public schools, one basic purpose was clearly to enact labor legislation. Despite threats of political retaliation by union spokesmen, two major laws were passed. The first, the Public Utilities Labor Relations Act, established procedures for dealing with crises such as the Vepco episode. The statute provided that no party to a public utilities labor dispute could engage in a strike or a lockout until two negotiating sessions had been held, with the governor empowered to act as mediator at the second conference if he deemed it desirable. If either party refused to submit to arbitration and a work stoppage impended, the governor was authorized to seize the facility and operate it in the name of the state until the dispute could be settled. The other, and more controversial, measure was a "right-to-work" law prohibiting the requirement of union membership as a condition of employment. The Tuck labor legislation was favorably received by most Virginians. Within several months the right-to-work law was federally sanctioned by passage of the Taft-Hartley Act, and before Tuck left office the utilities law successfully ended a pending strike by telephone employees.

In addition to labor unrest, Tuck faced a vastly increased demand for state services resulting from the war-induced population boom. Despite the restrictions of the "pay-as-you-go" principle, he was able to wheedle from the legislature appropriations sufficient to produce steady, if unspectacular, improvement in educational institutions, mental and physical health facilities, welfare, and highways. Still, the Commonwealth's expenditures in those areas consistently ranked near the bottom nationally. As one observer aptly put it, these increased appropriations often allowed the level of state services to rise only "from *abysmally* low to merely *too* low."

To secure even such modest gains and maintain a balanced budget, Tuck had to recommend a tax increase—an undertaking fraught with difficulties because of the determination of the Byrd leadership and the business community to maintain Virginia's vaunted reputation as a low-tax state. Specifically, the governor recommended to the 1948 General Assembly that corporate income taxes be raised 2 percent and that individual income taxes be raised ½ percent on incomes under $5,000 and 2 percent on incomes in excess of $5,000. The tax package prompted immediate, and in some cases vicious, reaction, led by the Richmond press. Despite the opposition of newspapers and much of the public, as well as unaccustomed resistance in the organization-controlled General Assembly, the tax increase was eventually enacted. Nevertheless, Tuck was shocked by the virulence of the opposition, especially since the most vociferous critics were often the very ones whose demands for improved state services made the increase necessary. "They called on me to preach the sermon, and I preached," Tuck said whimsically. "But when I passed the collection plate, they began to run out on me."

Although the Tuck governorship could not be called a reform administration, it did produce some progressive innovations. The creation of an agency to control water pollution, for example, anticipated by several decades the popular concern for environmental protection. There were also salutary changes in the prison system, including outlawing corporal punishment and phasing out the use of chains in road camps. The most ambitious reform involved reorganization of state government, prompted largely by newspaper revelations concerning the inordinate size of the bureaucracy—an embarrassment in view of the Byrd organization's dedication to frugality. The consolidation of seventy-two agencies into thirty, at an annual saving of well over a million dollars, was only a qualified success, though it did constitute the first appreciable attempt at reorganization since the thorough streamlining under Byrd some twenty years earlier.

Political activity during the Tuck governorship was by no means moribund, despite the pervasiveness of organization influence. In 1946 antiorganization wheelhorse Martin Hutchinson made a determined, albeit losing, run at Byrd in the Democratic senatorial primary; the same year, the Democrats held a spirited convention to select a successor to the deceased Senator Carter Glass, finally settling on then-Congressman A. Willis Robertson. And the volatile issue of poll tax repeal came to a head. For years antiorganization leaders had claimed that the tax aided the Byrd hegemony by keeping the electorate manageably small and that the organization manipulated payment so as to ensure that its partisans always qualified to vote. The Byrd-dominated legislature eventually approved a set of constitutional amendments abolishing the poll tax as a prerequisite for voting but giving the General Assembly power to set up other suffrage requirements. Accordingly, when the referendum was held in 1949, both pro–poll tax forces and those who feared what the Assembly might devise in its stead joined hands to defeat the amendments. The poll tax was retained in state elections until abolished by a decision of the U.S. Supreme Court in 1966.

By far the most controversial political development of the Tuck administration was the "anti-Truman bill." Though white Virginians prided themselves (with some justification) on the Commonwealth's relative lack of racial discord, many had become increasingly uneasy as demands for full equality grew in postwar years. In February 1948 Harry S. Truman proposed a sweeping civil rights program that included a permanent Fair Employment Practices Commission (FEPC), an agency which was anathema to southern conservatives, Tuck included. Though more of an old-line paternalist than a race-baiter of the Bilbo stripe, Tuck feared that increased federal involvement in socioeconomic matters (such as the FEPC) would erode the states' rights doctrine by which the South had long maintained its system of racial separation. Accordingly, in an extraordinary third appearance before the 1948 General Assembly, he blasted the Truman plan as portending "the final and complete destruction of the autonomy of not only the Southern states, but of all the states of the American union. . . . This is sufficient to create in America the counterpart of a Hitler or Stalin." Incensed that a Democratic president would make such a proposal, Tuck then set forth a plan for retaliation by revising state election laws. The most startling provisions would have kept the names of presidential candidates off the ballot (using only names of parties and electors) and, further, would have permitted a state party convention or a committee thereof to decide for whom the state's electoral votes would be cast, even after the election had been held!

No single proposal of the Tuck governorship provoked such a uniformly hostile reaction. One Richmond paper adjudged it "asinine and utterly immoral," while another asked incredulously, "Was there ever anything like it? Is this still Virginia?" In an impassioned speech before the General Assembly, antiorganization Delegate Robert Whitehead, damning the measure as "not legal, not honorable, and neither fair nor wise," queried: "Has the General Assembly assumed the position of the Ku Klux Klan, to march under a ballot bill contrary to our basic law?" Tuck admitted that the original proposal was poorly drafted and carefully explained that the intent of the bill was merely to ensure that the Democratic electoral vote not be cast for a candidate (e.g., Truman) repugnant to the majority of Virginia Democrats. The bill as eventually enacted still permitted a state party to instruct its electors for someone other than the national party nominee. Significantly, however, such change, if made, would have to be announced at least sixty days before an election, or the electors would automatically be committed to the national ticket; in addition, the names of all candidates were to be printed on the ballot.

Once the bill became law, the question was whether or not it would be used. At the Democratic national convention in Philadelphia in July 1948, Byrd, Tuck, and other organization leaders strove mightily to prevent Truman's nomination. The governor hoped first to nominate Dwight D. Eisenhower, but when the general proved unavailable, he and other members of the delegation cast their ballots for Georgia Senator Richard Russell. When, despite southern opposition, Truman was nominated, there was speculation that the Byrd organization might well invoke the "anti-Truman" law to select a more suitable candidate in Virginia—a prospect enhanced by the appearance in the field of the Dixiecrat J. Strom Thurmond. Ultimately, however, the organization did what came so naturally to it: nothing. In the breach, disaffected organization men were left to vote either for Thurmond (as did Tuck) or for the Republican Thomas E. Dewey. Antiorganization Democrats in the meanwhile formed a "straight-ticket committee" to work for Truman. The subsequent election of the feisty incumbent was thus construed as a defeat for Byrd regulars and left the antis in an unusually buoyant mood as they anticipated the 1949 gubernatorial election.

There were, in truth, signs that the Byrd hegemony might be deteriorating. Organized labor, for example, had been permanently alienated by the Vepco affair and the subsequent enactment of restrictive labor legislation. The black community was disenchanted by organization reaction to the Truman civil rights program, a development of increasing importance as larger numbers of blacks began to vote in the 1950s and 1960s. Liberal Democrats were alarmed by the "anti-Truman bill," and demographic changes were taking place that would eventually shift the locus of political power from rural areas, traditionally loyal to Byrd, to less conservative urban areas. Still, the Byrd organization was characterized by its resilience, and those who would have written its epitaph in 1950 were premature in their judgment.

As for Tuck himself, he left office enjoying immense personal popularity—at least among the bulk of the voting (i.e., white, conservative, nonunion) public. Moreover, he had grown greatly in the esteem of the man who mattered most in Virginia politics, the once-dubious Harry Byrd. "You will stand through all history to come," he wrote the departing Tuck, "as one of Virginia's greatest governors."

Out of public office for the first time in over twenty-five years (except for a few months in 1930), Tuck returned to South Boston in 1950 and, professing disinterest in any further office, rejoined his prospering law firm. But in 1952 he was elected chairman of the state Democratic party, a position he held for barely six weeks before resigning rather than endorse the presidential candidacy of Adlai Stevenson (whom he derisively labeled "the Truman candidate")—though not before excoriating the Truman administration as "government wastrels," "political rapscallions," "minions of vice and venality," and "political vultures." The following year he won a special election to fill the Fifth District congressional seat vacated by Thomas B. Stanley, who resigned to run for governor. For the next sixteen years Tuck held the seat, sometimes running unopposed, rather handily defeating those who dared to challenge him.

Tuck's congressional career—which included lengthy service on both the Judiciary and Un-American Activities Committees—was characterized by a hard line against Communism abroad and an insistence upon fiscal conservatism at home. Most of all, however, Tuck was an outspoken opponent of the civil rights revolution sweeping the nation. He had scarcely arrived in Washington when the epochal *Brown* decision was delivered, rendering unconstitutional the South's hallowed system of segregated public schools. Livid, Tuck denounced the Supreme Court as "nine reprehensible individuals gasconading in judicial ermine" and pronounced the decision "the worst thing that has ever happened since the foundation of the Republic." He had no patience with those who counseled even token compliance. "On this subject," he declared, "I am not a 'gradualist,' I am a 'neverist.' " He joined Byrd in the vanguard of the movement to thwart implementation of the decision, informing the senator that he was "in favor of putting up an impregnable wall of massive resistance and keeping it there."

When that effort ultimately failed, Tuck devoted himself to the task of trying to stay the burgeoning movement for civil rights legislation. Along with Senator Byrd and Congressmen Howard Smith and Watkins Abbitt, Tuck led the Virginia segment of the southern conservative phalanx that managed to delay, or at least water down, all such legislation for a decade. His most venomous attacks were against the proposed civil rights bill of 1964, a measure which he termed "heinous, obnoxious, . . . nauseating, . . . [and] repugnant to every concept of liberty." With vintage Tuck rhetoric he also lambasted the Civil Rights Commission. "It will," he predicted, "flare back to haunt those who empower it to intimidate, bullyrag and torment an already aggravated citizenry." Tuck's fulminations, in the end, proved unavailing as the Congress passed not only the 1964 bill but the 1965 Voting Rights Act and numerous other pieces of social legislation incompatible with what Tuck regarded as "sound states' rights doctrine."

Indeed, Tuck's entire congressional career was one of almost unrelieved negativism—of constant warring against ideas and programs whose time had come. It was thus with unfeigned relief that in May 1967 he announced his decision not to seek reelection. His eyesight dimmed by cataracts, distraught over the tragic death of his eldest grandson in a high school football game, and worried about his wife's failing health, he seemed truly glad to escape the Washington environment that had all along been alien to him. "I'll be happier at home," he said, ". . . back down there on my poor, rocky farm."

This retirement, unlike the one in 1950, proved to be permanent, notwithstanding suggestions that he seek election to the state legislature. He chose instead to pursue the leisurely practice of law in his old South Boston firm, which had now become a large one according to Southside Virginia standards. His interest in politics remained keen, though his participation amounted to only an occasional public appearance and a rare speech. Even such limited activity was curtailed after a stroke in late 1976 left him unable to walk without difficulty. From that point onward, his political involvement consisted of endorsing candidates he deemed suitably conservative—some of whom made the pilgrimage to his home to receive the benefaction of the man who had become (along with his friend Colgate Darden) the eldest of the Commonwealth's elder statesmen.

Bill Tuck's political career was a remarkable one in many respects, not least of all in its longevity; holding office almost continually from 1924 to 1968, he never experienced electoral defeat. Though he held a variety of offices, it was clearly as governor that he had found his métier and as governor that he would be remembered. "In any list of Virginia's finest governors of this century," declared his sometime nemesis the Richmond *News Leader,* "Mr. Tuck would rank one-two with Mr. Byrd, and take your choice." It was not so much what Tuck did—though some of his actions were surely significant—as how he did it, that engaged the attention of Virginians. He had no use, he said, for public officials who were always "dying of the can'ts." His own forthright approach, decried by some critics as impetuous or ham-fisted (or both), was likened by a more sympathetic observer to "a boisterous summer storm with deafening thunder, blinding lightning, and driving rains from which the land emerged rejuvenated, all sweet, green, smiling and amazed."

Throughout his career Tuck was something of an anomaly in that, while his conservative political philosophy was that of the aristocratic Byrd organization, his unabashed personality was that of a populist. A country boy by birth, and always one at heart, he remained utterly unaffected by high office. His gastronomic preferences ran to chitlins, collards, and cornbread—traditionally preceded by a generous quantity of bourbon tinctured but slightly with branch water. For entertainment, he enjoyed listening and dancing to country music. His humor was earthy and often self-deprecatory, as when he admitted that several of his gubernatorial mistakes had made him feel "like a one-legged man in a tail-kicking contest." Some of his escapades became nearly legendary: firing a pistol in the night air outside the Governor's Mansion in a playful, impromptu test of Capitol security; inviting sundry and unsuspecting passersby to have cocktails in the Mansion or to accompany him to the Old Dominion Barn Dance, a popular Richmond hoedown; sneaking away in an old, nondescript car to his rural Halifax cabin retreat, there to relax until anxious state police fetched him back to Richmond.

Accustomed as they were to conventional, colorless, staid political leaders, Virginians found Bill Tuck a rousing iconoclast—perhaps the closest thing to a folk hero ever to sit in the Governor's Mansion. It is fairly certain that, for better or worse, the Commonwealth had never seen a governor quite like him, nor ever will again.

SOURCES

Primary sources for the day-to-day events of the Tuck administration are major state newspapers. Pertinent collections of personal papers include those of Harry F. Byrd, Martin A. Hutchinson, and Robert Whitehead (all at the University of Virginia) and those of William M. Tuck (College of William and Mary). The Tuck Executive Papers (Virginia State Library) are helpful. Of utmost benefit were numerous personal interviews with Tuck, the notes from which are in the possession of the author.

For the national setting of the Tuck years, see Eric Goldman, *The Crucial Decade—And After: America, 1945–60* (New York, 1960) and Cabell Phillips, *The Truman Presidency* (New York, 1966). Basic to an understanding of state politics during the era is J. Harvie Wilkinson III, *Harry Byrd and the Changing Face of Virginia Politics, 1945–1966* (Charlottesville, 1968). Tuck's career is examined in William Bryan Crawley, Jr., *Bill Tuck: A Political Life in Harry Byrd's Virginia* (Charlottesville, 1978); his gubernatorial administration is analyzed more extensively in the same author's "The Governorship of William Munford Tuck, 1946–1950: Virginia Politics in the Golden Age of the Byrd Organization" (Ph.D. diss., University of Virginia, 1974).

Other University of Virginia dissertations germane to the Tuck era are Jonathan J. Wolfe, "Virginia in World War II" (1971) and Peter Ros Henriques, "John S. Battle and Virginia Politics: 1948–1953" (1971). Additional informative studies include Herman L. Horn, "The Growth and Development of the Democratic Party in Virginia since 1890" (Ph.D. diss., Duke University, 1949) and James R. Sweeney, "Byrd and Anti-Byrd: The Struggle for Political Supremacy in Virginia, 1945–1954" (Ph.D. diss., University of Notre Dame, 1973).

JOHN S. BATTLE

Governor of Virginia

1950–1954

JOHN S. BATTLE

Last Governor of the Quiet Years

Peter R. Henriques

John S. Battle was in many ways the archetypal governor of the Byrd era. Tall, easy-going but dignified, looking exactly as a governor should, Battle was both a longtime personal friend of Senator Harry F. Byrd and a staunch supporter of his organization. After a lengthy apprenticeship in the General Assembly, Battle presided over an eminently successful administration, leaving office even more popular than when he entered.

Born into an old and distinguished southern family, Battle traced his American ancestry back to 1654 when the first John Battle settled on the west fork of the Nansemond River. The most prominent of his ancestors was his grandfather Cullen Andrews Battle, a Confederate brigadier general from Alabama. Elected to Congress after the war, he was denied his seat and, disgusted with Radical Reconstruction, moved to New Bern, North Carolina. There, on July 11, 1890, his first grandson, John Stewart Battle, was born. General Battle's influence on his grandson was considerable, for the aging general lived with John's family until his death in 1905. As Battle put it, "I've been brought up on the War Between the States." It is not surprising that Battle became a conservative southerner, distrustful of strong central government, fearful of the ruinous effects of deficit spending, and a convinced segregationist.

John moved to Virginia as a toddler when his father, the Reverend Henry Wilson Battle, an eloquent Baptist clergyman, received a call from a church in Petersburg. Always eager to be a lawyer, Battle first enrolled at Wake Forest but transferred to the University of Virginia after his father became pastor of Charlottesville's High Street Baptist Church. Admitted to the university's School of Law in 1910, John graduated Phi Beta Kappa in 1913. A brief sojourn in Texas ended unhappily when he was stricken with rheumatic fever. Returning to Charlottesville, he recovered slowly and saw only limited service in World War I, primarily promoting war bond sales. He then commenced a small law practice with Lemuel F. Smith and formed an even more important partnership in 1918 with a neighborhood sweetheart, Janie Lipscombe, a union that was to last until Battle's death in 1972. In 1919 W. Allen Perkins, a well-established attorney impressed by Battle's talent, asked him to join him as a partner.

Battle devoted most of the 1920s to law, but in 1929 he decided to try for public office in order to make personal contacts that could increase his practice. Easily winning a House of Delegates seat, Battle arrived in Richmond in January 1930 just as Harry Flood Byrd was completing his term as governor. The two men soon became close friends, a friendship that would have great effect on John Battle's political career. Believing that he had accomplished his basic goal after serving two terms, in 1933 Battle decided not to seek reelection. Then fate, in the rather unlikely form of Franklin D. Roosevelt, intervened. President Roosevelt appointed longtime state Senator Nathaniel ("Bull") Early to a federal post, and Early suggested that Battle become his successor. Battle soon was nominated and elected. This election and subsequent senatorial campaigns reflect his personal popularity as well as the lack of vitality in Virginia politics. Although Battle won in 1933 and was reelected four times (1935, 1939, 1943, and 1947), he never once faced even token opposition in either the primary or the general election.

John Battle won quick acceptance into the Senate's clublike atmosphere, and his fifteen years in the upper house were notably successful. Dignified yet friendly, he was a great storyteller, enjoyed his whiskey, and became known as one of the Senate's best poker players. Battle, however, possessed much more than a likable personality; he was also a man of high intelligence and real ability who took his responsibilities seriously. He compiled a fine record and identified himself with some progressive legislation. Yet at no time did Battle desert the Byrd machine on an issue of crucial importance. He was in no sense a maverick, and like many conservatives, his social conscience was not as sensitive as his personal conscience. By 1946 he was chairman of the powerful Finance Committee, the most important of all standing committees of the Senate. There is no evidence to indicate that Battle was one of the inner circle of organization leaders who determined policy, but he was one of the machine's most capable lieutenants for translating that policy into legislation. His long apprenticeship successfully completed, John Battle sought the perfect capstone for his political career—the Virginia governorship. A pilgrimage to Senator Byrd's home in Berryville, probably early in 1947, won him Byrd's famous "nod." Once Battle received the senator's blessing, he believed he was virtually assured of being Virginia's next governor.

But the 1949 gubernatorial primary, the most exciting and hotly contested state race during the Byrd era, was enlivened by various unforeseen developments. Blatantly undemocratic attempts to keep President Harry Truman off the state ballot in 1948 backfired and seriously damaged the Byrd organization. Indeed, Truman's victory in Virginia appeared to many as a harbinger of the possible end to the Byrd era. Second, the anti-Byrd wing of the Democratic party had gained markedly in strength during the postwar years. Although still weak, these liberals posed a much more formidable threat because of their gubernatorial candidate, Colonel Francis Pickens

Miller. A courageous and eloquent leader, Miller not only had the desire but, more importantly, the time and the money to organize more effectively than ever before. Finally, the Byrd organization was badly split. Horace Edwards, the young, ambitious, and talented mayor of Richmond, held a powerful position in the Byrd hierarchy in the 1940s as chairman of the Democratic state central committee. The urbane Edwards used his post to cultivate support for his gubernatorial ambitions. Senator Byrd, increasingly miffed, saw Edwards as a threat to his leadership. Despite Byrd's polite entreaties to wait, Edwards entered the race, declaring his decision was "irrevocable."

Consequently, by the summer of 1948 (a full year before the 1949 primary) John Battle found himself facing both Miller and Edwards. By fall the field was further crowded by the entry of Petersburg businessman Remmie Arnold, a wealthy pen manufacturer. Known for many years as one of the worst "labor baiters" in Virginia, Arnold had the support of several prominent Dixiecrats and would draw whatever limited support he received from disenchanted elements on the far right. Still, these were votes the conservative Byrd organization could ill afford to lose. There was no primary runoff law, so a plurality would mean victory.

Battle's political career did not prepare him for these changed realities. Strenuous campaigning was foreign to his experience and contrary to his easygoing personality, and organization leaders became alarmed by his lackluster performance. Byrd, deeply concerned, soon was sending Battle sharp, critical messages: "You are no doubt aware that there is a great deal of dissatisfaction over the State because you have not been active enough in your campaign and that you have as yet hardly begun to form a state organization. . . . I cannot overemphasize the disastrous consequences that will result unless you undertake these things without delay and bring them to effective accomplishment." Benjamin Muse, perceptive editor of the Manassas *Messenger,* managed to catch the essence of the Battle-Byrd relationship in his witty editorial, "Candidates Passing By": "But first comes John Battle, and let us draw near for a better view. Unlike his antagonists, Battle is transported by a machine, and you should note the big piggy bank at his side. Each time the speedometer turns, he murmurs, 'Hail Byrd' and drops a penny in the piggy bank. This singular practice is symbolic both of the statesman's loyalty to One of Virginia's Greatest Sons and of his uncompromising devotion to the policy of pay-as-you-go." In short, Battle was Byrd's candidate. This did not mean that Battle was not his own man, but that organization leaders did not hesitate to make suggestions which Battle usually followed. This is illustrated in the development of the two major issues in the campaign—public schools and the labor question.

A man deeply involved in these matters, but working behind the scenes, was E. R. ("Ebbie") Combs, chairman of the powerful state Compensation Board, clerk of the Senate, and Byrd's acknowledged lieutenant and right arm. Perhaps the most astute politician in the Old Dominion, Combs had an uncanny ability to assess a situation and suggest the proper course of action. Horace Edwards, conscious of the Byrd organization's inadequate appropriations for education, had taken the unorthodox step of proposing a 2 percent sales tax to provide badly needed public school funds. Ebbie Combs developed a plan to undercut this proposal, and Battle unveiled it on April 10, 1949. In essence, $74 million was to be made available to localities for school construction in 1950. Of the $74 million, $30 million would be a gift from a newly discovered surplus in the state treasury. The other $44 million was to be made available in low-interest loans. Once announced, the plan became an essential part of Battle's campaign. Its major appeal was a promise to solve Virginia's single most pressing problem without increasing taxes, refuting Edwards's contention that only a sales tax could raise the needed funds. As Battle put it to the voters, "I ask you that one simple question that appears to me to be the entire school financing problem. Is it not more reasonable to use the money we now have than it is to levy additional taxes of any kind?"

Combs, one of the first to see the labor question as a potentially significant issue, also urged Battle not to seek labor support—despite his essentially sympathetic record on working-class issues. Combs wrote Byrd: "Practically all of the voters who will support Battle in the final analysis will react favorably to strong criticism . . . [of] the tactics of radical labor leaders and labor agitators. I cannot think of any issue upon which we could stir up as much interest for Battle as this stand would arouse." Senator Byrd agreed, and Battle soon demanded that Miller and Edwards make their views crystal clear on controversial antiunion laws passed under Tuck, laws Battle now staunchly supported.

In July, Battle charged that he had proof of outside labor interference on Miller's behalf and subsequently released a devastating letter written by James C. Petrillo, president of the American Federation of Musicians. In it, "Czar" Petrillo, with the exception of John L. Lewis the most hated labor leader in America, advised his union members in Virginia to vote for Miller. This irrevocably linked Miller with "alien" labor bosses, and nothing he could do in the remaining weeks would change that fact. Never mind (as the Norfolk *Virginian-Pilot* noted) that there were hardly enough Petrillo union members in the entire state "to elect a justice of the peace." Never mind that Miller publicly and completely disavowed the letter. Never mind that outside labor control was a bogus issue, as Governor Battle himself later admitted. Bogus issues are sometimes the most effective, and it is certain that the Petrillo letter dealt Miller's candidacy an extremely severe, if not fatal, blow.

The more effectively Miller was portrayed as a radical, the better Battle's chances became. The Byrd machine constantly warned Edwards's supporters that by voting for Edwards, who could not win, they were in fact voting for Miller, who might destroy Virginia. Intense pressure was put on organization supporters who had strayed to Edwards, and a great many returned to the fold. Furthermore, the Republicans, although they were holding their own primary the same day, were urged by one of their leaders, Henry A. Wise, to enter the Democratic primary and vote for Battle in order to "repel this unholy invasion by aliens into our domestic affairs." John Battle, a partisan Democrat who always voted a straight ticket, called Wise's statement "highly patriotic" and made it clear that he would welcome GOP support.

Battle emerged the victor on August 2, 1949, with 43 percent of the vote. Miller, with 35 percent, finished a respectable second. Edwards polled a mere 15 percent, his political ambitions permanently destroyed. Remmie Arnold with 7 percent did about as well as everyone but Remmie Arnold expected. Celebrating what he termed "the most momentous" election in Virginia history, Byrd wrote soothingly to the victor: "The result of the election is a tremendous personal tribute to you. You captured the confidence and respect, as well as the admiration, of the Virginia people in your campaign." And this was true. Hampered at first by a lackluster campaign style, Battle eventually won votes to his side by virtue of his experience, ability, and integrity. Quite possibly he was the only candidate who could have carried the machine standard to victory in 1949. Nevertheless, Battle won only with the absolutely essential aid of Byrd and his organization. As he took the oath of office on January 18, 1950, John Battle knew this better than anyone else. He would not forget it.

The key to Battle's successes and failures as governor can be found in his personality. He was a born conciliator and harmonizer. An extremely likable individual, Battle combined natural dignity with easygoing affability. Even his political opponents, in the privacy of their personal correspondence, rarely said an unkind word about him as an individual. This unique personality formed the basis of his excellent relationship with the General Assembly. He was on a first-name basis with nine-tenths of the legislators, and his remarkable ability to get along with them became the hallmark of his administration. Yet Battle's easygoing nature and desire for harmony also had a negative side which would limit his accomplishments. Contented with life, Battle felt no compulsion to seek dragons to slay or wrongs to right. One admirer, Guy Friddell, described him as "a big-boned man but his biggest bone was his lazy bone." Occasionally, Battle would even follow a course of action he personally believed to be mistaken because it was what Senator Byrd or other organization leaders wanted. The desire to please Byrd and to do a good job as governor usually presented no conflict for Battle. Yet sometimes a choice had to be made.

An example of such conflict arose during the 1950 General Assembly as the result of popular pressure to reduce taxes. The governor's stand on taxes was clear. In his inaugural address he had asserted, "I regret that I cannot recommend any decreases in taxes at this time." A month later he responded to a tax cut proposal with the words, "I don't think the taxpayers can hope for much relief. . . . We need every penny of revenue we can get." A week later a new tax reduction bill was introduced by none other than Harry F. Byrd, Jr. A boyish-looking thirty-five, derisively called "Sonny Boy" by his opponents, Harry, Jr., was by far the youngest member of the Virginia Senate, which he had joined in 1948. Byrd's bill tied tax refunds to future state surpluses. If state income exceeded estimated revenue by a certain percentage, then individuals and corporations would have their taxes reduced according to a specified formula.

Battle personally believed the Byrd measure was a "bad bill." However, he ultimately decided that in good conscience he could not oppose it. Young Harry's political reputation was at stake, and this was the governor's way of at least partly repaying the debt he felt he owed to the Byrd family. To make matters worse, Battle had to intervene to defend the bill from being weakened by an amendment proposed by Armistead Boothe limiting the measure to only two years unless repassed by the General Assembly. Boothe's effort narrowly failed; the Byrd proposal became law. The large surpluses of the 1940s continued, and for three years Virginia taxpayers received refunds totaling approximately $20 million. Such an amazing feat drew national attention. Young Byrd boasted, "Virginia has received a million dollars of favorable publicity as a result of the bill."

In fact, the Byrd tax bill was a disaster. Fiscally handcuffing Battle's administration, it drained off $20 million desperately needed to help alleviate pressing problems. Proponents claimed that common morality demanded that the surplus be returned to the taxpayers. Robert Whitehead, the most eloquent and informed critic of the Byrd machine, spoke most scathingly about the morality of the Byrd tax law:

> In reply to your statement about the moral issue involved, I have only this to say: When, as now, afflicted children in our mental institutions are forced to sleep on the floors; when, as now, the mentally disturbed patients in our mental hospitals incarcerated behind locked doors are expected to be restored to health and society on $2.02 a day; when, as now, persons suffering from tuberculosis are being put on the waiting list and denied admittance to our sanatoria because we do not have the beds to care for them; when, as now, public schools are swamped with children who are denied teachers meeting the minimum state requirements—all because we do not have the money—I say it is morally wrong to wilfully and deliberately deplete the state treasury by granting tax credits.

John Battle was not a reformer by nature. Nevertheless, supporting the Byrd tax bill was one of his most serious mistakes and sharply limited what he would accomplish as governor. The act continued to play havoc with Virginia's finances until finally repealed in 1956.

In only one area did Battle spend lavishly: public schools. The crux of his program was contained in House Bill no. 96, introduced early in the 1950 General Assembly, making $45 million available for school construction without requiring matching local funds during 1950–51. Battle defended these unmatched grants because some localities, often those most in need of new construction, could not match state funds, and consequently such a requirement would only aggravate a crisis generated by decades of neglect and the postwar "baby boom." Battle forces beat down all efforts to require matching funds and then passed the bill by lopsided majorities. It was the piece of legislation in which the governor took greatest pride. By the time he left office early in 1954 the state Board of Education had approved school construction expenditures for eighty-six counties and twenty-seven cities totaling approximately $132 million, and localities had spent an additional $120 million on their own. Certainly the school crisis did not end as a result of Battle's education program, and grave deficiencies remained. Nevertheless, by appropriating large sums of money and by initiating the program of unrestricted state grants, Battle at least pointed Virginia in the proper direction.

The governor saw another benefit in unrestricted state grants: they might help preserve Virginia's segregated school system in the face of federal court decrees. The Battle program was geared, in part at least, to shore up the state's "separate but equal" system of public education. Later, when Virginia went down the road of massive resistance against the *Brown* decision, some expressed surprise, yet there were numerous hints during the Battle years of willingness to go to extreme lengths to preserve segregation. By 1950 there were nine state-owned parks scattered across the Commonwealth, all of them, except one located in Prince Edward County, reserved exclusively for whites. Failing to win even limited access to the other parks, blacks filed suit in federal courts in 1951 to force Virginia to open its state parks to blacks on the grounds that the present system violated their constitutional rights under the Fourteenth Amendment. Governor Battle took a hard line against this new militancy and warned of dangerous consequences—including an end to Virginia's park system. Faced with the threat of federal action, the General Assembly drafted a bill designed to put the parks in private hands and empowering the governor to close them. Although these provisions fortunately never were utilized, prosegregation sentiment was so strong that the bill passed both houses with only a single dissenting vote.

No specific legislation was passed concerning public school integration during Battle's administration, but there was considerable speculation on the topic. In keeping with his habit of not seeking trouble, Battle adopted a do-nothing-and-hope-for-the-best attitude. Not only did he discourage "premature" legislation, he even refused to allow a study group to plan for the eventuality of an adverse court ruling. Summarizing Battle's lack of action, the Roanoke *World-News* wrote, "Virginia has taken an ostrich-like approach to the problem of school segregation."

Battle was lucky, and the storm did not break while he was governor.

He was not as fortunate in another crisis where race was also the central issue: the "Martinsville Seven," seven black youths sentenced to death for beating and brutally raping a white woman in January 1949. In and out of the courts during the next two years, the case became a cause célèbre of leftists who insisted the youths were "victims of a jimcrow frameup." As the case neared its tragic denouement, Battle was deluged with over 10,000 letters, some from as far away as the Soviet Union. Protesters came to Richmond in large numbers, and to Battle's credit he met with a delegation of their leaders. Around-the-clock prayer vigils were held in front of the Capitol, but such protests actually obscured the fundamental issue: the severity of the punishment. The tragic truth was that the seven faced execution because they were black. No white man had ever been condemned to death in Virginia for rape alone, even when the victim was white.

John Battle conscientiously and sincerely examined the case in an effort to see justice done. However, either his own racial philosophy blinded him to the fact that the men were to be executed solely because they were black, or prejudice prevented him from seeing anything particularly wrong with such an occurrence. Battle would have liked to have saved a couple of the youths less involved in the crime, but he did not want to appear to give in to radical protesters and eventually concluded there was nothing he could do. The final acts of the grim tragedy were played out in February 1951 in the largest mass execution for a single crime ever staged in Virginia.

Although Battle received much publicity, generally unwelcomed, for his role in the Martinsville Seven case, under a much more intense national spotlight at the 1952 Democratic national convention he had his "finest hour" as governor of Virginia. Many Virginians still remember John Battle's stunning speech, when, in Ebbie Combs's words, he "reversed a whole trend of events" and saved Virginia from being thrown out of the gathering. The facts are not quite as heroic as the memories, but Battle's role was still of fundamental importance.

Relations between Virginia's Democratic party and the national Democratic administration had deteriorated to such an extent that when Harry S Truman once entered a room in which Battle was standing, the governor deliberately left by a side door to avoid greeting the president of the United States. Then a long anti-Truman campaign, often abetted by Byrd, bore unexpected fruit on March 29, 1952, when the president suddenly decided not to seek reelection. A plethora of Democratic hopefuls quickly emerged, but only one man seemed likely to unify Democrats, North and South, right and left, Governor Adlai E. Stevenson of Illinois, and he had not yet entered the race. If the nominee was a real question mark, another question was whether the South might bolt to Republican Dwight D. Eisenhower. Two totally different and antagonistic strategies emerged at the Democratic national convention. The "unifier" strategy, espoused by moderates and conservatives, maintained that only a united party and southern electoral votes could defeat General Eisenhower. The opposing view, the "sectionalist" strategy, insisted the Democrats could not match Eisenhower's popular appeal and should stress instead a progressive party program that would strongly appeal to labor, blacks, and other minority groups. Such a strategy deliberately discounted the South, and its proponents were willing to anger the region's conservatives in order to ensure a liberal victory in Chicago and hopefully in November.

A clash was virtually inevitable and not long in coming. On the first day of the convention, Monday, July 21, the liberals succeeded in having a loyalty oath adopted—the Moody Resolution. The session was tumultuous, and Battle unsuccessfully demanded a roll-call vote. In reality the resolution did little more than ensure that the convention nominees would be placed on state ballots, something Virginia law already provided. On Tuesday the resolution was amended to make it so innocuous that even Deep South states like Alabama, Georgia, and Mississippi had no trouble accepting it. Only Virginia, joined by South Carolina and Louisiana, remained adamant.

With the convention leadership desperate for a compromise, the Virginians made it clear they would accept only total capitulation, for the Moody Resolution had played directly into the hands of Byrd and Tuck. They came to Chicago willing and perhaps even anxious to be thrown out and thus had little to lose. If they won their seats, something that seemed unlikely by Wednesday, they would win on their own terms. If the convention threw them out for refusing to sign the resolution, then the onus for the break would be on the national party. However, the split that Byrd and Tuck desired was viewed by John Battle with considerable misgiving.

Although Virginia delegates were denied the right to vote on Wednesday, they still retained their seats and remained on the official list of delegates. If they remained as spectators but not as participants, the dispute might simply fizzle out as balloting for the nomination began. To avert this possibility, opponents of the oath agreed to have Louisiana, the first of the three recalcitrant states on the roll call, yield to Virginia. Then Battle would submit a parliamentary inquiry to permanent chairman Sam Rayburn demanding a specific ruling on the status of the three states. It was nearly 7:00 P.M. on Thursday, July 24, when Louisiana attempted to yield to Virginia, but the entire Minnesota contingent challenged Louisiana's right to speak. Louisiana managed to yield, but the scene was chaotic.

Battle's long-awaited opportunity had finally come. Exhausted by days of intense activity, fully conscious of the high stakes, excited and nervous, Battle began, "Mr. Chairman, this is John S. Battle, Governor of Mississippi . . ." He quickly corrected himself, but the slip demonstrates the tremendous pressure he felt. Urged by his colleagues to go to the platform to explain Virginia's stand, Battle started in that direction. Ex-Governor William Tuck, buoyed by drinks at dinner and in a rebellious mood, also headed for the platform. Possibly he only wanted to give Battle moral support, but more likely he planned to give the convention a piece of his mind. Battle, completely absorbed in his own task, knew nothing of Tuck's intentions, and to that degree stories about "the great footrace" between Battle and Tuck are inaccurate.

After a brief discussion backstage, Rayburn recognized Battle. It was 7:22 P.M. John Battle, who had always dreamed of being a great orator like his father and grandfather, now fulfilled his dream before a national television and radio audience of perhaps 75 million people. Speaking with dignity and eloquence, he assured the convention that Virginia law required the nominees of the party's national convention be on the ballot. He continued to his central point:

> What, my Democratic friends, we in Virginia object to is the language of this Resolution under which it may be construed, as we construe it, that this Delegation and the Democrats of Virginia, insofar as we are able to commit them, would be committed to support any future action which might be taken by this Convention. We are unwilling, frankly, to take that Pledge. We have taken that position from the beginning. We do not recede from it now. We are simply reserving to ourselves the freedom enunciated by Thomas Jefferson—in whose County I happen to live—the great patron saint of this Party, who believed in freedom . . . Freedom of thought and freedom of action, and we are not going to sign any Pledge or any commitment which will prevent that freedom which we claim for ourselves and believe you would like for yourselves.

The speech lasted four minutes. By the time he had finished Battle had accomplished at least one noteworthy feat. The tumultuous convention was silent. If nothing else, Battle had won their attention. Although he did not budge from Virginia's original position, his tone was friendly and conciliatory. His speech contained no arrogance, insults, or threats. Still, moving as it was, the speech itself did not ensure Virginia's place in the convention. Indeed, it forced a sad and reluctant Sam Rayburn to rule that the three states had not complied with the rules.

Then Maryland's chairman, Lansdale G. Sasscer, moved that since Battle's speech was in "substantial compliance" with the Moody Resolution, Virginia be seated. Rayburn accepted the motion, and a crucial roll-call vote followed, but it caught many delegates by surprise, genuinely puzzled as to how they should vote. Illinois, for example, initially voted 45–15 against Virginia. Then key politicians realized that Estes Kefauver backers and northern liberals were trying to drive conservatives out of the convention to enhance the chances of the Tennessee senator. The Illinois delegation promptly reversed its vote, 52–8 for Virginia, a turning point in the struggle.

Chairman Rayburn patiently waited for enough states to change their votes to ensure victory. The final vote was 615 yes, 529 no. The Old Dominion had won its right to be seated and had won it on its own terms.

Battle's speech was of considerable significance in triggering the chain of events that followed. Certainly things would have been different if Tuck had taken the platform. In a sense, Battle went against Byrd's wishes. Yet Byrd was probably of a mixed mind about the outcome. Although "in a way" he wanted Virginia forced out, he undoubtedly was relieved that its delegates got both to make their point and keep their seats without any compromise whatever. Battle's performance at Chicago made him the hero of the hour to countless Virginians, 3,000 of whom turned out to welcome him home to Richmond. Battle's role in the national convention added greatly to his stature and popularity and gave him a kind of charisma of his own.

In the ensuing presidential campaign, Battle, fulfilling a pledge he made at Chicago, endorsed Adlai Stevenson and campaigned for him. Since neither Byrd nor Tuck backed Stevenson because of his connection with "Trumanism," Battle's actions established him as a man of independence, endearing him to the more liberal wing of the party. Still, he did it in such a way that he remained friendly with Byrd. After Byrd's famous October 17 speech against Stevenson, Battle played a less visible role in the campaign. Eisenhower's sweep of Virginia also helped maintain this cordial relationship. If Stevenson had won, Byrd might have resented Battle's action, but in the glow of victory he was anxious to let bygones be bygones and to avoid any major split in the organization with a gubernatorial race coming up in 1953. He wrote Battle a flattering letter, and their close and friendly relationship remained intact.

It should be emphasized that the drama of the Martinsville Seven Case and the excitement of the 1952 Democratic national convention were the exceptions and not the rule. Most of Battle's time as governor was taken up with the commonplace rather than the dramatic. A majority of his duties were of a ceremonial nature—greeting visiting dignitaries, addressing a local Kiwanis club, crowning a new Miss Virginia, meeting a group of eagle scouts, or raising money for a worthwhile charity. In the words of one Washington *Post* observer, "It is in this respect, I think Battle is at his best. Blessed with handsome features and a natural dignity, he has been a worthy leader and an unmistakably devoted public servant. He has been every inch a governor."

In 1954 Battle resumed his successful law practice in Charlottesville, but occasionally he found himself back in the spotlight. He was Virginia's favorite-son candidate at the 1956 Democratic convention. Although a convinced segregationist, Battle broke with the Byrd organization on massive resistance, serving a two-year term on the newly established U.S. Civil Rights Commission (1957–59) even though he often sharply disagreed with its conclusions. His political ambition did not die. In 1958 Byrd announced he would not seek reelection. Battle aspired to fill Byrd's seat—as did former Governor

Tuck. Fearful of the disruptive effects of such a race, Byrd changed his mind and ran for a fifth time.

In failing health, Battle saw his son, William C. Battle, win the Democratic gubernatorial nomination in 1969 only to lose, narrowly, in the general election to Republican Linwood Holton. After he suffered a stroke in 1970, Battle's health further declined, and he was admitted to a Charlottesville nursing home. He died there on April 9, 1972, at the age of eighty-one.

John S. Battle was the perfect man to govern Virginia in the last of the quiet years. With dignity, personal charm, and real ability, he was the kind of executive most Virginians wanted. By reflecting the Byrd organization at its best, Battle made Virginians proud of him and proud of their state. When he left office in January 1954 he was, as the Washington *Post* noted, "the most universally popular figure in Virginia public life." It was an accomplishment any man could view with satisfaction.

SOURCES

The Battle papers at the Virginia State Library and the University of Virginia are of limited use. Papers still in the Battle family are only slightly more helpful. The Harry F. Byrd and E. R. Combs papers (University of Virginia) are very revealing, as are the papers at the same repository of the major opponents of the Byrd machine—Francis Pickens Miller, Robert Whitehead, and Martin Hutchinson.

An excellent overview of Virginia politics in 1949 is available in V. O. Key's *Southern Politics in State and Nation* (New York, 1949). Also see J. Harvie Wilkinson III, *Harry Byrd and the Changing Face of Virginia Politics, 1945–1966* (Charlottesville, 1968); Francis Pickens Miller, *Man from the Valley: Memoirs of a 20th-Century Virginian* (Chapel Hill, N.C., 1971); Peter R. Henriques, "The Organization Challenged: John S. Battle, Francis P. Miller, and Horace Edwards Run for Governor in 1949," *Virginia Magazine of History and Biography* 82 (1974): 372–406; James R. Sweeney, "Revolt in Virginia: Harry F. Byrd and the 1952 Presidential Election," *Virginia Magazine of History and Biography* 86 (1978): 180–95; and Peter R. Henriques, "The Byrd Organization Crushes a Liberal Challenge, 1950–1953," *Virginia Magazine of History and Biography* 87 (1979): 2–29.

The most complete account of John S. Battle and his administration, including a full bibliography, is Peter R. Henriques, "John S. Battle and Virginia Politics, 1948–1953" (Ph.D. diss.: University of Virginia, 1971).

THOMAS B. STANLEY

Reluctant Resister

Ronald L. Heinemann

On May 17, 1954, the Supreme Court of the United States held that racial segregation in public education is "inherently unequal" and, therefore, in violation of the Fourteenth Amendment to the Constitution. This landmark ruling kindled a revolution in American life and, in particular, turned southern society on its head. For Thomas B. Stanley, who four months before had been inaugurated governor of Virginia, the decision shattered the calm he had hoped would distinguish his term and transformed it into a firestorm of acrimony and demagoguery not witnessed in the Old Dominion since the Funder-Readjuster clashes of the 1880s. Massive resistance became the watchword of the Byrd organization, dominating the political life of the state and diverting attention from more pressing needs.

Virginia could ill afford such a diversion, for it was in the midst of a social and economic metamorphosis of its own. Favored by location and low-tax fiscal policies, the Old Dominion had lured many new industries and residents in the postwar years. The population was becoming less rural, less conservative, less politically predictable, and less satisfied with state appropriations ranking Virginia near the bottom in education, mental health, and welfare expenditures. Leaders of the long-dominant Democratic organization, slow to respond to these conditions, chose Congressman Tom Stanley to preside over the new Virginia of the turbulent mid–1950s. Among the most conservative members of the machine, Stanley had little to recommend him except longevity of public service.

Thomas Bahnson Stanley was a twentieth-century Horatio Alger—poor farm boy, "runaway," bank teller, furniture manufacturer, millionaire, congressman, and governor. Born near Spencer in Henry County on July 16, 1890, he was the son of a Confederate veteran who, as a carpenter and self-sufficient farmer, provided his family of seven much love but little material reward. "Bahns," as Tom was called by friends, grew up knowing the value of hard work and a dollar. At age seventeen, dissatisfied with the drudgery of farm life, he left home over the protestations of his father for the West Virginia coalfields. Two months in the mines convinced him to return to the farm, but his ambition had not been stifled. Having pressed the meager educational facilities of his area to their limits, three years later he left home once again,

THOMAS B. STANLEY

Governor of Virginia

1954–1958

this time for Poughkeepsie, New York, to enroll at Eastman National Business College; he emerged in 1912 to begin his rise to fame and fortune.

During the next dozen years he held several bookkeeping and banking jobs, acquiring more responsibility and becoming a respected member of the communities in which he lived. However, it was his marriage in 1918 to Anne Pocahontas Bassett, daughter of the owner of Bassett Furniture Company, that proved to be the most propitious step of his career. Joining the Bassett Company two years later, he began to learn the furniture business. His future seemed secure, but in the tradition of the self-made man, Tom Stanley struck out on his own and established the Stanley Furniture Company in 1924. With sales of $800,000 in its first year, the company grew rapidly, and a small village, Stanleytown, was built for employees. But the depression of 1929 threatened to terminate Stanley's budding entrepreneurial career. Only the financial assistance of an old banking friend and extreme cost-cutting measures enabled the company to survive; Stanley himself took a 50 percent cut in pay, and his employees agreed to several pay cuts rather than be laid off. By 1933 there was a small profit, and within a decade Stanley Furniture almost doubled in size.

Although Stanley remained president of his firm until 1962, in these depression years he embarked upon a second career. After serving several years on the Henry County School Board, Bahns faced the pleasant dilemma in 1929 of being nominated for the House of Delegates by local Republicans as well as Democrats; being a lifelong Democrat, he accepted the call of Harry F. Byrd's party. He won the primary and general elections handily and was reelected eight times with little opposition.

Stanley was not an active initiator of legislation in Richmond, and his conservative stands caused the Roanoke *Leader* to label him "perhaps the most reactionary member of the whole legislature of Virginia." Mindful of the deficiencies of his own schooling, however, he became a strong supporter of public education, a commitment to be sorely tested during his governorship. Through his work with governors and House committees and his contacts with organization stalwarts Byrd and William M. Tuck, with whom his political future would be inextricably entwined, he discovered that loyalty and longevity were the requisites for eventual success. As one friend put it when renominating Stanley for the House in 1939, "If we keep him down there long enough, he may well become the State's first citizen."

In 1942 Stanley was elected speaker of the House, his ingratiating manner, which made few enemies and many friends, helping him defeat several rivals. He also demonstrated keen political sense by collecting written statements of support from a majority of delegates before the party caucus met. Able promotion of Governor Darden's legislative programs and his perpetual conviviality led to reelection in 1944 and 1946. Adhering to a recent three-term tradition for speakers, Stanley announced in August 1945 that he would not seek another term in the House in 1947. Coming on the heels of failure to receive Byrd's support for governor in 1945, this spawned rumors of an early political retirement. However, in March 1946, when Fifth District Representative Thomas Burch disclosed plans to retire, Stanley declared his candidacy for Congress on the same day. He easily won the primary and general elections, and the Republicans did not bother to contest his reelection bids in 1948, 1950, and 1952.

As in Richmond, Stanley's years as a Washington lawmaker were unspectacular. He introduced no major legislation and was not an active participant in floor debate. A party regular at first, he then tended to follow Byrd's lead, voting for the Taft-Hartley labor bill and most defense appropriations while opposing liberal measures. These stands ran counter to the views of most congressional Democrats, but Stanley remained more of a party loyalist than Byrd, continuing to endorse the national Democratic nominees in presidential races. A "watchdog" in the Byrd mold, Stanley fought excessive federal spending and the growing bureaucracy, was attentive to constituent needs, and in 1950 became chairman of the House Administration Committee. Nevertheless, Stanley's heart was not in legislative work or in Washington's fast-paced social life, and he was thankful when the long-sought "nod" finally came his way.

When he resigned from the House to run for governor in 1953, he was praised by several colleagues for his "warmth of personality," his "charming wife," his integrity, and his steadfast conservatism. In no small way these qualities were the basis for his success in Virginia politics. Tall and handsome, Stanley was a gregarious glad-hander who campaigned best among the people from whom he had risen; it was once said that he knew the names of ten of the first twenty people he met in any county seat in Virginia. Inarticulate and awkward in formal press conferences, he preferred person-to-person campaigning to political addresses and debates. Wealth gave him a certain sophistication, but he never forgot his poor, farm-boy roots, and membership in numerous organizations brought him a host of friends.

Stanley's affable manner reflected the comforts and amenities of his home life. His wife Anne, a petite and attractive native of Henry County, was (in their son's opinion) a vivacious, "tough little lady," who was a "splendid asset" to her husband's political career. The couple reared three children on a farm near Stanleytown where Tom constructed an English manor house called Stoneleigh, and Stanley eventually acquired two other farms, which he turned into thriving livestock operations. Robust, broad-boned, well-coordinated, and indefatigable, Stanley loved the out-of-doors, often spending his spare time hunting and fishing in Henry County. Business success enabled the Stanleys to become local philanthropists, beginning with the financing of Stanleytown's first school in 1928. They later donated a quarter-million-dollar recreation center to the town and supported construction of Stanley Library at Ferrum Junior College where Stanley was an active trustee.

Stanley was generous to the Virginia Democratic party as well. His financial contributions quickly caught the eye of its leaders, who likened his background to that of Harry Byrd. Both had converted the tenets of hard work and thrift into successful business careers, an experience which fashioned a mutual fiscal conservatism and confirmed for them the value of self-help and the folly of government interference. This conservative orthodoxy, combined with loyalty, money, and his wide victory margins, propelled Stanley into the front ranks of the organization. Even so, he was not an inner circle intimate. His relationship with Byrd was always cordial. They respected and liked one another, but Stanley's instincts were less political. Furthermore, he was somewhat unpredictable in public forums and thus was rarely consulted on major issues or strategies.

Stanley's accession to the governorship was clearly a matter of "a man whose time had come." There had been talk of his running in 1941 and again in 1945. After John Battle became a candidate in June 1948, apparently with organization approval, there was concern that Stanley might run even without the "nod." Byrd met with Stanley and he agreed to wait; nevertheless, he made it clear to the organization leadership that his turn was next. And in January 1953, with organization support, Tom Stanley announced that his hat was in the ring. Competition appeared in the forms of Charles Fenwick, state senator from Arlington, and W. Russell Hatchett, a Virginia Beach realtor whose candidacy proved ephemeral. Liberals, disheartened by a 1952 runoff law preventing a plurality winner in the primary, were reluctant to challenge the machine. Delegate Robert Whitehead of Lovingston announced his candidacy, subject to receiving ample campaign pledges, but withdrew when they were not forthcoming.

The primary campaign that followed was a lackluster one. The similarity of the Stanley and Fenwick platforms caused James J. Kilpatrick, editor of the Richmond *News Leader,* to label the candidates "Tweedledee and Tweedledum." The vitriolic editor privately urged Byrd to inject a little life into Stanley who, he said, was leaving a "vapid and innocuous impression. . . . So far he looks like a pathetically weak sister." Although both candidates were members of the organization, Fenwick was thought to be the more independent and somewhat liberal, prompting most of the courthouse crowd and the General Assembly to support Stanley. He won handily in July by a two-to-one margin. The general election, however, would be a different story.

Coming on the heels of Republican successes in state and nation the preceding year, the gubernatorial campaign of 1953 was reminiscent of that in 1929. Although Hoover's coattails had proved weak in the twenties, Virginia Republicans were hopeful that Eisenhower's popularity would overcome years of failure. Their hopes were further buoyed by selection of Ted Dalton of Radford as their nominee. Former Montgomery County Commonwealth's attorney, state senator for ten years, and Republican national committeeman, Dalton was a popular and vigorous campaigner known for his candor on the issues. He immediately put the Stanley campaign on the defensive by calling for repeal of the poll tax, lowering the voting age to eighteen, review of absentee voter laws, and revision of the state tax system. He appeared to be more flexible on public financing than Stanley and prudently suggested that Virginia should be prepared to act when desegregation cases before the Supreme Court were decided. Compensating for the dearth of grass-roots Republican organization and money, little of which was forthcoming from the national party, Dalton waged an issue-oriented campaign.

Stung by Dalton's hard-hitting tactics, Stanley rejected the vote for eighteen-year-olds but did not know what to do about the poll tax. On this and other issues he became ambiguous and evasive. Often he did not have time to answer questions, promised to say more later, or simply had "no comment." Feeling the Republican pressure, Stanley and the organization leaders switched to their own offensive, accusing Dalton of making wild promises, "pulling figures out of the air," and using "cry-baby tactics"; they labeled the GOP platform "asinine" and even waved the old flag of Black Reconstruction to frighten Old Dominion voters with memories of "carpetbaggers and Republicans." Stanley came out in favor of increased benefits for the elderly, higher teacher salaries, and a road equalization plan by which more highway money would be made available to the mountain counties. Late in the campaign he finally endorsed a referendum on the poll-tax issue, but this delayed gambit only confirmed his image as an inept, fumbling campaigner.

Behind the scenes, a prophetic correspondence was going on between newsman James J. Kilpatrick and Harry Byrd. Worried that the journalist might turn against the organization, Byrd cautioned that defeat in 1953 would leave the party open to the "radicals"; he defended Stanley as "an honorable man who will adhere to . . . sound principles." Kilpatrick, a friend of the organization, replied with a scathing critique of Stanley: "Throughout the whole year of campaigning—going back to last January—Tom never indicated the slightest ability to think for himself, to make tough decisions promptly, to speak knowledgeably about the State government. He has shown no imagination, no stature, no drive, nothing to recommend him to the voters. He has been wishy-washy, mealy-mouthed, half-hearted, equivocal; he has stumbled around over the simplest expression of opinion. He is not doing the Organization one damn bit of good. He isn't an asset, he's a liability, and Harry, damned if I think the Organization can afford a liability in the Governor's office for the next four years." Stating that he would editorially support neither Stanley nor Dalton, Kilpatrick criticized the machine for its perpetuation of a tired, inefficient bureaucracy and its inability to face the future by attracting "first class young people."

The final blow to Democratic complacency came in mid-October when Sidney Kellam, Democratic campaign director and longtime Byrd associate, was indicted with five others for conspiracy to avoid paying federal income taxes. Denying the charge, Kellam resigned his position, claiming the Republicans had trumped up the case to embarrass the state's Democrats. Nothing ever came of the case, and the indictment was withdrawn after the election. Ironically, the Kellam incident, instead of harming the organization, probably revitalized efforts to defeat a suddenly formidable opponent.

As the campaign moved into its final stage, Dalton raised one issue too many. Seeking an alternative to raising gasoline taxes to pay for highways, Dalton offered a "pay-as-you-use" program for road building to be financed with special construction revenue bonds totaling $100 million over a five-year period. Senator Byrd, who had played an insignificant role thus far, immediately branded the plan unconstitutional and said he would "oppose with all the vigor I possess this plan of Senator Dalton to junk our sound fiscal system based upon freedom from debt." Along with Governor John S. Battle and former Governor Tuck, he jumped into the fray to repulse this attack on "pay-as-you-go," the bedrock of organization orthodoxy. Said one Seventh District Democrat, "Dalton couldn't have hurt himself more if he'd come out for licensed prostitution." The Radford lawyer was portrayed as a "big spender," a label he tried to offset by pledging no tax increases, but the damage had been done. Stanley swept to a 43,000-vote victory, winning eight of ten congressional districts. Dalton, whom a friend described as "utterly devastated," attributed his defeat to an error of conviction.

Stanley's 10 percent margin of victory was the smallest ever for an organization candidate seeking statewide office. Nonetheless, it was still a substantial triumph, and it is not likely that Dalton's tactics in the last two weeks changed the outcome. Organization muscle and money, not issues, decided the result. Democrats outspent Republicans by almost two-to-one, with Stanley's personal contribution far exceeding Dalton's, $42,000 to $5,000. The diminished victory margin was attributable to Stanley's "colorless and disappointing campaign" and Ted Dalton's vigor. Bolstered by a temporarily reinvigorated Republican party, Dalton rode a wave of dissatisfaction reflecting the changing nature of Virginia society. Perhaps the real loser was Tom Stanley, who emerged a discredited politician, the figurehead of a political machine whose power seemed to be ebbing. Calls for new blood abounded; forces from within and without the machine were demanding change. Stanley's business experience and glad-handing politics had not prepared him for such challenges.

Thomas Bahnson Stanley's governorship did not begin auspiciously. On a warm, damp day in January 1954, he pledged his allegiance to the Virginia constitution and then proceeded to violate his major campaign promise by calling for a one cent per gallon increase in the gasoline tax. This move confirmed the fears of some that the governor was indeed inept and may well have cost him much of his influence with the General Assembly. Compounding his plight was the departure from the capital of the seventy-eight-year-old E. R. Combs because of ill health. Adviser to half-a-dozen governors, Ebbie Combs had been Byrd's man in Richmond, and his absence was critical.

The major controversy of the 1954 legislative session was fierce debate over retention of the Byrd Automatic Tax Reduction Law, allowing income tax credits for individuals and corporations when revenues exceeded budget estimates by 5 percent. New voices in the Assembly, largely from the neglected urban areas of Northern Virginia and Norfolk, demanded this money for schools and hospitals which, they claimed, were desperately needed. These "Young Turks" were youthful organization men dissatisfied with the standpattism of the machine; nor were they willing to serve the long organization apprenticeship of being seen and not heard. Stanley took no strong position, mildly favoring retention but claiming it was a legislative matter. At the eleventh hour a compromise was arranged, supported by the governor, which allowed for an appropriation of $2.2 million of the predicted $7 million in tax credit funds to be spent for teachers' salaries, colleges, and hospitals.

Although Stanley's impact on this debate had been negligible, several pieces of legislation received his vigorous support—a strengthened right-to-work law, increased appropriations for mental hospitals, a reduction in the number of holidays for state employees, and a study of the capital needs of Virginia for the next six years—all of which passed. Despite his lobbying efforts, the gasoline tax bill died in committee.

The spring of 1954 was notable for its ending and beginning of historical chapters. The Army-McCarthy hearings were winding down; Dien Bien Phu, a little-known outpost in northern Vietnam, fell to the Communists of Ho Chi Minh; and the Supreme Court, in its *Brown* ruling, reversed a fifty-eight-year-old decision that had legitimized racial segregation in America. The day after the Court's announcement was Stanley's finest in the Governor's Mansion. Calling for "cool heads, calm study, and sound judgments," he stated, "I am confident the people of Virginia will receive the opinion of the Supreme Court calmly and take time to carefully and dispassionately consider the situation before coming to conclusions on steps which should be taken." He contemplated no immediate action but indicated that he would meet shortly with state and local leaders to consider plans "in keeping with the edict of the court. Views of leaders of both races will be invited in the course of these studies." Politicians, editors, and school officials applauded the governor's moderation, but other Virginians were less jubilant. Within days the governor's office was deluged with hundreds of letters, some expressing fears of race-mixing and charging Communist plots. Garland ("Peck") Gray, who was to figure prominently in the massive resistance movement, urged Stanley to make a fight against the decision or face the "destruction of our culture" and "intermarriage between the races." He warned the governor not to counsel with educators, clergy, and Negroes. Most letters, however, were devoid of hysteria, and many commended the governor for his calm approach.

While informing his correspondents as well as the public that schools would remain segregated for the 1954–55 academic year, Stanley avoided precipitous action and met with a variety of groups, including the state Board of Education and prominent black leaders such as Oliver Hill and P. B. Young. He wrote to Gray, "The Court's decision, of course, was unwelcome and distasteful. I do not agree with the decision, but I believe defiance of the Court would tend to aggravate the situation and deprive us of the chance of coming to some understanding that would minimize the effects of the ruling on our social and educational system." Nevertheless, Stanley was beginning to retreat from his initial remarks, and by late June 1954 his public reversal was complete. He declared that he would use all means at his disposal to continue segregated education in Virginia; in lieu of that he suggested the possible repeal of section 129 of the state constitution which provided for the maintenance of public free schools. This shocked even the segregationists, who did not want to be portrayed as school closers.

What caused this shift is unclear. Failure of the Supreme Court to specify the timing or the method of carrying out its edict encouraged delay, evasion, and obstruction. In Virginia, as in the Deep South where the response from the beginning had been more critical, the forces of negativism overcame the voices of reason. Although most white Virginians preferred segregated schools, the equanimity with which they accepted token integration four years later suggests that a similar course might have worked in 1955 or 1956. But organization leaders perceived race as an issue with which to maintain their hegemony so recently threatened by Miller, Dalton, and the Young Turks. Massive resistance was designed, in effect, to revitalize a dying political machine.

There was more to this policy, however, than mere politics. Organization faithful, including Tom Stanley, believed separate-but-equal was the proper basis for race relations in the South. And the loudest voices sustaining this philosophy came from the Southside, heartland of the Byrd machine, where fears of race-mixing were strongest. The representatives of this region—Watkins M. Abbitt, William Tuck, Garland Gray, and Mills E. Godwin—were highly placed organization leaders whose views would become even more influential in the next few years. Political profit and racial conviction, therefore, along with resolve to counter another instance of federal intrusion, dictated the organization's response to desegregation. The governor merely followed that lead, abandoning his original moderate position.

In August 1954 he appointed a thirty-two-man Commission on Public

Education to design Virginia's answer to the recent Court decision. Composed entirely of General Assembly members, it was all white, all male, and devoid of educators. Stanley justified its makeup on the ground that the legislature would eventually have to deal with the question, but his selection exposed the primary objective: to maintain organization control. Only two Republicans were appointed; no liberals or Young Turks. All regions were represented, but membership was disproportionately weighted in favor of the Southside and the First and Eighth Districts, where blacks and whites were nearly equal in numbers.

Stanley had little to do with the commission eventually headed by Garland Gray. While it deliberated, Stanley was busy with plans (formalized a year later) for a modest construction program for mental hospitals, medical schools, colleges, and prisons financed out of general fund surpluses, to be increased by earlier payment of taxes. The governor lavishly praised this accelerated tax collection gimmick as a means of avoiding a sales tax and bond issues.

When the Gray Commission presented its plan to Stanley in November 1955, he wholeheartedly endorsed its recommendations for a local assignment scheme giving school boards discretionary power to assign pupils to schools for reasons other than race. In the event of school closings or integration, the commission suggested tuition grants enabling children to attend private schools. Since the Virginia constitution forbade use of public funds for private schooling, the report asked for a special session of the General Assembly to initiate steps to permit such grants. Viewed within the context of the times, the Gray Plan struck a reasonable chord, allowing localities to integrate if they chose but advocating legislation to help them avoid it if they wished.

Almost at once, the report came under attack. Blacks labeled it another subterfuge to circumvent the law, while moderates like Ted Dalton and Robert Whitehead feared tuition grants would undermine public education. On the other hand, segregationists feared the plan might allow some integration in the state. Among the latter were the Defenders of State Sovereignty and Individual Liberties. Formed in October 1954, the Defenders had a statewide following but were strongest in the Southside, particularly in Prince Edward County, the site of one of the original desegregation cases. Here the cries of "Integration—Never" were powerful enough to convince Byrd and others to reject the token integration of the Gray Plan and champion total defiance.

Stanley, once again, was caught in the middle by this about-face. A November special session of the Assembly authorized a statewide referendum to approve a constitutional convention which would legalize tuition grants for private education. Stanley became a vocal supporter of the referendum, which most observers saw as tantamount to a vote on the Gray Plan. He was backed in this campaign by the state Board of Education and former Governors

Darden and Battle. Confronted with charges that approval would lead to school closings, Stanley publicly renewed his pledge to maintain an efficient public school system. He called the Gray Plan "sound and moderate." With these assurances, the electorate overwhelmingly approved the convention by a two-to-one margin.

But even as voters were going to the polls, the limb was being sawed off behind Stanley. Although Senator Byrd had backed the referendum, he had remained silent on the other provisions of the plan, calling instead for flexibility. The day after the election, spokesmen for the Defenders publicly talked of shelving the Gray Plan, while Byrd, pointing out its weaknesses, privately told Stanley to go slow on implementation. On January 17 the governor announced that the Gray Plan would not be acted upon until the constitutional convention was over.

The regular General Assembly session of 1956 saw a new line of defense proposed—interposition. Based on John C. Calhoun's concept of state nullification, which invalidated unlawful federal action, interposition had been resurrected in the editorials of James J. Kilpatrick, an articulate spokesman for segregation and states' rights. Stanley, concerned with other legislation, was initially cool to an interposition resolution, but he eventually gave it his blessing, and it passed both houses easily. Although interposition had little legal significance, it did help to create a favorable climate for massive resistance.

While the Assembly concentrated on interposition, Stanley pressed for more money for public schools and mental hospitals and approval of the $109 million capital outlay program requiring accelerated tax collection, all of which he received. In an effort to reduce waste and inefficiency in the hospital system, he asked for and got authority to appoint a business manager responsible to the governor rather than to the hospital board, a first step in improving the abysmal record Virginia had compiled in mental hygiene.

In the midst of this session, Senator Byrd announced his plan for massive resistance to desegregation. The frustrations of twenty years of dealing with an encroaching federal octopus and the urge to prop up a faltering political machine combined to produce one of the saddest chapters in Virginia history. Without a lawyer's sense of the complexities of the issue, Byrd was encouraged to proceed by Kilpatrick's doctrine of interposition and by the margin of victory in the recent referendum. Although Stanley had had little to do with the shift to massive resistance, he now had to placate the public while a new plan of action was being mapped out. Throughout the spring, even after the constitution was amended to allow tuition grants, he adopted a "wait and see" attitude on a special session and reaffirmed his commitment to the separate-but-equal doctrine in all phases of Virginia life.

On July 2, 1956, Stanley, Gray, Tuck, Abbitt, and others met secretly with Senator Byrd in Washington to formulate Virginia's last-ditch response.

Three weeks later, the governor called an Assembly session for August 27 and announced that in response to the "overwhelming sentiment of the people of Virginia" and to events threatening "to destroy our constitutional system," he was urging a "total resistance line." State money would be withheld from any locality integrating its schools, and no assignment plan would be adopted permitting integration. The Gray Commission plan he had called "splendid" eight months before had been scrapped. Tom Stanley had at last defined his position. His back had been stiffened by new court decisions which portended greater federal involvement in state affairs. Furthermore, he was no longer on the outside looking in. He had been included in the crucial discussions of recent months, and his role in the upcoming Assembly would be substantial. Virginia's final solution would be known as the Stanley Plan.

When the General Assembly convened, passage of the Stanley Plan was not assured. The opposition, which included Colgate Darden, a majority of the state Board of Education, and one-third of the Gray Commission, charged it would destroy public schools. Advocates countered that their program was the only way to keep schools open, arguing that any integration would close them. Parroting the Defenders, the governor warned that integration could not be contained in schools but would spread insidiously throughout the Commonwealth. Thus, those who favored a local option assignment plan were frequently labeled "total integrationists."

To preclude an opposition victory, the resisters modified the Stanley Plan, giving the governor additional options before withholding state funds from integrated schools. A three-man pupil placement board under the governor's authority would attempt to circumvent the courts by assigning pupils to schools on criteria other than race. If a school was integrated by court order, the governor was authorized to close it temporarily and then attempt to reopen it on a voluntarily segregated basis. By shifting responsibility for school operations to Richmond and by creating new legal barriers, segregationists hoped the sweeping nature of the Supreme Court decision could be sidestepped; at the very least the process would be delayed by further litigation. Organization forces won, but more narrowly than they had hoped. Local option plans were defeated in the House, 59 to 39, and in the Senate, 21 to 17; the modified Stanley Plan was then passed by similar margins. In a vindictive effort to strike at its most bitter foe and reduce the number of lawsuits being prosecuted, the Assembly also passed bills designed to harass and undermine the work of the NAACP.

Stanley's governorship effectively ended with this special session. The remainder of his term was consumed by "watchful waiting" as the courts moved step by step to dismember the resistance plan and order school desegregation. Much of the tension in 1957 was relieved by the ceremonies of the office. Selected chairman of the National Governor's Conference the year before, Stanley presided over the meetings of the executive committee as well as the annual conference, held in Williamsburg. In August he received Virginia's Distinguished Service Medal for twenty-eight years of service to his state, and in October he welcomed Queen Elizabeth to the celebration commemorating the 350th anniversary of Jamestown.

Problems with the hospital system continued to confound him. Having placed fiscal management under his supervision, Stanley felt compelled to remove three hospital board members who had opposed this step; the commissioner of mental hygiene was also replaced when rumors of negligence continued. Hospital personnel and the governor differed frequently on whether newly instituted management practices actually improved patient care.

The final months of the Stanley term witnessed the countdown to school closings. Rulings of various courts overturned the pupil placement law, but Stanley refused to terminate operation of the placement board, claiming that any new legislation on the issue would have to be initiated by his successor. The situation was further inflamed by events in Little Rock, Arkansas, where Governor Orville Faubus denied blacks entry to the high school. The introduction of troops by President Eisenhower, an act Stanley labeled "totalitarian," undoubtedly hardened resistance in Virginia and proved fatal to the candidacy of Ted Dalton, who was soundly thrashed in the 1957 gubernatorial race by Democrat J. Lindsay Almond. Stanley interpreted Almond's victory as an expression of confidence in his handling of the school situation. In his final address to members of the General Assembly Stanley urged a continuation of the segregation policies they had evolved together, complimenting them—and indirectly himself—on preventing "up to this day a single instance of integration in any public school classrooms of this state." That would be the most fitting epitaph for his governorship. Breathing a sigh of relief, he departed for Stanleytown, leaving Almond the tattered remnants of the Stanley Plan with which to face the gathering storm.

Although he occasionally campaigned for friends, Stanley had promised his wife that the governorship would be his last public office. He continued as president of the Stanley Furniture Company until 1962 when he became chief executive officer and chairman of the board. Maintaining a spirit of public service, he chaired a commission that studied tax reform measures from 1962 to 1964. Otherwise, Tom Stanley pursued his lifelong interests in his community, church, and family. He died in 1970, a few days before his eightieth birthday.

By the standards of his predecessors, Tom Stanley performed well as governor. He continued the tradition of conservative business management of state affairs, leaving at his departure a $53 million treasury surplus. Improvements had been made in the administration of state hospitals, more money had been appropriated for schools, and highway and industrial development had been encouraged. If massive resistance had been an unpleasant intrusion,

Stanley had at least acted calmly and in accord with the popular will. Personally he always felt that the stable fiscal condition of the Commonwealth, the hospital improvements, and his dignified representation of Virginia to the outside world were his most significant achievements. While he might have handled the school crisis differently had he had a free hand, never once did he think he had acted improperly. He was, said his son, "a willing participant in massive resistance." For those who had worked with him in that effort, his stature increased with passing years.

Regrettably, Stanley's qualities of honesty, industry, and perseverance, while admirable, did not suffice in a time of crisis. The irony was that a man who seemed so well prepared for the office was, in reality, ill-equipped to lead Virginia in such a difficult period. His own inner drive to success, the development of executive skills, and twenty-three years of political experience had groomed him to be the kind of governor Virginians had come to expect over the preceding three decades; but changes within and without the Old Dominion demanded much more. A man of modest intellect, Stanley was overwhelmed by the complexities of an urbanizing Virginia on the brink of social upheaval. His many public reversals and evasions suggest indecisiveness or a dependence cultivated by organization politics; furthermore, he lacked political charisma. Simply put, Stanley was neither an innovator nor an inspirational leader, qualities that might have produced more able direction in the 1950s. If there be an apology for him, it is that his weaknesses were exploited by a self-serving organization. He merely endorsed the outdated and misguided policies presented to him. He exemplified the risks of a selection policy honoring men for loyalty and service rather than ability. Not without some justice, these flaws contributed to the final death of the Byrd machine a decade later.

SOURCES

The private papers of Thomas B. Stanley remain in the possession of the family and are unavailable for inspection, but the governor's Executive Papers (Virginia State Library) as well as the letter collections of Harry F. Byrd, Everett R. Combs, and James J. Kilpatrick (all at the University of Virginia) were helpful. The governor's son, Thomas B. Stanley, Jr., graciously submitted to a lengthy interview, and William M. Tuck, Colgate W. Darden, Carter G. Lowance, and James H. Latimer kindly responded to questionnaires sent them.

Major sources for this study were the Richmond *Times-Dispatch* and these books: J. Harvie Wilkinson III, *Harry Byrd and the Changing Face of Virginia Politics, 1945–1966* (Charlottesville, 1968); James W. Ely, Jr., *The Crisis of Conservative Virginia: The Byrd Organization and the Politics of Massive Resistance* (Knoxville, Tenn., 1976); Robbins L. Gates, *The Making of Massive Resistance* (Chapel Hill, N.C., 1964); and Benjamin Muse, *Virginia's Massive Resistance* (Bloomington, Ind., 1961). A book by Dorothy Cleal and Hiram J. Herbert, *Foresight, Foun-*

ders, and Fortitude: The Growth of Industry in Martinsville and Henry County, Virginia (Bassett, Va., 1970), provides some information on Stanley's early years in the furniture business. Warren Riggan's "A Political Biography of Thomas Bahnson Stanley" (M.A. thesis, University of Richmond, 1965) is superficial.

J. LINDSAY ALMOND, JR.

Governor of Virginia

1958–1962

J. LINDSAY ALMOND, JR.

The Politics of School Desegregation

James W. Ely, Jr.

No Virginia chief executive of the twentieth century proved more controversial than J. Lindsay Almond, Jr. A major figure during the massive
resistance era of the 1950s, he was instrumental in the movement away from
the school closing scheme. Thus, Almond was an important transitional
leader in the political life of the Old Dominion.

In many respects Almond's career was an American success story. The
future governor was born on June 15, 1898, in Charlottesville, where his
father was a railroad engineer. When Almond was six, his family moved to
rural Orange County to commence farming on a 250-acre tract. Young Lindsay did chores, learned to read at home under his mother's tutelage, and
received his elementary education at a one-room country school. An admirer
of Woodrow Wilson, Almond early became involved in politics. Before he
turned sixteen he was already taking an active part in county election campaigns. In addition, Almond manifested a sustained interest in public speaking and mastered the vanishing art of southern oratory. The Richmond *Times-
Dispatch* later described him as "a colorful phrasemaker and old-fashioned
pulpit-pounding type of orator." He entered the University of Virginia in
1917 as a member of the Student Army Training Corps but was discouraged
by low grades and, unable to afford tuition, served for a year as principal of
Zoar High School near his home. Then he entered the University of Virginia
School of Law and earned his law degree in 1923.

Almond began practice in Roanoke, handling a large number of criminal
cases. He loved trial work and perfected his technique of examining witnesses.
In 1925 two events occurred which profoundly influenced the course of Almond's life. He met Harry Flood Byrd, then campaigning for governor, made
several speeches for him, and gained his favor. In the same year Almond
married Josephine Katherine Minter, a Roanoke native. Keenly interested in
politics, she made Almond an ideal wife, and their long union was happy.
Although the Almonds never had children, they raised Mrs. Almond's orphan
nephew from infancy.

In 1930 Almond was named assistant Commonwealth's attorney for
Roanoke, and earlier support for Byrd paved the way in 1933 for his election
by the legislature as judge of the Roanoke hustings court. He was thirty-four

years old, one of the youngest judges ever named by the General Assembly up to that time. Almond presided over this challenging and busy tribunal until December 1945, acquiring both judicial experience and a reputation for fairness. In 1945 the congressional seat for the Sixth District became vacant, and the Democratic convention tapped Almond for the job. Elected easily, Almond generally voted on the conservative side, including support for the Taft-Hartley Act.

Almond fully expected to continue in the House of Representatives, but upon the death of Virginia's attorney general, Harvey B. Apperson, in 1948, Governor William M. Tuck and Senator Byrd urged him to accept the lower-paid post. The senator, eager to block an anti-Byrd candidate for the job, argued that having Almond on the ticket would strengthen John S. Battle in his forthcoming race for the governorship. Contrary to the advice of his wife, Almond resigned his seat in Congress and became attorney general in April 1948. Byrd made no promises concerning the future, but others around him hinted to Almond that he could have the Democratic gubernatorial nomination after Battle's term. Campaigning vigorously for Battle in 1949, Almond won a full term as attorney general. He also used his official position to help Battle with a controversial interpretation of election laws permitting Republicans to vote in the Democratic primary.

Almond always regarded himself as an adherent of the Byrd organization, but his relations with the inner circle were not close. His continued support of the Democratic national ticket prompted some degree of distrust during years when many Byrd loyalists tacitly or openly backed the national GOP. Almond gave colorful expression to his attitude in 1948: "The only sane and constructive course is to follow in the house of our fathers—even though the roof leaks and there may be bats in the belfry, rats in the pantry, a cockroach waltz in the kitchen and skunks in the parlor." Almond also manifested an independent streak on some issues. In 1951 he called for abolition of the poll tax at a time when the Byrd organization was committed to retaining the levy. Far more significant was the Hutchinson affair. In 1950 President Truman nominated Martin A. Hutchinson, a Richmond attorney, for a place on the Federal Trade Commission. An antiorganization Democrat, Hutchinson had been Byrd's opponent in the 1946 senatorial primary. Almond and Hutchinson had never been political allies, and Almond declined to testify on Hutchinson's behalf. Still, as a personal favor Almond wrote a letter supporting the nomination. Having cleared the matter with organization leaders, he was surprised to learn that Byrd was "highly offended." The Hutchinson letter placed a strain on Almond's association with Byrd, who ultimately blocked Senate confirmation of the appointment. In 1953, contrary to earlier suggestions to Almond, the Byrd organization named Thomas B. Stanley as the Democratic nominee for governor. Almond was again reelected attorney general, easily defeating Republican Walter E. Hoffman, who later became a federal district judge in Virginia.

Almond's long tenure as attorney general was eventful. During the Tuck administration he investigated violence in the mines of southwest Virginia. Under Battle, Almond became marginally involved in the bitter controversy about the Martinsville Seven, seven black youths sentenced to death for brutally raping a white woman. Almond handled the appellate phases of the litigation and sat with the governor in commutation hearings. When Battle rejected executive clemency, the defendants were executed.

After 1950 Almond was increasingly preoccupied with the school segregation question. He recognized that state schools "had been separate but not equal," yet he was "very sincerely wedded to the soundness of the separate but equal doctrine" and presented this view to the courts. Under his guidance Virginia prepared the most aggressive and skillful defense of separate schools offered by any of the states involved. When the lower court decision sustaining separate schools was appealed to the Supreme Court, Almond coordinated Virginia's defense with lawyers representing other jurisdictions. *Time* later described Almond as "one of segregation's ablest legal advocates."

Although disappointed by the 1954 *Brown* decision, Almond gained widespread publicity for his role in defending the state. Stronger politically than ever before, by 1956 Almond had resolved not to be denied a chance at the state's top job. Rejecting overtures that he accept a seat on the Virginia Supreme Court of Appeals, Almond announced his candidacy for governor on November 17, 1956, without first consulting Byrd. This was a break with Democratic party tradition that caught organization leaders by surprise. "I had the nomination locked up," Almond recalled. Through his official contacts as attorney general he had built up strong support among local officials and the middle and lower echelons of the Byrd organization, and soon endorsements were pouring in from state legislators and local officials. A bandwagon for Almond was under way despite the tardy announcement by state Senator Garland Gray, reputedly Byrd's choice, that he was also interested in the nomination. Only when Almond's political front was secure did he solicit Byrd's approval. Unlike his immediate predecessors Battle and Stanley, Almond obviously did not owe his nomination to the senator's influence.

Both Almond's 1957 campaign and his gubernatorial term were preoccupied with Virginia's response to the Supreme Court's school desegregation edict. As governor he inherited a program of massive resistance designed to halt school integration anywhere in Virginia by erecting a series of defensive obstacles: a board to administer a statewide pupil assignment plan and forestall integration with elaborate criteria and cumbersome procedures, and laws requiring the governor to close any school confronted with integration and to reorganize it (if possible) on a segregated basis. If all else failed, the governor was authorized, at his discretion, to permit a closed school to reopen with racial integration, but all state funds were then automatically cut off. A program of tuition grants was established so that students adversely affected by school closings could attend private schools.

Curiously, when massive resistance became law in September 1956, Almond was privately unenthusiastic and questioned its efficacy. He played no part in drafting the legislation and later maintained that he had advised Governor Stanley against the scheme. As attorney general, moreover, Almond issued a legal opinion that the Virginia legislature's 1956 interposition resolution, designed to assert state sovereignty as a defense against the *Brown* ruling, "is not a legislative enactment having the force and effect of law." Still, Almond was a segregationist and entered the campaign as a champion of massive resistance. Although a degree of ambiguity can be detected upon a close examination of his speeches, the average Virginian could have concluded he would oppose integration to the bitter end.

His Republican opponent for governor was Radford state Senator Ted Dalton, who had nearly defeated Stanley in 1953. A popular and respected legislator, Dalton had consistently opposed interposition and massive resistance. Yet he was no integrationist and favored as much school segregation as could be legally retained. Dalton urged locally administered pupil assignment permitting school districts to decide the question of integration in conformity with local wishes. Although Dalton repeatedly stressed that he favored separate schools for the races, he was almost immediately placed on the defensive. In an effort to seize the initiative, the Republican candidate warned that massive resistance would fail and lead either to wholesale integration or closing down of the public school system.

Almond and the Democrats mounted an energetic campaign. Aided by a wide variety of speakers, he and Byrd campaigned vigorously in all sections of the state. Democratic orators continually linked Dalton and the Republicans with such objects of opprobrium as Chief Justice Earl Warren, the NAACP, and school integration. Almond denounced Dalton's pupil assignment plan as a step "on the road to racial amalgamation." Democratic speakers even suggested that the Supreme Court might alter its opinion on school integration if Virginia and the South held fast. The Little Rock incident of September 1957 played directly into the hands of those favoring massive resistance. When President Eisenhower used federal troops to enforce school integration, reaction in Virginia was extremely hostile. Democrats unquestionably utilized Little Rock to bring the segregationist majority in Virginia to a fever pitch, but it appears that Almond was ahead of Dalton from the outset and would have been elected in any event. Given the nature of the dominant campaign issue and Almond's overwhelming press support, the election results were no surprise. In a record vote for a nonpresidential year, Almond crushed Dalton by nearly a two-to-one margin, 326,921 to 188,628.

The Republican nominee showed strength only in suburban areas of northern Virginia, a handful of mountain counties in the southwest corner of the state, and among black voters.

The Democrats were naturally jubilant. Byrd hailed the results as an "outstanding and decisive" victory which would be "recognized through the South and the nation as showing Virginia's determination to resist integration." Almond and the Byrd organization had successfully converted the gubernatorial campaign into a public referendum on the Supreme Court's integration edict. Considering that the Negro vote was largely for Dalton, it is obvious that the overwhelming majority of white Virginians, by perhaps as much as three to one, supported a candidate who seemed to promise that public schools would be closed before they would be integrated. Whatever Almond's private reservations about massive resistance, he somehow had created the impression that he would keep public schools open and segregated. Any failure on his part would be keenly disappointing to his strongest backers.

The early months of 1958, following Almond's triumph of the preceding November, were the honeymoon period for massive resistance. On inauguration day, January 11, Almond delivered a plea for the preservation of states' rights and limited government. "Weakened by this cynical phlebotomy, enervated by sweet anesthetic, the States," he warned "gradually are declining to the insignificant role of dependent Federal satellites." Touching on the school question, Almond rededicated himself to the fight for segregation: "Against these massive attacks, we must marshal a massive resistance." Yet he also stressed his support for public schools and argued that Virginia "ought not to rely on any Maginot Lines."

Almond's sizable victory gave him considerable influence in the General Assembly, and any private doubts he entertained about massive resistance were well disguised by his legislative recommendations. The lawmakers reaffirmed their intention to cut off state funds to integrated schools and tightened existing massive resistance legislation. At Almond's request, the General Assembly also enacted the "Little Rock" bill, which provided for the automatic closing of any public school patrolled by U.S. military force. Moreover, the legislators continued to probe both the financing and the activities of the NAACP. The most controversial item of the 1958 legislative session was a registration act requiring prospective voters to register on a blank sheet, using only the state constitution as an aid. Almond signed the measure, which was designed (as the governor subsequently conceded) to "hit the Negro voter harder than the white voter." "It was one of the most harmonious sessions," state Senator Mills Godwin wrote Almond. "Your firm leadership was unquestionably a major factor in the lack of enthusiasm on the part of the opponents." Almond would never again face a General Assembly so united under his guidance.

The segregationist tide was also apparent in gubernatorial appointments. In May 1958, after months of hesitation, Almond named William J. Story, Jr., school superintendent of South Norfolk, to the state Board of Education, thereby replacing a moderate member. Story, a strong supporter of massive resistance, had powerful backing from Southside Virginia. The appointment of Story assured a board majority favorable to resistance. "There was considerable pressure and I succumbed to it," Almond later declared.

The public schools completed the 1957–58 academic year without racial integration, but it appeared that Norfolk, Arlington, and Charlottesville would face final orders to desegregate in September. Everyone was surprised when the massive resistance showdown came in Warren County, a largely rural area in the Shenandoah Valley with only a modest Negro population. On September 8, 1958, the federal district court ordered black students admitted to Warren County High School at Front Royal. Four days later Almond closed the school and vested all authority over it in himself. Shortly thereafter the governor was obligated to seize and shut several schools in Charlottesville and Norfolk. Approximately 13,000 pupils were eventually left without classrooms, and despite emergency measures, thousands of them received no formal schooling.

Realizing that federal action was inevitable, the governor asked Attorney General Albertis S. Harrison to institute a test case before the Virginia Supreme Court of Appeals to determine the validity of tuition grant payments. Almond had little confidence that the courts would sustain massive resistance and during the fall of 1958 lapsed into silence on the issue. Periodically, though, he would deliver a rousing call for resistance, thereby advancing a public position completely at odds with his innermost thoughts. And there were limits beyond which he refused to move. Almond opposed any resort to violence and strongly denounced the Klan: "We certainly don't need the Klan in Virginia; we frown on the activities of the Klan and I hope our citizens do what they can to discourage its growth." Similarly, Almond rejected suggestions that localities forced to close white schools should also shut their Negro schools.

Finally, on January 19, 1959—the birthday of Robert E. Lee—massive resistance expired under a double legal reversal. Both the Virginia Supreme Court of Appeals and a three-judge federal district court declared the school-closing laws unconstitutional. The next evening Governor Almond responded over radio and television in one of the most famous political addresses of twentieth-century Virginia. Although Almond had expected the judicial setback, he delivered a blistering denunciation of integration and the federal courts and vowed to continue the struggle:

> To those of faint heart; to those whose purpose and design is to
> blend and amalgamate the white and negro race and destroy the
> integrity of both races; to those who disclaim that they are integra-

tionists but are working day and night to integrate our schools; to those who don't care what happens to the children of Virginia; to those false prophets of a "little or token integration"; to those in high places or elsewhere who advocate integration for your children and send their own to private or public segregated schools . . . let me make it abundantly clear for the record now and hereafter, as Governor of this state, I will not yield to that which I know to be wrong and will destroy every rational semblance of education for thousands of the children of Virginia.

With respect to his motives, Almond later conceded that there was "no rational answer." "I felt very deeply what I said. People cannot appreciate the pressures I was under at that time. I succumbed to inner frustration." Almond intended to demonstrate that he had done all he could, but the speech unfortunately fostered an illusion that the state still had some device whereby it could retain both public schools and total segregation. Almond unwittingly heightened the expectations of the resisters. "The speech made my position more difficult," Almond admitted. "I brought a lot of suffering on myself for that speech. I paid for it."

Making no additional public disclosure of his plans, Almond called a special session of the General Assembly to meet on January 28. When that body convened, the governor announced his surrender. He bluntly declared that the state was powerless to maintain strict segregation in public schools. Almond urged repeal of the massive resistance laws, as well as the compulsory school attendance law, and strongly backed a revised and broadened tuition grant program.

Tactically Almond's moves were sound; he caught the resisters by surprise. Had the governor notified key resister spokesmen before delivering his address, it appears unlikely that he could have mitigated their opposition or convinced them that his course was proper; he would also have run the serious risk that the resister bloc in the General Assembly might defeat his new program. As it was, Almond's dramatic shift doomed any revival of massive resistance. Most Virginia newspapers supported his conciliatory stance. Yet the resisters were keenly disappointed and turned upon their fallen hero with cries of "traitor" and "turncoat." Some suggested that Almond should resist integration to the point of being jailed for contempt of court, a move that might have a public relations advantage. Almond felt jail would serve no useful purpose. Here Almond's legal training and experience (of which the resisters had made so much) returned to plague them, for his professional career had conditioned him to accept judicial determinations—however distasteful they might be.

He also might have attempted to halt integration by liquidating the Old Dominion's public school system. Almond was aware of this painful alternative and subsequently remarked that "the only way to defeat integration was to close down every single, solitary school in this state and keep them closed." Many resisters wanted a popular referendum on maintaining public schools. The Richmond *News Leader* and a few other newspapers favored such a move, arguing it would increase the state's room to maneuver and thereby tighten the defense against further integration. By throwing his full weight against any referendum, Almond forestalled this maneuver and relegated the resisters to impotent rage.

On February 2, 1959, a handful of black students peacefully entered previously white schools in Norfolk and Arlington. Two days later Almond named a legislative commission to seek a school integration formula. Although the forty-man Perrow Commission, chaired by state Senator Mosby G. Perrow, Jr., of Lynchburg, included staunch resisters, a clear majority favored the emerging Almond position. Moreover, the governor worked closely with Perrow in tailoring the commission's report. No one was surprised when the Perrow Commission set forth in March a scheme intended to hold school integration to the lowest possible minimum. The recommendations of the commission, endorsed by Almond and largely adopted by a special session of the General Assembly, restored the compulsory attendance law on a local option basis and provided tuition grants, without regard to the course of public school integration, for the education of children at nonsectarian private schools. In addition, the legislature enacted a new pupil placement law, effective in March 1960, permitting localities to remove themselves from the jurisdiction of the Pupil Placement Board and handle their own student assignments. The Pupil Placement Board itself remained intact. The commission opposed any constitutional amendment dealing with public education, and a proposal to repeal the education section of the constitution was defeated 53–45 in the House of Delegates.

Using firmness and executive leadership, Almond saw to the enactment of much of the commission's work. At one point the Senate had to resolve itself into a committee of the whole to bypass a negative vote in the Education Committee. The session was bitter and perplexing, with bruised feelings all around, and one result was an irrevocable break between Almond and key Byrd lieutenants. Although Byrd was silent during the controversy, his son, state Senator Harry F. Byrd, Jr., was a vigorous opponent of Almond, and the fray threatened to rupture the organization.

The spring of 1959 was a curious time in the Old Dominion. Byrd loyalists and segregationists criticized the man they had made governor, Almond broke with old friends and embraced former foes, and the resister faction in the General Assembly split, one wing defecting to the local option plan it had previously denounced. Despite the governor's frequent statements that token integration would not succeed, this concept was at the heart of his new legislative proposals. Almond and the resisters really were clashing over how best to avoid massive integration, a debate over means, not ends. Integrationists were quick to recognize the shallow dimensions of the struggle. The Norfolk *Journal and Guide,* a Negro newspaper, observed that the "margin between the majority represented by Governor Almond and the minority represented by those now in open revolt against him is very slim. At heart both sides are segregationists—the real thing or the very real thing." Despite persistent skepticism, the Almond policy of containment appeared, for several years after 1959, to accomplish its objective. Indeed, when Almond left office in January 1962, less than 1 percent of Virginia's black pupils attended integrated schools.

For Almond the spring of 1959 was a season of temporary triumph and personal misgivings. By accepting even limited integration, the governor was constrained to turn his back on his deep belief in racial separation. In breaking with the Byrd organization, moreover, he quit the circle of the man he most revered. Alone and smarting from criticism, Almond sought to justify his conduct to Virginians—and perhaps to himself. He argued that he kept his word by offering the maximum possible resistance and, somewhat paradoxically, that he had saved public education. More telling was Almond's oratorical campaign to defend and bolster Virginia's public schools. He told a Warren County audience that Virginia could not "abandon public education and thereby consign a generation of children to the darkness of illiteracy, the pits of indolence and dependency, and the dungeons of delinquency." Yet most of his speech was a defense of his record in battling school integration. "I exercised every power at my command in the keeping of that promise," the governor declared. Almond wanted to have it both ways.

In the last analysis Lindsay Almond was a victim of circumstances largely beyond his control but aggravated by his own ill-considered remarks. He was in the wrong place when the roof caved in, and the resister bloc vented its anger upon him. Nevertheless, Albertis S. Harrison, Jr., who followed him as governor, provided a fitting guidepost to any study of the Almond years: "When the times judge Lindsay Almond, history will deal kindly with his administration." Whatever his personal foibles, at the crucial moment Almond demonstrated the courage to reach a hard decision and the political muscle to make it stick.

The year 1960 saw a continuation of the running battle between Almond and the Byrd camp. Almond guaranteed a lively Assembly session by requesting a record budget and a state sales tax to finance it. Arguing that property and personal income were taxed too heavily, he proposed a 3 percent sales levy, proceeds to be shared with localities. Senators Mills E. Godwin, Jr., and Harry F. Byrd, Jr., emerged as leading spokesmen for the anti-sales-tax bloc. The senior Byrd made no public comment, but it seems highly unlikely that his son and other close political friends would have contested the Almond plan without his approval. The battle lines soon resembled the lineup with regard to the Perrow Plan of the year before. By late January, Almond was charging that much of the opposition to the tax was prompted by his solution to the school problem. The governor often returned to this theme in the final weeks of the session; this was, in his words, "the politics of revenge." Recognizing the strength of opposition, the Almond administration hinted that it might accept a 2 percent sales tax, but in February the finance committees of both House and Senate killed the entire program. Almond struck back with a direct challenge to Byrd legislative leaders: "If these gentlemen want to play it rough that suits me, for the remainder of this administration, for the days that shall come after the close of this administration." The rift within the organization was widening, and the break between Almond and Byrd became irrevocable.

If Almond lost the sales tax, he did salvage one major victory with passage of his budget. A determined effort to reduce the budget was narrowly turned back in the upper house. Since the sales tax had been defeated, the General Assembly in its last day had to find $80 million in new revenue to match increased expenditures. In order to fill this gap the legislators voted new levies on cigarettes, cigars, and alcoholic beverages.

The 1960 presidential election provided more conflict between Almond and Byrd. The senator early expressed his support for Lyndon B. Johnson of Texas. When the state convention met in May, Almond, a supporter of John F. Kennedy, urged an uninstructed delegation to the national party gathering. Contrary to Almond's wishes, the state convention pledged Virginia's thirty-three national delegate votes to Johnson. Thus enfeebled, Almond was designated chairman of the delegation. Rumors that he was seeking a federal judgeship began to circulate at this time, and it was entirely plausible that Almond might extend his public career with a new national administration.

Virginia did not play an important role at the Democratic national convention in July. Almond called the party platform, with its strong civil rights stand, "very obnoxious" but squelched any talk of a Virginia walkout. Virginia's endorsement of Johnson could not halt the Kennedy drive to a first-ballot nomination, and Almond—at least—was happy with the outcome. The governor was doubly pleased when he was able to deliver a seconding speech for Johnson, the man he recommended to Kennedy for second spot. In highly visible contrast with most Virginia officials, Almond threw himself into the Kennedy campaign. Many observers believed that a Kennedy victory in the Old Dominion would boost Almond's political stock, but Republican Richard M. Nixon carried the state by some 42,000 votes.

Almond's final year as chief executive was relatively quiet, and he took no part in the Democratic primary to select his successor. From time to time the newspapers speculated about Almond's future plans, and virtually the entire Virginia press agreed that he ought to be given a judicial post. In April 1962 Kennedy submitted Almond's nomination as judge to the Senate. Byrd stalled a hearing on the nomination for more than a year, but in the end

Almond was duly confirmed. He served on the Court of Customs and Patent Appeals until he retired in 1973, assuming senior judge status. The court, composed of five judges, exercised a nationwide jurisdiction over appeals involving customs questions, patents, and trademarks. Issues concerning the patenting of inventions were frequently argued before the tribunal, and Almond regularly wrote opinions. Since the court sat in nearby Washington, D.C., he continued to live in Richmond. With his appointment to this specialized tribunal Almond quit political life and gradually faded from public view.

A tall, gregarious man with a keen sense of humor, Almond spent an eventful career in law and politics. Yet his controversial public role should not obscure Almond's unassuming private life. Active in the United Lutheran church, he lived unpretentiously, having never amassed wealth from the modest salaries paid Virginia officials and federal judges.

Almond's gubernatorial term cannot be accurately assessed in terms of the usual list of legislative and administrative accomplishments. His period as chief executive was so completely dominated by the race question that Almond had little opportunity to leave a mark in other fields. His 1960 budget, with its call for a sales tax, was a courageous attempt to address the need for better services and increased revenue. Moreover, Almond somehow found time to call a statewide conference designed to promote industrial growth in the Old Dominion. Still, his place in history must ultimately rest upon his handling of school desegregation. Here Almond's political independence was to prove his greatest asset. Repudiating earlier commitments to massive resistance, he contributed to the ultimate resolution of the crisis. Only when the explosive race issue subsided could Virginia move on to other problems. This gain, however, was achieved at a steep personal price.

SOURCES

Scholars should consult Almond's Executive Papers (Virginia State Library) and the papers of Harry F. Byrd and James J. Kilpatrick (both at the University of Virginia). For Almond's years as the state's chief legal officer, see the annual *Opinions of the Attorney General*.

A complete account of Almond and massive resistance can be found in James W. Ely, Jr., *The Crisis of Conservative Virginia: The Byrd Organization and the Politics of Massive Resistance* (Knoxville, Tenn., 1976). For biographical material, see James Harvie Wilkinson III, *Harry Byrd and the Changing Face of Virginia Politics, 1945–1966* (Charlottesville, 1968); Benjamin Muse, *Virginia's Massive Resistance* (Bloomington, Ind., 1961); and Charles McDowell, Jr., "J. Lindsay Almond, Jr.: New Virginia Governor Excells as an Orator," *Commonwealth* 25 (Jan. 1958): 9. For Almond's role in the school desegregation cases, see Richard Kluger, *Simple Justice* (New York, 1976).

ALBERTIS S. HARRISON, JR.

Governor of Virginia

1962–1966

ALBERTIS S. HARRISON, JR.

Transition Governor

Virginius Dabney

Albertis S. Harrison, Jr., addressed himself to the industrial development of Virginia with marked success. The Commonwealth made exceptional material progress during his administration, and this progress, in turn, brought significant advances in educational and cultural realms. Harrison also sought to play down the school integration issue, and thanks in part to his endeavors, racial tensions cooled while he was governor. In these respects (and in others as well) his tenure constituted a transition phase from the reactionism of the massive resistance era to the relatively progressive climate of the mid-1960s.

The future governor was born in Brunswick County, Virginia, on January 11, 1907, the son of Albert Sydney ("Albertis") and Lizzie Goodrich Harrison. The eminent Harrison family had produced a signer of the Declaration of Independence and two presidents of the United States, but Harrison's immediate family was by no means affluent. His father farmed; his mother taught school. The Harrison homeplace was 275 acres in extent, and there were 1,500 additional acres. "Farming still smacked of the way it was done in colonial times when I was a boy," Harrison recently said. "You had all the advantages of that way of life." An only child, he did the usual chores around the place, but some of them, notably milking cows, did not appeal to him. He termed it "about the meanest job that was ever devised by man" and added, "By devious ways I was able to opt out of this as soon as possible." His father had a warm, relaxed personality; his mother was more dynamic and intense. Both were Methodists, and the family regularly attended Antioch Methodist Church. The Harrisons bent every effort to give their son a college education and decided years in advance that he would go to the University of Virginia and take law, all entirely in accord with his own wishes.

When Harrison entered Alberta High School, his mother "kept his feet to the fire," saw that he did his lessons, and to a substantial degree was responsible for the good record he later achieved as a college student. A few months before the end of his senior year he transferred to Lawrenceville High, since it was accredited and Alberta was not, and graduated at the age of sixteen.

In the fall of 1923, wearing his first pair of long pants, Harrison enrolled at the University of Virginia, which he attended for the next five years. "It took me about two years to get oriented and find out what it was all about," he admits. Even so, he eventually compiled a creditable academic record. His ability as a speaker stemmed, in part, from the debates of the Jefferson Literary Society in which he participated. President of the "Jeff" the year he was graduated in law, he was also a member of Delta Sigma Phi and won a place on the editorial board of the prestigious *Virginia Law Review,* serving as its Virginia editor the year he got his degree.

While a student at Lawrenceville High, Harrison had met the attractive Lacey Virginia Barkley. Although she said many times that she would never marry a lawyer or a politician, she and Harrison were wed in 1930 and set up housekeeping in a Lawrenceville apartment. A son and a daughter were eventually born to the couple, and there are now six grandchildren.

Also in 1930, at the age of twenty-five, Harrison ran for Commonwealth's attorney of Brunswick County. As he later explained, "I was not 'urged by countless friends' to become a candidate, as politicians sometimes claim. The only people who asked me to run were my parents, who thought it was high time that I made some money." Fortunately, his father was a first cousin of W. Emory Elmore, veteran clerk of the Brunswick County court and acknowledged local spokesman for Harry F. Byrd. This connection certainly did no harm to Harrison's political prospects. His opponent, also a Byrd man, was apparently overconfident in his contest with young Harrison, who campaigned hard and won. This 1930 contest was the only time he faced opposition for Commonwealth's attorney, a position which he held for the next sixteen years, excepting war service.

At the outbreak of World War II, Harrison enlisted in the navy and was commissioned as a lieutenant (j.g.). He served in Florida and then at Fifth Naval District Headquarters in Norfolk. His legal talents were well utilized, first as defense counsel and subsequently as judge advocate in general courts-martial. His duties kept him from the combat zone, naturally enough, and he says that during the conflict he "never heard a shot fired in anger." Mustered out at the end of the war, Harrison resumed his duties as Commonwealth's attorney. In 1947 he decided to run for the state Senate from the Seventh District (Brunswick and Mecklenburg counties) and handily defeated Shelton H. Short, Jr., of Mecklenburg for the seat. Serving in the Senate for a decade, Harrison was never opposed for reelection.

Senator Harrison, a down-the-line supporter of Harry F. Byrd's organization, by virtue of an ability and willingness to play the game with the insiders became one of the rising stars of that entrenched machine. Emerging as one of the Senate's most influential members, he was named to a number of important committees during his various terms. Standing with the conservatives, Harrison aligned himself with what he called the "hard-nosed group."

His relations with the organization's "Young Turks," who were more independent thinking, were polite but not particularly cordial.

In 1948, the year Harrison entered the Virginia Senate, Harry Truman made his tumultuous and spectacular reelection bid. There was much antagonism to Truman among members of the Byrd organization, especially because of his civil rights program. Reflecting this hostility, Governor William M. Tuck, with Senator Byrd's approval, sponsored legislation designed to keep Truman's name off the Virginia ballot. Harrison, who had always supported the national Democratic nominees, made no outcry against this extraordinary proposal, but intense and widespread objections from other quarters soon forced backers to beat a hasty retreat. Despite Senator Byrd's "golden silence" in the ensuing campaign, Harrison refused to abandon the Democratic ticket. Instead, he reluctantly supported Truman's uphill struggle to remain in the White House. Indeed, Harrison continued to function as a Democratic regular for another quarter century, supporting the party's national candidates until he voted—at last—for Republican Richard M. Nixon in 1972.

Harrison thus clung to his traditional Democratic loyalties and was equally reluctant to discard another long-established feature of southern life, racial segregation. The civil rights issue loomed ominously after the Supreme Court required integration in the public schools in its 1954 *Brown* decision. Convinced that white Virginians would not accept such racial mixing immediately without violence, Harrison determined to slow the progress of integration by all legal means. He served as a member of the Gray Commission, appointed by Governor Thomas B. Stanley in 1954 to find means of circumventing the Supreme Court's controversial ruling. Initially adopting a moderate stance, Harrison and his associates produced a report suggesting that various political subdivisions should decide for themselves whether to integrate their schools. U.S. Senator Byrd, however, opposed this local option approach, and moderation succumbed to intransigence. Massive resistance became the order of the day.

As a good lawyer, Harrison knew that the jerry-built massive resistance mechanism could not stand the ultimate test in the courts. But he was, and is, of the opinion that this effort, including temporary school closings, bought time during which the people of Virginia could be persuaded to accept the inevitable, without violence. Furthermore, Harrison explains frankly that any member of the General Assembly, and especially one from the Southside, had to be "against integration" to survive politically. Lending his backing to massive resistance, Harrison also fell into line in support of the obstructionist principle of "interposition," exhumed in 1955 from political battles of the late eighteenth and early nineteenth centuries. According to this theory, a state could interpose its sovereign authority between its citizens and the federal government and thereby preserve states' rights. Acting in an atmosphere of near hysteria, the General Assembly passed an interposition resolution by overwhelming majorities in both branches. Although Harrison later professed to recognize the basic futility of this action, he did not join with two Senate colleagues who opposed the resolution.

The Lawrenceville lawmaker had stood with the Byrd machine in the initial phase of the massive resistance debate, and his loyalty was soon rewarded. He was elected attorney general of Virginia in 1957, even though he had not intended to run. Howard C. Gilmer, the organization's first choice, withdrew in the face of charges that as a federal district attorney he had employed improper procedures for marketing life insurance. Byrd persuaded Harrison to take Gilmer's place on the ticket, and he was elected easily.

Attorney General Harrison had the responsibility of representing the Commonwealth in the litigation involving massive resistance. This he did with considerable skill and effectiveness, perhaps because he was more objective in his attitude than Byrd and many other members of the machine. Harrison's pragmatic approach is readily apparent in his correspondence with Senator Byrd during the late 1950s. He argued that school closings in Norfolk, Charlottesville, and Warren County had effectively demonstrated a determination to resist integration, but he advised the senator in August 1958 that admission of blacks to white schools was probably inevitable.

Meanwhile, Harrison was working to develop a more constructive approach to school integration problems, and he and Governor Almond soon came to see eye to eye on issues raised by the Supreme Court. A Richmond meeting of business and industrial leaders with both men in December 1958 helped Almond begin to back away from all-out resistance. This group argued that new industries would not settle where public school closings were threatened and insisted that Virginia's image was being severely damaged by the state's racial policy. Harrison encouraged the businessmen to continue efforts to create a more constructive climate of opinion in the Commonwealth.

With a cool head in a hot controversy, the attorney general aided the governor in preparing and filing a defense of the state's racial policies before Virginia's Supreme Court and in federal court. In early January 1959, two weeks before both courts outlawed massive resistance, Harrison accurately predicted the outcome in a letter to Byrd. Governor Almond then decided—in a move endorsed by Harrison—to yield to the inevitable and allow some integration, a departure opposed by Byrd and other last-ditch segregationists. Under heavy police protection, black children entered previously white schools in Norfolk and Arlington on February 2, 1959. There were no disorders. Seeking a new legislative alternative to defunct massive resistance, Governor Almond, again in close cooperation with Harrison, appointed a commission headed by state Senator Mosby G. Perrow, Jr., of Lynchburg which recommended a local-option, "freedom of choice" plan. This seemed to both Almond and Harrison the most workable policy under the circumstances, and they set to work to achieve its implementation.

It is a tribute to the attorney general's powers of persuasion that he finally convinced Senator Byrd that this revised strategy would have to be supported. In April he cautioned Byrd against further defiance of judicial decisions, maintaining that this could only lead to disorder and bloodshed. There was, he observed, no alternative to obeying the courts. Governor Almond was now persona non grata for giving in to federal decrees, and the burden of clearing the path for the new approach fell to Harrison. Complicating matters still further, Harrison wanted to be Virginia's next chief executive, and he needed Byrd's blessing to attain that goal. It was a delicate task, but Harrison eventually prevailed—with positive results for the Commonwealth and for his own career as well. Massive resistance gave way to freedom of choice, and Byrd bestowed the "nod" on the Lawrenceville lawyer when the time came to choose a successor to Almond. Although complex maneuvers played a role in his advancement, Harrison was the logical choice in 1961. He had served creditably in the state Senate and as attorney general, and his middle-of-the-road approach to Virginia's racial difficulties appealed to a wide spectrum of Virginians, including organization moderates, Young Turks, and even some conservatives who recognized that the Old Dominion had reached the end of the resistance path.

In the 1961 primary Harrison was opposed by Lieutenant Governor A. E. S. Stephens of Isle of Wight in a lively contest. On the ticket with Harrison were Mills E. Godwin, Jr., candidate for lieutenant governor, and Robert Y. Button for attorney general. Rounding out the Stephens slate were state Senator Armistead Boothe, leader of the Young Turks, for lieutenant governor and T. Munford Boyd of the University of Virginia law faculty for attorney general. Stephens, an organization product, had offended hard-core segregationists during the massive resistance backdown and compounded his sins by attacking Byrd in a Winchester speech delivered before the senator's friends and neighbors. This proved to be a serious blunder and left little doubt who would win the primary. Harrison waged a dignified campaign and captured the Democratic gubernatorial nomination, 199,519 to 152,639. The Byrd machine had been fully mobilized in his behalf from one end of the state to the other, and he encountered only nominal Republican opposition in November. Harrison's triumph constituted one of the last statewide victories for the Byrd organization.

The near hysteria of massive resistance had faded when Harrison became governor in 1962, and he was able to address problems other than race. Although Harrison displayed little flamboyance, he struck a decidedly progressive note in his inaugural speech. "If I were to fix one goal for Virginia during the final decades of this century," he declared, "it would be the expansion of the minds of our people within the tradition of the Virginia character."

Suggesting that "in times past we have not expanded sufficiently our intellectual and cultural horizons," he called upon the Commonwealth to become more receptive to "our changing world" and to adjust "wisely and realistically to the social and economic changes of our times." Harrison noted that he had deliberately omitted all mention of race in his address, and he added a highly significant observation: "The progress that is so necessary to Virginia and the programs that I ask you to consider were designed for the welfare and happiness of all Virginians, irrespective of their race, color, or creed."

When Harrison took office Virginia was far behind almost all other states in expenditures for education, health, welfare, and similar services. There was an obvious need to raise and spend more tax dollars for such programs, and the newly inaugurated governor saw industrial development as the most effective means to expand the state's revenue base. Traveling throughout the United States talking to top businessmen and also hosting them at the Governor's Mansion, he always presented the same message: investors would find a hospitable business climate in Virginia and a right-to-work law enabling workers to get jobs without having to join a labor union. The chief executive lent the full prestige of his office to this campaign, taking industrial promotion into his own hands and sponsoring changes in the tax laws to remove what he saw as inequities in Virginia levies on business and industry. At the close of his administration Harrison estimated that one-third of his time had been devoted to this development crusade.

Success crowned the governor's endeavors. In December 1965 he announced that the Commonwealth's outlay of $3 million to attract industry during his four years in office had been rewarded by "more than $900 million in new manufacturing plant investment, 150,000 total new jobs, $750 million in new payrolls, over 300 manufacturing plants, and more than 325 major expansions." In contrast to the exploitative "New South" booms of previous eras, these new industries generally had good wages and responsible management. Factories for the production of chemicals, tobacco, electronics, tires, textiles, and razor blades proliferated in rural as well as urban areas, adding much needed diversification to the state's economic life. Reflecting these developments, the Commonwealth's per capita income rose during Harrison's term from $1,894 to $2,373, a jump which placed Virginia in a virtual tie with Florida for the highest per capita income in the Southeast.

Buoyed by increased revenues from economic growth, the state treasury also benefited from a Harrison-sponsored withholding tax on individual incomes which yielded unexpectedly large returns. A surplus of $100 million had accumulated by the end of his term, creating the budgetary climate for dramatically increased expenditures. The 1966 General Assembly, for example, was able to appropriate nearly $264 million more for essential services than in 1964.

Educational outlays soared during Harrison's administration. Hundreds of new public schools were built, and a new program of postsecondary technical education was instituted, along with a greatly expanded branch college service. Five branch colleges were opened during the Harrison years, as well as a technical college in northern Virginia. Two additional technical colleges were in process of being established by the end of the governor's term, and he had recommended appropriations for six more such institutions. Harrison also fulfilled his commitment to expand "the minds of our people" in another significant way. Favorably impressed by visiting scholars at Charlottesville and Lexington, Harrison expressed a desire to encourage other institutions of higher learning to draw men and women of great eminence to their campuses. Accordingly, during his term the General Assembly provided matching funds for colleges and universities wishing to implement similar programs.

In addition to these educational breakthroughs, Harrison's emphasis on progress manifested itself in a successful tourist campaign. The legislature significantly increased appropriations for tourist advertising, and the Commonwealth also launched a media campaign to improve its image. And visitors to the state found the highways improved, because motor vehicle fees were increased to finance the arterial road system, and interstate highway construction was stimulated as well.

Harrison's performance with reference to educational and economic matters was praiseworthy, but his record on racial affairs was mixed. On the plus side, he played a major role in reopening the public schools of heavily black Prince Edward County, closed since the U.S. Supreme Court had ordered them integrated in 1959. Harrison was unwilling to force the schools to open, preferring that the issue run its course in the courts. On the other hand, he feared that the total absence of public schooling in Prince Edward might lead to a court test which would destroy the Commonwealth's tuition grant program, a last echo from the massive resistance era. To restore Negro education he worked quietly to ensure the success of an unofficial federal-state plan launched at the instigation of President John F. Kennedy. Under this arrangement the Prince Edward Free School Foundation was established with private funds. Harrison persuaded former Governor Colgate W. Darden, Jr., to head the foundation board that provided the county's black children with schooling in 1963–64, one year before the Supreme Court ordered Prince Edward public schools reopened.

Harrison also managed to maintain public order during the civil rights disturbances of the mid-1960s. His unruffled approach and executive firmness served to minimize the potential for violence. Less creditable was his unwillingness to appoint blacks to even semiprestigious posts in his administration. He professed to be unable to find qualified Negroes and asserted that he was searching constantly for such persons. Unimpressed by these claims, a delegation from Hampton Institute presented the governor with a long list of blacks they deemed qualified. Harrison was so effusive in thanking them that they left with the conviction that he would soon announce a number of significant appointments from the list. Nothing of the sort happened. Harrison also adopted a less than vigorous stand on the reemergence of the Ku Klux Klan. He issued a characteristically low-keyed criticism of the organization near the end of his term, observing mildly that the KKK had nothing to contribute to the solution of the Commonwealth's problems and expressing his belief that it would have "little appeal" for Virginians. Again, Harrison's views placed him well to the rear in the civil rights revolution of the 1960s, although it can be argued that his cautious approach may have contributed to the desirable goal of calming racial antagonisms.

The governor's reticence in such matters undoubtedly stemmed in large measure from his continued involvement with the conservative Byrd machine, which maintained its hold on Virginia during his term. Harrison continued to admire Byrd—in spite of occasional differences on policy matters—and enjoyed excellent relations with the organization-dominated General Assembly. The senator did not seek to control or dominate Harrison, who later claimed that he "could count on the fingers of one hand the number of phone calls he made to me while I was governor." Harrison appointed Harry F. Byrd, Jr., to the U.S. Senate when the senior Byrd retired from that body because of ill health late in 1965. This proved to be a highly significant appointment, of course. The conservative "Young Harry" won reelection to the post in his own right in 1966, 1970, and 1976 and emerged as a major influence in Virginia politics.

Harrison thus acted to preserve significant elements of the Byrd legacy, but his four years were also marked by developments setting the stage for the final erosion of organization strength. Federally ordered redistricting of legislative and congressional districts to provide more equal representation and a constitutional amendment eliminating the poll tax in federal elections did much to transform the political face of the Old Dominion. The increased influence of rapidly growing urban areas and the enhanced role of blacks and poor whites meant that the days of the once-invincible Byrd machine were numbered.

These actions of Congress and the courts brought added burdens to Harrison. He had to call three extra sessions of the General Assembly to cope, respectively, with the anti-poll-tax amendment to the federal Constitution, state legislative redistricting, and congressional redistricting. Maintaining his traditional belief in states' rights, Harrison did not relish the necessity of making these basic changes, but he perceived no alternative to complying with the demands of the national government. All in all, Harrison estimated that these (and other) federal intrusions probably doubled his work load as the state's chief executive. The growing role of the federal government, the new political power of blacks and urbanities, and the awakening to the need for greater state services served to mark Harrison's as a transition administration, the bridge to a new era.

Conservative Virginians blamed much of the social turmoil of the mid-1960s on liberal Democratic administrations in Washington, but Harrison remained loyal to the national party throughout his term. Indeed, he and others planned to offer a mild endorsement of President Johnson's reelection bid during the 1964 state Democratic convention in Richmond, but Senator Byrd objected, and the party's resolutions committee prepared a noncommittal report concerning the presidential race. When Harrison read this proposal to the convention, the large pro-Johnson contingent booed loudly and offered a substitute motion. After bitter debate, it carried by a close vote, a major defeat for the Byrd organization and a definite signal that its influence was on the wane. Both Harrison and Lieutenant Governor Godwin subsequently campaigned for Johnson, and with their help he carried Virginia—the first national Democratic aspirant to do so since Truman in 1948. Black and urban votes had overcome those of rural segregationists.

The cooperation between Harrison and his lieutenant governor would yield even more positive results in later years. Harrison's conciliatory attitude permitted Godwin to moderate his hard-line conservatism and develop the popular base for a successful gubernatorial bid in 1965. Harrison also laid the groundwork for one of Godwin's most important accomplishments, the enactment of a state sales tax. In his final message to the General Assembly, Harrison urged the immediate adoption of such a tax and worked closely with his successor's administration in the subsequent drive to achieve that goal.

Governor and Mrs. Harrison left the Executive Mansion in January 1966 a much appreciated couple. Mrs. Harrison possessed unusual warmth and charm, and she and her husband had entertained tastefully. They had improved the mansion's physical appearance, and Mrs. Harrison had participated in the preparation of an attractive illustrated booklet concerning the historic structure. They returned to a brick house in Lawrenceville they had built in 1935, across the street from Saint Andrews Episcopal Church where they had been married and two doors from the apartment where they had begun housekeeping more than a third of a century before.

But Harrison's service to the Commonwealth was far from over. In September 1967 Governor Godwin named him to the state Supreme Court (a post which he filled ably until he retired on December 31, 1981). In 1968 Godwin appointed him to chair an eleven-man commission created to recommend changes in the Virginia constitution. This group undertook the first stem-to-stern overhaul of the state's organic law since the convention of 1901–2. Lewis F. Powell, Jr., who served on the commission before his elevation to the U.S. Supreme Court, says Harrison "presided over the commission with a sensitive combination of firmness and deference to the views of its members. His wide knowledge of the constitution and statutes of Virginia—and of the specific needs for revision in the fundamental law—proved immensely helpful to the commission and to our staff of able lawyers." The recommendations of Harrison and his associates, approved by two successive sessions of the General Assembly, were overwhelmingly ratified in the popular referendum that followed. Reflecting the guiding principles of Harrison's public life, the commission sought to make the constitution more responsive to contemporary and future needs—all the while maintaining a balance between tradition and change. The resulting document, much shorter and more succinct than its predecessor, declared education to be a fundamental right of every Virginian, guaranteed education of "high quality," and imposed on the General Assembly the duty to intervene and provide such schooling if any locality should fail to do so. General obligation bonds for the construction of college and university buildings, schools, hospitals, penal institutions, recreational facilities, and harbor installations were authorized (subject to reasonable restrictions). The new constitution guaranteed the civil rights of all citizens and required periodic legislative reapportionment. Progressive in tone and content, the commission's handiwork provided additional proof of the advent of a new day.

In 1969 Justice and Mrs. Harrison moved from their Lawrenceville home to one which they built in a grove of oaks near the Meherrin River, four miles to the westward, known as Saddletree Farm. Containing 1,100 acres, the estate embraces part of a 2,907-acre tract patented by Lieutenant Governor William Gooch to Henry Harrison in 1732.

Albertis S. Harrison, Jr., has made significant contributions to the progress of Virginia as a legislator, governor, jurist, and constitutional reformer. While he was the Commonwealth's chief executive, his cool, undramatic approach to issues sometimes created the impression that he was letting things drift, and his reluctance to express himself forcefully on controversial questions occasionally led to strained relations with the press. "Newsmen had a rough go with Harrison," according to Carl Shires of the Richmond *News Leader*. "He could say less with more suave words than anybody they'd seen in the Mansion for years." Even so, Harrison's relaxed and unobtrusive manner of dealing with the problems of the day may well have served Virginians better than a more flamboyant or dogmatic executive style.

The Old Dominion was still lagging badly at the end of Harrison's gubernatorial term, but he had brought the Commonwealth to the threshold of far-reaching advances in education and industrialization and had given it a new relationship with federal authority. Although not bold or dynamic, he clearly understood the needs of his era and possessed the political insights and the personal qualities for meeting those needs. As the conservative Byrd machine fell apart, Harrison established the tone for a new, more progressive era. The transition was tranquil; flexibility and accommodation prevailed.

Avoiding extremes, the urbane lawyer from Lawrenceville set the stage for the moderate administrations of Mills Godwin and Linwood Holton.

SOURCES

Clipping files of the Richmond *Times-Dispatch* and *News Leader* are a rich source of information concerning Harrison's career. Editorials in the *Times-Dispatch* (Jan. 9, 1966) and the *News Leader* (Jan. 15, 1966) give appraisals of his administration. Correspondence between Attorney General Harrison and Senator Harry F. Byrd, 1957–60 (Byrd Papers, University of Virginia Library, box 244), affords insight into the relationship between the two men in the era of massive resistance. Correspondence and personal interviews with Harrison, political writer James Latimer, and U.S. Supreme Court Justice Lewis F. Powell, Jr., were extremely helpful.

See also J. Harvie Wilkinson III, *Harry Byrd and the Changing Face of Virginia Politics, 1945–1965* (Charlottesville, 1968); Robbins L. Gates, *The Making of Massive Resistance: Virginia's Politics of Public School Desegregation, 1954–1956* (Chapel Hill, N.C., 1962); James W. Ely, Jr., *The Crisis of Conservative Virginia: The Byrd Organization and the Politics of Massive Resistance* (Knoxville, Tenn., 1976); and Robert C. Smith, *They Closed Their Schools: Prince Edward County, Virginia, 1951–1964* (Chapel Hill, N.C., 1965). Gay Neale, *Brunswick County, Virginia, 1720–1975* (Richmond, 1975), traces the history of the county and provides the milieu in which Harrison grew up.

MILLS E. GODWIN, JR.

Governor of Virginia

1966–1970

1974–1978

MILLS EDWIN GODWIN, JR.

A Man for All Seasons

James L. Bugg, Jr.

Few political leaders have equaled Mills Godwin in comprehending the anatomy of Virginia politics or in translating into reality the aspirations of their constituents. His two gubernatorial terms presented diverse challenges which he met with great effectiveness. The only man chosen twice by Virginia voters as their governor, he was elected first as a Democrat and then as a Republican. Godwin made the cause of public education his own during his first stay in the Governor's Mansion, so much so that he earned the title of "the education governor." Scarcely less significant were improvements in other services. Godwin's most singular achievement lay, however, in freeing his tradition-bound state from the dead hand of the past. His second administration spanned the restless mid-1970s, a period when disturbed voters insisted upon increased economy and accountability in government and demanded relief from what many perceived as an overgrown and unconcerned bureaucracy. The test of Godwin's leadership now lay in the essentially negative role of conserving inadequate resources, maintaining fiscal integrity, slowing government growth, and restoring public confidence. Of necessity, his second administration dealt with mundane issues; even so, his activities in an era of unrest provided additional evidence of his ability as a leader.

Mills Edwin Godwin, Jr., grew up in rural Nansemond County in the Virginia Southside, where his ancestors had settled three hundred years earlier. Born at Holladay's Point on November 19, 1914, he spent his early years on the family farm, fishing and hunting, frequently accompanied by the children of the black tenants who worked his father's land. When he was thirteen, his family moved to the village of Chuckatuck where he headed the young people's group at the local Christian church, played basketball and baseball on high school teams, was elected class president, and developed skill in debating. In the fall of 1931 Godwin enrolled in the recently established Norfolk Division of the College of William and Mary. The following year he transferred to the main campus in Williamsburg where he waited tables to help pay for his education, compiled a better than average academic record, and took an active interest in student activities, baseball, and debating. In 1934 he entered the University of Virginia School of Law. Although he passed the state bar in 1937, a ruptured appendix delayed his acquisition of the law degree until the following year.

The fledgling lawyer joined the Suffolk legal firm of his cousin Charles B. Godwin, Jr., soon met and married Katherine Thomas Beale, a teacher newly arrived in Chuckatuck, and settled into the life of a young country attorney. World War II altered this pattern. Undecided whether to join the navy or the Federal Bureau of Investigation, he applied to both. A favorable response from the latter marked the beginning of a three-year tour as a special agent in St. Louis, Norfolk, and Richmond. When the war ended, he returned to his practice and Chuckatuck, having accumulated two commendations for meritorious service and a heightened respect for law enforcement.

Following a path familiar to young lawyers, Godwin participated actively in community affairs. Joining a multitude of organizations, he began a particularly notable career in Ruritan, leading to the national presidency of that organization. In 1947 he won the House of Delegates seat for Suffolk and Nansemond from a veteran stalwart of the Byrd organization. Both he and his father were Byrd supporters, and his uncle, state Senator Charles Moses of Appomattox, held a leadership position in the Byrd faction. To his surprise, however, he found no warm welcome in Richmond. He had defeated an organization incumbent, and the House leadership showed its displeasure with "less than the best" committee assignments. The following year Godwin compounded his difficulties by supporting a relative, Horace Edwards, in the Democratic gubernatorial primary against John Battle, the successful organization candidate. As a lawmaker, Godwin conscientiously attended to the needs of his constituents, faithfully supported the legislative programs of Governors Tuck and Battle, and took an increasing interest in highway safety, environmental problems, and public education.

In 1952 Godwin won an uncontested election to fill a vacancy in the state Senate for the district which included the cities of Suffolk and Franklin and the counties of Nansemond, Isle of Wight, and Southampton. After numerous committee assignments, he eventually won a seat on the coveted Finance Committee, broadening both his perception and his influence. Passing years brought membership on various study groups and on the governor's budget advisory committee—all testifying to his progress toward a leadership role in the organization. Indeed, as the organization's troubles multiplied in the turbulent 1950s, the Nansemond senator rendered increasingly important service. He faithfully supported the primary tenets of Byrd orthodoxy: "pay-as-you-go" financing, balanced budgets, and moderate taxes. But he also worked quietly to persuade the organization to adopt a less rigid conservatism. Although he endorsed the junior Byrd's automatic income tax credit law of 1952 to return to taxpayers any surplus remaining at the end of each biennium, in the 1954 session Godwin played a leading role in developing a compromise between the "Young Turks" and die-hard conservatives which appropriated one-third of the $7 million surplus for education and returned the remainder to taxpayers.

The U.S. Supreme Court's epochal *Brown* decision outlawing segregation in the public schools prompted Godwin's emergence as a principal architect of massive resistance, one of a select group of hard-core obstructionists opposing any integration whatsoever. His Senate speeches on this subject attracted more criticism than any other aspect of his political career and continued to haunt him in subsequent decades. Not a racist in the classic negrophobic mold, he did not urge deliberate defiance of the law, nor did he manifest hostility toward blacks as individuals or as a group; instead, his actions were directed exclusively toward delaying and minimizing integration by legal means.

The *Brown* decision, in Godwin's judgment, represented a flagrant abuse of judicial power and violated the historic rights of the states. Perhaps equally important, he believed that integration would open "the door to the inevitable destruction of our free public schools," and "Virginia could not go forward without the public schools." Thus Godwin, after briefly supporting the moderate Gray Commission plan for local option, soon was employing his considerable oratorical abilities to justify massive resistance. Opposing every attempt at local option, he declared that he and his associates would never retreat "from our stand of no compromise on our principle of total segregation in Virginia."

For a time they enjoyed complete success. But in the fall of 1958 school closings in Norfolk and Charlottesville provoked mounting opposition from business, labor, and citizens' groups, and in January 1959 state and federal courts forbade the closing of schools to avoid integration. Faced with these developments, Governor Almond created the Perrow Commission to establish local option. Godwin, a member of that body, joined eight other dissenters in issuing a minority report calling for elimination of the constitutional requirement for the maintenance of public schools. In contrast to some of his colleagues, Godwin never apologized for his role in massive resistance. Virginians, he declared, needed time to "adjust to what inevitably had to happen." He later admitted that "we waited too long to do some of the things we should have done in earlier years to assure full equality of opportunity in education for our Negro children," and as governor he would do much to "right the wrongs." Even so, the stigma of involvement in abortive massive resistance would remain.

Yet, because of, or in spite of, his role in massive resistance Godwin's political fortunes continued to improve. In 1961 he became the candidate for lieutenant governor on a ticket headed by Albertis S. Harrison, Jr. In a hard-fought primary he received the support of the organization, while liberals, many moderates, organized labor, and blacks supported his opponent, Armistead Boothe. The ensuing battle placed two able, articulate and experienced politicians on opposite sides, one symbolizing tradition and the other reform. Godwin characterized his opponent as "the great apostle of integration," the "darling" of union bosses and liberals, the "original big spender." Boothe responded that Godwin was an "architect of massive resistance" who placed the preservation of segregation above that of schools. This excessive campaign rhetoric led commentator Charles McDowell to note that the voters were "actually asked to believe that one side is a bunch of wild revolutionaries working for socialist bosses, and the other side is a bunch of reactionaries running errands for Senator Byrd when they aren't otherwise occupied closing schoolhouses." The victorious Godwin won a landside majority in the Southside but failed to carry southwest Virginia and the urban areas of northern Virginia, south Hampton Roads, and Roanoke.

The next four years represented an important transition period for Virginia and for Godwin. Past glories and traditional values began to receive less emphasis in his speeches and improved state services more. Gradually the view emerged that Godwin's conservatism did not preclude the necessity for change, and his emphasis on party loyalty during the 1964 presidential campaign did not go unnoticed. Suddenly Virginians were discovering a moderate Godwin who articulated an exciting new vision of a developing "program for progress." A program stressing a diversified economy, quality education, and concern for humane values, it promised significant advances in state services as varied as mental health and cultural development, conservation and urban renewal, port development and community colleges. When he announced for the governorship in 1965, not only the organization leadership but moderate and liberal Democrats and, surprisingly, organized labor and the two largest black political organizations were in his camp.

Perhaps the new image can be explained as the pragmatic move of a superb politician adept at evaluating popular mood, yet equally significant was the fact that Godwin's now mature political philosophy embraced principles underlying the program he advocated. Godwin often described himself as a conservative in fiscal affairs and a moderate "in relation to those services, and to the extent thereof, that government ought to provide for its citizens." The test of any public official, in Godwin's opinion, was the judgment required to provide essential services—and the wisdom to understand that government could not meet all needs, solve all problems, or create a bureaucratic utopia.

Godwin's principal opponent in the 1965 gubernatorial race was an articulate and attractive young Republican from Roanoke who dreamed of a new and dynamic party far removed from Goldwater conservatism. Linwood Holton pictured Godwin as a massive resister and defender of the status quo, a follower of Byrd who shared the senator's penny-pinching economics. Godwin countered by preaching the gospel of economic diversification, quality education, improved social services, and urban renewal. Not surprisingly, many of his more reactionary Southside neighbors refused to support him. Bitterly opposed to the civil rights activism of the Johnson administration and the federal judiciary, a sizable contingent of voters in Godwin's home district deserted him for the recently formed Conservative party. Although Godwin won the election, the Conservatives denied him a majority. He carried Richmond, the Tidewater cities, the Southside, and the Southwest and received the strong backing of labor and the blacks. But he lost the large and rapidly growing northern Virginia area, as well as the Richmond suburbs and a substantial portion of the Shenandoah Valley. His 47 percent plurality was approximately 10 percent above the total vote for Holton. But Conservative nominee William J. Story captured one-third of the ballots in Godwin's home district and obtained an impressive 13.4 percent of the statewide vote.

Both growing Republican strength and the desertion of former Democrats to the Conservatives spelled future difficulties. In spite of this, Godwin entered office with a confidence born of long experience and tested leadership abilities, a friendly Assembly, and a prosperous economy. He assured his fellow Virginians that they stood on the threshold of a bright future. He was unaware of the impending demise of the organization which had nurtured him.

During his first term as governor Godwin encountered personal tragedy, outstanding success as chief executive, and disappointment in the role of party chief. Unable to have children of their own, the Godwins in January 1954 adopted an infant daughter, Becky, who rapidly became the center of their lives. In August 1968, while swimming at Virginia Beach, she was struck by lightning and died four days later. After the funeral the governor remained secluded for a week. "It was not easy to give her up," he later recalled. "We faced up to what we had to face." Godwin had suffered the most grievous tragedy of his life.

Becky's death represented a dark moment in a four-year term marked by success. In many respects Godwin's first administration provided a textbook example of the art of leadership. It began on a cold, January day in 1966 as the new governor delivered what was perhaps his finest address. He stirred the emotions of listeners as he issued an urgent call for action: "If there is a watchword for our time, it is to move, to strike out boldly, to reach for the heights."

Godwin's objective, a program to move Virginia into a position of leadership among the states, involved expansion and improvement of state services, economic growth and development, urban renewal, and revision of the antiquated state constitution. Success depended on a significant increase in revenue which only a state tax on sales (the last major untapped source of funds) could satisfy. Consequently, Godwin urged the Assembly to initiate a 2 percent statewide tax, which localities might supplement by an additional 1 percent. Half of the state tax would be returned to the localities, and the state levy would automatically rise to 3 percent on July 1, 1968—thus committing the Commonwealth to long-term support for the proposal. This move sparked bitter and lengthy debate revolving around the distribution formula, failure to exempt food and nonprescription drugs, and, above all, departure from the long-established tradition which prohibited a legislative body from binding its successor. Patiently responding to his critics, Godwin defended the sales tax and skillfully employed every resource at his command. In the end, the Assembly approved the tax with its controversial escalator clause, as well as a companion measure imposing a 2 percent tax on automobile sales—the proceeds to be earmarked for highway construction.

Since this was no final solution to revenue problems, Godwin was forced to make an even bolder recommendation: abandonment of pay-as-you-go financing, one of the most sacred principles of Virginia political orthodoxy. In January 1968, he advocated capital funds bond issues for higher education and mental health. Assembly approval of $80 million in bond sales for these purposes transferred the contest to a popular referendum. Announcing a bipartisan campaign, Godwin urged state politicians, government officials, and business and community leaders to join in an intensive effort to rally support for the bond issues. A small army of Virginians answered the call, but Godwin was the moving force and mastermind. When voters gave their overwhelming approval, congratulatory messages poured in to praise the "masterful" leadership of a governor who, with "wisdom, foresight and ability," was moving Virginia into a "new era."

With adequate revenue assured, Godwin assigned first priority to the advancement of public education at all levels. Although he had long been interested in educational matters, he now began to preach the gospel of educational opportunity with the zeal of a convert. Knowledge, he proclaimed, was the "great equalizer of our time," the "surest road to . . . equality of citizenship." Through the acquisition and application of knowledge, the state could "realize its immense potential for industrial and cultural development, for our general well-being, for the very survival of all we hold dear." During Godwin's term state aid for public schools more than doubled, minimum salaries for teachers rose significantly, and state aid was extended to kindergartens and summer schools. Appropriations to colleges and universities increased by more than 100 percent, and the equivalent of sixty-two acres of new instructional space was added. The growth of kindergartens at one end of the educational ladder and new graduate programs, graduate scholarships, and increased emphasis on research at the other demonstrated the scope of his educational commitment.

Godwin's plans to create a statewide community college system ran into legislative opposition, but he eventually won approval of six two-year campuses, the nucleus of a system which expanded rapidly to twenty-three community colleges on thirty-two campuses. Indeed, Godwin's efforts stimulated the development of every public college and university in the state. New facilities expanded enrollments, and more adequately equipped libraries and laboratories improved the quality of instruction. In Richmond, the new Virginia Commonwealth University (an amalgam of Richmond Professional Institute and the Medical College of Virginia) opened in 1968 to provide additional educational opportunities in one of the state's fastest growing metropolitan areas.

Godwin also took the lead in seeking more adequate budgets to upgrade mental health care and to improve other state services. He actively supported efforts to reorganize and strengthen agencies dealing with water resources and pollution, and his administration designed programs to return welfare recipients to a self-supporting basis. Appropriations to welfare, corrections, conservation, public safety, ports, and state parks increased substantially. In four years the state budget rose by approximately 42 percent, and no major area of state activity was unaffected. In addition, the governor completed the first major reorganization of state government since the Tuck administration.

The Godwin program also stressed economic growth to provide jobs and to finance continuing expansion of state services. Since improved transportation facilities would accelerate industrial expansion, Godwin took the lead in getting state subsidies for port development, budget increases to hasten construction of interstate and arterial highways, and federal funds to subsidize airport construction. During his term almost $20 million was invested in port facilities, and the state added 480 miles of interstate highways and 600 miles of arterial roads. The governor, much like Harrison before him, became chief salesman in a search for new markets and new industry. Gracious in manner, well-informed and hospitable, he moved easily in executive circles and proved an able advocate at annual luncheons held in New York and in Chicago. In 1967 and 1969 he led trade missions to Europe, dispensing Virginia products, promoting the state as a site for branch plants, advertising its tourist attractions, and encouraging the use of its ports. In 1969 he officially opened a European trade office in Brussels (a "Virginia Consulate"), an innovative step for an American state. Industrial investment during the Godwin years exceeded a billion dollars, and when he left office tourists were spending $840 million annually in the state. These advances created 60,000 new jobs and increased by 25 percent the income of the average Virginian. The state now had a model growth program, one recognized across the nation.

In his search for new industry the governor emphasized the stable political climate of Virginia, and maintenance of law and order became another major theme of his first term. The mass violence of the late 1960s for the most part bypassed Virginia. The 1968 Assembly approved a stringent riot control law, and Godwin immediately served notice that both the state police and the Virginia guard were trained and equipped to deal with civil disobedience. Godwin viewed the 1968 Poor People's March on Washington as a threat to public order and displayed even greater contempt for self-proclaimed revolutionaries, on and off college campuses, and for national leaders who failed to

380 MILLS E. GODWIN, JR.

maintain order. Radicals, he proclaimed publicly, would not be tolerated in Virginia. In October 1966 Godwin responded equally firmly to embryonic Klan activity. Within a year informants supplied information that resulted in prosecution of six Klansmen and conviction of four. Stymied by prompt and effective executive action, the Klan threat dissipated as quickly as it had arisen.

Efforts to deal with individual crime met with less success. The governor appointed an able (if somewhat controversial) professional, Otis A. Brown, to head the Division of Welfare and Institutions. He strongly backed Brown in establishing a youthful offender diagnostic center, a juvenile offenders' camp, and six regional juvenile courts that placed greater emphasis on the rehabilitation of young lawbreakers. Reforms at the state penitentiary promised some long-needed improvements but fell far short of solving the problems there. And in spite of Godwin's "urgent attention," crime statistics in the cities continued to rise.

The urban crisis presented complex problems. Rapidly mounting population increased the need for expanded public services; budgets grew faster than resources; state restrictions on local taxing powers and annexation resulted in local deficit financing; suburban communities became havens for those fleeing the central cities; migration patterns brought economic and racial changes to core cities that threatened their continued viability. Godwin viewed the problems of the suburbs and central cities as interrelated and contended that future progress of both depended upon the continued health of each. Yet his efforts in 1966 to create planning districts encompassing cities, counties, and towns were rejected by the General Assembly. Three years later, he warned of eventual disaster if local officials continued to sponsor the development of independent suburban communities adjacent to core cities.

The governor's efforts to modify Virginia's 1902 constitution did, however, win approval. In February 1969 Godwin reported the recommendations of an eleven-man commission to a special session of the Assembly, strongly supporting most of the proposed revisions, particularly that the state discard the pay-as-you-go financial straitjacket, provide a more flexible debt policy, and continue the one-term gubernatorial tradition. By mid-April the lawmakers had devised compromises satisfactory to both the governor and the General Assembly and had approved the proposed constitution. The new document expanded considerably the amount the state could borrow, provided for annual legislative sessions, devised a procedure to remove unfit judges, liberalized voting qualifications, limited the appointive power of judges, permitted localities to liberalize certain tax provisions, and retained the prohibition against successive terms for the governor. Voter approval came easily in the fall of 1970, and this success was a final capstone to Godwin's program. "I know of nothing," he declared, "that is going to be more important to the long future of Virginia."

Many factors explain Godwin's phenomenal success. He came to the governorship at a time when the state was both prosperous and calm. The racial antagonisms of previous years had cooled, legislative realignment had weakened the traditional rural conservative dominance, and the emotional and political climate favored fundamental change. Of equal importance was the governor's ability to unite a diverse group of legislators with their own particular interests and ambitions. He brought to the governorship a spirit of excitement, a feeling of movement, of confidence in his leadership. "Anyone who has any doubts that Virginia will move forward in the next few years," wrote a Richmond legislator, "need only come to the Capitol and sense the rapport that is developing between the General Assembly and a Governor who has demonstrated he has the ability and courage to lead."

Godwin's relations with the federal government were less cordial. The civil rights legislation of the mid-1960s, an important part of Lyndon Johnson's Great Society program, he believed both unwise and unconstitutional. Godwin joined other governors in protesting the Johnson administration's practice of ignoring the states in administering these programs and took the initiative in an unsuccessful attempt to remove Virginia from restrictions of the federal Voting Rights Act. Godwin aimed his strongest criticism at the Department of Health, Education, and Welfare and fought with the limited weapons at his command the new affirmative action requirements pointing toward total integration of schools. As HEW turned increasingly to quantitative measurement, racial balance, and busing to implement its objectives, Godwin strongly condemned "arbitrary procedures" that he feared would threaten the upgrading of public education in Virginia. Quality schools required increased funding, which needed the support of those who were deserting public schools because of HEW demands. As an ever-larger number of whites enrolled their children in private schools, their interest in public education declined. The governor's plea for moderation went unheeded, and he was eventually reduced to joining fellow governors in a futile protest, this time against busing.

Even more disappointing to the governor was his inability to prevent the dissolution of the Democratic coalition which had placed him in office. First to break away were the blacks. Their leaders believed rightly that they had played a significant role in the Godwin victory, and they considered their rewards both too few and too long delayed. In contrast, Godwin remained on reasonably amicable terms with organized labor through much of his term. Although he had reservations about some of the goals of the state AFL-CIO, he broke precedent by addressing its 1966 state convention. But labor, too, eventually disagreed with him over the election of his successor. The industrial-financial establishment continued to back Godwin, yet even this group divided in the next gubernatorial race, many seeing the Republican party as a vehicle for the restoration of Byrd conservatism.

The process of dissolution began in the 1966 primary when a liberal coalition emerged in the Eighth Congressional District to back George Rawlings against organization stalwart Howard W. Smith. Moreover, liberals and moderates united behind Armistead Boothe and William Spong to oppose Harry Byrd, Jr., and A. Willis Robertson for the U.S. Senate. Smith and Robertson failed to survive the primary, while Rawlings lost to a Republican in the fall election. Godwin noted the defeats and urged the party to unite on the broad middle ground which he believed his administration had staked out. The governor participated actively in the 1967 General Assembly elections; and, although the Republicans made modest gains in the Southwest, the Valley, and northern Virginia, a still united Democratic party could claim another victory.

But beneath the surface unity, the forces of dissolution continued to gain strength. A faction under the leadership of Henry Howell was determined to remake the party in the liberal image of its national counterpart. The very antithesis of Godwin in background, in philosophy, and in temperament, Howell had initiated a series of successful rate cases which won rebates from utilities and insurance companies. He was equally successful in persuading the U.S. district court to require Godwin to restore some $11 million in federal funds the state had diverted from their intended purpose of aiding school districts "impacted" with the children of federal personnel. Opposed to school closings during massive resistance and sympathetic toward collective bargaining, he easily united blacks, labor, and antiestablishment populists under his banner. An irrepressible extrovert, he possessed in full measure the energy, aggressiveness, and charisma required to lead a populist crusade. Although they bore little resemblance to each other, Senator Spong found Howell and Godwin strangely alike in one respect; neither could "participate in anything without taking it over."

Godwin believed Howell an unfit candidate for governor, and he had no intention of relinquishing party control to the leader of a liberal faction eager to impose on Virginia the same "fiscal folly" which he believed the national Democrats had inflicted on the nation. Certain that victory in the 1969 gubernatorial election depended on uniting the conservative and moderate factions of the party, the governor devoted his efforts to achieving this objective. However, he failed, and in the primary liberals backed Howell, moderates supported William Battle, and conservatives endorsed Lieutenant Governor Fred Pollard. Although he probably preferred Pollard, Godwin refused to endorse any candidate; but when the close vote between Battle and Howell required a runoff, the governor backed Battle. Once committed, he campaigned actively and played a crucial role in the moderate candidate's victory.

A tired Battle entered his third campaign against a well-organized, well-financed, and buoyantly optimistic Linwood Holton, the Republican aspirant. Howell advised his supporters to vote as they pleased, and a group of Richmond conservatives organized to campaign for Holton. The Republicans imported both President Richard Nixon and Ronald Reagan to rally support for their ticket. The voters, commentator Charles McDowell noted, were being asked to "brace themselves for a Holton-Nixon-Reagan-labor-populist-liberal-conservative alliance." And he added: "What is Virginia politics coming to?" Godwin might well have pondered the same question. Again he campaigned actively for Battle. And when his candidate lost, the governor found the voters' mood both puzzling and disturbing: "On the one hand our people seem immensely pleased at what has been accomplished [by the Godwin administration]. But in the next breath they express the feeling that it is time for a change." Noting that Holton had benefited from both conservative and liberal defections, Godwin added that Virginia politics was becoming increasingly difficult "to understand or explain." To a close political friend he confided that there were "certain implications from the voting . . . that ought not to be ignored. We had some defections from the right . . . but if the control of our party ever gets into the hands of the real liberal element, we will see tremendously large defectors—perhaps even including me."

When his term ended in January 1970, Godwin returned to Nansemond County to resume his law practice, manage his 500-acre farm, and accept directorships in several corporations and a major bank. Denied even a delegate's seat in the 1972 state Democratic convention, he watched from the sidelines as his party moved toward the McGovern disaster in the fall election. When liberals also seized control of the Virginia Democratic party, an embittered Godwin broke ranks to support Republican Nixon in the presidential race. He even agreed to serve as advisory chairman of the Virginia Committee for the Re-election of the President. Nixon won a massive victory; the moderate Spong, caught between the Republican tide and division in Democratic ranks, lost his Senate seat to an obscure Republican, William Scott. Two years earlier a brilliant young strategist, Richard Obenshain, had gained control of state Republican machinery from the moderate Holton forces and had proceeded to remold the party into a new, conservative image which was proving attractive to an increasing number of Democrats. As 1973 opened, Republicans claimed not only the governorship and one of the two U.S. Senate seats (independent Byrd held the other) but seven of Virginia's ten congressmen and a growing minority in the Assembly as well. With a well-filled treasury, increasingly effective organization, and the impetus of recent victories, they needed only a strong gubernatorial candidate.

Political events of the previous year established the pattern for the 1973 race for governor. Howell, strongly backed by organized labor, blacks, urban and suburban liberals, and a large youth contingent, planned a return engagement. Obenshain Republicans, with the financial and organizational support for a conservative renaissance, turned to Godwin as the man most likely to defeat Howell. With promises of support and pleas that only he could rally Virginia conservatives and moderates in a common defense of traditional values, they persuaded a reluctant Godwin to enter the battle against his old antagonist.

Both men announced as independents, although Godwin, in June, accepted the nomination of the Republicans and joined their party. Throughout a major part of the campaign he pictured Howell as an ultraliberal who favored school integration, busing, and gun control and who opposed the state right-to-work law. Godwin led in early polls, but then Howell forged ahead. Efforts of professional consultants to assist Godwin proved only partially successful, since his obvious hostility toward Howell made him seem negative and even vindictive at times and reduced his effectiveness as a campaigner. Howell proved an aggressive and adept challenger who castigated his opponent as a "Republicrat," a former leader of the Byrd organization who catered to the privileged few in the top echelons of both parties and failed to understand the problems of the average Virginian. Howell returned Godwin's distrust with interest, his playful jabs of the early campaign turning into bitter and exaggerated charges as the election date approached. Indeed, both candidates tended to substitute personal attacks and distortions for dispassionate discussion of relevant issues and, as a result, bored the electorate into a state of apathy. "Its tougher than hell to get anybody to give a damn," remarked one frustrated Republican legislator in the midst of the campaign.

The sales tax issue attracted the most interest, and Howell almost made it a springboard to victory. But in the final weeks Godwin acquired new momentum, and he eventually won by the narrowest of margins as more than a million Virginians split their votes almost evenly. Godwin carried six of ten congressional districts, forty-nine of ninety-six counties, and twenty of thirty-nine cities. He swept the suburbs, carried the rural areas by smaller margins, and lost heavily in the central cities. Several factors contributed to the Godwin victory. Richard Obenshain not only engineered a highly successful telephone campaign that got Godwin supporters to the polls but cooperated with Republican national committee staff in a last-minute television blitz. Howell also committed two errors which cost him dearly: he unveiled an ill-advised tax program neutralizing his most effective issue and published a September poll showing him well ahead which stirred languid Republicans into action. Finally, in the last weeks Godwin shifted to a more informal style and placed increasing emphasis on a positive program.

In his second inaugural the governor noted that the people of Virginia were breaking with an ancient tradition of one-term governors and added, "I am humbled to be the instrument of that departure." James M. Thomson, the House of Delegates majority leader who would soon emerge as a major administration foe, welcomed "home an old pro—with a great deal of relief." But there was a difference, for Godwin now was a Republican. Indeed, as he began his second term in January 1974, he faced a vastly different environment—no longer completely trusted by the party he had left, not fully accepted by the party he had joined. In his first administration he had opened new vistas and mapped new directions that excited and inspired both participants and observers. Now he faced the necessity of consolidating gains already achieved, of conserving resources, of slowing momentum instead of increasing it. Patience and self-restraint were the characteristics now demanded, not daring.

Inevitably, some enthusiastic supporters would become critics, disillusionment would replace ardor, complaints would grow about a lack of innovation, of initiative, of leadership. Gradually the thesis developed of a governor less competent, less creative, and less successful. Godwin believed such an interpretation unjust. "You can only compare the way the circumstances of each administration were handled," he observed. The new problems, he noted, were severe and varied, and they "tested our mettle." The problems were indeed severe, for the governor faced a series of emergencies in the corrections system, energy, the economy, and the environment which would make crisis the keynote of the second administration as progress had been the watchword of the first.

For years Virginia had neglected its penal system, and the days of reckoning had arrived. An ancient and obsolete penitentiary in Richmond was supplemented by assorted farms, juvenile detention centers, and road camps scattered around the state, many makeshift and hardly fit for human habitation. To the undertrained, underpaid, and undermanned staffs rehabilitation was a concept but poorly comprehended and largely ignored. First offenders and hardened criminals were thrown together, and primitive medical treatment and occasional inhumane treatment threatened both physical and psychological health. Reacting to these conditions, a federal judge in 1971 ordered sweeping reforms designed to safeguard the constitutional rights of prisoners and fined top prison officials when they ignored his orders. These actions ended many flagrant abuses but also limited the ability of prison officials to deal with unruly prisoners. In January 1974, as Godwin returned to office, the State Crime Commission and a Richmond grand jury spelled out the full extent of the crisis, condemning the penitentiary as a "bankrupt institution" and emphasizing the loss of effective control by officials and the rapid increase in the number of escapes.

Involved in a grim race against time, Godwin struggled to eliminate abuses and upgrade the system. The governor established a new Department of Corrections with separate divisions to handle adult services, youth services, and probation and parole. He imposed more stringent furlough regulations, ordered the receiving unit transferred from the penitentiary to the Goochland

State Farm where first offenders could be segregated from hardened criminals, and arranged for a floor in the Virginia Commonwealth University
hospital to be used as a medical ward for prisoners. In addition, he hired
qualified consultants to map out additional reforms and persuaded the Assembly to appropriate funds to renovate prison facilities and initiate a rehabilitation school system. In June 1974 Godwin appointed Jack F. Davis as director
of the new Department of Corrections. Although inexperienced in the corrections field, Davis proved to be an able administrator. Higher salaries, a better
qualified staff, modern business methods, and new probation, furlough, and
work release programs emphasizing rehabilitation did much to restore discipline and improve morale. Prison escapes decreased dramatically. Indeed,
Davis and the governor wrought a minor miracle by revamping a system in
serious trouble.

The governor also addressed himself to other law enforcement problems—although with less success. In his first address to the Assembly he
advocated more stringent laws against violent crime, rigid law enforcement,
and quick and certain punishment, particularly through the reinstatement of
the death penalty for a limited number of serious crimes. Responding to
Godwin's appeal, the 1975 Assembly approved a mandatory death penalty
for the murder of a kidnapped victim, murder-for-hire, and murder by a
prison inmate. In 1976 the crime of premeditated murder in the commission
of rape or armed robbery was added to the list, and in 1977 the Assembly
approved the death penalty for the murder of on-duty police officers. Demanding stiffer penalties for rapists, prison escapees, repeat offenders, and
other felons, the governor urged legislators to overhaul the penal code. These
recommendations sparked spirited debate, yet in the end he found support for
a major part of his program, and the criminal code was revised in 1975. Two
years later the governor could note with some satisfaction that the crime rate
had decreased and that the "number of negative headlines with respect to our
corrections program" had declined.

The problems of penal reform and crime prevention coincided with a
second crisis involving energy, already approaching its climax when Godwin
took office. An embargo on the sale of Arabian oil during 1973 had created a
scarcity of oil in the United States. Reacting to the situation, Godwin appealed to federal authorities for larger allocations, requested major oil companies to provide additional gasoline for the hardest-hit areas, and ordered
state police to investigate a threatened strike of retail dealers. Eventually, in
mid-February 1974 he initiated mandatory rationing restricting the purchase
of gasoline to alternate days. An increased allotment, combined with the odd-
even purchasing, reduced the shortage, and the end of the Arab embargo
permitted Godwin to suspend mandatory rationing two months later.

Nevertheless, the governor recognized that energy was an ongoing problem and established a new State Energy Office to control, conserve, and distribute energy resources. In November he assembled some three hundred industrial and governmental executives to discuss the persisting effects of the energy shortage on the state's economy. Events soon demonstrated the wisdom of Godwin's continuing concern. The winter of 1974–75 brought a natural gas shortage centered in western Virginia and the Danville area. Faced with the shutdown of industries, the governor appealed to both the Federal Power Commission and the Federal Energy Commission for additional natural gas. Again the crisis passed, but Godwin's interest in the problem continued. "I personally think," he declared, "that our life style may have to be changed. . . . We are just not going to have plentiful energy sources available. . . . We are going to have to conserve."

The crisis receded during the mild 1975–76 winter, but the following year was one Virginians would long remember. The first of a series of cold waves hit in November. Again the governor took stern measures, limiting the use of natural gas by most nonresidential customers, restricting businesses to a forty-hour week, and making the setting of thermostats above 65° an illegal act subject to fine and imprisonment. Purchases of additional oil and natural gas relieved the immediate crisis, and Godwin allowed his orders to expire after the severe weather abated in mid-February. Perhaps, as his critics charged, the governor overreacted, but there can be no doubt that his efforts brought home to every Virginian the reality of the problem.

The energy shortages of the mid-1970s paved the way for a severe economic recession. Godwin believed that such difficulties demanded maintenance of a balanced budget without resorting to increased taxes, and this approach dictated a temporary brake on expansion and improvement of state services. He told the 1975 Assembly that in a "winter of insecurity," conservation of available resources must be the paramount consideration. For four years the governor kept the budget in a precarious balance but at the expense of state services. This meant reduced agency budgets and school aid, temporary freezes on hiring and new highway construction, and the transfer of funds already appropriated for new buildings to the operating budget. He demanded more prudent management and conservation of state funds and served notice that new programs, regardless of merit, would be postponed. Clearly and specifically he stated his opposition to deficit financing in any form: "I've staked out my position in this matter and I shall stay with it, because I believe in it."

The governor's mail indicated broad support for his views. Legislators also followed his leadership, although with increasing reluctance. Democratic spokesman James Thomson accused him of changing from a do-something to a do-nothing executive whose only policy was retrenchment. Godwin characterized the debate as one between those who believed the state should limit expenditures to available resources and those who advocated the federal government's solution of deficit financing. His opponents charged that "Mills the Munificent" had turned into "Mills the Miser."

By 1976 the necessity for new capital construction at state institutions became so critical that Godwin proposed new taxes on beer sales, on coal severance, and on dividends paid by Virginia corporations and banks, with the revenues from these sources to be used at colleges, mental hospitals, and prisons. The defeat of a major portion of this proposal forced him, the following year, to recommend the issuance of bonds for these purposes. He submitted five proposals totaling $125 million to pay for improvements in higher education, mental health, parks, and ports. After receiving the overwhelming support of the Assembly, he launched an aggressive bond campaign which won voter approval in November 1977. Not until the latter part of 1977 did an economic upturn provide a growing surplus which allowed the governor, on the eve of his departure in January 1978, to recommend significant budget increases for virtually all state agencies. Godwin interpreted this development as vindication of his lonely but determined stand.

Along with economic recession, Godwin also encountered stunning environmental crises. Floods ravaged thirteen southwest Virginia counties in April 1977, and a severe drought afflicted almost the entire state the following summer—all necessitating emergency relief measures. These problems, however, paled before the tragic implications of the Kepone disaster. This unfolding story brought into sharp relief an incredible mosaic of corporate irresponsibility, indifference to health and safety standards by federal and state officials, violation of federal law by a municipality, and long-term injury to an important segment of the Virginia economy.

Life Science Products, Inc., a Hopewell firm closely related to Allied Chemical Company, in 1974 began manufacturing a chlorinated hydrocarbon called Kepone. Produced in an abandoned gas station, this highly toxic chemical soon became a major threat to public health and safety resulting in heart-wrenching illness for employees and their families. Contaminated water dumped into the James River created one of the worst ecological disasters in the nation's history. The James was found to be contaminated for sixty miles, and Godwin ordered an end to fishing in the river and in nearby regions of the Chesapeake Bay. Some 1,500 fishermen found their livelihood destroyed, and an equal number of seafood packers and assorted interests were also affected. Godwin rendered what assistance he could through state and federal agencies, and in February 1976 he sent the Assembly a proposal to inventory all dangerous substances manufactured in the state, to expand the authority of state agencies regulating production of such substances, and to provide both civil and criminal penalties for violation of public health requirements. The Assembly gave swift approval, but the damage had already been done.

For the remainder of his term the Kepone problem plagued the governor as pollution of the James continued.

Godwin must have regarded his continuing problems with HEW as almost as persistent and insoluble as Kepone. This time the issue was additional integration in higher education. The governor, maintaining that the state was in full compliance with the law, pledged renewed efforts to increase the number of minority faculty and students in predominantly white colleges and universities, and HEW approved a more moderate desegregation plan which provided a temporary truce. Three years later, under prodding of federal courts, more extreme demands were again enumerated, and Godwin left office with the problem unresolved.

As a Republican governor forced to deal with an overwhelmingly Democratic Assembly, Godwin found the art of diplomacy essential. His wide acquaintance among legislators was an asset, and his pledge that he "would be a governor first and a politician second," elicited a favorable response. The 1974 and 1975 sessions in most respects went smoothly. The Assembly gave the governor most of what he requested—and refused to approve what he opposed. But before the end of the second session Godwin engaged in tests of strength with Democratic leaders in both houses. He emerged the victor in the crucial battle on fiscal policy, but there was growing criticism of a lack of positive executive leadership.

Again, in 1976, much of the governor's modest program was accepted. But from the first day of the session a crisis developed as Democratic moderates and liberals combined to gain control of the Senate. Although leadership in the House of Delegates did not change, Majority Leader Thomson also was determined to contest executive influence, and the session soon demonstrated a lack of unified goals and discipline. As the governor's influence declined, no force emerged to control the new rivalries and dissensions that arose to compete with long-established antagonisms between the two legislative chambers. The battle for dominance soon centered on the manner of securing additional funding for capital improvements. It ended in a confrontation between the allies of Thomson and those of the governor in the House of Delegates, with neither group able to gain the upper hand. Indeed, the result demonstrated clearly the difficulties inherent when opposing parties control the executive and legislative branches of state government. In the last two years of his term Godwin increasingly used the veto to prevent passage of legislation he deemed unwise. Yet, in spite of increasing restlessness and the threat of revolt, the Assembly generally supported his recommendations.

Godwin's long association with the Assembly partially explains the willingness of many legislators to accept his leadership; also important was the governor's seeming indifference to party labels. Philosophy, to Godwin, was more important than labels, and he made no secret of his willingness to campaign "for those who share my convictions and views." In August 1974 he announced his support of all ten incumbent congressmen—including three conservative Democrats. In the 1975 Assembly campaign the governor stated his position even more bluntly: "I do not intend to oppose Democrats whose political philosophy coincides with my own." When independent Senator Harry F. Byrd, Jr., ran for reelection in 1976, Godwin not only urged Republicans to endorse the senior senator but announced his own support irrespective of party action.

Not all Republicans admired the governor's continued loyalty to old political friends or approved of his tendency to ignore party labels in his appointments to state boards and commissions. A GOP committee chairman in western Virginia noted that the governor's lack of partisanship in appointments did not make defending his administration "any easier in the Roanoke Valley." Richard Obenshain assured the critics that Godwin did not ignore the Republican personnel committee: "To be sure, not all of our recommendations have been followed. But very few people, I believe, would have expected, in view of the broad coalition which elected him and the strong personal attachments resulting from his life-time in politics, that all of our recommendations would have been accepted." Both Obenshain and his successor as state chairman, George McMath, worked actively to eradicate dissension and to unify party support behind the governor. In defense of his record Godwin noted that he had worked closely with the party leadership and made more Republican than Democratic appointments. Moreover, he argued that the success of his program depended on the support of Democratic legislators and that he could not ignore his supporters, whatever their party affiliation. He might have added that his conversion to Republicanism brought the party substantial benefits as Virginia conservatives turned increasingly to Godwin as their leader and spokesman.

When his term ended in January 1978, the governor closed his active political career with a feeling of satisfaction and quiet pride. For three decades he had served Virginia well. Without apology and without regret he had battled with consummate skill—as legislator and governor, as Democrat and Republican—for principles and policies that reflected the ideals and the heritage of his native state. He had devoted his life and his considerable talents to its service, and he had been rewarded with its highest honors. No man loved the Commonwealth more, and few understood better the deep wellsprings of its strength.

History may well accord Godwin a place second only to Harry F. Byrd, Sr., as the architect of political development in twentieth-century Virginia. If so, his reputation will depend primarily on the accomplishments of his first administration. Yet the manner in which he confronted the different, and equally difficult, problems of his second term should not be overlooked. He met the crises thrust upon him with courage and decisiveness, marks of true leadership. Above all, he battled for fiscal integrity amid mounting pressures for deficit financing and saw his judgment vindicated by the solid victory of his Republican successor, John Dalton. After attending a Norfolk dinner organized by friends and supporters to honor Godwin and his wife upon his retirement, commentator Guy Friddell noted that "historians might be bemused at the contrasts in Godwin's thirty year public career—but to those present he was simply a man for all seasons."

SOURCES

Readers seeking additional information should consult the Godwin Executive Papers (Virginia State Library) and the Godwin personal papers (College of William and Mary). Also see the Harry F. Byrd Papers (University of Virginia) and the Henry Howell Papers (Old Dominion University).

Articles by James Latimer and Charles McDowell in the Richmond *Times-Dispatch* are especially helpful, as well as material in other contemporary newspapers. Also consult these published works: M. Carl Andrews, *No Higher Honor: The Story of Mills E. Godwin, Jr.* (Richmond, 1970); J. Harvie Wilkinson III, *Harry Byrd and the Changing Face of Virginia Politics, 1945–1966* (Charlottesville, 1968); James W. Ely, Jr., *The Crisis of Conservative Virginia: The Byrd Organization and the Politics of Massive Resistance* (Knoxville, Tenn., 1976); Jack Bass and Walter DeVries, *The Transformation of Southern Politics* (New York, 1976); and Larry Sabato, *Aftermath of "Armageddon": An Analysis of the 1973 Virginia Gubernatorial Election* (Charlottesville, 1975) and *The Democratic Party Primary in Virginia: Tantamount to Election No Longer* (Charlottesville, 1977).

LINWOOD HOLTON

Governor of Virginia

1970–1974

LINWOOD HOLTON

An Idealist's Demise

J. Harvie Wilkinson III

Linwood Holton, first Republican governor of twentieth-century Virginia, was also the first governor since World War II not to emerge from the ranks of the Byrd organization. He was perhaps the least formal, and certainly the most progressive, of Virginia's modern chief executives. Along with Jimmy Carter of Georgia, Holton belonged to a school of "New South" governors who would deliver their region into a new day of racial harmony and moderation. All spoke the language of racial justice, and none fought the battle under heavier fire than Linwood Holton.

Fundamental to the Holton governorship is an understanding of its origins in mountainous southwest Virginia, in his boyhood a region of poor roads and poorer schools, hardscrabble farms, and coal—a blessing and a scourge: what it gave in income and employment it took in black lung and collapsed mine shafts, in scarred hillsides and half-deserted mine towns. To most Virginians, southwesterners were outsiders. Lee County, for example, was closer to the capitals of eight other states than to Richmond. Distance, however, was more spiritual than physical. Mountain folk cared little for Tidewater-Piedmont traditions; the Southwest, in fact, reveled in its irreverence. Since the terrain never accommodated plantations or slaves, the black man was rarely seen. By 1950 not a single county southwest of Roanoke was 10 percent black. On occasion, blacks and mountaineers shared common distrust of the Byrd organization and desire for a broader franchise and poll tax repeal. There was no affection for the black in the Southwest, simply less preoccupation with him. As a result the region was freer to develop other priorities: jobs, roads, and schools.

Finally, the Southwest cradled modern Republicanism. "The Blue Ridge mountains," noted Alexander Heard in 1952, "plowing up the counties of western Virginia, western North Carolina, [and] eastern Tennessee . . . outline the heartland of the Republican South." The highlanders were Republicans by heredity. Readjusters, C. Bascom Slemp, and Ted Dalton all were heroes in this region. Dalton's platform against Stanley in 1953 was so progressive that Francis Pickens Miller, Virginia's chief anti-Byrd Democrat, termed it a "genuine Democratic document" and invited his followers to back the Republican. Heir to the Dalton mantle was Linwood Holton. Unschooled in Byrd courthouse politics, unsteeped in the mannered customs of eastern Virginians, Holton brought to office different preconceptions and priorities, a folksier style and a freer hand. Not that he was ever radical or undignified. But in comparison to Battle, Stanley, Harrison, or Godwin—the gentlemen of the Byrd organization—Linwood Holton was of a different mold.

He was born near the Kentucky line in Big Stone Gap on September 21, 1923. His father was president of a small coal-hauling railroad. Holton's childhood was comfortable, not plush; "we always had what we wanted, but nothing to splurge," his mother remembered. During the depression years, Big Stone Gap was still backcountry where, noted one reporter, "WPA programs paved the streets, but cows still wandered in them." At Big Stone Gap High, one teacher recalled, Holton was a cantankerously curious pupil, someone who "liked to raise the questions in class and argue about the answers." And he was into everything: on the football, track, and debating teams, secretary-treasurer of the senior class, and business manager of the yearbook, the *School Bell*.

From high school Holton went to Washington and Lee, where he majored in commerce and graduated in 1944. After a navy tour as a submarine officer in World War II Holton attended Harvard Law School, earning his LL.B. in 1949. He wavered momentarily between Maine and Virginia, then decided on Roanoke, the town nearest home with possibilities for a sizable law practice and a strong political base. After practicing briefly with the firm of Hunter and Fox, Holton became a founding partner of Eggleston, Holton, Butler, and Glenn. But law was always secondary. "I was determined to be governor from the beginning," Holton admits, and "hoping I'd be the first Republican."

In 1953 Holton wed Virginia Harrison ("Jinks") Rogers, a Wellesley graduate who had worked in Belgium and Washington as an intelligence analyst for the CIA. The match gave Holton three things: establishment connections (Jinks's father, Frank Rogers, was a distinguished Roanoke attorney and prominent Byrd Democrat); four children (Tayloe, Anne, Woody, and Dwight); and an extroverted spouse for whom campaigning came instinctively. Warm, smart, and urbane, Jinks Holton would campaign for her husband in a motor home named the "Hi Jinks." As Virginia's First Lady she would help organize conferences on the teaching of reading skills and intelligent use of the family food dollar.

By the 1950s Holton was deep into politics as chairman of the Roanoke's Republican committee. But the party was still faintly disreputable. When Byrd Democrats assumed leadership of the state campaign for Eisenhower, Republican regulars were to remain out of sight. Given such attitudes, Holton's run for the House of Delegates in 1955 was a triumph in all but fact; he lost by a scant 340 votes out of 15,000 cast. Eisenhower's use of federal troops in Little Rock spoiled a repeat bid in 1957—not just for Holton but for gubernatorial candidate Ted Dalton as well. Yet Holton persisted. In 1961 he managed the gubernatorial campaign of Republican Clyde Pearson, who suffered another predictable loss.

Party strategy was to field candidates without hope of winning; even losing efforts built party organization and personal followings. Thus Holton ran for governor in 1965 primarily to become better known. His chief opponent, Lieutenant Governor Mills Godwin, was a seasoned Byrd Democrat and to all appearances unbeatable. But Holton waged a spirited campaign charging that Virginia was "hoarding" a $100 million surplus "while neglecting schools, roads, and other public needs." But Godwin himself ran a progressive race, and aversion to all Republicans in the aftermath of the Goldwater debacle of the previous year helped mass blacks, labor, and moderate Democrats together with the old Byrd organization behind him. Nevertheless, Holton garnered 212,207 votes to Godwin's 269,526. Three years later the 1968 presidential campaign placed Richard Nixon in Holton's debt. Holton served on a six-man committee that handled Nixon's nomination bid at Miami Beach, and he became a regional coordinator for Nixon's fall campaign, capitalizing on the president's success and preparing for his own race the following year.

Virginia politics in 1969 scrambled old myths with new realities. The Byrd machine legend continued strong, even as its candidates suffered stunning defeats. No organization candidate for statewide office survived the Democratic primary; its choice for governor, Fred Pollard of Richmond, miffed conservatives with a compliment to Hubert Humphrey and received but 23 percent of the vote. Although moderate William Battle won, the shocker was the close second-place finish of state Senator Henry Howell of Norfolk, a populist whose shrill vow to "Keep the Big Boys Honest," to roll back utility rates and insurance premiums, and to repeal the sales tax on food and patent medicines attracted a curious black, labor, and Wallaceite following. Alarmed both at Howell's success and his platform, establishment figures, led by Governor Godwin, jumped behind Battle in a bitter primary runoff which he narrowly won, 226,108–207,505.

Battle's primary victories cost him dearly in the fall election. The Democratic left sulked or—as in the case of labor and blacks—tended to endorse Holton, not from enthusiasm for the Republican nominee but to bury, once and for all, the hated Byrd machine. "We've been waiting a lifetime to kill the Byrd machine," explained AFL-CIO president Julian Carper, "and this is our chance, and we're going to do it." Battle likewise suffered defections on the right. Almost five hundred conservative Richmond-area Democrats suddenly turned Republican. Their backing brought Holton votes, respectability, but above all money. And the mystery of Battle's political identity persisted. To the left, he was a Byrd Democrat, to the right a Kennedy Democrat. In truth, he was a Spong Democrat (after U.S. Senator William Spong), which was somewhere in between. But as Battle himself noted, the middle-of-the-road was a dangerous place if the traffic got too heavy on either side.

Holton, for his part, dared not disrupt his motley coalition. His campaign slogan—"It's Time for a Change"—said both nothing and everything and served as a lure for disenchanted voters of every stripe. On the issues, the candidates differed imperceptibly. Holton, if anything, was the more fiscally adventurous with an ill-considered plan to refund the sales tax on food at a rate of $9 per year to every Virginian. But Holton's main pitch was his party. It was only fair, he suggested, that Republicans have their chance to govern after nearly a century of Democratic rule. In the end, it took Richard Nixon's blessing before a roaring crowd of 6,500 in Roanoke the week before the election to give Virginia its first Republican governor since William Cameron switched to the party back in 1884.

Holton won by 65,000 votes (480,860 to Battle's 415,695). Ironically, two young, moderate Democrats, J. Sargeant Reynolds and Andrew P. Miller, defeated Holton's running mates, H. D. ("Buzz") Dawbarn and Richard D. Obenshain, for lieutenant governor and attorney general. Holton's own victory margin came from Republican strongholds in the Shenandoah Valley and the Roanoke environs but, above all, from the suburbs where Republicanism was the coming fashion in the South. By best estimates, Holton also claimed some 37 percent of the statewide black vote. His chief inroads were in Richmond; the traditionally Democratic black precincts in Tidewater and rural Virginia gave Battle 75 to 80 percent of their vote.

Holton's election reflected the emergence of new realities in Virginia politics. The smaller, more manageable electorate of the Byrd era was gone. The 1969 election, the first gubernatorial contest without a poll tax, attracted over 915,000 voters, a 63 percent increase over four years before. Voting power shifted further from Harry Byrd's county courthouses to cities and suburbs as Virginia's six largest metropolitan areas cast over 54 percent of the vote. Television surpassed courthouse word-of-mouth as the chief medium of campaign communication. Holton spent the unprecedented sum of $500,000, a goodly part for television spots in the closing days. Finally, the winners in 1969 were not the staid gentlemen of the Byrd dynasty but, as the Washington *Post* noted, "young, personable, able, new to statewide prominence, and moderate or liberal in their political views. It is hard to think of a more dramatic change in a state's politics."

Yet the losses of his running mates made Holton's victory seem more a personal than a party one. Holton's coattails did raise Republican representation in the 100-member House of Delegates from 11 to 24, primarily because of a gain of eight seats in northern Virginia. Such gains, however, proved temporary; by 1975 the party's House strength sagged back to 17. Even so, Holton's election signaled that the main political event was now the autumnal general election, not the summer Democratic primary; more than twice as many votes were cast in the 1969 general election as in the August runoff. And Holton's appeal hastened party realignment along the "conservative-Republican, liberal-Democrat" national model, a pattern that would surface more clearly in statewide races of the 1970s. Ironically, it was this last contribution to two-party politics that returned to haunt Holton.

"The skies wept a little," wrote Charles McDowell of Holton's inauguration, but "there was no thunderbolt, no deluge, no cataclysm of any kind" to mark the end of eighty-four years of Democratic rule. Even "George Washington kept his seat on his horse atop the famous statue in [Capitol] square." For two days and nights, Richmond was awash in Republican revelry. But the new Governor's inaugural address heralded change beyond that of party affiliation. The southern venerables went unmentioned; instead, three Yankee gentlemen—John Gardner, then chairman of the Urban Coalition, Daniel Webster, and Abraham Lincoln—were quoted by name. Holton's speech was short, activist, progressive. And there was no mistaking its central theme:

> Here in Virginia we must see that no citizen of the Commonwealth is excluded from full participation in both the blessings and responsibilities of our society because of his race. . . .
>
> As Virginia has been a model for so much else in America in the past, let us now endeavor to make today's Virginia a model in race relations. Let us, as Lincoln said, insist upon an open society "with malice toward none; charity for all." . . .
>
> . . . . Let our goal in Virginia be an aristocracy of ability regardless of race, color or creed.

Holton moved at once to put words into practice. His first executive order read: "I will not tolerate nor will any state official tolerate racial or ethnic prejudice in the hiring or promotion of state employees." And he prodded private industry to follow suit. By the end of his administration black employment in state government rose 25 percent, to approximately 18 percent of the work force. Holton's most visible black appointments were William Robertson to his executive staff as director of consumer and minority affairs and Ernest Fears as the nation's first black head of a statewide Selective Service System. To his later regret, Holton did not appoint a black to the board of visitors at the University of Virginia or to a judgeship of a court of record (where the governor makes only interim appointments). In general, however, so many blacks were named to state boards and commissions that Capitol reporters began calling them FBEs—"First Blacks Ever."

The new governor struck a handsome pose: sandy-haired, a bit bald at the crown, ruddy features set by a broad forehead and broad shoulders. His personality is less easily described. He could be stubborn, moody, and ill-tempered to subordinates. He was vain, fond of attention and perquisite, teased by vague longings for the vice-presidency and beyond. As governor, he was pulled toward the play of the rich: the world of yachting and saunas, of posh resorts and private tennis courts. Yet he was also a man of strong principles, and state government fascinated him in the manner of an avid and devoted hobbyist. A sense of humor was never far off. Possessor of ever playful eyes and ready grin, he was as quick to laugh at himself as at others. It was this folksy, ebullient Holton that caught the public eye. Writers called him "The Happy Governor." Holton, wrote Norfolk *Virginian-Pilot* columnist Guy Friddell, was as pleased "with his work as a boy baiting a fishhook on a Saturday morning." "The Holton administration," recalls his press secretary Staige Blackford, "was a departure from the somewhat stuffy, formal, and regal governorships of the past. Can you imagine, for example, seeing Mills Godwin walking around the Governor's office in his stocking feet? In short, I think Holton gave us a bit of what could be called Camelot on the James."

To some, this new Camelot was as resistible as Camelots elsewhere. And the conservative disenchantment, which began with style, shifted rapidly to substance. The year 1970—the most eventful in the Holton administration— pitted the governor against three cherished symbols of Virginia conservatism: tobacco, neighborhood schools, and the name of Harry Byrd.

Holton's chief proposal to the General Assembly was to increase the "harmless little old tax" on cigarettes from 2½ to 5 cents a pack. Special taxes in Virginia reflect sectional politics. Southsider Godwin sought in his second term to tax the Southwest's main product, coal. Holton, the southwesterner, proposed taxing a Southside product, tobacco. Truly the crop of Virginia conservatism, tobacco was grown in the state's most conservative rural region, and cigarettes were manufactured in the state's most conservative metropolis. Many national tobacco companies had major plants in Richmond, and tobacco executives peopled the city's affluent and fashionable West End. Undaunted, Holton blithely advertised the cigarette tax increase as a $28 million "pot of gold" which would permit development of Virginia's port facilities and the immediate state assumption of 90 percent of local welfare costs. The tobacco industry, he argued, would not suffer; even after the increase forty-five states would still have higher cigarette taxes than Virginia. Mobilized against the increase were not only tobacco executives and labor leaders but the Richmond business establishment, the Richmond newspapers, the Virginia Farm Bureau, and the state AFL-CIO. The Senate passed the measure, 26 to 13; the House Finance Committee crushed it, 15 to 5.

Though the Assembly scuttled the Governor's cigarette tax and his $9 per person food tax rebate, it did approve Holton's recommendation for an additional 4 percent tax on alcoholic beverages—a levy with an estimated annual yield of $14 million. And the session was generally progressive in outlook. With the governor's firm support, the lawmakers provided both the first funds for community mental health centers and for unified development of rival Hampton Roads ports under a central Virginia Port Authority. Ironically, the session's most symbolic moment involved a bill that never passed.

The more liberal Virginia Senate killed by a single vote a House-backed antibusing measure, denounced by Senator Henry Howell as a throwback to the days of massive resistance.

In many maneuverings of the Democratic legislature, the new Republican governor was no more than a bystander. His signal achievement was to persuade the General Assembly to appropriate $7.8 million which, together with $17 million in federal matching grants, aided construction of local sewage treatment plants. Holton's personal relationships with most legislators remained friendly and cooperative. "Likeable, intelligent, but inexperienced," was Democratic House majority leader James M. Thomson's view of Holton after the 1970 session. "His relations with the Democratic-dominated legislature were generally harmonious," reporter Helen Dewar noted at the end of his term, "but this stemmed in part from the fact that Holton, a novice in legislature maneuvering, rarely tried to overplay his hand." Befriending the opposition, Holton sensed, would hasten enactment of pet programs and convince skeptical Virginians that Republicans could, after all, govern well.

The summer of 1970 brought Holton's second—and more serious—breach with Virginia conservatism. In March 1970, partly to avoid the more liberal electorate in the Democratic primary, Senator Harry F. Byrd, Jr., announced he would seek reelection as an independent. The Republicans faced the dilemma of doing nothing or nominating a candidate who might split conservatives and elect a liberal Democrat. Byrd, of course, might have resolved the matter by turning Republican. But despite conversations Holton had with Nixon and White House overtures to Byrd, the senator refused to become a Republican or to commit himself to vote with the GOP to organize the Senate. The most Byrd said was that he would "welcome a Republican endorsement." For some, this was more than enough. Pro-Byrd forces at the state Republican convention made certain that the senator had more banners, buttons, and posters than all the Republican candidates combined. They wanted the convention to take no action, in effect tacitly endorsing Byrd. But all this reckoned without Holton's eleventh-hour intervention. At a banquet speech the night before the voting, he pleaded for a real Republican candidate: "I've seen speculation in the papers that you'll go home having done nothing. Frankly, I can't believe it. We're the biggest, strongest, and the best party in Virginia . . . I can't believe we'll do nothing. Doing nothing would be like having the biggest, shiniest, newest fire engine and not taking it to the fire." Next day, while a confident Holton left to play tennis, the delegates handily rejected a no-action resolution and nominated little-known Delegate Ray Garland of Roanoke to oppose Byrd.

The fire engine speech may have been the most momentous of Holton's career. His decision blended profound conviction, personal egotism, and a touch of political self-interest. Holton's fight for a two-party system in Virginia had been largely a fight for an alternative to the Byrds. Now that the system had arrived, the governor was not about to watch the Republicans go begging after a Byrd. To sit passively, Holton sensed, was to lose public respect and, in particular, the goodwill of blacks and labor. Yet Holton's shiny fire engine of June was, by November, irrevocably smudged. So was the governor's judgment in tackling the most famous name in Virginia politics with one of the most obscure. Senator Byrd won easily with 53.5 percent of the vote. Liberal Democrat George Rawlings captured 31 percent and Holton's candidate, Garland, 15 percent. The results suggested that Nixon's southern strategy, based on converted Byrd Democrats and Wallace supporters, offered more hope than the moderate, "mountain-valley" Republicanism of Linwood Holton.

Garland's (and thus Holton's) demise and Byrd's victory were assisted by the resurgence of racial controversy. The 1960s witnessed great progress in Virginia, not only because of economic prosperity but because race tensions, for the most part, remained in the background. But by 1970 several Virginia cities faced lawsuits demanding student busing to desegregate public schools. The Richmond area was especially disturbed by suggestions that the city school district, almost two-thirds black, be combined with the mostly white suburban counties of Henrico and Chesterfield. "It's getting to the point where federal courts and the federal government will only listen to the mob," one lawyer told a crowd of 2,500 in Chesterfield. "So if we have to get a mob, let's get a mob."

Despite cries to intervene in the suits, Holton refused, fearing such action might place the state under court order to assign pupils itself. To anguished conservatives, this stand was a dodge. Not only did the governor refuse to intervene, on the opening day of classes he escorted his thirteen-year-old daughter Tayloe to predominantly black John F. Kennedy High School, the one assigned her under the court busing plan. The First Lady took two younger Holtons, Anne, twelve, and Woody, eleven, to Mosby Middle School, where they were the only white pupils in their respective classrooms. "They're going to give this as much leadership as you can expect from 11 to 13-year-olds," Holton noted, "which is right much." He did not mention that he could have sent the children to any public school in Richmond. The Governor's Mansion was on state, not city, property and thus technically exempt from any busing order. It was the most public moment of the governor's entire life, front-page news throughout the nation. The Washington *Post* praised Holton for "the kind of leadership long needed in Virginia, across the South, and in every area where desegregation is a problem." Blacks for once, said the Richmond *Afro-American,* felt they were "a part of the whole." The most lavish praise came from Colgate Darden, who called Holton's actions "the most significant happening in this commonwealth during my lifetime."

Conservatives, led by the Richmond daily newspapers, resented the governor's failure to speak out against busing. The Richmond dailies, Holton countered, "wanted me to stand up on the Capitol, face toward Washington, and shake my fist." Confronted with a court order there was no way to stop, Holton's first concern was "to keep schools open and make sure they survived." Although schools remained open, many whites sought private schooling, moved from city to county suburb, or kept their children home. Richmond business leaders subsequently cited busing as a chief reason for an accelerating population decline. Yet, given a situation he personally opposed and had not created, Holton acted admirably. Racial violence was largely averted. By a single dramatic gesture, Virginia's heritage of massive resistance yielded to compliance with the courts and open public schools.

The next year, 1971, was much quieter for Governor Holton. The General Assembly was busy with redistricting and with bringing the Virginia Code into conformity with the new state constitution. Holton, for his part, was strangely passive. He presented the Assembly only innocuous requests, partly, he said, because of an anticipated $16 million budget deficit. Democrats challenged these predictions and presented proposals to aid hard-pressed localities. A compromise of sorts finally emerged whereby the Assembly appropriated $21.5 million, largely for local sewage treatment projects, but delayed for six months state assumption of local welfare costs. Holton, who had embraced such aid to localities just one year earlier, appeared momentarily Byrd-like in his fiscal caution.

The year belonged, tragically, to the lieutenant governor. Holton liked J. Sargeant Reynolds (in contrast to Attorney General Andrew Miller, whom he labeled "something of a cold fish"). And Reynolds was the prince of Virginia politics, advancing from delegate to state senator to lieutenant governor in rapid succession. Wealthy, intelligent, boyishly handsome, he was the clear favorite for governor in 1973. He had about him a special wit and charm: "My father [Richard Reynolds of Reynolds Metals Co.] told me that under no conditions could I buy the office of lieutenant governor. . . . But he said I could rent it for four years." Yet Sargeant Reynolds was the Virginia governor that never was. On Sunday, June 13, 1971, two weeks before his thirty-fifth birthday, he lay dead of an inoperable brain tumor.

In the months following discovery of Reynolds's illness, his true mettle had shown. Despite cobalt treatments, his talk remained lighthearted and keen. He even treated his affliction lightly, noted the Norfolk *Virginian-Pilot,* "as when he startled a clergyman, who was about to open a Senate session with prayer, by suggesting, smiling, 'Put in a word for me.' " A memorable moment came near the end, at the Wakefield shad planking, that annual gathering of "good old boys" in Harry Byrd's Virginia. Reynolds's subject that spring afternoon was court-ordered busing. It must not return Virginia to massive resistance; this time, Reynolds said, the law must be obeyed: "You can't condemn the scraggly-looking kids on college campuses, lecture them on being part of the system, and then turn on the system when it renders decisions with which you don't agree. . . . If coming down here to the shad planking in Southside Virginia and making such statements spells political doom for me—so be it. At least I will have had the very warm feeling of having . . . said what I thought needed . . . saying." "Oh God," said Bill Battle on learning of his death. "I hadn't allowed myself to think he could die. . . . Sarge was a young man with the world in his hand. . . . How do you say it's over?" But it was little people, the small clutches of black Richmonders gazing at the casket, who felt the keenest loss. "I voted for him every time," said one elderly black. "He was a good man—a good man and a just man."

Three candidates ran in the special November election to replace Reynolds: state Senator Henry Howell, Delegate George Kostel of Clifton Forge, and Delegate George Shafran of Arlington. Howell, concluding that the Democratic convention would be stacked against him, ran as an independent. Kostel, a Democrat, won the backing of old-line conservatives. And Shafran, the Republican, was the candidate of Linwood Holton. Howell won with 362,371 votes, mainly from the left; Kostel placed second with 334,580 votes, mainly from the right; and the moderate Shafran, with but 209,861 votes, was savaged in the crossfire. To Shafran's patron in the Governor's Mansion, the returns of 1970 and 1971 sent distressingly similar signals. Holton's dream of a two-party system had succumbed, momentarily, to the politics of formlessness, dominated by independents with robust personal followings. Virginians had preferred both ends of the political spectrum— right (Byrd) and left (Howell)—to the middle ground occupied by Holton and the moderate candidates fielded by the Republicans. More ominously, the Garland and Shafran losses shattered Holton's political standing before the midpoint of his term and just before the start of the 1972 General Assembly, at which the governor was to present his most ambitious program.

Meanwhile Holton was setting new directions in appointments to dozens of boards, agencies, and commissions. In contrast to courthouse cronies and prominent businessmen of the Byrd era, Holton favored greater diversity. Together with the stylish Cynthia Newman, his choice as secretary of the Commonwealth, he sought appointees from neglected regions such as the Southwest and northern Virginia. He named more blacks and more women to state posts and appointed the first student member to the board of visitors of the University of Virginia. Republicans naturally received more patronage. Yet the rank and file, thirsty for preferment after years on the outside, wanted still more. "When they fuss at me for not making appointments that please them," the governor replied, "I tell them, 'If this Administration succeeds, you've got a two-party system. If this one fails, I don't know what will happen.' " Holton also sought talent outside Virginia. Among his best finds was Vernon Hill, lured from Oregon to shape up the Division of Motor Vehicles. Another avid suitor for that post was Richard Obenshain, Holton's running mate for attorney general and the articulate leader of the Republican party's conservative wing. Holton recalls that his chief assistant urged him to "bury Dick Obenshain in DMV." Holton refused and named Hill—to Obenshain's deep chagrin.

Holton appointments left their greatest impact in pollution control. With the energy crisis still in the future, the Holton years favored ecological progress. The governor seized the opportunity; environment ranked second only to race relations as an area of priority and accomplishment. Symbolic of the new day was Noman Cole, a smart, aggressive, and abrasive nuclear engineer who was Holton's choice as chairman of the State Water Control Board. Under Cole's leadership the board directed localities and private industries to stop polluting public waterways and passed tough water purity standards for future sewage treatment projects. Holton backed his chairman against local protests and persuaded the legislature to spend greatly increased sums for sewage treatment plants. When combined with federal matching funds, the locality's share of sewage treatment construction was reduced from 70 to 20 percent. The object, Holton always said, was to make Virginia's rivers "swimmable again."

Holton's credentials as an environmentalist were tarnished by a controversy over Green Springs, once referred to as "Holton's Vietnam." Only with respect to executive stubbornness is the parallel apt. Green Springs was a collection of historic homesites in Louisa County which Frederick Hartt of the University of Virginia called "a living textbook of the history of rural architecture in Virginia, a succession of buildings of high quality from the early 18th and 19th centuries unmatched in the state for its completeness." For this community, Holton planned a twentieth-century prison—a diagnostic and reception station—part of the replacement of the antiquated state penitentiary in Richmond. Although Holton faced strong opposition from national and state groups, he would not be moved. When federal aid was blocked, Holton determined to proceed with state funds. More thousands of state dollars were thrown into contesting lawsuits brought by Green Springs residents. Only upon Holton's departure from office was the matter resolved. Governor Godwin, in one of his first acts of office, announced the state would seek another site. And Green Springs, still under siege, prepared to fend off vermiculite mining projects.

Convening in the midst of such controversies, the 1972 Virginia General Assembly differed from those of the Byrd era. It was younger: 50 of its 140 members were freshmen. It was more moderate and the first in which urban legislators held a clear majority. And, as House Speaker John Warren Cooke observed, "the political climate at the 1972 General Assembly was unique. The Governor was a member of the Republican Party, the Lieutenant Governor was an Independent, and the Assembly itself was overwhelmingly Democratic." Yet the prevailing atmosphere was more harmonious than hos-

tile. Holton regularly breakfasted and conferred with the legislative leadership. For its part, the Assembly diluted and modified more often than it
rejected his proposals.

On fiscal matters, the Assembly proved the more cautious partner. It
passed a $5 billion state budget, roughly a 30 percent increase over the
previous biennium but nearly $120 million less than Holton requested. It
endorsed the governor's proposals to boost the gasoline tax from 7 to 9 cents
per gallon and the corporate income tax from 5 to 6 percent, but not his call
for a substantial personal income tax increase; a compromise of sorts raised
rates from 5 to 5.75 percent on taxable personal income over $12,000. Hol-
ton's environmental program fared less well. His pleas for a Department of
Natural Resources, legislation to protect Virginia's wetlands, and a tough
strip mining law were either scuttled or gutted by amendment.

Antibusing resolutions passed the Assembly, but so did an open-housing
law, the first of its kind in the old Confederacy. From the beginning, open
housing and antibusing were skillfully linked. "We all know busing is the
result of ghetto living, of the restrictions on free movement," spoke Delegate
Ferguson Reid, one of three blacks in the Assembly. "If you want to solve the
problem of busing, you need to solve the problem of open housing." The bill
duplicated in most respects the federal Fair Housing Act of 1968, and its
tougher provisions were deleted by the Senate. Yet passage—by large margins—was itself symbolic, and the governor was largely a bystander. Sensing
overexposure on racial issues, Holton feared open support on his part might
prove counterproductive. Upon passage, however, he hailed it as "the most
important piece of legislation to pass this Assembly since the Civil War." The
governor's hyperbole notwithstanding, legislators reacted to busing in a spirit
other than massive resistance.

Holton's top priority for the 1972 session was a proposal for a Governor's
Cabinet, reorganizing state agencies into six major departments—each headed
by a secretary appointed by the governor at a salary of $30,000 or more a
year. The six fields were administration, commerce and resources, education,
finance, human affairs, and transportation and public safety. The idea originated with a 1970 study which found that about half of the 150 state agency
and department heads reported directly to the governor and intruded on his
time. The proposal barely survived Assembly objections that it would add "a
new layer of bureaucracy" and passed only with the help of prominent Democrats. But passage was no more than a structural first step. It remained to be
seen whether able cabinet officers could be recruited and given adequate
responsibility and staff support and, above all, whether subsequent governors
would insist, as Holton did, that individual agency heads report through
cabinet officers in their respective areas.

The irony of Holton's governorship was that policy successes seemed
abruptly offset by political losses. At the 1972 Republican convention, con-

servative Richard Obenshain ousted Warren French, a Holton loyalist, from the state chairmanship by the astonishing margin of 769 to 288. Holton, anticipating his friend's defeat, left the convention to play tennis. One month later, at a meeting of the Republican state central committee in Charlottesville, conservatives swept secondary party posts as well. The problem was, Republican rank and file wanted more patronage jobs, were distressed by the Garland and Shafran defeats, and distrusted Holton the "liberal," particularly on race. "I've always been a supporter of the governor," Delegate Jerry Geisler confessed, "but he got too far to the left. . . . The governor's thinking doesn't represent a majority of Republicans in the state or the traditional Republican viewpoint. To get back to the center we've got to move to the right."

Move they did. The 1972 convention wrought a profound change of character in the Virginia Republican party. From its mountain-valley bastions, the party had historically been a progressive force, a moderate alternative to the conservative machine of Senator Byrd. Now Obenshain, a devotee of Senator Barry Goldwater, had different ideas. Virginia's parties, he believed, must realign themselves to reflect the positions of their national counterparts. Obenshain's theory of realignment was assisted by a takeover of the state Democratic party that year by followers of Henry Howell and Senator George McGovern. Capitalizing on this development, Obenshain pledged to make the Republican party a "comfortable new home" for Byrd Democrats fleeing the liberal takeover of their party. Yet this trend simultaneously made uncomfortable the blacks, labor leaders, and assorted moderates Holton wished to attract to the Republican standard.

The 1972 convention forecast a conservative hegemony in Republican politics that lasted, with but minor interruptions, for the remainder of the decade. And the conservative Republican record in statewide races was one of remarkable success. Congressman William Scott, benefiting from Nixon's coattails, McGovern's unpopularity, busing fever, and a $200,000 "loan" fron financier J. Stetson Coleman, upset incumbent Democratic Senator William Spong, a capable but unexciting moderate whom Scott painted in a last-minute media barrage as an advocate of gun control and the federal Voting Rights Act. The next year, in a major victory for Obenshain's strategy for realignment, former Byrd Democrat Mills Godwin ran successfully for governor as a Republican. In 1976 party conservatives sent a delegation favoring Ronald Reagan to the national convention in Kansas City, declined to nominate a Republican candidate against Senator Byrd, and then helped make Virginia the one southern state to support Gerald Ford in the fall. In 1977 John Dalton, unaligned with either party faction, succeeded Godwin as the third straight Republican governor. And in 1978, after U.S. Senate nominee Obenshain died tragically in a light-plane crash, John W. Warner picked up the conservative Republican banner and beat Democrat Andrew Miller in the fall. As conservative successes began to mount, Holton's influence further declined. He became an outsider in Republican politics even before the close of his term.

The irony was that this Republican governor—spurned by his party as too liberal—was in many respects no liberal at all. He was an activist governor, in part because he believed vigorous state government might reduce Washington's role. No spendthrift, Holton sought more efficient, less costly ways of running state government. He supported a firm Vietnam policy and talked tough on campus protest. And he sought racial progress not with new legislation or bureaucracy but by setting examples of personal goodwill. How liberal, finally, was the Nixon loyalist who, despite the president's growing coolness, kept faith unto the end? "The president was still saying directly to me and to others that he didn't know about these things," Holton said of Watergate. Not until "the big tape came out" and Nixon left office, "did I begin to realize it was such a sick situation."

The final months of Holton's term were undramatic. His "inclination," wrote Helen Dewar, "is for public relations, not the back room give-and-take of legislative maneuvering. This never showed more than now, his last full year in office." Because of his lame-duck status, the erosion of his party base, and Democratic domination of the legislature, Holton's was not a commanding presence. He did, however, strike a notable blow for equal educational opportunity by encouraging the 1973 Assembly to appropriate an additional $31 million to Virginia's less fortunate school districts. A companion provision required localities to spend a minimum of 80 cents per $100 of market value of local real estate for public education. The targets of this last measure were conservative rural counties, mainly in the Southside and Piedmont, which had underfinanced public education for years. The Assembly refused, however, to permit regional planning districts for assorted area services. "Future assemblies will have to recognize that the regional approach is the only approach to the complexities of local government," Holton advised the lawmakers in a farewell message. For the moment, however, such talk only aroused suburban fears of annexation or school consolidation with central cities and their ever-growing populations of black and poor.

Holton left office more popular with the public than with his party, better liked in northern Virginia, western Virginia, and Tidewater than in Richmond or Southside. For Holton himself, the rest was rather sad. He was assistant secretary of state for congressional relations for a while, a mere go-between for Secretary Henry Kissinger and leading members of the Senate. Next he practiced law with the Washington firm of Hogan and Hartson but felt restless and bored. Then, in a comeback attempt, Holton sought the 1978 Republican nomination for the U.S. Senate. In the convention balloting, the former governor finished third behind Richard Obenshain and John Warner, men who had not before held elected office. But he exited with dignity and grace. His family, Holton told convention delegates, was "very happy to join with you in welcoming me to the status of the elder statesman." Returning to private life, he became vice-president and general counsel for the American Council of Life Insurance in Washington, D.C.

Holton's place thus rests with his governorship and not, as with many politicians, on long service in a variety of posts. Clearly his impact was not that of Byrd in the 1920s or Godwin during his first term, but he belongs, to steal a phrase, with "the best of the rest." His legislative achievements— cleaner waterways, a cabinet form of government, funds for poorer schools— were constructive but not extraordinary. Yet they are not his legacy. At his best Linwood Holton exemplified what we should value most in politicians: personal decency, an intelligent approach to problem-solving, some consciousness of the future, the courage of leadership, and the ability to place public interests above partisan ones. Thus the great Holton contributions were symbolic and intangible: a new air of openness in state government, two-party democracy in action, and, above all, racial understanding through personal tolerance and goodwill.

"In the early 1970s," Ken Ringle of the Washington *Post* has written, "two of the hottest new political properties in the nation were the Democratic governor of Georgia and the Republican governor of Virginia. Both were small town natives of the rural South; men in their mid-forties who had sprung from political obscurity to the governor's mansion on their second try." Both Linwood Holton and Jimmy Carter spoke of racial justice, and "pundits predicted that both men were headed for bigger things." But, of course, "the pundits were only half right."

Historians will wonder why Holton's was a career of such foreshortened impact, and why on the threshold of his great dream of two-party competition in the South, Holton forfeited his role in the form that competition would take. His demise was partly the result of commendable convictions: the determination to work well with Democrats in the legislature, to make competent appointments, to field Republican opposition to Byrd, and to light Virginia a new way on matters of race. But partly it was the result of the governor's own blindness to the realities of party power in American politics. Holton, while governor, inhabited that dream world where good government automatically makes good politics, and where lofty policy decisions somehow become detached from the need to remember first names, placate precinct chairmen, send messages of congratulations or condolence, or, if the governor cannot personally do those things, have lieutenants around who will. Yet in Holton the ideal and the intensely practical never quite conjoined. The lesson of Linwood Holton is that it may never be enough simply to govern well.

SOURCES

The most helpful sources on the Holton governorship are daily newspapers, especially the Richmond *Times-Dispatch,* Norfolk *Virginian-Pilot,* and Washington *Post.* Also see pertinent issues of the *University of Vir-*

ginia News Letter. Letters from Staige Blackford, Holton's press secretary, and Raymond Boone, editor of the Richmond *Afro-American,* were helpful, as was an interview with Holton (September 22, 1977).

Lively sketches of the governor include Don Hill, "67th Governor of the Commonwealth of Virginia: Linwood Holton, Jr.," *Virginia Record* 92 (Jan. 1970): 8–16, 113–16; and Shirley Bolinaga, "The Happy Governor," *The Commonwealth* 37 (Aug. 1970): 23–27. The Holton-Nixon relationship is discussed in Frank Rich, "Decency and Loyalty: Linwood Holton Learns the President's Views," *Washington Monthly* 5 (April 1973): 47–54. Glenn Scott, "Springs of Controversy," *The Commonwealth* 38 (Dec. 1971): 23–27, provides an interesting look at the Green Springs controversy.

Among books see Jack Bass and Walter De Vries, *The Transformation of Southern Politics* (New York, 1976); Weldon Cooper and Thomas Morris, eds., *Virginia Government and Politics* (Charlottesville, 1976); Ralph Eisenberg, "Virginia: The Emergence of Two-Party Politics," in William C. Havard, ed., *The Changing Politics of the South* (Baton Rouge, La., 1972); Neal Pierce, *The Border South States* (New York, 1975); Larry Sabato, *The Democratic Party Primary in Virginia: Tantamount to Election No Longer* (Charlottesville, 1977) and *Virginia Votes, 1969–1974* (Charlottesville, 1976); and Alexander Heard, *A Two-Party South?* (Chapel Hill, N.C., 1952).

About the Editor

EDWARD YOUNGER was born in Pindall, Arkansas, in 1909. He earned his B.A. degree in history at Central University of Arkansas in 1932. For the next five years he taught in the public schools of his native state and in Oklahoma, where he met and married one of his co-workers, Barbara Badgett. A daughter, Ellen Badgett Younger, was born to them.

Mr. Younger received his M.A. in history at Oklahoma State University in 1938 and his Ph.D. at George Washington University in 1942. Serving in Naval Aviation during World War II, he rose to the rank of lieutenant commander and, at the end of the conflict, was assigned to the faculty of history and government at the U.S. Naval Academy. Shortly thereafter, in 1946, he became a member of the Corcoran Department of History at the University of Virginia.

Mr. Younger's thirty-three years at the university were marked by continued advancement through the academic ranks, including service as department chairman (1962–1966), Dean of the Graduate School of Arts and Sciences (1966–1969), and appointment as Alumni Professor of History. These years were further highlighted by a Fulbright lectureship at Allahabad University in India; work as a State Department American specialist in India, Nepal, and Pakistan; service as a NATO lecturer in Paris; a visiting appointment to the Ernest J. King Chair of Maritime History at the U.S. Naval War College in Newport, Rhode Island; and delivery of the J. P. Young Lectures in Memphis, Tennessee.

In addition to publishing articles and reviews in scholarly journals, Mr. Younger wrote one book and edited another before beginning work on this volume. His biographical study, *John A. Kasson: Diplomacy and Politics from Lincoln to McKinley* (Iowa City: State Historical Society of Iowa, 1955), won the Phi Beta Kappa Prize at the University of Virginia. He established his reputation as an editor with *Inside the Confederate Government: The Diary of Robert Garlick Hill Kean, Head of the Bureau of War* (New York: Oxford University Press, 1957), a Civil War Book Club selection.

As a graduate instructor, Professor Younger directed 68 doctoral dissertations and 140 masters theses—a record unparalleled at the university and in the state. His services were recognized by receipt of the Governor's Award, the Raven Society Award, and appointment to an honorary membership in the Virginia Historical Society. Becoming ill early in 1979, he died at Pavilion X, East Lawn, his home on the university grounds, in June of that year.

Ever and in all circumstances a gentleman, Mr. Younger personified an ideal of courtesy, grace, and concern for the welfare of others. This book, most of whose authors were his students, is a testament to his abilities, his character, and his enduring influence.

Notes on the Contributors

F. N. Boney (B.A., Hampden-Sydney College; M.A. and Ph.D., University of Virginia) is Professor of History at the University of Georgia.

James L. Bugg, Jr. (B.A., Hampden-Sydney College; M.A. and Ph.D., University of Virginia) is Professor of History at Old Dominion University.

Walter T. Calhoun (B.A., Lynchburg College; B.D., Vanderbilt University; M.A., University of Nebraska) is Associate Professor of History at East Carolina University.

William B. Crawley, Jr. (B.A., Hampden-Sydney College; M.A. and Ph.D., University of Virginia) is Professor and Chairman of the Department of History at Mary Washington College.

Virginius Dabney (B.A. and M.A., University of Virginia) is a professional historian residing in Richmond, Virginia. He is a former editor of the Richmond *Times-Dispatch*.

James W. Ely, Jr. (B.A., Princeton University; LL.B., Harvard Law School; M.A. and Ph.D., University of Virginia) is Professor of Law at the Vanderbilt University School of Law.

Alvin A. Fahrner (B.A., Hampden-Sydney College; M.A. and Ph.D., University of North Carolina) is Professor of History at East Carolina University.

Henry C. Ferrell, Jr. (A.B. and M.A., Duke University; Ph.D., University of Virginia) is Professor of History at East Carolina University.

Joseph A. Fry (A.B., Davis and Elkins College; M.A. and Ph.D., University of Virginia) is Associate Professor of History at the University of Nevada, Las Vegas.

Thomas E. Gay, Jr. (B.A., Tampa University; M.A. and Ph.D., University of Virginia) is Professor of History at Edinboro State College.

Alvin L. Hall (B.A., Randolph-Macon College; M.A. and Ph.D., University of Virginia) is Associate Professor of History and Dean of the School of Continuing Education at Virginia State University.

ROBERT T. HAWKES, JR. (B.A., Randolph-Macon College; M.A. and Ph.D., University of Virginia) is Assistant Professor of History and Dean of the Division of Continuing Education at George Mason University.

RONALD L. HEINEMANN (B.A., Dartmouth College; M.A. and Ph.D., University of Virginia) is Professor and Chairman of the Department of History at Hampden-Sydney College.

PETER R. HENRIQUES (B.A., Trinity College; B.D., Princeton University; Ph.D., University of Virginia) is Associate Professor of History at George Mason University.

EDWARD L. HENSON, JR. (B.A., Virginia Military Institute; M.A. and Ph.D., University of Virginia) is Professor of History at Clinch Valley College.

PATRICIA HICKIN (B.S., Richmond Professional Institute; M.A. and Ph.D., University of Virginia) is a professional writer and researcher in Richmond, Virginia.

JOHN S. HOPEWELL (B.A., Washington and Lee University; M.A. and Ph.D., University of Virginia) is Instructor in History at The Collegiate Schools in Richmond, Virginia.

ROBERT R. JONES (B.A., M.A., and Ph.D., University of Virginia) is Professor of History and Dean of the Graduate School at the University of Southwestern Louisiana.

JACK T. KIRBY (B.A., Old Dominion University; M.A. and Ph.D., University of Virginia) is Professor of History at Miami University (Ohio).

WILLIAM LARSEN (B.A., Brigham Young University; M.A. and Ph.D., University of Virginia) formerly chaired the Department of History at Radford University. He now manages a tree farm near Christiansburg, Virginia.

RICHARD G. LOWE (B.A., University of Southwestern Louisiana; A.M., Harvard University; Ph.D., University of Virginia) is Professor of History at North Texas State University.

JAMES TICE MOORE (B.A., University of South Carolina; M.A. and Ph.D., University of Virginia) is Associate Professor of History at Virginia Commonwealth University.

JOHN H. MOORE (B.A., Hamilton College; M.A. and Ph.D., University of Virginia) is a professional writer in Washington, D.C.

CHARLES E. POSTON (B.A., University of Richmond; M.A., University of Virginia; J.D., College of William and Mary) is an attorney at law in Norfolk, Virginia.

HARRY W. READNOUR (B.A., Oklahoma State University; M.A., George Washington University; Ph.D., University of Virginia) is Associate Professor of History at the University of Central Arkansas.

WILLIAM A. RHODES (B.S., Virginia Polytechnic Institute; M.A., University of Virginia) is Assistant Professor of History at Germanna Community College.

STUART I. ROCHESTER (B.A., Loyola College of Baltimore; M.A. and Ph.D., University of Virginia) is Associate Historian with the United States Department of Defense.

CRANDALL A. SHIFFLETT (B.A., St. Johns University, Minnesota; M.A. and Ph.D., University of Virginia) is Assistant Professor of History at Virginia Polytechnic Institute and State University.

MINOR T. WEISIGER (B.A. and M.A., University of Virginia) is Director of Research for the Republican Party of Virginia.

J. HARVIE WILKINSON III (B.A., Yale University; J.D., University of Virginia) is editor of the Norfolk *Virginian-Pilot*.

L. STANLEY WILLIS (B.A., Hampden-Sydney College; M.A. and Ph.D., University of Virginia) is Professor of History at Clinch Valley College.

JONATHAN J. WOLFE (B.A., Hendrix College; M.A. and Ph.D., University of Virginia; B.S., Pharmacy, University of Arkansas) is Staff Pharmacist at Doctors' Hospital in Little Rock, Arkansas.

Index

DATE DUE